Ancient China and the Yue

In this innovative study, Erica Brindley examines how, during the period 400 BCE–50 CE, Chinese states and an embryonic Chinese empire interacted with peoples referred to as the Yue/Viet along its southern frontier. Brindley provides an overview of current theories in archaeology and linguistics concerning the peoples of the ancient southern frontier of China, the closest relations on the mainland to certain later Southeast Asian and Polynesian peoples. Through analysis of Warring States and early Han textual sources, she shows how representations of Chinese and Yue identity invariably fed upon, and often grew out of, a two-way process of centering the self while decentering the other. Examining rebellions, pivotal ruling figures from various Yue states, and key moments of Yue agency, Brindley demonstrates the complexities involved in identity formation and cultural hybridization in the ancient world and highlights the ancestry of cultures now associated with southern China and Vietnam.

Erica Fox Brindley is Associate Professor of Asian Studies and History at the Pennsylvania State University. She is the author of *Music, Cosmology, and the Politics of Harmony in Early China* (2012), *Individualism in Early China: Human Agency and the Self in Thought and Politics* (2010), and numerous articles on the philosophy, religions, and history of ancient China.

Ancient China and the Yue

Perceptions and Identities on the Southern Frontier, c. 400 BCE–50 CE

Erica Fox Brindley
Pennsylvania State University

CAMBRIDGE
UNIVERSITY PRESS

University Printing House, Cambridge CB2 8BS, United Kingdom

One Liberty Plaza, 20th Floor, New York, NY 10006, USA

477 Williamstown Road, Port Melbourne, VIC 3207, Australia

314-321, 3rd Floor, Plot 3, Splendor Forum, Jasola District Centre, New Delhi-110025, India

79 Anson Road, #06-04/06, Singapore 079906

Cambridge University Press is part of the University of Cambridge.

It furthers the University's mission by disseminating knowledge in the pursuit of education, learning and research at the highest international levels of excellence.

www.cambridge.org
Information on this title: www.cambridge.org/9781107446816

First published 2015
First paperback edition 2018

A catalogue record for this publication is available from the British Library

ISBN 978-1-107-08478-0 Hardback
ISBN 978-1-107-44681-6 Paperback

Contents

Figures, maps, and tables

Figures

Maps

Tables

Preface

The problem with "China," "Chineseness," and "sinicization"

This book, at its core, aims to shed light on identities that many people seem to take for granted. What does it mean for someone to be Chinese, Vietnamese ("Viet" is the ancient pronunciation of "Yue"), or Southeast Asian? As a person of Eurasian descent, I've been taught to say that I am a mixture of seven different European ethnicities on my father's side – Welsh, Irish, Swiss, German, English, Scottish, and Dutch – and only one ethnicity on my mother's side: Chinese. Clearly, something is amiss. After all, it is not as though the genes on my European side are any more differentiated than they are on my Asian side. What if my mother had instead stressed my heritage as Shaoxing-ese, Hakka, Nanping-ese, Shandong-ese, Cantonese, Taiwanese, Chaozhou-nese, Hokkien, and Hainnanese?[1] This latter way of discussing one's "Chineseness" may seem unfamiliar or absurd to the contemporary ear, but why would such a way of carving up one's East–West bloodline be any less valid than the "7+1 = 8" formula that my parents taught me, which is generally accepted by people on both sides of the Eurasian Continent? The way we conceive of ethnicities in China reflects not only the West's engagement with China as an allegedly monolithic culture with a homogeneous history and people, but also a sinocentric way of viewing, constructing, and reconstructing Chinese identity from within the Chinese mainland and its far-flung diaspora as well.

Every form of identity carves boundaries and assembles some aspects of the self into a package that distinguishes itself in a particular way. While calling oneself "Chinese" functions no differently than any other type of identity, the category of "Chinese" is distinctive in a few ways. First, it is massive in its scope and the sheer number of diverse peoples that it covers. The contemporary label "European" may at first glance seem comparable with the term "Chinese," and yet, even with all the recognized diversity of

[1] I have just randomly made up and picked a few possible ethnic groupings that seem to correspond in specificity to the European labels.

the "Europeans," such a term may not even approach the geographical and ethnic scope of what is encompassed by "Chinese."[2] Being "Chinese" assumes an ethnic identity that is intimately linked to a vast cultural history. Even though such a tradition narrates its history according to a continuous, linear trajectory starting from legendary heroes at the dawn of civilization to modern times, such a simplified history is still incredibly broad and inclusive. There are few types of cultural identification in the rest of the world that can compare in terms of inclusivity, except perhaps the relatively recently constructed identity "the West," which, intriguingly, often contrasts itself with "the East," and locates its roots in ancient Hellenic culture dating from Homeric times. Even in the case of so-called "Western" culture, one would be hard-pressed to discuss it in the singular, as Chinese culture is often presented, and as though there were but a single, continuous ethno-political entity dating from the ancient sages to today.

Also outlandish is the claim that Chinese people all somehow share the same genetic heritage. While a myth of shared descent is characteristic of many ethnic claims, any historian of China will quickly realize that thinking about Chinese people in terms of a single ethnicity is especially fraught with problems. This is due to the relative permeability throughout the ages of the boundary between what was considered to be inside and outside, or what was Hua-xia (or Han or Chinese) or not, as well as the all-inclusive manner in which Chinese imperial states gobbled up and incorporated those surrounding them into the administrative and cultural fold of the Chinese state.

Chineseness is often expressed these days in terms of the Han ethnicity. Both ethnonyms, "Chinese," and "Han," are exceedingly problematic and to a large extent informed by modern notions of the nation.[3] Scholars have worked on various concepts of Chineseness during specific periods of Chinese history, and some have even used databases to collect data on various usages of ethnonyms such as "Han," from the earliest available records.[4] But to date, no comprehensive account that provides an arc for the development of Chinese concepts of an ethnic or cultural self has been forthcoming.

[2] Another interesting comparison might be to "South Asian," or "Arab."

[3] See Lydia Liu, *The Clash of Empires: The Invention of China in Modern World Making* (Cambridge: Harvard University Press, 2006), p. 80. For the recent history of ethnic and racial classification schemes, see Thomas Mullaney, *Coming to Terms with the Nation: Ethnic Classification in Modern China* (Berkeley: University of California Press, 2010), and Frank Dikötter, *Discourse of Race in Modern China* (Stanford: Stanford University Press, 1994).

[4] Ma Rong at the Institute of Sociology and Anthropology at Peking University has compiled an extensive database of uses of the term "Han" throughout Chinese history.

So that we might come to terms with what it means to be Chinese or Han, I offer the following suggestions: rather than assume that "large, continuous, and homogeneous" was the natural state for China and its peoples, I ask that we take a close look at the ways in which such qualities have historically been fought for and only accepted after much time and contestation, if wholly or at all. As for the notion that "Chinese" is a relatively homogeneous and stable identity, I suggest that we focus on the mechanics of one's identification with Chinese culture as one way of deciphering when, where, and how individuals think of themselves and others as Chinese as opposed to smaller, more local forms of ethnic or regional identification (such as Chaozhou, Hakka, Hokkien, Taishan, Fuzhou, and Putian). By examining the mechanics of Chinese identity as it functioned in history, we will break down the act of identifying oneself or another as Chinese (or, in this book, we will use the more relevant labels of "Hua-xia" or "Zhu-xia," "Central States," etc.) into component parts. Such parts consist in the various functions and reasons for naming, presenting, and maintaining a sense of self and other within specific contexts. In this book, for example, our focus on contexts of naming and constituting self and other – which, to a large extent, concern relationships of power – will help us better understand how an appeal to a single, unified identity such as the Hua-xia has been part of the political and cultural landscape of China since ancient times.

This book examines the predecessor to the Chinese self – the Hua-xia – by offering a case study of the cultures and peoples associated with its ancient southern frontier: the Yue/Viet. It pores over the pre-imperial and Qin-Han period (221 BCE–220 CE) textual corpus, pitting conceptions of Yue identity against the presumed central identity of the Hua-xia, or Zhu-xia. Analyzing rhetorical strategies, common tropes, and other types of representations of the other, I show the extent to which articulations of the self and Yue other were shaped by specific contextual needs or political exigencies. In addition, I provide an extensive discussion of the various geographies and nomenclature of Yue, as well as a review of current theories in linguistics and archaeology concerning the ancient peoples and regions of the southern frontier that are traditionally linked to the Yue. This establishes a non-textual background for the study of Yue identity in the ancient South, which in turn casts the textual evidence in relief, helping reveal the limitations and biases of our literary sources on the Yue.

By revisiting the question "What is 'Chinese'?" via the question, "Who were the 'Yue'?" in the pre-modern history of the South, I touch upon general questions relating to processes of identity construction, preservation, and destruction in the early history of East Asia. My abiding hypothesis is that early empires and the imperial logic of centrality – the latter of which began well before the actual establishment of the Qin Empire in 221 BCE – played an important role in the unification of a Hua-xia center and self, and, hence, the construction of marginal others in the process. The logic of centrality and centeredness, which was accompanied by a cluster of cosmological concepts such as harmony, universality, and the gravity of the central body, served as an underlying and foundational conceptual framework for constructing the self and other.

Critical to such an analysis is the question of how the logic of centrality relates to the historiographical conceit of sinicization, or, the notion that cultures along the periphery of the Central States regions assimilated into Hua-xia culture by adopting it wholesale. Should we accept at face value its implicit assumption that Hua-xia peoples and cultures from the North swept across the Southlands with such political, military, and cultural force that the Southerners were naturally swayed and won over by it? The model of sinicization, which functions much like Confucius' depiction of the gentleman whose *De*-virtue 德 blows over petty people like wind over grass, is clearly a gross oversimplification of modes of cultural change in Chinese history. Yet it remains a stalwart paradigm that has not been rectified, ousted, or challenged significantly, at least not for the early period. In this book, I emphasize ways in which early authors of classical Chinese texts center the Hua-xia self while decentering the other, thereby showing how the model of sinicization is intrinsic to Hua-xia perspectives on the other from very early on. This will help contextualize the very tools of historiography that we have inherited and that continue to exert a force in scholarship today.

The importance of the Yue – or, at the very least, local peoples inhabiting the South (who may or may not have identified as Yue) – as powerful actors in the ancient past serves as testament to the immense diversity and complex history of the East Asian mainland. As this book will show, certain scholarly approaches, as well as the many textual sources on the Yue themselves, are mired in identity politics and enmeshed in the interests of various nationalities and/or ethnic and social groups. The history of peoples associated with the term "Yue" has thus been swallowed up not just by time, but also by a dominant historiography that assumes that sinicization was the core, triumphant process at work. This book will offer a reformulation of the sinicization paradigm while also helping chisel away at incumbent interpretations of China – its history and identity – as a monolithic (i.e., "large, continuous, homogeneous") whole. Through the lens of how the Yue other was constructed, described, discussed, and studied, I will establish a space for understanding the extent to which diverse, indigenous inputs and agents from the South featured in the very creation of Hua-xia and Yue identities.

In examining modes of constructing the self and southern other, we shed light on the very ways that the history of Chinese engagement in the South has been written. I do not ask that we completely throw out the model of sinicization, but I hope that we would approach it critically and come to terms with the ways in which it may be shaping our understanding of the past. If there is historiographical merit to the concept of sinicization, then it is only after the boundaries of time and place have been constructed and the limits and extent of such a process have been set. On the other hand, perhaps Hua-xia culture never really dominated in the South until the last 500 years or so. If the logic of Hua-xia centrality and its concomitant notion of sinicization lead us to a false understanding of the early history of identity relations in that region, then we will need to establish an alternative model of understanding southern and Hua-xia interactions: perhaps by redefining what Hua-xia meant in the context of the early history of the South (i.e., by viewing it as a constantly evolving concept), or by delving into the concepts of local cultures, syncretism, hybridity, and syncretic/hybrid cultures in more detail.

Acknowledgments

While researching and writing this book, I have wandered a bit off the path with which I am most familiar – that of the ancient classics, philosophy, and intellectual history of China. On other academic shores I found a lively crowd of Southeast Asianists, especially those working on Vietnam, who welcomed me warmly and have been extremely gracious and supportive colleagues ever since I began this project. Archaeologists and linguists as well have mentored me with much patience and persistence, and scholars of frontier studies have generously supported this project. I feel very fortunate to have had a chance to interact with people who are so passionate about what they do and eager to help others at the same time.

Some of my first contacts were in the studies of Vietnam. Stephen O'Harrow, Keith Taylor, Michele Thompson, and Liam Kelley were each very responsive to my early articles on the ancient Yue and never hesitated to pass on suggestions for readings or to discuss certain points of Vietnamese history and language with me. At first I corresponded with these folks impersonally by email. One can imagine my pleasant surprise, therefore, when I met them one by one over the years and realized that they were each in person as delightful and helpful as they were via email. The first time I met Keith Taylor at an Association for Asian Studies panel, we found a nearby Vietnamese café and talked avidly about Vietnamese history for at least an hour. I am grateful to Michele Thompson for sharing her expertise on Southeast Asia and Vietnam during our many hours of chatting and hanging out in Singapore together (along with Nam Kim) in the summer of 2012. I am also grateful to Stephen O'Harrow for his friendship, support, and correspondence. When I sought Stephen out in Hawaii, he took me on a Chinatown adventure that started with the search for fish paste, took me through the bowels of Hawaii's extensive Chinatown, and ended with a cheap bowl of Thai noodles on the other end. I was impressed to hear him speaking to various vendors in Cantonese, Vietnamese, and Mandarin during his quest for that elusive fish paste. And many thanks to Liam

Kelley for his support and keen criticism of approaches to the early history and historiography of Vietnam. The works he has sent my way have spared me much time, insofar as I did not have to track down the source for every type of claim – myth or historical fact – concerning ancient Vietnam. Liam has also helped me with issues of textual reliability and confirmed that the ancient Chinese sources that I was taking as primary were indeed more representative of the early period than the earliest textual sources in Vietnamese, which are written over a millennium after the earliest Chinese sources.

My study of the ancient ethnonym Yue/Viet has taken me into unknown disciplinary waters in search of a general understanding of the background of the southern peoples. I would have most certainly drifted off or been sunk if not for the valuable and patient guidance of leaders in the fields of Asian archaeology and linguistics, some of whom became informal mentors to me. In archaeology, I owe much of what I know to the dedicated help of Jiao Tianlong, Francis Allard, and Alice Yao. All three have responded to my incessant queries about archaeology and have influenced my understanding of current debates in archaeology by sending me relevant articles, reading over rough chapters or passages of writing, and otherwise advising me on approaches to or ways of thinking about archaeology. Francis Allard's work on archaeology in the Lingnan 嶺南 region has been of incredible use and significance to my own. He helped me conceptualize the material situation in the ancient South and kindly dedicated his time to reading and commenting thoughtfully on multiple rough drafts of my chapter on archaeology. Alice Yao has guided me deftly in the archaeology of southwest China and the relationships between such an area and the South. She and Francis have both helped me think through some of the important methodological approaches in archaeology and directed me to the most interesting questions relevant to my inquiry. I am so grateful for their dedication and patience.

I could not have had a better introduction to the archaeology of the ancient southern frontier without Jiao Tianlong. Tianlong's monumental assistance on my 2012 trip to southern China allowed me to gain first-hand insight into the archaeological cultures of the ancient Southerners and even acquire hundreds of pictures of important sites and artifacts to boot. I am indebted to him for taking the time out of his busy schedule to travel with me from Fuzhou to Wuyishan, showing me and his students at Xiamen University how archaeologists hit the road with open minds and adventurous spirits, sifting patiently through the earth's sloughed-off layers of skin for material proof of our forebears, their stories, activities, and passions. This was no cerebral exercise of reading and writing as my job as historian tends to be. Instead, it was about physically going to each and every site; walking over, beside, under, and past ancient walls, foundations, and burial mounds; and examining and testing shards, remains, soil samples, and rocks. Experiencing the past in this way was certainly very different from the experience of poring over books or copies of bamboo strips to gain insight into another's thoughts. I thank Tianlong as well for pointing me to much of the relevant scholarship on the ancient Wu-yue and Min-yue regions.

My six months in Hawaii in 2011 offered an occasion to meet with the king of Austronesian linguistics, Bob Blust, who further helped me gain an understanding of the Austric hypothesis, as well as the origins of Austronesian languages in and around ancient Taiwan/Fujian. In linguistics, I also wish to extend special thanks to Bill Baxter for his dedicated guidance on the linguistic panorama of the ancient East Asian mainland. As my main mentor early on in this project, Bill helped bring me up to speed on some of the basic controversies and approaches in the historical linguistics of Asia. Especially fruitful was his help explaining some of the fundamental concepts put forth in several key articles dealing with the Austro-Asiatic and Austronesian language families. Bill has also been responsive to the questions I have had over the years concerning Chinese or Asian linguistics; I am very grateful for his help, patience, and insightful responses to my elementary questions.

Laurent Sagart, another leading figure in Chinese historical linguistics, also extended a helpful hand in guiding me in current linguistic theories and recent work on the origins of and possible interactions among East Asian and Southeast Asian languages. He read through a later draft of my linguistics section and was able to point out errors and recommend further readings on areas and issues that I had previously neglected. I especially thank him for his generous help, the many articles he sent me, and the email exchanges we were able to have before this book was sent off to the press.

If I still do not completely comprehend the details of the many linguistic debates introduced to me by Bill Baxter, Laurent Sagart, and Bob Blust, or the archaeological work introduced to me by Jiao Tianlong, Francis Allard, and Alice Yao, and if I somehow fail to present the pressing concerns and debates of archaeologists and linguists adequately in this book, it is certainly all my own fault, reflecting my own limitations as an outsider to these disciplines, and not the commitment of my colleagues to my education in these areas.

My official entrée into the field of Southeast Asian Studies occurred in the summer of 2012 at a conference in Singapore, supported by ISEAS and organized by Victor Mair, on China and its southern neighbors. The conference provided a great forum for meeting a host of people who are working on very interesting facets concerning all sorts of cultures and civilizations associated with the maritime networks that connected mainland Southeast Asia and China to the islands of the Pacific and the rest of the Eurasian Continent, especially India. I was particularly thrilled to have finally met the great Wang Gungwu, a true gentleman as well as scholar of prodigious mental capacity and scope, whose 1958 book on the Nanhai trade inspired and informed this book and my entire outlook on the role of the South China Sea in East and Southeast Asian history. I would like to thank the other participants in the conference – Andrew Abalahin, Sylvie Beaud, Andrew Chittick, Hugh Clark, Rebecca Shuang Fu, Derek Heng, Liam Kelley, Nam Kim, Li Tana, Yi Li, Victor Mair, Sean Marsh, Tansen Sen, Tan Chin Tiong, Michele Thompson, Geoff Wade, and Takeshi Yamazaki – for providing me with a better sense of connections between China Studies and Southeast Asian Studies and the interesting problems they are working on in relationship to the maritime networks and cultures of (mostly) the pre-modern periods.

I am indebted to the American Council of Learned Societies for awarding me a Charles A. Ryskamp Research Fellowship. This generous award helped fund a year's worth of additional research time and travel in 2011–2012, which allowed me to meet and work with key linguists, archaeologists, and scholars during a short stint in Hawaii. In addition, I am thankful to Penn State for the sabbatical year they just granted me in 2013–2014, during which I was able to finish up the rough draft for this book. The two reviewers of this book gave me insightful comments that shaped the final product in tangible ways. And I would like to thank the American Council of Learned Societies and Chiang Ching-kuo Foundation for their generous support of a conference that I co-hosted with Kathlene Baldanza at Penn State University on April 12–13, 2013, "Maritime Frontiers in Asia: Indigenous Communities and State Control in South China and Southeast Asia, 2000 BCE–1800 CE." The many stimulating discussions by the participants of this conference helped contribute to my overall understanding of frontier issues in pre-modern China and Southeast Asia. Participants included Hugh Clark, Wu Chunming, Eric Henry, Michael Puett, Francis Allard, Jiao Tianlong, Kate Baldanza, Greg Smits, John Whitmore, Tansen Sen, Wingsheung Cheng, Billy So, Robert Antony, Liam Kelley, Niu Junkai, Michele Thompson, Sean Marsh, James Anderson, Magnus Fiskesjö, Ronnie Hsia, Victor Mair, Stephen O'Harrow, and Paul Smith.

Lastly, without the help and support of colleagues, friends, and family, as well as wonderful caretakers and teachers for my children, I would never have had the time or energy to complete this book. I thank in particular Xiao-bin Ji for being on call for quick, last-minute discussions and clarifications of confusing passages in Chinese histories. I thank Dan Shultz for helping me make the three maps for this book, as well as Cynthia Col and Julene Knox for their superb work on indexing and copy-editing, respectively. I also thank Michelle Rodino-Colocino, Todd Colocino, Eric Hayot, and Chunyuan Di for local support in State College, and I am indebted yet again to Derek Fox, my husband, for his efforts at sharing the Sisyphean task of childrearing with me

Note on the text

Parts of Chapter 5 were originally published as "Barbarians or Not? Ethnicity and Changing Conceptions of the Ancient Yue (Viet) Peoples (c. 400–50 B.C.)," *Asia Major* 16.1 (2003), 1–32. Parts of Chapters 8 and 9 of this book, as well as one of the political timelines in Part II, were originally published in "Representations and Uses of Yue 越 Identity Along the Southern Frontier of the Han, c. 200–111 BCE," *Early China* 33 (2009): 1–35. A version of the section on hairstyles in Chapter 6 was published as "Layers of Meaning: Hairstyle and Yue Identity in Ancient Chinese Texts," in Victor Mair and Liam Kelley, eds. *Imperial China and Its Southern Neighbors* (Nalanda-Srivijaya Series), Singapore: Institute for Southeast Asian Studies, 2015. The author thanks the publishers from *Asia Major, Early China*, and the Institute for Southeast Asian Studies for their permission to reprint material from these works in this book.

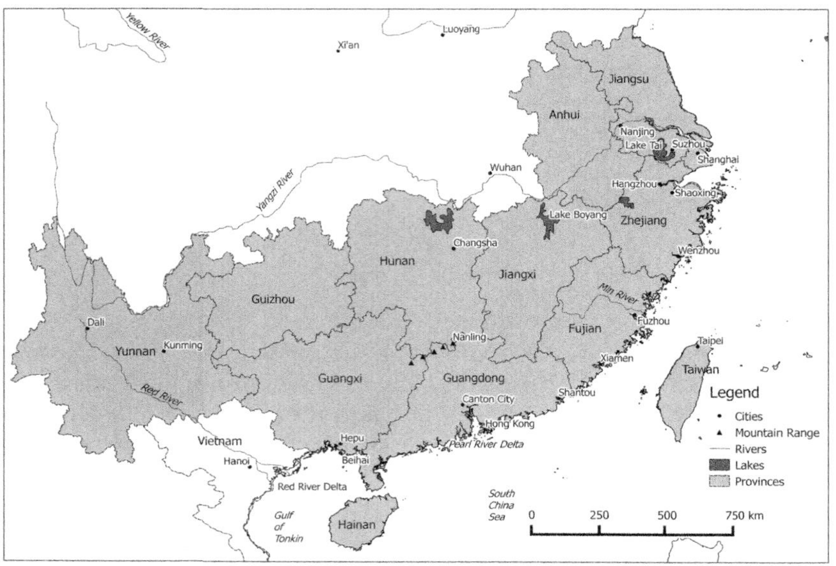

Map 1: Provincial map of modern south China and Vietnam (drawn by Dan Shultz).

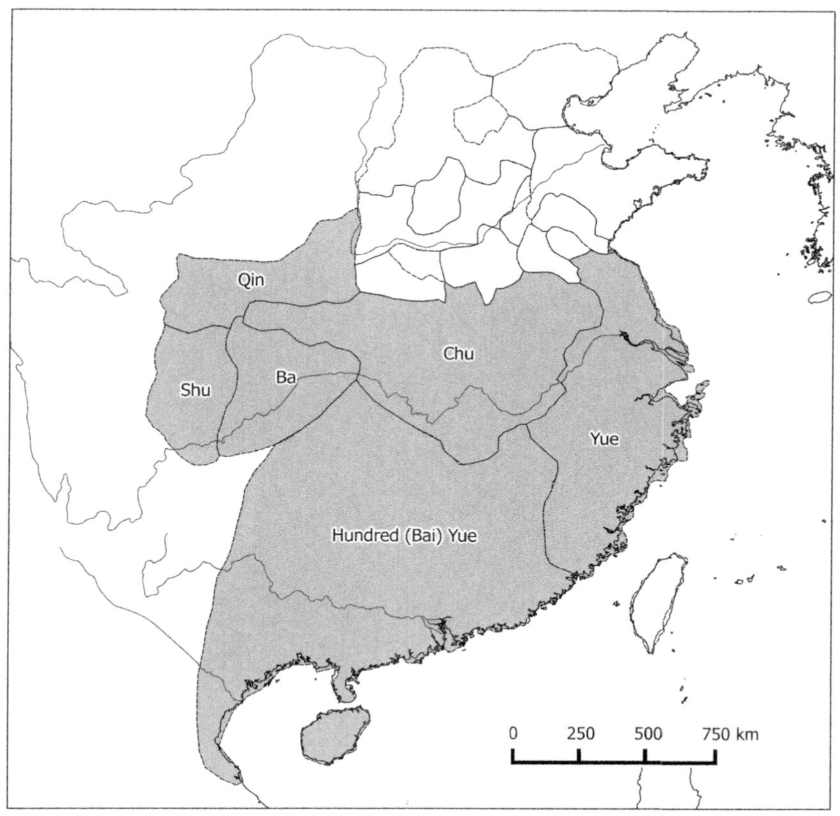

Map 2: Warring States China, 350 BCE (drawn by Dan Shultz).

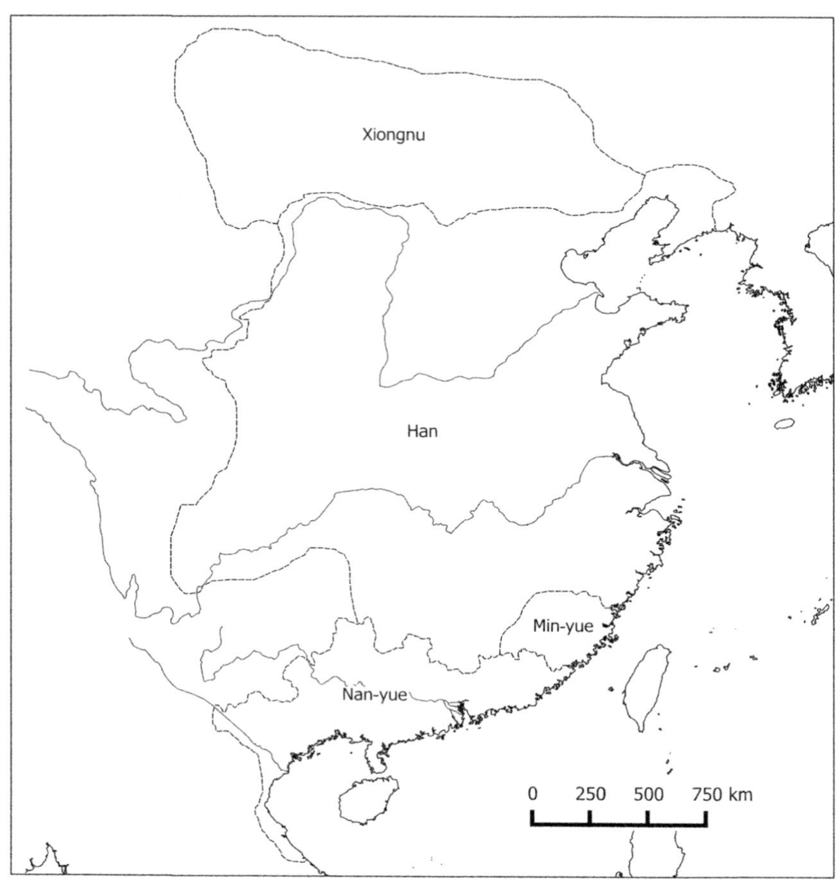

Map 3: Early Han era, 200–111 BCE (drawn by Dan Shultz).

Part I

Orientations: definitions and disciplinary discussions

Introduction: concepts and frameworks

This book is rooted in a great irony of Chinese history: what was once considered the dreaded ends of the earth during the classical and early imperial periods over time came to represent the epitome of Chinese culture. The ancient Yue 越, with its associated peoples, cultures, and lands, was transformed in the Chinese South from other to self, foreign to familiar, theirs to ours, and non-Central States to "China." Cantonese, the language spoken in modern Hong Kong and Guangdong Province, as well as other neighboring areas, is referred to as the "Yue language," even though it is primarily a Sinitic language and not what the natives of the region would have spoken in early times.[1] Chinatowns throughout the world attest to the far-flung influence of the Sinitic Yue legacy. Even the identification of the Han Chinese as Tang ren (唐人 people of the Tang Dynasty), used mainly by overseas Cantonese and some overseas Min-nan and Hakka peoples and referring to all Chinese as a whole, is linked to the South. Lastly, many renowned scholars of the second millennium CE either came from the South or lived much of their lives there. In addition to the exodus of elites during certain major periods of northern turmoil or conquest, extensive migrations to south China, along with the unending trickle of northern migrants seeking political refuge, farmland, and business opportunities throughout the first and second millennia CE, helped transform the entire Southland from native Yue to Sinitic Yue and, hence, to what could be understood in some contexts as quintessentially Chinese.

Meanwhile, in Vietnam – or "South of Yue" – people see themselves as descendants of the Yue and use Yue history and identification as a means of distinguishing themselves from the Han or Chinese people and state. The story of the naming of the state of Vietnam during the early 1800s reflects the ways in which the identification of "Yue" was contested and

[1] Its links to the native, non-Sinitic languages of the region remain largely unrecognized and understudied.

negotiated on both sides of the Sino-Viet border to make claims to Han and non-Han legacies.[2] Most histories of Vietnam include a dedicated section to the ancient kingdom of Southern Yue (during Han imperial times) as a critical part of early Vietnamese history.[3] Vietnam's strategic co-optation of the culture and history associated with ancient Yue provides an alternative example of how the term has been altered and reused in a different guise to support identity and nationalism.

Both Chinese and Vietnamese cultures share the valuable history of the Yue. Peoples from both regions and later eras interacted with the various meanings of Yue from the ancient tradition to help decide on important matters of identity and politics. But what was this ancient tradition of Yue that they interacted with? What were the various meanings associated with the term, its peoples, and cultures? This book sheds light on how, even in ancient times, people fashioned and refashioned their own identity and that of the Yue, long before the rise of either concepts of "China" or "Vietnam." It describes the contours of a relationship – that between the Hua-xia 華夏 (the blossoming, or efflorescent Xia [of the Xia Dynasty]) self and the descriptions of their alien Yue counterparts to the far southeast and south.

Given the nature of the ancient accounts I will be looking at, all of which derive from texts and were recorded in Chinese, we will not be able to garner very much about how Yue people self-identified or expressed themselves. This raises an important question: How does a historian of texts go about investigating a group that left no written record but nonetheless helped deeply shape the dominant group's self-identity and historical trajectory? The answer, I believe, lies in the stated goals of my inquiry and narration of the past. Instead of providing a straightforward, factual account of who the Yue were and how they thought of and grouped themselves, I aim to show how early Chinese texts reveal a different reality about the Yue. Such a reality describes not who they were exactly or how they identified or grouped themselves (although this is sometimes hinted at), and not even what they said or thought about themselves. Rather, such a reality contains a substantial degree of imagination – by viewing the foreign other through the warping lens and

[2] See Kate Baldanza, *The Ambiguous Border: Debate and Negotiation in Sino-Viet Relations in the Fifteenth and Sixteenth Centuries*, forthcoming, for a thorough retelling of how Vietnam got its name. As Baldanza narrates, the reigning Emperor of the Nguyễn Dynasty of Vietnam, Nguyễn Phúc Anh, proposed the name "Nanyue [Southern Yue]" to the Jiaqing Emperor of the Qing, requesting the latter's acceptance and formal recognition of it. This name was summarily rejected by the Qing because it might have been perceived as laying claims to the then-Qing provinces of Guangdong and Guangxi.

[3] See Keith Taylor, *The Birth of Vietnam* (Berkeley: University of California Press, 1983).

perspectives of an ever-changing self, we reveal important aspects about how a certain culture wished to see, build up, and maintain its own self-image.

This retelling of the Yue suggests that the making of Yue as an identity or concept in ancient texts is akin to an activity – a process – of comparing oneself to the other, of gazing into what were perceived as the depths of otherness so as to reveal, maintain, mitigate, or strengthen some perceived aspect of the Hua-xia self. Indeed, the relative absence of the Yue voice and perspective in the texts of ancient China makes it impossible to answer, let alone ask, certain questions. But this does not render the texts themselves useless. By focusing our inquiry on perceptions and representations of identity, I hope to let the texts tell us what they can about the ancient past. Rather than test what the Hua-xia said about the Yue as people or cultures in terms of an objective reality, or assume that what they said about the other was true in fact, I examine how the term "Yue" was meaningful as a label, which in turn says much about what the ancient Chinese thought about both themselves and the alien others to their South.

Coming to terms with how the 'Yue' in ancient accounts were described helps us piece together the ways in which the Hua-xia people constructed their own identities vis-à-vis southern difference. Such an inquiry should help us understand how southern peoples and cultures were perceived in ways unique to the southern frontier and its special environments. It is by elucidating characteristics of the southern other – and asking why such characteristics were chosen to be worthy of mention or discussion in the first place – that the representations of the self emerge in sharper focus. We thus begin to fathom the limits of the presentation of both self and southern other in the ancient textual tradition.

Changing concepts of Yue and Hua-xia identity would have played a large role in shaping real, concrete political actions and policy. Thus, the study of Yue identity not only provides a deeper understanding of the intellectual history of North–South cultures and encounters. It can also serve as a backdrop to the history of human action and the eventual transformation of the ancient South into something both quintessentially Chinese and Vietnamese.

Ethnicity plays a key role in our inquiry. Most frequently, the type of identity that casts Yue as a foil to Hua-xia is ethnicity. Even though the term "Hua-xia" (sometimes also "Zhu-xia," or, "the varied Xia") ostensibly has political connotations by pointing to the many descendants of a so-called Xia polity (c. 2000–c. 1600 BCE), authors of Warring States times (c. fifth–third century BCE) did not use such a term for its political value. Instead, they invoked Hua-xia as an identity that transcended contemporary, political, or state groupings.[4] Similarly, even though the term "Yue" is also related to a prominent political state in later Zhou times (sixth–fourth centuries CE), such a term also comes to transcend political boundaries as it develops in the literature as a southern foil to the Hua-xia.

Viewing Hua-xia and Yue primarily through the concept of ethnicity will center our discussion around cultures and a sense of their inherited or acquired group identities, rather than any and all forms of identity. To be sure, we will have to address political identity to a certain extent, especially when exploring the multifaceted ways in which terms associated with the Yue are used in the literature. But by searching for Hua-xia and Yue as ethnonyms, or analyzing them in terms of what we would call "ethnicity," we can formulate a more precise theory concerning the origins of Chineseness as an ethnic concept. We can also better observe how ethnicity was maintained and preserved in the early history of China.

Jonathan Hall, a scholar of ancient Hellenistic identity, has proposed a useful definition of ethnicity that is grounded in the notion that ethnicities, while there might be a strong biological component, are at base constructed categories. Ethnicity, for Hall, grounds identity in a shared myth of descent and a shared association with a specific territory.[5] As thus conceived, ethnicity is an open, malleable social construction capable of changing with time and place. Such a definition is general enough to allow for varying claims on ethnicity but specific enough to distinguish ethnicity from other forms of identification such as nationality, kinship, and culture. It is important to note that one's sense of shared, ethnic territory is often not separate from one's sense of shared descent, as original ancestors are necessarily locatable to a specific place and time. In this book, I expand upon Hall's concept of ethnicity to include the following three criteria: a shared myth of descent, a shared association with a specific territory, and a shared sense of culture. This way of understanding ethnicity renders problematic any conception of Chineseness as a primordial, essential, and, indeed, biological marker of much significance.

[4] The traditional understandings of Chinese history start with the Xia Dynasty, followed by the Shang and then the Zhou. While the existence of the latter two have been confirmed through archaeological and textual data, the existence of the Xia as a polity or dynasty is still much contested by scholars. K. C. Chang believes that there is good reason to think that the Xia corresponds to an archaeological culture called the Erlitou 而里頭, which dates to 1900–1350 BCE. See K. C. Chang, "China on the Eve of the Historical Period," in Edward Shaughnessy and Michael Loewe, eds., *The Cambridge History of Ancient China* (Cambridge: Cambridge University Press, 1999), pp. 71–73.

[5] Jonathan Hall, *Ethnic Identity in Greek Antiquity* (Cambridge: Cambridge University Press, 1997), p. 32.

The criterion of a shared sense of descent helps clarify that ethnicity can be dependent "not so much on real descent as on the symbols of descent and the individual's belief in them."[6] It also helps distinguish ethnicity from other identifications such as nationality and culture, more strictly understood. Nationalities can be based solely on geography (territory) and politics, but ethnicities are different because they incorporate a group consciousness, mythic or not, of one's origins and ancestors. Similarly, ethnicities can be distinguished from culture insofar as they include a notion of shared descent. Many people can share the same culture, defined as the shared habits and practices of people living in similar environments, without having to share the same myth of descent.[7] But when a people shares a myth of descent, a geographic location, as well as a sense of culture, it is fair to refer to them in terms of ethnicity.

Inscribing difference: identity as an ascribed taxonomic landscape

Judith Butler has famously referred to identity as performance, or stylized acts.[8] Identity can indeed be fruitfully discussed in such constructivist terms, and in this book I subscribe to a thoroughly constructivist way of approaching the concepts of identity and ethnicity. But rather than focus on formulations about performance and the dramatic act of expressing the self and other, I wish to draw our attention to larger social, cultural, and political processes of labeling, inscribing, classifying, and delimiting others. For example, of the ancient Yue peoples and cultures we know very little about the performative, stylized acts of identity enacted by the Yue themselves, especially with regards to the active construction of their own self-identity. We are mostly only privy to descriptions written by Hua-xia elite outsiders about the Yue, or to the act of ascribing identity to someone outside the self. Even though "performance" is a perfectly acceptable way of understanding such a manner of constituting the Hua-xia self through the Yue other, I am not convinced that it

[6] Mark Elliott, *The Manchu Way: The Eight Banners and Ethnic Identity in Late Imperial China* (Stanford: Stanford University Press, 2001), p. 17.

[7] Culture and ethnicity can be deeply related, thus making it difficult to distinguish between the two. Sow-theng Leong points to competition with others as a factor that helps carve an ethnicity out of people with a shared culture. While she does not give a definition of ethnicity, she provides us with a possible source or reason for its emergence, along with its clear connection to culture. Sow-theng Leong, *Migration and Ethnicity in Chinese History: Hakkas, Pengmin, and Their Neighbors*, Tim Wright, ed. (Stanford: Stanford University Press, 1997), pp. 19–20.

[8] Judith Butler, *Gender Trouble: Feminism and the Subversion of Identity* (New York: Routledge, 1990).

appropriately encapsulates the more cerebral act of inscribing and mapping that characterizes the written, cognitive forms of creating taxonomic schemes of self and other. For this reason, while I acknowledge the power associated with viewing identity as performance, I prefer in this book – especially given the types of sources we have for analyzing identity construction in ancient Chinese texts – to use metaphors of inscribing, mapping, categorizing, and delimiting that seem to be more relevant to the written nature of our sources.

There seems to be an inherent tension and interaction between the performance of one's own self-identity in real-life time and the inscriptional ossifying of the self and non-self in written genres. In the former, there is an assumption of the multiplicity of the self; it is opaque and fluid, uncertain until the moment at which it is expressed outwardly as an act and performance. Yet even in its crystallization in the moment, there is always an assumption that, just as time inevitably progresses forth, so too the self will change and move with it.

In the case of constructing the self and other through certain written genres, one's intention is often to create a myth of something that transcends the momentariness of time, to record and create a lasting impression in time-as-duration and time-eternal, not ephemeral or moving time. The objective here is to carve out an image with definite spatial attributes in indefinite time, minimizing the temporary nature of the self by transforming momentary and liquid performance into a solid incarnation of difference. Thus, when a self ascribes traits to another through writing, it etches out an entire landscape of distinctions between self and other, sometimes without fully realizing the extent to which the very inscription of self or other implies both that which is carved out and that which fills the background and, indeed, the entire canvass. This concept of identity as a "still life," or essentialized and congealed self couched in an ascribed, taxonomic landscape of other, is what I will explore when trying to express the contours of ancient tropes, arguments, or other types of formulations of the Hua-xia and Yue.

Habits of nomenclature

While the bulk of my analysis revolves around terms such as "Hua-xia" and "Yue," there are other ways of referring to the self and southern other that will no doubt give rise to a bit of confusion. Let us first discuss the problems associated with references to the "Hua-xia" self and how such a term links to current conceptions of Han or Chinese identity. During the time frame examined here, the Chinese self is conceived of in a variety of ways. Politically, the people representing the Central States voice usually saw themselves as belonging to the "Zhou" sphere of ritualized interaction. Even early empires such as the Qin and Han based their shared sense of history in the Zhou and its predecessors, and so there is little need to debate the existence of such a political and cultural identification.

Today, the majority of Chinese identify themselves as being of Han ethnicity. This ethnonym has a complicated history, although its origins as something that describes the Hua-xia peoples is relatively recent, perhaps dating from Tang times and proliferating only during the Mongol-ruled Yuan Empire (1271–1368 CE).[9] In fact, throughout much of Chinese history, peoples inhabiting what is now the Chinese mainland were sometimes referred to by their dynastic identities such as the "Han," "Tang," "Song," "Yuan," "Ming," and "Da Qing." But the use of such dynastic labels usually referred to a person's political or official relationship to the state, not their ethnic identity. In later periods, some of these identities were picked up by people in China and elsewhere to refer to the Chinese as an ethnicity (e.g., "Han" was a label used later in both China and Japan, and "Tang" was used in Japan to refer to the Chinese).

During the Han Empire, the term "Han" came into use by outsiders such as the Xiongnu to refer to people of that dynasty – people who worked for or who came under the fold of the Han regime. It was therefore not an ethnic identity. While the compound, *Han ren* 漢人 (Han person) appears several times in Sima Qian's *Shi ji* (c. 100 BCE, *Records of the Office of the Grand Historian*), the use of "Han" to designate an ethnic or cultural group, as in *Han zu* 漢族, rather than political officials affiliated with the Han Empire does not appear until around the sixth and seventh centuries CE, in texts such as the *Shuijing zhu* 水經注 (Commentary on the Classic of Waterways) and the *Beiqi shu* 北齊書 (History of the Northern Qi, completed in 636).[10]

More relevant for the ancient time period in question is the ethnonym, "Hua-xia," which later in history became subsumed under many different kinds of ethnic identities associated with Chinese culture and people, such as the "people of the Tang (唐人)," "people of the Han (漢人)," the "Chinese (中國人)," etc. Most of the Hua-xia people were situated in what were known as the Central States (*zhongguo* 中國) or Central Plains (*zhongyuan* 中原) region – that is, in the region surrounding the Wei and

[9] See Endymion Wilkinson's *Chinese History: A Manual* (Cambridge: Harvard University Asia Center, 1998), pp. 96–97, 682–688, 694–704, 722–725.

[10] Wolfgang Behr, "'To Translate' is 'To Exchange' 譯者言易也 – Linguistic Diversity and the Terms for Translation in Ancient China," in N. Vittinghoff and M. Lackner, eds., *Mapping Meanings: The Field of New Learning in Late Qing China* (Leiden: E. J. Brill, 2004), p. 178.

Yellow River valleys in what is now north-central China.[11] Some intellectuals of these regions, notably the Ru ritual specialists (such as Confucius and his disciples), consistently invoked a shared myth of descent that transcended political boundaries within the above-mentioned region. In addition to Hua-xia, another term used during the Warring States period to refer to this ethnic group is "Zhu-xia" 諸夏 (the many, or various [descendants of] Xia), or "Zhou" (周, referring to the cultural legacy of this dynasty). That these three terms – "Hua-xia," "Zhu-xia," and "Zhou" – represent an ethnic and not merely a cultural or political category can be most clearly seen in the *Analects*, which we will discuss in greater detail in Chapter 5.

Another important point in this study concerns the false notion that "China" or the "Chinese" in ancient times stands for anything that is in conflict with or distinct from what is "southern." For example, when we assume a southern person was Chinese simply because he or she was not native to the region, we do a disservice to the hugely diverse array of cultures and peoples who inhabited the southern regions who were neither strictly Hua-xia nor native and whose mixed cultural identities were in a constant state of flux. Indeed, perhaps the term "local" is a better word for anyone who lived for a significant period of their life in the South, whereas "Hua-xia" and "Yue" are better at designating perceived cultural or ethnic identifications.

While the ancients often saw themselves in terms of the great Hua-xia versus Yue divide, our analysis of the situation need not always embrace or describe reality using such crude distinctions. I try in this work to emphasize hybridity and identities in flux. One way to gain a sense of the fine-grain and complexity of the situation is to break down such giant nomenclatures as Hua-xia and Yue into more specific names of groups and peoples, especially as they are reflected in the sources. I sometimes

[11] While I will usually refer to the Chinese as "Hua-xia" in this book, I will also make use of other terms provided us by the primary sources of the period, such as "Zhu-xia," or people of the Central States or Central Plains. I will try to be specific about semantic scope and context when invoking certain markers of identity, although such a goal is not always easy, given that the sources themselves are usually tremendously unclear on such matters.

The toponym "Central States" can be defined during Warring States times as a vague reference to those states that occupied the regions around the Zhou heartland in the Wei and Yellow River Valleys. General usage of the "Central States" also suggests that these states were full-fledged members of the Zhou political sphere, and, intriguingly, it does not include interstitial states of the same geographic region in which large portions of ethnic groups resided, such as those associated with the four directions –the Rong, Di, Man, Yi. The position of Chu as a Central State appears to be indeterminate, although my sense is that it is usually considered an outlier because of its high population of southern Man-yi peoples.

refer to what others before me have called "China" as the "Central States," which connotes a smaller, more north-central region of the East Asian mainland. When referring to political entities, I invoke the specific dynasty or regime (Chu, Qin, Han, Southern Yue, Min-yue, Eastern Yue, Wu, Wei, etc.) in question, whether such entities were associated with Hua-xia or Yue. And specific ethnic terms such as Yu-yue, Luo-yue help us zoom in on regional particularities as well. My use of such ethnic and political terms is not meant to deny that there was continuity of identity among these various southern regimes and peoples, but merely to add to the specificity of my study and demonstrate the incredibly transient nature of identities – despite attempts by authors to congeal and fix them.

Framework for this study

In the study of frontier histories of China, there is a consistent focus on its northern and northwestern frontier.[12] This is not surprising, given the constant and often intense military conflicts between the agricultural areas associated with the Central Plains region and the more nomadic, steppe regions whose peoples seemed to be perpetually in motion and not infrequently at war with their southerly neighbors. To be sure, throughout history, large ethnic and political groups from China's northernmost regions such as the Rong 戎, Di 狄, Xiongnu 匈奴, Tabgatch (Tuoba Xianbei 拓拔鮮卑), Khitans 契丹, Jurchen 女真, Mongols, and Manchus continuously played a role in shaping, guiding, creating, or even dictating the policies and actions of various Chinese states. Much of the scholarship on these peoples makes clear that China as we know it was in part defined

[12] A few representative examples provide an adequate picture of this scholarly emphasis on the historical northwest. Joseph Fletcher, Owen Lattimore, Pamela Crossley, Mark Elliott, James Millward, Laura Hostetler, Jonathan Lipman, and Dru Gladney have done extensive work on Chinese and Inner Asian, Sino-Manchu, and/or Sino-Muslim relations from Qing to contemporary times. For ethnicity and/or foreign relations in pre-Qing China, scholars such as Jonathan Skaff, Thomas Barfield, and Morris Rossabi hover around the northern frontier, as they analyze Khitans, Jurchens, and Mongols in relationship to the "Han" peoples of the Tang through Yuan periods. More than a few scholars from the disciplines of art history or religion during the Six Dynasties period address the issue of Chinese ethnic relationships with Central Asian warlords and leaders in historical perspective. For early imperial China, Nicola di Cosmo and Marc Abramson focus primarily on the northern and western frontier areas and distinctions among ethnicities and nomadic groups from Central and Northern Asia. Nicola Di Cosmo's book on pre-Han and Han relationships to "steppe" cultures that practice pastoral nomadism provides an important starting point for understanding the early history of China's northern frontier. See Nicola Di Cosmo, *Ancient China and Its Enemies: The Rise of Nomadic Power in East Asian History* (Cambridge: Cambridge University Press, 2002). See also the work of Wang Mingke 王明珂 on frontiers and the northern Qiang peoples before the Han.

through its various interactions with the nomads and influences along its northern frontier, some coming from very far away along the Silk Roads spanning Eurasia.

The current study serves as a counterpoint to the work already being done in northern frontier and Silk Roads studies. It observes the creation of Chinese identity through a different lens, one that is directed southward at the southern frontier of the Central Plains civilizations. Rather than tell a story of long-distance travel by camel, horse, and caravan across great stretches of dry terrain and parched earth, the story of the South is one of wet, riverine, and coastal cultures that involve boats, canoes, swimming, and sea creatures. These cultures participated in their own Silk Road – perhaps better referred to as a maritime highway – that connected Eastern Eurasia to Southeast Asia, Japan, India, and beyond to Africa and the Middle East. And, as did their Silk Road counterparts in the North, theses southern, maritime cultures engaged in an endless feedback loop of cross-cultural, cross-ethnic encounters that helped throughout the centuries define Chinese identity as a whole.

In his 1958 book on the subject Wang Gungwu convincingly demonstrates the importance even during pre-imperial eras (Warring States times) of the Nanhai (South Sea) trade network – a vast network of interactions in the South China Sea and toward India – based on luxury goods such as pearls and rhinocerous tusks.[13] No doubt, this trade network formed the backbone in the development not only of Southeast Asian cultures and polities, but also of early cultures and polities along the southern frontier of China, Taiwan, and possibly Japan as well. To ignore the role of the mainland's southern frontier and its maritime connections with the rest of the world would be to omit a vital component in the shaping of Chinese and other identities and cultures on mainland East Asia. It is time for scholars to correct the bias toward northern frontier studies and pay attention to ways in which the pre-modern southern frontier was also a hotbed of cross-cultural interactions, ethnic assimilation and strife, and identity formation and flux.

For contemporary periods, the bulk of scholarship on ethnicities focuses on the southwestern frontier, in the regions of Yunnan, Sichuan, and Guangxi Provinces, where a multitude of ethnic minorities still reside.[14] Even though the ancient northern frontier and the modern

[13] Wang Gungwu, *The Nanhai Trade: Early Chinese Trade in the South China Sea* (originally published in 1958 by the *Journal of the Malayan Branch of the Royal Asiatic Society*; Singapore: Eastern Universities Press, 2003), pp. 1–9.

[14] Anthropological work on China generally hovers around the southwestern frontier, near the borders of Tibet, Burma, and Vietnam. See representative works by Joseph Rock, Sow-theng Leong, Stevan Harrell, and Ralph Litzinger. See also works by authors in

southwestern frontier differ significantly from what we encounter in the ancient South, some of the methodologies these sub-fields use for investigating cross-cultural interactions and the ethnic other can be usefully applied to the question of Hua-xia and Yue identity. At times, it will be useful to draw upon insights learned through contemporary, anthropological studies of cross-ethnic encounters in southwestern China or current Southeast Asia to discuss the issues at hand.

We begin this book by laying out a general background to Yue studies. In addition to an overview of the received political history of various Yue states, I discuss linguistic and archaeological evidence to provide a better sense of the problem of the Yue and the difficulty in understanding who the Southerners on the ancient frontier might have been. Here, one of my main goals is to magnify the problems concerning the use of the term "Yue" as a presumed entity in such social science fields. Later chapters of this book present perspectives on the ancient Chinese textual repertoire for talking about the Yue and identity. A main line of inquiry into the early textual records involves the extent to which ideological statements, rhetoric of cultural dominance and superiority, and certain tropes of the savage other found in the ancient Chinese textual sources can be taken at face value – as representative of what actually happened or existed along the southern frontier. It is in these sections that I offer a critical glimpse of what the sources say, asking why they say it, and providing my own explanation of the literature in light of the larger Hua-xia cultural tradition and sense of self in which statements about the Yue are couched.

Recent historiography on the Yue

Recent historiography on the Yue comes in many flavors. While each general region in China – typically divided according to contemporary provinces or cities like Hong Kong or Guangxi Province; or by perceived ancient regions such Min-yue; or by archaeological sites such as the tomb of the king of Nan-yue – usually has a book or two dedicated to the history of the region, city, or site, it is less common for authors to write histories of the entire southern frontier. One might think that the hundreds of volumes on Bai-yue (Hundred Yue) history would cover this frontier, but, alas, coverage and synthetic interpretation of the larger picture are not the same. Most volumes concerning the Bai-yue involve detailed studies of very specific questions or sites; they do not perform the meta-level interpretive work that is necessary to show whether or not this region

Stevan Harrell, ed., *Cultural Encounters on China's Ethnic Frontiers* (Seattle: University of Washington Press, 1996).

hung together as a coherent space of cultural, ethnic, commercial, and political networks.

To date, there are about a handful of more monumental works concerning the history of the South, and they were all written well over thirty-five years ago.[15] While none of these works looks at Yue identity in detail, each provides a general framework for understanding migration, trade, and settlement patterns along the southern frontier. The most important Chinese scholar to write on the South was Xu Songshi 徐松石, who wrote primarily in the first half of the twentieth century.[16] Xu contributed to an understanding of the history of regions surrounding contemporary Guangdong and Guangxi Provinces and produced a seminal study of three various ethnic groups of the South, called *Research on the Tai, Tong, and Yue Peoples*.[17] In this latter work, Xu links the ancient South (including areas in the Red River Delta) with languages related to the Tai linguistic group (in particular, the Zhuang language), thereby establishing an important connection between south China and Southeast Asia. Xu's works provide the basic background to the work of many Western scholars of south China and Vietnam. While it still represents an important introduction to the peoples and histories of the region, its emphasis on data from early twentieth-century minorities in China limits the book's value for contemporary scholars. In addition, Xu – writing in the 1930s – could not make use of useful archaeological and linguistic advances that we have since benefitted from.

Herold Wiens' *China's March Toward the Tropics* is one of the first Western works to attempt a large-scale history of the settlement and migration patterns, as well as colonial tendencies, of Chinese peoples in the Southland. Basing his work on the work of Xu Songshi and Wolfram Eberhard, who published a series of works on ethnicities and local cultures in China's South, Wiens recounts the approximately 2,500-year recent history of migration and settlement along the southern frontiers of China.[18] He explains this settlement according to a general pattern of

[15] See Herold Wiens, *Han Chinese Expansion in South China* (Hamden, CT: Shoe String Press, 1967); C. P. FitzGerald, *The Southern Expansion of the Chinese People* (New York: Praeger Publishers, 1972); and Wang Gungwu, *The Nanhai Trade*. For a comprehensive, monumental study of the history of Vietnam, see Taylor, *The Birth of Vietnam*.

[16] Xu Songshi 徐松石, *Yue jiang liu yu renmin shi* (History of the Yue River [Pearl River] Delta Peoples) 粤江流域人民史 (Shanghai: Zhonghua shuju, 1939).

[17] Xu Songshi, *Taizu, Zhuangzu, Yuezu kao* 泰族僮族粵族考 (Research on the Tai, Tong, and Yue Peoples) (Beijing: Zhonghua shuju, 1946).

[18] Herold Wiens, *China's March Toward the Tropics: A Discussion of the Southward Penetration of China's Culture, Peoples, and Political Control in Relation to the Non-Han-Chinese Peoples of South China and in the Perspective of Historical and Cultural Geography* (Hamden, CT: Shoe String Press, 1954); Wolfram Eberhard, "Kultur und Siedlung der Randvolkers China," *T'oung Pao*, Supplement to Vol. 36 (1942).

commercial and agricultural migration, in conjunction with military conquest and colonial policies, which sets the scene for the fully successful sinicization of the entire region. The metaphors Wiens employs are of masculine dominance, which include the imagery of penetration, unstoppable marching, impregnation, ravage, and rape on the part of the Han-Chinese from the North; and submission, subjugation, and meek surrender to conquest by the southern peoples.[19] Such forceful and heavy-handed language aside, Wiens' overarching theory of migration and military first, and then culture (only as an easy second) is interesting and persuasive insofar as it makes a strong case for robust and steady influxes of peoples and conquests from the North. However, I find Wiens' work far too simplistic, insofar as he uncritically accepts much of the biased record of Chinese successes found in Chinese historiography and dynastic histories.

One of the more sophisticated studies of the history of the South is C. P. FitzGerald's *The Southern Expansion of the Chinese People*, published in 1972.[20] FitzGerald counters Wiens' dramatic history of human conquest and migration with a more natural metaphor of "seepage" and "overflow." Taking China to be a giant reservoir of people that cannot be contained and must burst forth across as much territory as possible, FitzGerald sees cultural change occurring first with pioneering individuals, and only later as a function of top-down imperial efforts and cultural power stemming from the elites in society:

> The picture of Chinese southern expansion into the borderlands ancient or modern is not therefore one of a violent imperial conquest which brought in its train a new dominant culture. It is rather a pattern of seepage, of slow overspill from the great reservoir which was China, and which grew ever greater by the absorption of the former borderlands, and then spread still further into new regions. It was a combination of trading penetration, peasant and small urban settlement, enriched by the injection of exiles of higher education, and only finally, or at a late stage, consummated by political control and incorporation in the Chinese state.[21]

One aspect of FitzGerald's narrative, which helps explain his account of Chinese seepage into the frontiers, involves the initial transformation of culture by local elites. FitzGerald hypothesizes about the linguistic "sinicization" of a region and infers from such a model a larger pattern of cultural change on the whole:

[19] See especially the language of sinicization used on pp. 159–161, 194, and otherwise throughout Wiens, *China's March Toward the Tropics*.

[20] FitzGerald, *The Southern Expansion*. [21] *Ibid*., p. xxi.

The local language borrows from Chinese many terms which it did not use before, adds many new words for new artifacts and for ideas which it has now to express. Gradually it becomes a quasi-Chinese dialect, pronounced in a fashion almost unintelligible to Han Chinese, but none the less [*sic*] strongly marked by Chinese linguistic influence. It is not written, only spoken. As the wealthier members of the community begin to seek education, they turn to Chinese literature as the sole medium of expression open to them. They become bilingual, and later, perhaps, abandon the native language altogether. Those who have reached this stage are considered to be "Chinese." In this sense many millions of southern Chinese are the descendants of peoples who were once quite alien both in speech and custom.[22]

This fascinating passage reveals a few key claims about the alleged mechanics of sinicization along the southern frontier. First, wealthier, intellectual natives wished to embrace Chinese language by borrowing previously unknown terms. This practice resulted in the transformation of the local elite language into a "quasi-Chinese dialect." The written language also became more accessible to such natives, and so they turned to Chinese culture – via Chinese literature – as a "sole medium of expression." It is at this point that such elites abandoned the native language, which was already a "quasi-Chinese dialect," signifying the final stage of sinicization among this group of people. The transformation from native to Chinese, at least for elite natives, was complete.

Such an account of sinicization differs significantly from Wiens' story. It lends much more power first to language and then to culture than the largely economic, agricultural, and military narrative that Wiens presents. It also renders elites into the primary agents of cultural change, rather than peasants, merchants, and soldiers. Despite these general differences, FitzGerald's story assumes the model of sinicization every bit as much as Wiens'. However, because FitzGerald provides an elaborate hypothesis of linguistic sinicization, his use of the term "sinicization" seems rather appropriate, considering that the Chinese language was indeed eventually adopted widely in the South (except in Vietnam and among southern minorities). FitzGerald also provides connective tissue linking linguistic sinicization to cultural sinicization, thereby making his claims for the latter all the more persuasive.

Another contribution of FitzGerald's book is its broad view of history as a holistic system of networks and influences, even from regions not directly connected to the South. For example, FitzGerald contends that the steppe regions of north China serve as critical factors in China's relationship to its southern frontier;[23] and, similarly, he explains Vietnam's victory as an independent kingdom in the second millennium

[22] *Ibid.*, p. xvii. [23] *Ibid.*, pp. 1–3.

CE largely in terms of its role as a buffer for potentially hostile Khmer forces farther south. In both these examples, FitzGerald uses the logic of large-scale geopolitical forces to explain historical contingencies and outflows into local, southern regions. His work thus weaves detailed analysis of the mechanics of local, cross-cultural transformations with larger understandings of global influence to create an interesting and powerful account of sinicization in the South.

Another monumental early contribution to the study of the southern frontier is Wang Gungwu's 1958 account, *The Nanhai Trade: Early Chinese Trade in the South China Sea on Economy of the South China Sea.* This work provides a detailed overview of the history of maritime trade between China, the South China Sea, and even the Indian Ocean. Its interest is not so much in the question of sinicization or cultural change along the frontier as in the extent to which the Chinese peoples and states were involved, from a very early date, in the global trade of the South China Sea that linked China with India and numerous kingdoms in-between. And while Wang is very careful to distinguish among the various types of actors in this trade – the Chinese affiliated with the central government (exiled or displaced governors or high officials from the North), interpreters (court eunuchs who may have previously had local, southern ties – as erstwhile prisoners of war), Yue maritime merchants and groups, the so-called "Chams" in the region of Rinan during the later Han, local peoples in every region who help supply merchant ships and keep them company, tribal chieftains, as well as Guangdong and Tonkin natives – he nonetheless charts out a China-centered history of economic maritime involvement, and does little to explore cross-cultural exchanges and the transformation of identities across time.[24] His work thus provides a crucial framework for developments and activities in the region, but it does not bring us closer to understanding the changing nature of Chinese and Yue identities in the early period.

More recent work takes on pieces of the long history of the South, either by period or region.[25] Keith Taylor's 1983 masterpiece on the history of

[24] Wang Gungwu, *The Nanhai Trade*, see especially pp. 13, 16, and 19.

[25] For background in the Southland starting just before or around the Sui-Tang imperial period, see Edward Schafer, *The Vermilion Bird: T'ang Images of the South* (Berkeley: University of California Press, 1967); and Charles Holcombe, "Early Imperial China's Deep South: The Viet Regions through Tang Times," *T'ang Studies* 15–16 (1997–1998): 125–156. For the Song and Mongol periods, see the various works of Hugh Clark, James Anderson, and Sean Marsh. Hugh Clark, *Portrait of a Community: Society, Culture, and the Structures of Kinship in the Mulan River Valley (Fujian) from the Late Tang through the Song* (Hong Kong: The Chinese University Press, 2007), and *Community, Trade, and Networks: Southern Fujian Province from the Third to the*

early Vietnam centers itself around the Red River Delta and the associated myths or creation stories of the peoples in that region.[26] Basing much of this history on sources that were written by Vietnamese literati during the thirteenth through fifteenth centuries CE, some of which derive from Tang administrators in the region, the stories are too far removed from the period they purport to represent to serve as veritable accounts of Han and pre-Han times.[27] In general, it is fair to say that such a view of Vietnamese history is every bit as fused with the creation of a Vietnamese ethnic and political culture as are the early legends of the sage rulers in the Hua-xia culture of Warring States and early imperial China.

Taylor is on firmer ground when he discusses the history of actual kingdoms such as the Nan-yue and Han control over the Red River Delta. A virtue of recounting this history – based largely on classical Chinese texts such as the *Shi ji*, *History of the Han*, or *Later Han History* – with an eye to Vietnamese history is that it forces one to move beyond standard sinocentric claims to this history, thus revealing the inherent biases of such an ethnocentric approach. Indeed, Taylor presents all this material concerning the Red River Delta, Nan-yue, and regions slightly north of Vietnam, as part of the larger history of Vietnam. A problem, however, is that he shifts the perspective from sinocentric to Viet-centric, and so he does not escape the basic problem of an ethnocentric bias in historiography. Furthermore, the Viet-centered approach taken by Taylor is not written according to a history of the ancient meanings of Yue as Viet, which is more the approach of this book. It is rather a Vietnam-centric account that bases itself on a later, ethnocentric and nationalistic, and, hence, highly selective understanding of Yue/Viet heritage and history.

Thirteenth Century (Cambridge: Cambridge University Press, 1991); James Anderson, *The Rebel Den of Nung Tri Cao: Loyalty and Identity Along the Sino-vietnamese Frontier* (Seattle: University of Washington Press, 2007), and "A Special Relationship: 10th–13th Century Sino-Vietnamese Tribute Relations and the Traditional Chinese Notion of World Order," Ph.D. dissertation, 1999, University of Washington. See also Sean Marsh, "Facing South: Geographies and the Colonization of Song China's Southern Frontier," Ph.D. dissertation, forthcoming University of California, Davis.

[26] Taylor, *The Birth of Vietnam*. Taylor's updated volume, *A History of the Vietnamese* (Cambridge: Cambridge University Press, 2013), continues to tell a grand history from the multifaceted perspectives of the peoples inhabiting the Red River region.

[27] An important source that Taylor draws extensively from is the *Lĩnh Nam chích quái* 嶺南摭怪, which dates to the fourteenth century. The *Đại Việt sử ký toàn thư* (大越史記全書 Complete Historical Records of Đại Việt), one of Taylor's main sources, was commissioned and completed during the fifteenth century and is derivative of earlier sources, but probably not much that was earlier than the Tang period. I am indebted to Liam Kelley for his research into the historicity of these Vietnamese sources and for alerting me to the utter lack of indigenous (non-Chinese) textual sources for the period that I work on. Private conversation, 11/4/2011.

Another contribution to the history of the Southland can be found in Edward Schafer's 1967 book, *The Vermilion Bird: T'ang Images of the South.*[28] Primarily limited to the Tang period and to the Lingnan region that was home to the Nan-yue (Schafer refers to it as "Nam-viet") in early Han times, this resource provides an encyclopedic discussion of peoples and their various ethnicities and religious worldviews, along with information concerning natural resources and landscapes associated with the South. Filled with details of southern exotica, curiosities, and oddities, this book provides an excellent, panoramic view of the region without venturing too much into interpretive synthesis of any event or theme. The effect is more of a mapping out of people and things, as well as some events, in time, rather than an explanatory account of the history of any single ethnicity or group. As such, Schafer's work on the South, while delightful and of great value, does not provide a higher-level interpretive framework for understanding Hua-xia and Yue relations or dynamic transformations of identity and ethnicity.

While Schafer focuses his history on Southern Yue and its legacies around the Lingnan regions, Hans Bielenstein provides us with a theory of sinicization concerning the ancient Yue region around Fujian, often referred to as "Min-yue," although the region went by many different names in history.[29] Bielenstein's statements concerning the relative lack of easy overland access to Fujian appear to be true, and such a factor may have indeed played an important part in early Qin-Han imperial decisions to pay less attention to the region. However, his claim concerning the gradual, peaceful migration into and sinicization of the region has yet to be challenged. Without further data on the long history of this region, we cannot assume such an easy, wholesale replacement of native practices and beliefs, merely because of the gradual and unceasing arrival of Sinitic migrants from the north.[30]

The current inquiry adds to this sparse collection of studies on the southern frontier by providing a critical account of Yue ethnicity during Warring States and early imperial times. While circumscribed in time period (roughly 450 years from c. 400 BCE to 50 CE), it offers a synthetic interpretation of how self-identity was constructed and preserved in relationship to the Yue other. The geographic scope implied by the study of the term "Yue" is massive, and the hermeneutical problems

[28] Schafer, *The Vermilion Bird.*

[29] Hans Bielenstein, "The Chinese Colonization of Fukien Until the End of T'ang," in Soren Egerod and Else Glahn, eds., *Studia Serica Bernhard Kargren Dedicata* (Copenhagen: Ejnar Munksgaard, 1959).

[30] Hugh Clark is helping to fill in such a gap in his writings on the history of Fujian primarily during the Song period. See especially Clark, *Community, Trade, and Networks.*

considerable. Nonetheless, it is important to transcend the highly specialized, regional, or site-specific nature of current Bai-yue scholarship from Asia and to complicate and refine frameworks for understanding the history of the South as represented by the monumental works discussed above. By analyzing the way the ancients viewed a large swath of their southern frontier – through the lens of Yue – we at once confront the notion of a unified southern people and try to understand why Central Plains writers might have viewed and depicted themselves and the other in such a manner.

1 Who were the Yue?

The ancient expanse of peoples who were associated with the term "Yue" is enormous, consisting in over 3,200 kilometers of coastline and its inland routes from Shanghai all the way down to central Vietnam. Naturally, such an expanse was home to a wide variety of ethnically, culturally, and linguistically diverse peoples. Any survey of the early literature demonstrates that the term "Yue" encompassed vastly different sets of people, depending on who was using the term as well as how and when they were using it. Given its status as a generic, fluid marker for certain groups of the South, the term "Yue" would appear to be of limited use in learning about its peoples. Yet because of its historicity – because ancient authors of the Central States invoked it and meant something when doing so – it is worth understanding in and of itself. In addition, as a historical concept and category of identity, the Yue of the South help to define the self – the Hua-xia or Central States agent – shedding light on how the construction of the Chinese or Sinitic self was unique and localized, so that what would eventually come to be known as "Chinese" of the South was not at all equivalent with what would eventually come to be known as "Chinese" farther north.

The term "Yue" is the modern, Mandarin pronunciation of what in Chinese used to be phonetically closer to "Viet" ("Ywat" in Middle Chinese). This term is the same that is used in the present-day name for Vietnam, as well as the historical Nam-Viet (Southern Yue) – from which the name "Vietnam" derives.[1] Yue/Viet (hereafter: Yue) was a name used

[1] Yu-yue 於越 is the longer version of the ethnonym, Yue 越. *Yu* is a prefix that occurs frequently in the indigenous languages attributed to the Yi and Yue peoples of eastern and southern China. Such prefixes were often dropped in later Sinitic references but are maintained in some early texts. See also Meacham, "Defining the Hundred Yue," *Indo-Pacific Prehistory Association Bulletin 15*, Chiang Mai Papers, Volume 2 (1996), p. 99; C. Michele Thompson, "Scripts, Signs and Swords: The Viet Peoples and the Origins of Nom," *Sino-Platonic Papers* 101 (March, 2000), p. 17. Thompson cites Jeffrey Barlow's thesis that the Yue were identified by their association with a large, battle axe (*yue* 鉞), which serves as a cognate for Yue. (p. 22.) Rao Zongyi, citing the *Da dai li ji* (Ritual Records of Dai the Senior), further claims that the term "Yue" can be a loan character for

by ancient peoples from the Central States (i.e., the largely Sinitic, or Chinese-speaking world) to designate a wide array of coastal and southern indigenous peoples inhabiting areas south of the Yangzi River.[2] Who were the peoples associated with this term? Did they constitute a single ethnic, political, archaeological, or linguistic culture, or were they heterogeneous on most of these fronts?

We do not know, for the most part, what the Yue – the peoples inhabiting these southern lands in the first millennium BCE – actually called themselves, nor are we aware of the types of ethnic and cultural distinctions they drew among themselves. We do know, however, that they possessed cultures and spoke languages that were radically different from those of the Central States. It is likely that the languages of these Yue peoples served as the ancestors of later Southeast Asian and most Oceanic languages and groups. The sheer linguistic difference between the Sinitic forms of language spoken closer to the Central Plains region around the Yellow and Wei Rivers and the Austro-Asiatic, Hmong-Mien, or proto-Austronesian that were spoken around and south of the Yangzi River is dramatic and supports what all sources suggest to be the case: that the peoples inhabiting the ancient Southland were drastically different from their northern counterparts.

Upon hearing the term "Viet," or "Vietic," one might immediately think of the Vietnamese people and their history and culture.[3] In its early history, however, the term "Yue" does not seem to be limited to a single type of people, ethnicity, or even culture. Depending on the historical period and context, "Yue" could refer to ancient peoples associated with the eastern (*yi* 夷), southern (*man* 蠻), southeastern, or even – in part – southwestern "tribes," or "barbarians."[4] Indeed, the term "Yue"

qi 戚 and vice versa. Rao Zongyi, "Wu Yue wenhua," in *The Bulletin of the Institute of History and Philology Academica Sinica* 41.4 (1969), note 2, p. 628. "*Yuenan*," or Vietnam, was first bestowed as a name for the nation of Vietnam by Manchu rulers of the Qing in 1802. Holcombe, "Early Imperial China's Deep South: The Viet regions through Tang times," *T'ang Studies* 15–16 (1997–1998): 133.

2 I choose the pronunciation "Yue" and not "Viet" so as to avoid singular, exclusive association with what now constitutes the Vietnamese state and people. Even though the modern-day Chinese pronunciation is still not neutral, I hope that by using it I can mitigate against the dangers of anachronistically projecting current, nation-based identities onto the past.

3 Eric Henry uses "Vietic" for all things associated with the term, "Yue." He thereby tightly links Vietnamese culture with the Yue past, which is warranted in some ways. However, I wish to avoid suggesting the equivalence of the ancient Yue and the modern nation state of Vietnam, as the former was a much broader and vaguer term that potentially applied to thousands of different groups across the entire southern frontier. See Eric Henry, "The Submerged History of Yue," *Sino-Platonic Papers* 176 (2007): 1–36.

4 That the Shandong Peninsula was also somehow implicated in the coastal cultures that later became known as "Yue" can be seen in some of the historical references to or descriptions of what would usually be considered "Yue" as "Yi." E. G. Pulleyblank

implicated the entire eastern and southern/southwestern coastal region of mainland East Asia, extending from as far north as the regions around modern-day Shanghai and Lake Tai (Taihu 太湖) near Jiangsu and Zhejiang Provinces, all the way down through Fujian, Guangdong, and Guangxi Provinces to include the northern part of contemporary Vietnam. The only regions of the South not connoted by Yue were the mountainous, far southwestern regions of Sichuan, Yunnan, and parts of Guangxi, which the Chinese referred to by other terms.

Even though the term "Yue/Viet" makes up part of the name for the current state of Vietnam, Vietnam is only a part of the story. Keith Taylor has noted that the current population of Vietnam is more likely to have stemmed from the regions around modern-day Vietnam itself than from the old Yue regions of China (which during imperial Han times included what is now northern Vietnam).[5] Current scholarship, however, muddies such a picture by uncovering the extensive ties that certain areas in Vietnam had with migrant populations from south China (earlier, from the southwest regions and, later, very clearly, from Fujian after the first millennium CE).[6] While ruling classes of the state of Yue in southeast China did migrate southward, and conceivably some of them into Vietnam over time, it may not be plausible to claim that the bulk of the current population of Vietnam migrated from other places.[7] Rather than the mass migration of peoples, cultural migration may have been the

discusses important ethnic changes in Shandong in his article, "Zou 鄒 and Lu 魯 and the Sinification of Shandong," in Philip J. Ivanhoe, ed., *Chinese Language, Thought, and Culture: Nivison and his critics* (Chicago: Open Court, 1996), pp. 39–57.

5 See Keith Taylor's refutation of Leonard Aurousseau's migration theory of the Yue peoples. Taylor, *The Birth of Vietnam* (Berkeley: University of California Press, 1983), pp. 314–315.

6 The tight connection between the Min people of Fujian in later periods of history and the founders of the first Vietnamese states around and after 1000 CE – indeed the tight connection between elite cultures of south China and Vietnam – attest to this ongoing network of influence. I thank Liam Kelley for this insight, who draws upon the works of Edward Schafer, *The Vermilion Bird* (Berkeley: University of California Press, 1967), pp. 48–79, and Hugh Clark, *Community, Trade, and Networks: Southern Fujian Province from the Third to the Thirteenth Century* (Cambridge: Cambridge University Press, 1991).

7 This type of claim is echoed in Mark Lewis' more general comments concerning the immobility of the peasants as opposed to the elite in "Warring States: Political History," in Edward Shaughnessy and Michael Loewe, eds., *Cambridge History of Ancient China: From the Origins of Civilization to 221 BC* (Cambridge: Cambridge University Press, 1999), p. 649. Some possible moments of increased southward migration of Yue and Central Plains peoples into the Red River region include the conquest of Yue by the state of Chu in 333 BCE (although it is doubtful that the Yue elite/people of the Yangzi Delta region actually migrated any farther south than Fujian and eastern Guangdong at the time); the establishment of the Southern Yue kingdom in the late third century BCE; the conquest of the Southern Yue by Han in 111 BCE; and throughout the Han in the periods covered by this book.

predominant connection between Vietnam and the southern coast of what is now China. At the very least, one can say that the Yue/Viet cultural traditions, including the nomenclature "Viet," were exported to the region because of the close maritime and regional connections among southern cultures throughout the prehistoric and historic periods.

Despite demonstrating the extensive scope of the Yue/Viet in ancient times – well beyond the confines of what the modern term "Vietnam" may suggest – this book implicates Vietnam and Vietnamese culture in an important way. Traditional Vietnamese historiography, dating from the fourteenth and fifteenth centuries CE, considers the Viet to be the cultural heritage of the Vietnamese, especially since Han era times when areas around the Red River Delta were incorporated administratively into the fold of the Han Empire. There may be reason to connect the current peoples of the Red River regions primarily with ancient peoples from inland Sichuan, Yunnan, and even Guangxi Provinces, as these regions shared a similar Bronze and Iron Age culture. This is especially apparent from giant, Bronze Age drums associated with the Dong Son culture of ancient Vietnam, whose geographical scope stretches from southwestern China and Vietnam to Indonesia and beyond. These drums are particularly associated with the Red River Delta region and areas of Guangxi, Yunnan, and Vietnam.[8] Notably, however, regions of Sichuan and Yunnan were linked in ancient times to other ethnonyms or place names such as Ba 巴 and Shu 蜀, and Yelang 夜郎 and Dian 滇, not the Yue.[9] Despite apparent cultural connections between these southwestern regions of ancient China and Vietnam, the ancient Yue were also likely to have played a significant role in the shape of early Vietnamese history. This is especially the case since the very concept of the Viet peoples and cultures was eventually absorbed by the people of the Red River region, and so, at the very least, the Yue played a significant role in the imagined creation of Vietnamese identity.

[8] Robert E. Murowchick, "The Interplay of Bronze and Ritual in Ancient Southwest China," *JOM* 42.2 (1990): 44–47.

[9] For an account of the greater area of Shu from an archaeological perspective, see Robert Bagley, ed. *Ancient Sichuan: Treasures from a Lost Civilization* (Princeton: Princeton University Press, 2001). See also Rowan Flad, *Salt Production and Social Hierarchy in Ancient China: An Archaeological Investigation of Specialization in China's Three Gorges* (Cambridge: Cambridge University Press, 2011). For the ancient Shu (in the Sichuan Basin) and Ba (in Sichuan near Chongqing to the Three Gorges region, and as far southwest as Guizhou and Yunnan), see Rowan Flad and Pochan Chen, *Ancient Central China: Centers and Peripheries Along the Yangzi River* (Cambridge: Cambridge University Press, 2013), pp. 71–73; 140–143. For archaeological work on ancient Yunnan, see the work of Alice Yao, "Culture Contact and Social Change Along China's Ancient Southwestern Frontier, 900 B.C.–100 A.D.," Ph.D. dissertation, University of Michigan, 2008.

The Yue people of ancient times are also relevant to the modern peoples of island Southeast Asia and Oceania. If the ancient Chinese had been aware of the geographic extent of the types of peoples they were calling "Yue" on the mainland, then they would have realized that some of the people they were calling the "Yue" who inhabited the southeastern seaboard were likely to have been the mainland counterparts to the Austronesians on Taiwan. Robert Blust has recently demonstrated with elegance and force that Taiwan had been the original homeland of the Austronesian-speaking peoples, who are represented on the island today by its various aboriginal peoples.[10] Taiwan was also the likely jumping-off point for such peoples, who later set out on one of the largest and most expansive migrations in history. As history tells us, the natives of early Taiwan disembarked during Neolithic times from Taiwan and set about on a series of intensive maritime migrations across the entire Pacific and Indian Oceans, eventually coming to colonize much of Oceania, as well as the many islands of the remote Pacific, such as Tahiti and Hawaii.[11] Given that the southeastern Chinese mainland was likely the homeland of the native inhabitants of Taiwan, one may be justified in thinking about the groups of people on Taiwan as akin to the "Yue" in southeast coastal China.[12] Therefore, in studying the history of the Yue on mainland East Asia, we are addressing the likely history of proto-Austronesian peoples who were linguistically related – possibly even genetically and culturally related, too – to the greatest maritime colonizers of the pre-modern world.

As for the peoples of Southeast Asia, this history is also important because some of the Yue were likely to have been not only genetically related to modern-day Southeast Asians, but in many ways ancestral as well.[13] A variety of disciplines have demonstrated that the coastal peoples – likely the proto-Austronesian-speaking peoples just mentioned – were carriers of cultures, material goods, and languages that became incorporated into the fabric of a wide variety of cultures across Southeast Asia.

[10] Robert Blust, "The Austronesian Homeland: A Linguistic Perspective," *Asian Perspectives* 26 (1984/5): 45–67.

[11] Peter Bellwood, "Austronesian Prehistory in Southeast Asia: Homeland, Expansion, and Transformation," in P. Bellwood, J. Fox, and D. Tryon, eds., *The Austronesians: Historical and Comparative Perspectives* (Canberra: Australian National University, 1995), pp. 96–111.

[12] Tianlong Jiao's work on the Neolithic and Bronze Age cultures of Fujian and the islands off its coast are rendering these ancient cross-straights connections clearer. See Tianlong Jiao, *The Neolithic of Southeast China: Cultural Transformation and Regional Interaction on the Coast* (Youngstown, N.Y.: Cambria, 2007).

[13] Peter Bellwood, "Asian Farming Diasporas? Agriculture, Languages, and Genes in China and Southeast Asia," in M. Stark, ed., *Archaeology of Asia* (Blackwell Publishing, 2006), pp. 96–118.

Many may have migrated back from Taiwan to the coastal regions of southern China, northern and central Vietnam, Hainan, and elsewhere, establishing settlements of Austronesian-speaking peoples across the coasts of the South China Sea and propagating their genes, languages, and cultures.[14] Early trade networks and paths of migration were undoubtedly sufficient to have exposed many coastal communities to their influence. This is especially the case for the island communities of Southeast Asia.

Peninsular Southeast Asia also likely incorporated peoples who had been subsumed under the category of "Yue" by the ancient Chinese, and a certain sub-group of the Yue may even have been the direct ancestors to peoples who now speak Mon-Khmer and Thai languages.[15] The very fact that "Yue" was a designation for both southeastern/southern (around modern-day Jiangsu, Zhejiang, Fujian, and Guangdong Provinces), and some southwestern peoples (around modern-day Guangxi Province and northern Vietnam), means that the term seems to have crossed over a substantial linguistic divide between the Austronesian or proto-Austronesian-speaking cultures of the South (largely represented in the coastal communities) and the Austro-Asiatic-speaking cultures of the South (perhaps more inland and/or linked to the Southwest). In any case, it seems clear that "Yue" was a term that included a variety of peoples that we today might otherwise wish to divide or chop up in a multitude of ways.

One must also not forget the obscured, ancient relationships between peoples who are now designated as "minority, non-Han, non-Vietnamese (many of whom James Scott has recently called 'inhabitants of Zomia' – the mountains and highlands of China and Southeast Asia)," and their Sinitic neighbors who migrated from the North, who interacted with them but also helped push them to the margins and mountain tops. The scope of this book does not touch upon the history of lowland and highland interactions among various ethnicities of the South, mostly because there is little textual evidence for such interactions in the early period that I examine, and the archaeological data have yet to be acquired and synthesized more broadly. But it is nonetheless important to keep in

[14] Laurent Sagart has proposed a unique hypothesis that the Tai-Kadai language family has a much more direct descent from early Austronesian forms on Taiwan, and that a certain sub-group of Austronesians on that island may have migrated back to the mainland (coastal areas near modern-day western Guangdong and Guangxi) and settled there, thus repopulating the mainland with a certain form of Austronesian language. See our discussion of this hypothesis in Chapter 2. Laurent Sagart, "The Higher Phylogeny of Austronesian and the Position of Tai-Kadai," *Oceanic Linguistics* 43 (2004): 411–444.

[15] Peter Bellwood, "The Origins and Dispersals of Agricultural Communities in Southeast Asia," in I. Glover and P. Bellwood, eds., *Southeast Asia: From Prehistory to History* (London and New York: Routledge Curzon, 2004).

mind that lines of ethnic difference, even in the ancient period, were not merely drawn according to geographic region, state, ancestry, or shared culture, but perhaps also between highlanders and lowlanders who often inhabited the same general geographic sphere.

Given the importance of the Yue to many types of East Asian, Southeast Asian, and Pacific/Oceanic peoples, one would expect the history of this ethnonym and the peoples associated with it to be better understood today. However, quite the opposite is true: remnants of ancient Yue cultures have been transmitted only in oblique ways, through archaeological discoveries and brief mentions of the Yue in ancient Chinese texts. The term "Yue" survives today in the name of the Vietnamese state (*yue nan* 越南, or, "Viet south" – "Viet of the South," – as the Vietnamese likely took it; or "South of the Viet" – as the Chinese likely took it) and the Sinitic dialect now spoken in the province of Guangdong (*yue yu* 粵語).[16] The fact that material cultures associated with indigenous southern peoples seem to have changed rather rapidly once extensive contact with Central States migrants and colonialists began, along with the fact that linguists are unsure which languages the Yue peoples actually spoke, means that it is difficult to trace the existence, development, and disappearance of what may have been many Yue cultures and languages in Asia's long history. Clearly, much of the problem lies in the fact that "Yue," as used in our sources, usually sheds light on Hua-xia formulations of the other and is less illuminating with respect to the histories of southern peoples in Asia as perceived by themselves.

Hawaiian history serves as an example of how the history of Yue is all but unknown to most people around the globe, even to those for whom it may be quite relevant. Most modern Hawaiians have never heard of the Yue peoples, yet some of the Yue types of people were likely to have been the mainland version of their ancestors on Taiwan, who later spread out not just over the South China Sea but to far-flung islands and locations across the Indian and Pacific Oceans (as far west as Madagascar and as far east as the Hawaiian islands). Even so-called distinctive Yue cultural traits, such as stilt houses, tattooing, wearing the hair short, and excelling

[16] The term "Yue" that is associated with the Cantonese language, cultures, and peoples (粵) has been glossed since Han times as the Yue 越 that is the subject of this book. In the story about the naming of the state we now know as "Vietnam," it is interesting to note that the Nguyen ruling clan had originally proposed naming their state "Namviet" – after the former empire/state along the southernmost border of the Han, but that the Qing government did not wish to allow for any confusion with their own territories in Guangzhou and Guangxi (erstwhile centers for Southern Yue statelets), suggesting the inversion, "Vietnam" instead. See Kathlene Baldanza, *The Ambiguous Border: Debate and Negotiation in Sino-Viet Relations in the Fifteenth and Sixteenth Centuries*, forthcoming, for more on this story.

in swimming (among a variety of others), which likely had been transmitted by mainland Southerners to descendants far and wide throughout history, are never traced back to the Yue, but to other peoples and later ethnonyms, such as the Polynesians of Oceania, the Li of Hainan, the Zhuang of China's Guangxi Province, the Vietnamese of the Red River Valley, etc. Only in the last fifty years have scholars in archaeology, linguistics, history, and various other fields begun to piece together the puzzle of the ancient Yue peoples and their relationships to later historical identities and groups.

The ancient South

The southern regions of the East Asian mainland were inhabited by a multiplicity of peoples and cultures, some of which are only now emerging in a more distinct fashion through archaeological work and new discoveries. The kingdom that attained perhaps the most sustained power in pre-imperial China was that of Chu, an expansionistic state on the southern edge of the Central States heartland, which at times encapsulated the Han River region, the Nanyang Basin, and areas of the Upper Huai and western Huainan.[17] Another unique area of development occurred in the southwestern region, near modern-day Sichuan, under the Warring States names of Shu 蜀 and Ba 巴.[18] And, most relevant for this volume, the Wu-yue 吳越 regions of the southeastern edge of the Central States – around Lake Tai and modern-day Jiangsu and Zhejiang – had been inhabited by peoples of the so-called Yue culture. After the downfall of the state of Yue caused by Chu (333 BCE), many princes and members of the aristocratic elite fled to areas even farther south – into regions of modern-day Fujian, and possibly even Guangdong and Guangxi Provinces (it is less likely that they went even farther west and south, into the northern reaches of modern Vietnam, although one cannot rule out this possibility). Some of the native Southerners over whom these ousted Yue elites generally ruled were known by Sinitic-speaking peoples as the "Bai-yue (百越 Hundred Yue)," but no doubt, given the breadth of the category, the people they dubbed "Bai-yue" were mostly ruled by local, native chieftains and lords.

[17] See Barry Blakeley, "The Geography of Chu," in Constance Cook and John Major, eds., *Defining Chu: Image and Reality in Ancient China* (Honolulu: University of Hawaii Press, 1999), pp. 9–20.

[18] See the various essays in Bagley, *Ancient Sichuan*, as well as the discussion in Steven F. Sage, *Ancient Sichuan and the Unification of China* (Albany: State University of New York Press, 1992).

While there are substantial differences among the Man-yi 蠻夷 (Southern others) populations associated with Chu, those associated with the southwest regions of Shu and Ba, and those associated with the Bai-yue, one might wish to speak more generally of the relationship between the entire ancient South and the Han Empire, comparing it to the relationship between the Han and Xiongnu along its northern frontier.[19] Southern and northern frontier regions were considerably less populated than the Central Plains heartland. Despite sparse populations, northern confederations were much stronger from a military standpoint than the kingdoms in the far South. These latter kingdoms were generally overpowered by the military men arriving from the Central States regions who would use their strength and superior military organization to maintain control over local inhabitants. In addition to effectively using military technologies and modes of organization from farther north, such enterprising men would adopt administrative techniques associated with empire-building in the Central States regions to bolster their political base and claims to rule.

Unfortunately, in the South, as opposed to the North, the states that were created were not sufficiently strong militarily to withstand a concerted attack from their Han neighbor to the north. This was true despite the fact that these states could be massive and economically vibrant, and were often able to maintain independence and put up a good fight against a northern onslaught for several years or even decades.[20] This general weakness vis-à-vis the Han Empire no doubt affected the story of cultural interactions between Han and the Yue. However, the question of whether Han military dominance translated wholesale into cultural dominance and sinicization in the South, especially during Han times, remains to be explored in more detail.

Identities of significance: Yue, Bai-yue, Man-yi, Ou, and Luo

Identities are notably difficult to pin down, always shifting over time and wholly dependent on one's perspective or vantage point. Yue identity in

[19] For discussion of the northern Han frontier, see Nicola Di Cosmo, *Ancient China and Its Enemies: The Rise of Nomadic Power in East Asian History* (Cambridge: Cambridge University Press, 2002).

[20] Many scholars simply disregard the history of military resistance in the South, considering the latter to have "had little political coherence or military might," and using such reasons to explain the eventual colonial successes in the South of various "Chinese" states from the North. Magnus Fiskesjö, "On the 'Raw' and 'Cooked': Barbarians of Imperial China," *Inner China* 1–2 (1999): 141–142. I disagree with this interpretation and would advance other reasons, such as shifts in demographics from north to south over centuries and two millennia, to discuss the eventual colonization of the South.

the ancient South proves to be particularly difficult to analyze, not least because the literature from the period usually depicts Yue as an ascriptive, as opposed to a self-proclaimed, identity, or autonym. This means that those who are being called "Yue" might not have seen themselves as "Yue," and even if they did self-identify as such, they most certainly would not have thought of themselves as "Yue" in the same way that Sima Qian or other Central States authors thought of them as "Yue."

Yue identity is also elusive because it appears to refer to so many different peoples and regions of the East Asian mainland, at times referring broadly – through the reference, "Bai-yue" – to the entire swath of what now includes China's southern provinces and northern Vietnam. More than a dozen ethnographic compounds existed in the early literature using the term "Yue" or referring to a group that was considered by Chinese authors to belong to Yue communities or lineages.[21] As outlined above, Yue areas extended roughly from contemporary northern Vietnam up through Guizhou, Guangxi, and Canton, and on to Fujian and even Zhejiang on the East China Sea. If one refers to the ancient Spring and Autumn/Warring States state of Yue, that was probably centered around the Hangzhou and Shaoxing area of modern-day Zhejiang Province, extending up through Shanghai. Farther south, the actual Han period kingdom of Southern Yue – distinct from the more eastern Han period kingdoms of the Eastern Yue, Eastern Ou, or Min-yue – was geographically massive, covering a distance roughly from Canton Province through the northern reaches of contemporary Vietnam.[22]

Our sources reveal a Central States bias of referring to most peoples at the extreme southern periphery of the mainland as the Bai-yue.[23] This

[21] Some of these compounds will be discussed below, but because of time we will not be able to examine or even explain the background of most of these terms. Some of the most common compounds are as follows: Yu-yue 于越, Gan-yue 干越, Min-yue 閩越, Dong-ou 東甌, Dong-yue 東越, Nan-yue 南越, Xi-ou 西甌, Luo-yue 駱越, Yang-yue 揚越, Dian-yue 滇越, Teng-yue 騰越, and Yue-xi 越巂, among others. For a simple overview of these compounds in early textual references, see Wu Chunming 吳春明, 从百越土著到南岛海洋文化 (Maritime Cultural Interactions between the Indigenous Yue in Southern China and Austronesians in Southeast Asia and the Pacific) (Beijing: Wenwu, 2012), pp. 74–79.

[22] That is, Southern Yue laid claim to a great geographical region, but just how much of that area was actually under its control, and how one defines "control" of a region in such a time and place, are other tricky questions.

[23] For an example of the many places still considered to be the homelands of the Yue peoples, see Chen Guoqiang 陳國強 *et al.*, *Bai Yue minzu shi* 百越民族史 (Beijing: Zhongguo shehui kexue, 1988). This book also includes the aboriginal peoples of Taiwan (the ancestors to all Polynesians) as Yue. For more on the shifting terms "Yue" and "Hundred Yue," see Brindley, "Barbarians or Not? Ethnicity and Changing Conceptions of the Ancient Yue (Viet) Peoples (c. 400–50 B.C.)," *Asia Major* 16.1 (2003): 10–15. As mentioned above, the connection with Vietnam is not trivial, especially since the peoples of such a region later would look back upon the ancient Yue (*Viet*)

name denotes both difference – *bai* (百 hundred) referring of course not to an exact count but to the fact of many, variegated Yue peoples – and similarity, insofar as all such Southerners indiscriminately fell into the category of Yue. It is also a relatively late term; the first and only occurrence to Bai-yue that I have found in the Warring States occurs in the compendium, the *Lüshi chunqiu* (呂氏春秋, Mr. Lü's Spring and Autumn Annals), datable to 239 BCE and written for the Qin ruler who would later become the First Emperor.[24] In texts dating to the Han, the occurrence of Bai-yue is more frequent, although also not ubiquitous, appearing a couple dozen times total in historical sources such as the *Shi ji, Yantie lun* (Discourses on Salt and Iron), and *Han shu* (Han History).

The Bai-yue were strewn across the entire South and Southeast. One of our key figures to be examined, Zhao Tuo 趙佗, mentions some groups of Yue people in terms of the small kingdoms as far west as Guangxi and northern Vietnam, referred to as the Western Ou 西甌, and Luo 駱 (the latter also known historically as Ou Luo 甌駱, or Au Lac in Vietnamese historiography).[25] Such groups were lumped into the category of "Bai-yue" by the Sinitic peoples to the north even though they may have had tenuous affiliations with so-called Yue peoples farther east.

Aside from the terms "Yue" and "Bai-yue," there are also references to *Man* 蠻, *Yi* 夷, or the compound Man-yi 蠻夷. These terms appear as a more generic reference to aliens of all types associated with the South, especially from the perspective of the traditional Central States cultures at the "center." As we will see below, people of Central States origins refer to the Yue as both "Yue" and "Man-yi." Other references to Man-yi in the state of Chu, for example, include Chu natives under the rubric of Man-yi.[26] The same applies for the southwestern kingdoms of Ba 巴 and Shu 蜀.[27] For this reason, it is perhaps fair to say that while the Yue were usually considered to be Man-yi, not all Man-yi were considered to be Yue. In general, the Yue were a specific sub-set of Man-yi who seem to have been associated with much of southern and southeastern China (especially the coastal parts), as far west as contemporary Guangxi and northern Vietnam.

In its earliest usages, the ethnonym Yue referred to a kingdom on the southeast periphery of the Central States during the Eastern Zhou period

cultures and kingdom of Southern Yue (*Nam Viet*) in terms of their own origins and the naming of their state, *Viet Nam*.

[24] "Shi jun 恃君" chapter of *Lüshi chunqiu*.

[25] *Shi ji*, 113.2969. For more on the history of the Au Lac kingdom, see Taylor, *The Birth of Vietnam*.

[26] See Constance Cook and John Major, eds., *Defining Chu: Image and Reality in Ancient China* (Honolulu: University of Hawaii Press, 1999), pp. 2–3.

[27] See, for example, *Shi ji*, 116.2991.

(770–221 BCE for the Eastern Zhou period, c. sixth–fourth century BCE for the Yue state). In actuality, both the states of Wu 吳 and Yue (Wu slightly to the west of Yue, around Lake Tai and modern-day Wuxi City) are historically associated with Yue peoples and cultures. The geographical scope of the states of Wu and Yue varied depending on the time period. As Mark Lewis notes, aside from areas where walls were built, it is very difficult to ascertain precise borders in any of the Eastern Zhou states, especially given the fact that borders shifted considerably over time.[28] Eric Henry postulates that there must have been much fluidity in the boundaries of Yue, especially since the rulers of the Wu-yue cultures were known for their peripatetic, rather than record-based, style of rulership.[29] In fact, given this lack of a record-based system of government, it may not even be appropriate to speak of a fixed capital of Yue in early Warring States times, but to think of the power centers of the state as dispersed across various locations and around a certain region (like Shaoxing).[30] Rather than try to claim any fixed boundaries for either Wu or Yue, it may be more appropriate for us to imagine them as ever-shifting and loosely bounded polities.

For the most part, however, the state of Yue was situated to the southeast of the more central states of the Zhou political sphere, just south of the mouth of the Yangzi River (including northern Zhejiang and southeastern Anhui), while Wu was situated on the Yangzi River, east of the state of Chu and west of Yue.[31] The capital of Wu was Gusu 姑蘇 (located in modern-day Suzhou), while the capital of Yue was located in various places, including Kuaiji 會稽 (located near modern-day Shaoxing); Lang Ye 琅邪 (in modern-day Shangdong – a location intended to represent Yue authority during its period of hegemony over the Central States), and in the state of Wu.[32]

Notably, the term "Bai-yue" was not the functional term used to describe all southern aliens, which was reserved for *Man* or Man-yi. Indeed, as this study will show, the term "Bai-yue" seems to possess a more culturally and ethnically laden significance than these directional terms for "alien from the southern direction." Insofar as it attempts to

[28] Lewis, "Warring States: Political History," p. 593.

[29] Eric Henry, "The Persistence of Yuè in Southeast China," paper presented at the AAS Annual Conference in Hawaii, March 31, 2011, pp. 9–10.

[30] Private conversation with Eric Henry, 10/30/2013.

[31] For the location of Yue, see Lothar von Falkenhausen, "The Waning of the Bronze Age: Material Culture and Social Developments, 770–481 BC," in Edward Shaughnessy and Michael Loewe, eds., *Cambridge History of Ancient China: From the Origins of Civilization to 221 B. C.* (Cambridge: Cambridge University Press, 1999), p. 526.

[32] The date for the move of the capital to Langye is 468, according to the information provided in the *Bamboo Annals*. See Henry, "The Submerged History of Yue," pp. 10–13.

describe a type of people that are loosely related to each other via certain cultural, linguistic, or ethnic traits, the term "Bai-yue" resembles "Yue" as an ethnonym, rather than a generic derogation of southern barbarians (as is suggested by Man-yi).[33]

The label "Ou 甌" was used to designate a certain Yue group in the South as well, one which likely inhabited the area around modern-day Guangxi and northern Vietnam. Sometimes, in texts that roughly date from the Qin and Han periods on, we also find the label, "Luo 駱," associated with the Western Ou people.[34] As Tan Shengmin 覃聖敏 points out, there are many controversies concerning whether or not the Luo were one and the same people and culture as the Western Ou (with different designations corresponding to variant usages in different time periods), or whether they were separate, neighboring, but distinct groups.[35] In the *Shi ji*, especially Chapter 113 on the Southern Yue, the term "Luo" is invoked in two different ways. In one passage, we find an intriguing reference, allegedly by King/Emperor Zhao Tuo of the Southern Yue himself, saying that "the [peoples of] the Western-ou 西甌 and Luo-luo 駱裸 kingdoms all call me 'king' 其西甌駱裸國亦稱王."[36]

[33] Surprisingly, many Western scholars believe these terms (Yue and Bai-yue) to have no cultural value at all other than generic value as derogatory terms for southern barbarians. They often place them within the category of "Man," "Di," "Rong," and "Yi," which were the typical appellations for aliens of the four directions. See Hugh Clark, *Portrait of a Community: Society, Culture, and the Structures of Kinship in the Mulan River Valley (Fujian) from the Late Tang through the Song* (Hong Kong: The Chinese University Press, 2007), p. 17; and Michael Churchman, "'The People in Between': The Li and Lao from the Han to the Sui," in Nola Cooke, Li Tana, and James Anderson, eds., *The Tongking Gulf Through History* (Philadelphia: University of Pennsylvania Press, 2011), p. 69.

[34] The earliest appearance of the term to designate a Yue peoples occurs in the *Lüshi chunqiu*, dating to around 239 BCE. Contemporary Chinese tend to think of certain minority groups present today such as the Zhuang 壯, Miao 苗, Yao 瑤, Dong 侗, Buyi 布依, and Li 黎 (of Hainan island) as having descended from these southern Yue groups, but which minority groups get included and which do not is entirely tentative and not based on documented evidence. Preferring instead to think that there was intermixing with outsiders (migrants from the North) throughout history, I will not discuss the history of current ethnicities in China's southwest and the Southeast Asian mainland in terms of direct and distinct lines of descent from Yue predecessors. Clearly, however, it is likely that those being dubbed the "Yue" in ancient times were the ancestors of all sorts of peoples currently living in southern China, Southeast Asia, and Oceania.

[35] Tan Shengmin 覃聖敏, "Xi-ou, Luo-yue Xinkao 西甌駱越新考," in Zhongguo Baiyue Minzushi Yanjiuhui, ed., 中國百越民族史研究會, *Baiyue Yanjiu* 百越研究 (Nanning: Guangxi Kexue Jishu Chubanshe, 2007), pp. 1–19.

[36] *Shi ji*, 113.2970. Note that there is a major minority group, called the Yi 彝 or Lolo (written variously as 猓猓, 倮倮, and 羅羅), that still inhabits the rural, mountainous areas of modern-day southwestern China (Sichuan, Yunnan, Guizhou, and Guangxi Provinces), parts of Vietnam and Thailand. The term "Lolo" is the alleged autonym for these peoples, and the Loloish languages they speak belong generally to the Tibeto-Burman language family.

This is similar to a slightly earlier passage that mentions both Western Ou and Luo (not Luo-luo) 西甌、駱 as though the two were distinct and separate from each other. In all the other mentions of Luo in this chapter, however, the two appear together and might be misunderstood as a compound referring to a single group: Ou-luo 甌駱 (Au Lac).

My best interpretation of this confusing use of Ou and Luo is that "Ou" in these instances refers to the "Western Ou" kingdom, which in Hua-xia eyes appears to have been distinct but physically nearby or similar to the Luo-luo kingdom in some significant way. Certainly, our Han sources suggest that the Luo people are Yue as well. This is especially the case since these smaller kingdoms were united under the confederation referred to as "Southern Yue" during the early Han Empire, but it is also true because our Han sources refer to the two famous rebels the Zheng/Trung sisters (rebelled 41 CE) as both "Yue" in addition to "Luo."[37]

Scholars have written extensively on the possible connections between the meaning of these various graphs for "Luo" and the geographical and cultural traits of the area and people they allegedly describe, but I would warn against making too much of possible semantic connections.[38] This is because the term may in fact simply be a transliteration of a term in the native language of the people themselves. As Tan points out, "*lok*" means "bird" in the Zhuang language, a modern language of the Tai group that some scholars believe is the descendant of the Yue language.[39] Since different graphs of similar pronunciation were used, this suggests that it was the sound of "luo," or "lue" that may have been the dominant factor in labeling these people. For this reason, the name "Luo" may simply be a reference to their native word for "bird," which could have served as the group's totem, and which is featured heavily in the bronze drums for which the region is famous.

[37] After much discussion of the literature, Tan Shengmin concludes that the confusion surrounding the term "Ou-luo" lies in the likely fact that these were two different branches before the third century BCE – the Western Ou occupying the northern reaches of Guangxi and environs, and the Luo-yue inhabiting the southern reaches of Guangxi. (Note that "Luo-yue" is not used at all in the *Shi ji*, so Tan would be more accurate to talk about a southern group called "Luo-luo" instead of "Luo-yue.") With the arrival in the area of the First Emperor of Qin's forces, Tan suggests, the two separate groups joined together to form a united front against the outsiders, thereby becoming what were known as Ou-luo peoples. Tan Shengmin, "Xi-ou, Luo-yue Xinkao," p. 18. I am wary of this interpretation because the textual evidence from the period is not detailed enough to back it.

[38] The term "luo" (also pronounced "lue"), meaning "foothill," describes the peaks and gorges 山麓 of the region well. Another graph was used to indicate the Luo, 雒, which in ancient times also sounded the same as *luo* 駱. The graph used in the fifteenth-century source, the *Đại Việt sử ký toàn thư*, is 貉. Liam Kelley, "Tai Words and the Place of the Tai in the Vietnamese Past." *Journal of the Siam Society* 101 (2013): 55–84.

[39] Tan Shengmin, "Xi-ou, Luo-yue Xinkao," pp. 2–3.

The question as to why the term "Ou" was used to describe two different sets of Yue peoples, thousands of kilometers apart from each other (one in Fujian, the other in Guangxi/northern Vietnam), still remains to be answered. To date, I have found no decisive explanation. Perhaps the two groups shared some type of outward, distinguishing marker, such as a particular pattern or placement of a tattoo, which made Sinitic peoples group them into the same category. Perhaps the shared use of the term is purely coincidental, and that each group referred to themselves using a term in their own language that sounded similar to non-native speakers. Perhaps they were actually the same branch of people, some of which had broken off to migrate westward along the coast.

The problem with "Chinese" and "Vietnamese" identities

Constructions of Chinese identity, which are accompanied by cultural memes, metaphors, and the rhetoric of civilized society, resemble what Lydia Liu has called the "invention of China in modern world making."[40] Yet, clearly, the use of an overarching ethnic identity to unify a majority group and absorb real differences into a single, imagined manifold is not merely a technology of modern times. In China it finds its origins in historical mythologies of identity dating to Zhou times (c. 400–222 BCE) and spearheaded by the Ru, the Confucians. Propagated during the Warring States period and epitomized by Sima Qian's *Shi ji* of the early Han period, these mythologies posit the existence of a continuous and homogeneous Hua 華, Xia 夏, Hua-xia 華夏, or Zhu-xia 諸夏 people who trace their roots to the ancient sage kings. Such mythologies do not admit much to the ways in which Chinese identity itself was influenced and altered by other, alien groups and identities.[41] Rather, they present the

[40] Lydia Liu, *The Clash of Empires: The Invention of China in Modern World Making* (Cambridge: Harvard University Press, 2004), pp. 75–81. Liu shows how the super-sign "Zhongguo/China," was adopted as a form of self-identity only in modern times. Since the term "China" stems from either the Sanskrit or Persian words for "China" (*cina, chini*, respectively), it was a toponym used by others and thus not a part of the indigenous Chinese repertoire of self-identifications.

As Charles Holcombe puts it: "The tendency to project modern ethno-national identities into the remote past and assume that they are somehow eternal and immutable, however understandable, is a (dangerous) fallacy." Charles Holcombe, "Early Imperial China's Deep South: The Viet Regions through Tang Times," *T'ang Studies* 15–16 (1997–1998), p. 133.

[41] Sima Qian draws up a simple lineage for the Hua-xia people that traces back to the Three August Rulers and the Five Emperors, then to the Three Dynasties of Xia, Shang, and Zhou. *Shi ji*, 1–5.1–171.

Hua-xia self as a single, grand patriline stretching back into the depths of historical imagination; indeed, to the beginning of culture, civilization, and all things good.

One does not even need to examine the historical record of China very closely, however, to realize that the history of mainland East Asia is far from being a story of a monolithic empire that possessed control over much of the mainland from the earliest periods through 1911. In the 2,000 years from the first millennium BCE to the first millenium CE, and through at least the late sixth century CE, the primary political reality of the regions south of the Yangzi was that of independent or semi-independent kingdoms – some quite massive and powerful – all existing in an interactive sphere linked by overland routes and a plethora of maritime and riverine routes as well. Dominant states and cultures in the South such as Chu, Wu, and Yue during the Eastern Zhou; Min-yue and Southern Yue before and during the Han; Shu and Wu after the fall of the Han; the Eastern Jin at Jiankang (modern-day Nanjing); and the various southern regimes of the Southern Dynasties period (Liu Song, Southern Qi, Liang, and Chen Empires, 420–589 CE) had served as autonomous kingdoms and empires alongside other dominant northern states, not to mention neighboring kingdoms around and beyond the South China Sea.[42]

No doubt, the local peoples and cultures of these southern states would have been influenced substantially by legacies of what became Chinese culture, especially during and after the great influx of migrants to the South during the Eastern Jin period (317–420 CE). But this does not mean that locals and migrants in these southern regions did not continue to create and recreate their own sense of ethnicity, history, culture, and even political traditions. Moreover, even though all of the above-mentioned states helped contribute to the history of what is now China, many leaders of these states and their peoples – especially in the earliest periods –notably did not identify themselves as Chinese according to any of its various historical labels. In the cases when some of these Southerners did consider themselves to be Chinese (especially if they and their ancestors were migrants from the North), it is important to note the likelihood that they construed their identity in ways that

[42] See Cook and Major, *Defining Chu*. See also Rafe de Crespigny, *Generals of the South: The Foundation and Early History of the Three Kingdoms State of Wu*, Asian Studies Monographs, New Series No. 16 (Canberra: The Australian National University, 1990). For the Southern Dynasties, see Mark Edward Lewis, *China Between Empires: The Northern and Southern Dynasties* (Cambridge: The Belknap Press of Harvard University Press, 2009); and David Graff, *Medieval Chinese Warfare, 300–900* (New York: Routledge, 2001).

differentiated them from their counterparts in the North, or that they concurrently identified in some ways with the masses of ethnic others among whom they lived.[43]

Notions of pan-cultural, ethnic, and political Chinese identity were present from the earliest Confucian formulations of culture, and they were consolidated by the extraordinary successes and accomplishments of dynastic houses that unified large portions of the East Asian mainland and standardized much of the literary cultures of the unified regime. References to such Chinese identities are indeed abundant in the historical literature, but, even still, what it meant to be Chinese was constantly changing, and the boundaries associated with each Chinese identity had always been in flux. For example, in this book, we will not refer to the Chinese as "Chinese" (after all, "*zhongguo ren* 中國人" was not the reigning term for ethnicity at the time, but a political reference to a person as coming from the Central States) but as "Hua-xia," since that was a common term formulated in reference to the self at the time.

The history of the evolution of ethnic terms in China is important to the investigation of Yue culture at hand because the term "Yue" was ultimately, like so many other Asian identities once linked to the Chinese mainland, subsumed under the greater Chinese ethnicity that absorbed, displaced, and was transformed by it. In other words, Yue history in China morphed into a history of southern and coastal China (and separately as Vietnam), rather than a history of Yue peoples and cultures.

Accompanying this great effacement of a history of alterity along the southern frontier in China is the concomitant supremacy of the notion of sinicization, which, while certainly a major force in East Asian history, is much more complicated than the simple notion that all things "Chinese" took over all things "non-Chinese." In fact, the story of the interaction of cultures and ethnicities, even in ancient times, was one in which becoming Chinese or Hua-xia was an artificial, simplistic label for a much more complicated reality. Taking sinicization as the default assumption about culture change in the South thus fails to address the particular, local contributions of the Yue to transformations in both local identity and Han culture at large.

From the perspective of Vietnamese historiography, the concept of the nation state similarly obstructs one's view and understanding of the history of the ancient Yue. As Liam Kelley's work on the invented traditions of Vietnamese mythology demonstrates, medieval and modern scholars and elite created what the Vietnamese today praise as sacred,

[43] See Liu, *The Clash of Empires*, p. 80.

Vietnamese traditions that were allegedly passed on for generations through the folk.[44] In other words, various forms of cultural and national identity, embraced by the elite of Vietnam, helped invent a vision of the Vietnamese as utterly independent from their mainland neighbor(s) to the north and rooted in their own, local founding mythology. The ancient Yue, while certainly a part of that founding mythology, complicate and challenge such a vision of the nation because of their spatial reach across all of what is now southern China and northern Vietnam. A critical understanding of the Yue, therefore, would require that people abandon notions of the autonomous nation state to embrace a history of identity that knows nothing of such contemporary boundaries.

While Vietnamese historical sources generally accept the fact that Vietnam was ruled for the most part by larger empires to its north until its unification by Đinh Bộ Lĩnh in 968 CE, scholarship that is informed by nation-based Vietnamese identity politics usually posits a core language and national identity that is inexplicably present from the beginning of history. This mythology of national identity locates the source of Vietnamese history in the Red River Delta, and links an early, archaeologically attested Iron Age culture – the Dong Son – to the state of Văn Lang. It is noteworthy that the state of Văn Lang is not attested in early Chinese textual sources, but only first appears in the *Đại Việt sử ký toàn thư* 大越史記全書 (*Complete Historical Records of Đại Việt*), dating to the fifteenth century CE. Thus, there is little textual proof – aside from the known fact that complex societies and kingdoms existed in the first millennium BCE in the Red River Delta region – that an ancestral Vietnamese ethnicity existed at the time.[45]

The fiction that contemporary national and ethnic identities reached far into antiquity and have enjoyed seamless and homogeneous existences since then has obscured our understanding of the early development of many heterogeneous states and cultures in what is now southern China, Vietnam, and Southeast Asia. In short, it is because scholars and lay people disagree about divisions of identity – ones that do not at all correspond to the ancient or historical realities – that we sometimes fail to fathom the interconnected history of the entire south China and Southeast Asia/Oceania macro-sphere. In this book, I use an exploration of Yue identity as a means of opening up one small window onto a

[44] Liam Kelley, "The Biography of the Hong Bang Clan as a Medieval Vietnamese Invented Tradition," *Journal of Vietnamese Studies* 7.2 (2012): 87–130; and "Inventing Traditions in Fifteenth-century Vietnam," paper presented at "Imperial China and its Southern Neighbours," June 28–29, 2012, Singapore.

[45] Liam Kelley, "Tai Words."

complicated history of identity construction between the Chinese self and the Yue other. I hope that such an exploration will further shed light on the dizzying array of rich, intertwined cultures and peoples involved in one of the most important maritime networks of the ancient world.

Yue as a concept representing the riverine and maritime South

Despite the innumerable differences and local variation of cultures in the South, it makes sense to study the history of the entire southern frontier as a single unit. Why? Because, just as the interactions and clashes between nomadic (or semi-nomadic) economies and agricultural societies might be said to help define a northern frontier, a southern frontier may be defined as well by considering the interactions between Central States agricultural communities and their connections to southern cultures enmeshed in a vast riverine and maritime network. Indeed, the South and Southeast share much geographically and climactically, especially when compared to regions north of the Yangzi, as many southeastern/ southern cultures took part in a larger coastal, marine, mercantile, and agricultural (predominantly rice) economy. Given the distinctive economies both to the north and south of the Central Plains, each frontier is worth considering on its own as a unit. It is only when we take the larger perspective of southern frontier studies and not merely regional-specific studies (such as Fujianese or Cantonese history) that we see larger patterns of influence and thus begin to fathom the unique ways in which Central Plains peoples interacted with the southern frontier.

Rather than building walls, as Central States peoples often did in the North, people north of the Yangzi generally turned southward whenever troubles in their homeland arose.[46] In times of peace, as well, Central States involvement in the Southland was one of continuous southward migration and expansion in an effort to capture the economic benefits of a lucrative sea trade in luxury and natural goods. Such a process was defined not by nomadic raids and military excursions and defense, but by necessity as well as the enterprising and pioneering desires of the people. Unwilling migrants set up a new life in the South, bringing their old customs and languages with them. Willing migrants saw the South as a gateway to the riverine and oceanic treasures of the world, and

[46] C. P. FitzGerald provides a narrative of the Chinese expansion into the Southland in terms of a holistic understanding of what was happening in north China as well. *The Southern Expansion of the Chinese People* (New York: Praeger Publishers, 1972).

they often risked their lives or made considerable sacrifices to be a part of it.[47] Indeed, commercial opportunity, maritime mobility, and escape into the seas or far-off southern regions seem to have played a key role in defining the patterns of change and interactions along this frontier.

The fact that the southern regions are speckled with rivers that empty themselves out into the sea, and that every main southern entrepot possessed some significant connection to a waterway and river or ocean-going trade, demonstrate an intriguing parallel with the northern frontier. The fluidity and extreme mobility of goods and, sometimes, people in both maritime regions to the South and nomadic, horse- and camel-driven regions to the North make both southern and northern frontiers similar in interesting ways. Both frontiers have for thousands of years been zones of essential interaction between cultures defined by distinctive types of economy – nomadic and agricultural on the one hand, and maritime and agricultural on the other.

Wang Gungwu has called the thriving trade along the coasts of the South China Sea and Gulf of Tonkin the "Nanhai trade."[48] Other scholars have recently begun to discuss it in terms of the "maritime silk road," "maritime highway," or "feather route," which stretches past "Nanhai," or the "South China Sea," to India and beyond. Andrew Sherrat shows that Bronze Age southern China was part and parcel of a series of important trade and cultural networks across the ancient Southeast Asian mainland:

> By the closing centuries of the first millennium BC, a chain of sophisticated bronze-working cultures existed between the southern border of Han China and the Gulf of Thailand, whose products were distributed as far south as New Guinea. Just as in Europe an "amber route" connected urban consumers at one end of a supply-chain with populations at the other end of a continent . . . so it has been suggested that a "feather route," supplying bird-of-paradise feathers across the whole extent of Southeast Asia, carried these exotic items as far as China – bringing prosperity to trading-centres along the route.[49]

[47] Wang Gungwu, C. P. FitzGerald, and Herold Wiens have all discussed the history of southern China and provided a framework for understanding this history in terms of migration and colonization. In particular, FitzGerald discusses Chinese expansion in terms of a "private pioneering venture." See *ibid.*, p. xxi. See also Wang Gungwu, *The Nanhai Trade: Early Chinese Trade in the South China Sea* (originally published in 1958 by the *Journal of the Malayan Branch of the Royal Asiatic Society*. Singapore: Eastern Universities Press, 2003); and Herold Wiens, *Han Chinese Expansion in South China* (Hamden, N.J.: Shoe String Press, 1967).

[48] Wang Gungwu, *The Nanhai Trade.*

[49] Andrew Sherratt, "Foreword" in Ian Glover and Peter Bellwood, eds., *Southeast Asia: From Prehistory to History* (New York: Routledge Curzon, 2004), p. xix.

Unimpeded access to this trade in a variety of highly sought-after goods – goods that were often the exclusive endowments of sub-tropical and tropical climates – made control of the southern regions of vital importance to the Central States.

Thinking about areas around and south of the Yangzi River as major entrepots of civilization – regions that could in some ways rival those from the Yellow River Valley – has important historical implications. For example, the notion of indigenous, southern inputs in cultural change may help explain how the advanced state of Chu – a political tour de force during the Eastern Zhou period that primarily occupied the Yangzi River regions – attained such levels of power and technological, administrative sophistication.[50] Indeed, it is not out of the question that Chu colonialists were building the strength of their state upon the vestiges and legacies of multiple, rich, and flourishing civilizations from the South and Southwest (such as the ancient Yue, Shu, and Ba, among others), in addition to influences from the North. At the very least, scholars must begin viewing the early history of China and Southeast Asia as informed and influenced in a primary way by linguistic, material, technological, and cultural advancements from the Yangzi River peoples and their southerly neighbors.

Because the southern frontier acts as a critical counterpoint to the history of the northern frontier in understanding the history of China, and because it serves as an entry point for understanding the crucial history of the maritime highway, it is important to try to address the entire panoramic scope of the ancient Yue as primary representatives of the ancient, coastal frontier. Going beyond specific Yue groups to piece together a macro-history of Yue identity provides us with one way of linking the distinctive cultural traits and economies of southern peoples with the cultures from farther north.

Yue identity and the Yue voice

Since only very few self-representations of the Yue people exist in ancient Asian literature, it becomes very difficult to examine Yue self-identity according to the voice of self-proclaimed "Yue" people. We do not have much evidence demonstrating the existence of a written language associated with the Yue. Tantalizing records of inscriptions and a form of proto-script associated with the Yue include symbols found on pieces of Liangzhu pottery (Liangzhu was a third millennium BCE Neolithic

[50] For more on the ancient state of Chu, see Cook and Major, *Defining Chu*.

culture that many scholars think were likely predecessors to the Yue), symbols (numbering in the hundreds) found on geometric pottery in various places throughout ancient "Yue" lands, a so-called "bird script" inscribed on many ancient Yue bronze swords,[51] and about a dozen records of as-yet undeciphered inscriptions on rock cliffs from throughout Fujian.[52]

The various symbols from Neolithic cultures cannot yet be called "writing," insofar as there is no clear connection between such visual images and representation of a spoken language. As for the "bird script 鳥篆" (or "bird-worm script 鳥蟲篆") on Yue bronzes, these were artistic, decorative embellishments of the sinitically based seal script that derived from Shang times and became especially popular during the late Spring and Autumn and Warring States periods. Such a script was not unique to Yue, as many other southern states such as Chu, Wu, Song, and Xu used it, and it most certainly did not represent the Yue language, but, rather, the written lingua franca of royals and elites: classical Chinese. Lastly, the undeciphered inscriptions found on rock cliffs in the Jiulong River Valley of Zhangzhou, Fujian, are associated with "an unusual burial practice that placed the dead in boat-like coffins that were then interred in niches in the cliff-face."[53] Given the funerary, ritual applications of the inscriptions in question, it is just as likely that they were to be understood as apotropaic symbols that helped ward off evil forces, and therefore should not necessarily be taken as writing or as indicative of a full-fledged writing system.

The only textual documentation of a Yue voice in its own language (but nonetheless using the Sinitic script) occurs in two inscrutable inscriptions on Zhou period bronze bells, which scholars claim signify attempts to

[51] See announcements on a newly discovered sword of the king of Yue, Zhuji Yushi (越王者旨於睗剑). http://usa.chinadaily.com.cn/culture/2011-06/26/content_12781329.htm

[52] Luo Chia-li, "Coastal Culture and Religion in Early China: A Study through Comparison with the Central Plain Region," Ph.D. dissertation, 1999, Indiana University, p. 29. For a brief discussion of the rock inscriptions, of which only one (in Zhangzhou) is extant, see Hugh Clark, *Portrait of a Community*, pp. 171–172, and 379 note 1.

[53] Clark, *Portrait of a Community*, pp. 171–172. For a detailed discussion of the boat-coffins excavated from the cliffs of the Wuyi mountain range (Fujian), see Delphine Ziegler, "The Cult of Wuyi Mountain and its Cultivation of the Past: A Topo-cultural Perspective," *Cahiers d'Extrême Asie* 10 (1998): 255–286; especially pp. 261–264. It is interesting to note that the practice of using boat-coffins in mortuary ritual was common throughout various early tribes in insular Southeast Asia, indicating a likely connection between the inland Fujian aboriginals of the Wuyi Mountains and the Austronesian seafaring groups who populated insular Southeast Asia. See Rosa Tenazas, "The Boat-coffin Burial Complex in the Philippines and its Relation to Similar Practices in Southeast Asia," *Philippine Quarterly of Culture and Society* 1.1 (1973).

write the local Yue language using Chinese script, and in an ancient Yue song, "Yueren Ge 越人歌" (The Song of the Yue Boat-woman), attributed to a traveler to Yue from the state of Chu in 528 BCE, who allegedly transcribed it phonetically into Chinese characters.[54] Scholars do not understand the former, the two bell inscriptions, but the latter, the Yue song, has yielded some valuable information. Shangfang Zhengzhang, a linguist, hypothesizes that it reflects an early form of Tai in the Tai-Kadai language group.[55] Since at the time there seems to have been no written form of the language in question, the author provided readers with a phonetic transliteration of the Yue lyrics, along with a Chinese translation of it. Such a Chinese translation, however, "gives little indication as to which transliterated syllable corresponds to which Chinese word," so that it is very difficult to ascertain the language group to which such a language belonged.[56] Thus, though the Yue song found in the *Shuo yuan* provides some hints into one of possibly many Yue languages, it is merely a tantalizing glimmer that is highly filtered through the Chinese language. Similarly, the presentation of the song in the Yue voice does not in itself preclude the likelihood that the style and content of the song had been greatly influenced by Zhou lyrical forms or poetical models. It is therefore difficult to make any definite statements about Yue culture from it.

Other fragments of the Yue voice can be found throughout the textual record of the late Zhou and early imperial periods, becoming more frequent as Hua-xia cultures from the North came into more direct contact with Yue peoples and cultures. The highest frequency of quotations, usually by distinguished men of certain Yue polities, occurs in texts datable to the Han Empire, such as the *Shi ji*, the *Yuejue shu* (The Glory of Yue), and the *Wuyue chunqiu* (Spring and Autumn Annals of the States of

[54] Note that the Yue boat song was found in Liu Xiang's 劉向 *Shuo yuan* 說苑 (Garden of Sayings) of the Han period. For information on the two bell inscriptions, see Lothar von Falkenhausen, *Chinese Society in the Age of Confucius* (Los Angeles: Cotsen Institute of Archaeology, University of California, 2006), p. 283.

[55] Shangfang Zhengzhang 鄭張尚芳, "Decipherment of Yue-Ren-Ge," *Cahiers de Linguistique Asie Orientale*, 20 (1991): 159–168. For a critical statement on Zhengzhang's hypothesis, see Laurent Sagart, "The Expansion of Setaria Farmers in East Asia: A Linguistic and Archaeological Model," in A. Sanchez-Mazas, R. Blench, M. Ross, I. Peiros, and M. Lin, eds., *Past Human Migrations in East Asia: Matching Archaeology, Linguistics and Genetics*, Routledge Studies in the Early History of Asia (London: Routledge, 2008), p. 141.

[56] Tsu-lin Mei and Jerry Norman, "The Austroasiatics in Ancient South China: Some Lexical Evidence," *Monumenta Serica* 32 (1976), p. 277. For a brief linguistic study and translation of this song (into Japanese), see Izui Hisanosuke, "Ryu Eko 'Setsu En' Kan ju ichi no Etsuka ni tsuite 劉向'說苑'卷十一の越歌について," *Gengo Kenkyuu* 22/23 (1953): pp. 41–45.

Wu and Yue).[57] In most of these cases, speakers are educated men of the ancient Yue region who were well-versed in the culture and norms of the Central States. They most likely possessed a very complicated relationship to the masses of indigenous peoples still populating the area. Eric Henry hypothesizes, for instance, that the compilers of the geographical sections of *The Glory of Yue* (Chapters 3 and 10) had served in some capacity as tour guides for Han officials in the area.[58] If that is true, then such persons appear to have had extensive knowledge of elite Han habits and Yue locales, as well as local customs. Nonetheless, even supposing that such authors had had direct contact or extended experience and ancestral ties with the Yue peoples, we cannot always assume that such voices reflected typical Yue concerns or culture.

The elusiveness of the Yue voice is also apparent from archaeological data. We will discuss problems associated with the study of Yue material culture in Chapter 3, but for now it suffices to state that the relationship between material remains and the "voice" or "identity" of a culture is extremely problematic. While remains in tombs do form a kind of biographical representation of an individual, a tomb's structure, contents, as well as the very modes of presenting itself all stem from a variety of social sources, thereby creating a multifaceted account of the life, voice, identity, and culture of the deceased. No doubt, local, indigenous practices and beliefs will have found a way of being expressed in such contexts, but whether or not we are in a position to understand the limits of intentionality behind, say, the placement of a particular local object or the usage of local materials or a local form, is another matter altogether.

Another complicating factor in trying to uncover some sort of Yue identity through material remains is that much of the archaeological data on Yue that we possess is, like the textual corpus, biased in terms of the social status and political connections of the individuals represented by such material remains. Palaces, lavish tombs of elites, and shipping docks associated with broader network commerce are all arenas that suggest a bias in favor of the elites and the socially, economically, and politically privileged. Because of such biases and limits, we must approach the Yue other as carefully as possible, making good use of data and details that hint at a proper context for understanding.

[57] Eric Henry points out, for example, that the *Wuyue chunqiu* "introduces a couple of disyllabic phrases in the language of Yuè, but doesn't translate them," assuming that locals would understand them as is. Eric Henry, "The Submerged History of Yuè," p. 20. For a recent translation of the *Yuejue shu*, see Olivia Milburn, *The Glory of Yue: An Annotated Translation of the* Yuejue shu (Leiden: Brill, 2010).

[58] Henry, "The Submerged History of Yuè," p. 18.

2 Linguistic research on the Yue/Viet

This chapter examines some of the current linguistic scholarship pertaining to the peoples who inhabited the ancient southern portions of the East Asian mainland. The discussion, as well as the one on archaeology in the next chapter, is intended to provide context and help us understand who the ancient Chinese writers may have had in mind when they wrote about and described the Yue other. Rather than simply summarize the voluminous data on the subject, which would be too unwieldy for our introductory purposes, I try to offer a critical perspective that highlights a few main controversies, regions, theories, and approaches to the study of these ancient peoples and cultures. Naturally, our current methods of using linguistic and archaeological evidence to ascertain similarities and differences among groups vary greatly from the ancients' ways of perceiving such things. This means that even though we may declare linguistic and material similarities among certain groups of ancient peoples, those living at the time would not have categorized or grouped people according to such criteria. Simply put, their perceptions of the linguistic and material cultures of the Yue would not have been coterminous with either current linguistic and material data or our interpretations of such data.

It is therefore important to distinguish between the ancient peoples who inhabited the South – whom we now study primarily through the social sciences and sciences (since these were illiterate peoples) – and the "Yue" – whom the ancient Chinese perceived to have inhabited the southeastern and southern frontier of their known world. Even though these two groups may at times overlap quite a bit, keeping them conceptually distinct is important because it allows us to reinforce the notion that "Yue" is an ancient construction, the parameters of which may not always be accessible to us in the present. It underscores the fact that to the ancient Chinese, "Yue" was a specific type of category that was unique to the ways in which they perceived and grouped together similarities and differences among people.

Linguists working on the languages of ancient Asian peoples generally agree that the people referred to as the "Yue peoples" in ancient China were not a Chinese-speaking people. Of the five phyla of languages associated with the ancient mainland, including Sino-Tibetan, Hmong-Mien, Tai-Kadai, Austro-Asiatic, and Austronesian, the latter four were all linked to the South, including the regions to the southeast that were the homeland of the erstwhile state of Yue.[1] While we will discuss each of these four southern phyla and their possible connections to so-called Yue peoples, we will do so by presenting Tai-Kadai in relationship to Austronesian, a language group that today has no remaining native speakers on the Chinese mainland. Our reasons for this doing will become apparent in that section below.

The main question for the study of the "Yue," then, is, did the peoples designated by this term predominantly speak pre- or proto-Austronesian (which, as we will see, may have included Tai-Kadai groups), Austro-Asiatic, Hmong-Mien, or all of the above? First, let us consider what we do know about the early history of these language families, and then we may reconsider the situation in light of the term "Yue" as presented in the textual record.

Pre- and proto-Austronesian languages and their relationship to Tai-Kadai

Prior to the most recent global, colonial expansion of Indo-European languages, Austronesian (AN) languages reached the widest geographical scope of any language group in the world, spanning an area that extended from Madagascar to Easter Island, and including most of insular Southeast Asia and the Pacific islands.[2] Contemporary linguists have generally come to agree with Robert Blust's theory that the island of Taiwan was the homeland for all Austronesian languages, on account of its being the seat of the most diverse spread of non-extinct Austronesian languages.[3] The

[1] L. Sagart, R. Blench, and Alicia Sanchez-Mazas (2005). "Introduction," in L. Sagart, R. Blench, and A. Sanchez-Mazas, eds., *The Peopling of East Asia: Putting Together Archaeology, Linguistics and Genetics* (London: Routledge Curzon, 2005), pp. 1–14.

[2] P. Kirch, "Peopling of the Pacific: A Holistic Anthropological Perspective," *Annual Review of Anthropology* 39 (2010): 131–148.

[3] Robert Blust, "The Austronesian Homeland: A Linguistic Perspective," *Asian Perspectives* 26 (1984/5): 45–67. If the homeland were on the East Asian mainland near or in Fujian, which is highly likely, then current, linguistic evidence of its presence has been lost due to the effective linguistic sinicization of the peoples of that region over the course of thousands of years. Inferences about the homeland of the Austronesian-speaking peoples are made using a comparative approach that examines the geographical distribution of member languages and critically determines the internal branching, or sub-grouping, of member languages. The vast AN sub-group, Malayo-Polynesian, includes all the AN languages outside the twenty-one or twenty-two indigenous languages of Taiwan. As Blust explains,

sea-faring, pre-literate peoples of Taiwan were responsible for one of the largest and most extensive pre-modern migrations in the world. From their small island, for example, AN-speaking peoples made various maritime forays, ultimately leading them to colonize far-flung islands of the Pacific such as Fiji (c. 1000 BCE), Hawaii (c. 800–1000 CE), and New Zealand (c. 1250 CE), to make contact with the New World, especially South America (as early as 1000 CE), and to sail west to settle in Madagascar (c. 500 CE).[4]

In recent years more evidence has been mounting that there was significant back-and-forth travel between the southeastern, coastal regions of Fujian on the Chinese mainland and Taiwan.[5] The peoples inhabiting southeastern China, especially the coastal regions of southern Zhejiang and Fujian, were therefore very likely to have been the mainland counterparts to the AN-speaking peoples on Taiwan.[6] Archaeological evidence suggests that groups of coastal peoples left the their homeland in Fujian sometime during the fourth millennium BCE to establish settlements on Taiwan.[7] Since the southeast coast of China is the most probable candidate for the proximate mainland origins of the Austronesian-speaking peoples on Taiwan, it is safe to assume that the peoples of this coastal region who remained on the mainland and did not out-migrate to Taiwan at that time shared with their counterparts on Taiwan a pre-Austronesian linguistic foundation. Thus, at the

based on the application of the "principle of least moves," since the greatest diversity of AN languages occurs in Taiwan, "it follows that the AN homeland was most likely on or near the island of Taiwan." Robert Blust, "Austronesian Culture History, The Window of Language," in Ward H. Goodenough, ed., *Prehistoric Settlement of the Pacific* (Philadelphia: American Philosophical Society: 1996), p. 30.

[4] These dates are based on the most recent consensus, summarized in Kirch, "Peopling of the Pacific." According to the reigning theory, the Austronesian-speaking peoples on Taiwan were first thought to have migrated to Luzon in the Philippines. Later groups spread out to mainland and island Southeast Asia (and possibly the southern Chinese coast from the Pearl River to Red River Deltas around Hong Kong and Vietnam). Once in Indonesia, the Austronesian-speaking peoples migrated into Near Oceania and Remote Oceania in at least two separate pulses of migrations more than a millennium apart. See Robert Blust, "Austronesian Culture History," pp. 29–30.

[5] Peter Bellwood, "Southeast China and the Prehistory of the Austronesians," in Jiao Tianlong, ed., *Lost Maritime Cultures: China and the Pacific* (Honolulu: Bishop Museum Press, 2007).

[6] Robert Blust, "The Prehistory of the Austronesian-speaking Peoples: A View from Language," *Journal of World Prehistory* 9.4 (1995): 461. As Blust hypothesizes about the mainland prehistory if AN: "Taiwan probably was settled from the adjacent mainland of China. Since attested migrations rarely if ever result in the removal of an entire population, it is likely that speakers of PAN [proto-Austronesian] or its immediate antecedent were found on both sides of Taiwan Straight and on the intervening Pescadores (P'eng-hu) Islands by the late seventh millennium B.P."

[7] *Ibid.*, p. 461. See also Peter Bellwood, "Southeast China and the Prehistory of the Austronesians."

very least, we can assume that the mainland counterparts to the linguistic cultures of Taiwan were pre-Austronesian, and that such people were likely to have continued to inhabit the southeastern regions on the mainland even after certain groups of them departed to Taiwan.

Both the linguistic and archaeological data on early AN cultures are in relative agreement with each other. They show the following: that early AN-speaking peoples (c. 4000 BCE) on/around Taiwan cultivated both rice and fox-tail millet (*Setaria italica*), lived in timber houses raised on piles, had domesticated pigs, and dogs, and perhaps chickens, practiced true weaving, used the bow and arrow, and made pottery.[8] While some of the later AN speakers who inhabited tropical regions farther afield lost some of this cultural and technological capital, it is important to note that the early pre-Austronesian speakers who were thought to inhabit the southeastern Chinese mainland were an agricultural Neolithic society not too technologically distinct from other agricultural groups on the East Asian mainland. Indeed, many of the later, textual descriptions of Yue peoples speak of agriculturalists who lived in stilt houses and are intimately connected to the water and coasts, which seems to bolster a link between textual references to the Yue people and data concerning ancient southern, coastal peoples from the social sciences.

Laurent Sagart proposed in 2004 what some Austronesianists consider to be a controversial claim. If true, however, it has the potential to be field-changing and of great relevance to our understanding of the peoples inhabiting ancient south China. Sagart argues that the Tai-Kadai (TK) language group, which includes tonal languages spoken today in south China and Vietnam (like Zhuang, Gelao), Assam, Burma, and Southeast Asia (including modern-day Thai and Lao, among other tribal languages) is a daughter branch of proto-Austronesian (PAN). He bases his argument on shared innovations of numerals 5–10 in TK and proto-Malayo-Polynesian (PMP; a daughter of proto-Austronesian), as compared to other AN languages on Taiwan.[9] Furthermore, he claims, early peoples from Taiwan (and possibly the Philippines) migrated back to southern China in ancient times to settle the coastal regions well beyond Fujian.

[8] Robert Blust, "Austronesian Culture History," p. 31. For more on fox-tail millet and a possible Sino-Tibetan connection in even earlier times, see Laurent Sagart, "The Expansion of Setaria Farmers in East Asia: A Linguistic and Archaeological Model," in A. Sanchez-Mazas, R. Blench, M. Ross, I. Peiros, M. Lin, eds., *Past Human Migrations in East Asia: Matching Archaeology, Linguistics and Genetics*, Routledge Studies in the Early History of Asia (London: Routledge, 2008), pp. 137–139.

[9] Laurent Sagart, "The Higher Phylogeny of Austronesian," *Oceanic Linguistics* 43 (2004): 411–444. The following talk supports Sagart's claims: R. Blench, "The Prehistory of the Daic (Tai-Kadai) Speaking Peoples and the Hypothesis of an Austronesian Connection," presented at EURASEAA, Leiden, 3rd September 2008.

The genetic relationships between Tai-Kadai and other language families are still contested. Tai-Kadai was formerly considered to be a Sino-Tibetan language, but, in 1942, Paul Benedict rejected this idea, writing an influential article detailing some striking similarities in basic vocabulary between Austronesian and Tai-Kadai and suggesting a genetic link. Benedict's idea took a while to be accepted by the mainstream, but, in recent years, scholars have increasingly produced evidence that Tai-Kadai is indeed related to Austronesian in some way.[10] But whereas many linguists might admit to a genetic relationship between TK and AN as coordinates, or sister languages, only Sagart has gone so far as to claim that the genetic relationship is much closer than previously thought: that TK is a daughter or sub-group of an East Formosan clade of AN.[11] This claim is important because it means that a proto-Austronesian-speaking people migrated back from Taiwan (and possibly the Philippines) to the coastal regions of south China some time between the third and second millennia BCE. It further suggests that the actual scope of pre- and proto-Austronesian languages may have extended along the entire southeast coast, from the coastal regions around Zhejiang all the way down to the Pearl River Delta near modern-day Hong Kong, and then extending beyond to Guangxi, Hainan Island, and possibly northern Vietnam, depending on the view to which one subscribes.

Key Austronesianists, such as Blust, do not accept Sagart's theory because of the significant degree of dissimilarities in the vocabulary of TK as compared to other sub-groups of proto-Austronesian (PAN) – in particular, a sub-group Sagart calls "Muish," which is separate from other AN sub-groups on Taiwan and includes Malayo-Polynesian, Kavalan, and Ketagalan/Basai).[12] As Blust points out, even confirmed sub-groups of PAN that are lower down in the phylogeny than the branch where Sagart places TK retain many more resemblances to PAN than TK.[13] He

[10] In PMP, the words for "eye," "die," and "bird" are similar to the Thai words (PMP: **mata* "eye," **matay* "die," and **manuk* "bird"; Thai: **ta*, **dap/*dtai*, and **nk*). Paul Benedict hypothesized that Thai had just dropped the first syllable of these forms. Since it is unlikely that a language simply borrows terms for such basic vocabulary, linguists tend to assume a genetic relationship rather than a contact relationship. See P. Benedict, "Thai, Kadai, and Indonesian: A New Alignment in Southeastern Asia," *American Anthropologist*, New Series, 44.4, Part 1 (1942): 576–601.

[11] For the claim that TK and AN are coordinates, see Weera Ostapirat, "Kra-Dai and Austronesian: Notes on Phonological Correspondences and Vocabulary Distribution," in Sagart *et al.*, eds., *The Peopling of East Asia*.

[12] Sagart, "The Higher Phylogeny of Austronesian," pp. 428–430.

[13] Blust points out: "TK languages (Buyang 布央 being the most striking single case) share maybe 15 potential cognates with other 'Muish' languages such as Tagalog or Malay, while most Formosan languages – which lie outside Sagart's 'Muish' group and so are more distantly related – share 200–300 cognates with languages like Tagalog or Malay." Personal communication with Robert Blust, 9/9/2011 and 9/16/2011.

further contends that Sagart fails to convincingly establish the fact that TK shares innovations with the AN languages in Sagart's own so-called "Muish" sub-group. It is important to note that Sagart has since (2008) abandoned Muish and replaced it with "Puluqish," a group in which he includes Amis, Paiwan, Puyuma, and proto-Malayo-Polynesian. Puluqish gets its name from the innovation of **puluq* replacing earlier forms for "ten."[14]

According to the principles used by linguists to develop language phylogenies, judgments about linguistic sub-groupings are to be based on shared innovations, not overall similarities. It is sometimes the case, after all, that certain forms of language contact make a language appear to be more distantly related to another than it actually is. If we are to accept Sagart's analysis of numerals 5–10 as innovations, then his claim to a revised higher phylogeny of the Austronesian language may very well be justified.[15] Blust's counter-argument concerning the lack of a sufficiently convincing number of cognates is grounded primarily in claims about overall similarity, not shared innovations, so it does not strike against the fundamental core of Sagart's insights.[16] And even though Blust still finds

[14] Laurent Sagart, "The Expansion of Setaria Farmers," pp. 150–152.

[15] Further evidence for Sagart's theory that TK and AN are genetically related, and that they share innovations with proto-Malayo-Polynesian (PMP, the most prominent PAN sub-group originating from Taiwan), can be found in the Buyang 布央 language, a recently discovered Kadai language spoken in the Yunnan–Guangxi border region. By retaining the *ma*-syllable in the above-mentioned words for "eye," "die," and "bird," which is not present in other Tai languages, Buyang appears to serve as a missing link between Tai and AN. All of these data suggest that we may not wish to dismiss the notion that TK and PMP share innovations, which would further suggest that both language groups may similarly derive from PAN as daughter language groups. Li Jinfang 李锦芳, *Buying yu janjiu* 布央语研究. 北京市 ： 中央民族大学出版社 (Research on Buying Language) (Beijing: Zhongyang People's Publishing, 1999).

[16] While many advances have been made to disambiguate the numerous strands of history concerning AN-speaking peoples from the various Southeast Asian and Pacific islands, there is still much work remaining to reconstruct the history of what must have been an intensive connection between PAN-speaking peoples on Taiwan with those who remained on the East Asian mainland in the first place. Similarly, more work needs to be done to uncover data on those who may have returned to the mainland after an extended settlement in Taiwan (i.e., those TK-speaking inhabitants of Guangxi, Hainan, and beyond). Indeed, there appears to be somewhat of a communication gap between scholars of mainland "China" or "Vietnam" on the one hand, and those working on island Southeast Asia and the Pacific islands on the other. Such a gap is best reflected in the fact that scholars in China who work on Yue or Bai-yue studies generally tend to be archaeologists who do not necessarily contribute to the linguistic history of AN languages, while AN experts around the globe focus, for the most part, on the island histories of AN, and not at all on its possible mainland histories. This is understandable, however, given the ultimate disappearance of Austronesian-speaking peoples on the Chinese mainland (excluding the TK languages of tribal peoples in the Southwest).

Sagart's claims for shared innovations to be unconvincing, he has not yet provided a formal publication that explains why.

That TK languages would have fewer overall similarities with PAN than confirmed sub-groups of PAN lower down on the phylogeny can be explained by the special history of TK languages. If TK languages migrated out of Taiwan and back to the coastal regions of Guangdong, Guangxi, Hainan, and (possibly) Vietnam, they would simply not have had a development that resembled anything like the fate of other PAN languages that migrated out to the Philippines and other islands in Southeast Asia.[17] The TK languages on the Chinese mainland would have had a much more vigorous and extended contact experience with other mainland Austro-Asiatic or Sinitic languages that were nearby. Indeed, this vigorous and extended language contact would have made the TK languages appear to be more distantly related to PAN than other PAN sub-groups that are lower down in the phylogeny, even though they may be (according to Sagart) rather closely related to it. The relative absence of all but the most basic Austronesian vocabulary in TK does, in fact, suggest such a history, and so it is not far-fetched to believe that TK had been relexified by other languages, first by something Austro-Asiatic-related, and later by Chinese.[18]

If Sagart is right and TK is another offshoot of PAN, then it behooves linguists to follow up on this important finding and help establish a method for understanding the development of Austronesian languages in environments of extremely high linguistic heterogeneity and heavy contact, such as that of mainland East Asia in pre-historical and early historical times. Sagart's theory is intriguing for our purposes of understanding the possible realities behind the term "Yue" because it suggests a meta-linguistic sphere – PAN and AN – ranging far and wide along the mainland coast of ancient China that is genetically linked: the Tai-Kadai languages traditionally linked to southwest China and continental Southeast Asia share the same "ancestral DNA," so to speak, with the indigenous languages of ancient southeastern Fujian and Taiwan. Sagart's theory provides a linguistic basis for viewing the southerners – from the far southeast coast to the coastal regions around Vietnam – as similar to each other, possibly helping explain the elusive connection that early Chinese made between the Yue from southeastern regions such as Fujian and the Yue from southwestern regions such as Guangxi and northern Vietnam.

[17] I am grateful to Bill Baxter for pointing this out to me.

[18] I thank Laurent Sagart for this clarification.

Even if Sagart's theory of Tai-Kadai out-migration from Taiwan back to coastal southwest China were false, then one may still have reason to think that a significant portion of the ancient coastline from Zhejiang to Vietnam was inhabited by pre-AN-speaking peoples in ancient times. In the same article on Tai-Kadai, Sagart further hypothesizes about the connections between the ancient peoples inhabiting the Pearl River Delta region and the Fujian coastal region, taking us back to pre-Taiwan (pre-3500 BCE) times in Fujian. He states:

> it is likely that the passage to Taiwan did not exhaust the pre-AN population of the Fujian coast. More likely, this population continued expanding along the coast in a southwesterly direction toward the Pearl River delta, even after a group of them had crossed to Taiwan. Their archaeological traces SW of Fujian are perhaps seen in the Pearl River delta, although direct evidence of agriculture there has so far not appeared . . . I disagree with Tsang when he concludes that "the Pearl River Delta of Kuangtung is most probably the source area of the Tapenkeng Culture in Taiwan." I think it more likely that both cultures are descended from a common precursor on the Fujian coast.[19]

This statement, which Sagart himself admits is still speculative, presents an interesting scenario of how peoples and their languages migrate and change. Coastal regions are areas of extreme mobility, and whole populations almost never migrate completely leaving no one behind. Thus, while one may wish to label the languages of Fujian before the c. 3500 BCE out-migration to Taiwan "pre-Austronesian," there is enough evidence from archaeological digs to support the notion that PAN languages that developed on Taiwan may also have returned (repeatedly) to coastal Fujian, and that regardless of whether Fujian and Taiwan were both homelands to Austronesian, or whether it was just Taiwan, the constant back-and-forth of peoples post-3500 BCE from Taiwan to Fujian would have brought full-fledged Austronesian back to the mainland near Fujian. We would therefore be justified to think that the common precursor to Austronesian on Taiwan was a language family spoken along the Fujian coast (pre-AN), and that such a language family continued to develop from 3500 BCE in relationship to proto-Austronesian (PAN) inputs from Taiwan. This would make the entire region of the Fujian coast a PAN-speaking area in pre-historic times.

What does this discussion means for our study of the category "Yue"? It appears that the ancient reference to the Bai-yue, which referred to a diverse group of Yue south of the Yangzi from east to west, may have had some backing in a linguistic reality. The Chinese claim of perceived unity among the Yue may have been influenced by a linguistic unity. Of course,

[19] Sagart, "The Higher Phylogeny of Austronesian," pp. 439–440.

as mentioned above, it is highly unlikely that the ancients perceived language similarities and differences in the same way today's linguists determine them, but it is possible that such a linguistic unity in ancient times may have expressed itself outwardly through shared cultural, physical, or other material traits. If coastal, cultural, linguistic, and biological attributes linked to PAN speakers were indeed factors in marking the Yue from Hua-xia peoples (as well as from other groups – especially southwestern groups such as Shu and Ba), then perhaps we cannot so quickly dismiss the notion of "Yue" as utterly without a basis in the reality of ancient southern cultures.

We may imagine that in the pre-historical period much of the coastal portion of ancient southern East Asia was populated by groups of people who spoke a form of pre- or proto-Austronesian language. As Sagart speculates: "Unfortunately the evidence is too scarce to permit a direct identification of the affiliation of the Yuè language. My guess is that it, like PAN, was descended from the language or languages of the Tánshíshan-Xitóu culture complex.[20] This would make it an extinct group within the eastern branch of the wider STAN [Sino-Tibetan, Austronesian] phylum."[21] To the ancient Hua-xia from farther North, these pre-AN- and PAN-speaking peoples and their cultures may have seemed to express some sort of ethnic or cultural coherence – enough, at least, for the Hua-xia to lump them all together under the rubric of the "Hundred Yue." Regardless, scholars of China and continental Southeast Asia need to take note that the history of the Austronesian-speaking peoples – well-known for their forays throughout Southeast Asia, the Pacific, and other parts of the world – is one that also includes the southern portions of East Asia.

Austro-Asiatic and the Austric and STAN hypotheses

"Austro-Asiatic" (AA) denotes a large linguistic group that is most relevant to continental Southeast Asian languages but which also has some distribution over parts of Bangladesh and India.[22] Contemporary

[20] These are Neolithic archaeological sites that designate a larger archaeological culture (the Tanshishan culture), located in modern-day Fujian near the lower reaches of the Min River, and dating to approximately 5500–4000 BPE. See Tianlong Jiao, *The Neolithic of Southeast China: Cultural Transformation and Regional Interaction on the Coast* (Youngstown, N.Y.: Cambria, 2007), pp. 9–10.

[21] Sagart, "The Expansion of Setaria Farmers," p. 145.

[22] The two families conventionally associated with Austro-Asiatic are Mon-Khmer for Southeast Asia and Munda for India. See Roger Blench, "Stratification in the Peopling of China: How Far Does the Linguistic Evidence Match Genetics and Archaeology?" Paper presented at the symposium, "Human Migrations in Continental East Asia and

languages such as Khmer, Vietnamese, Mon, and languages scattered throughout continental Southeast Asia, India, and southwest China are represented by this group. Many linguists have proposed possible homelands for AA that include areas as diverse as southwestern China, the coastal region north of the Bay of Bengal, or Yunnan in southwest China.[23] Recently, Gérard Diffloth has presented faunal reconstructions that argue for a tropical origin of AA, suggesting that it may have been indigenous to continental Southeast Asia.[24] However, much of the ancient regions of southern China, Burma, and Southeast Asia were also important for biodiversity, and so, without more forthcoming evidence, it becomes difficult locate the homeland with much specificity. In general, however, contemporary Austro-Asiatic-speaking peoples are more generally associated with the far western reaches of the South – not the Southeast, where the Yue were predominantly situated.

In an influential 1976 article, linguists Jerry Norman and Tsu-lin Mei suggest an Austro-Asiatic language background for the Yue cultures that sprang up in southern and southeastern areas during the Neolithic and Bronze Ages, and perhaps even well into the Warring States (464–221 BCE).[25] They cite references to individual Chinese terms that possessed Austro-Asiatic derivations, and they show how such terms were variously linked in the received literature to the South (the state of Chu), as well as to the people of Yue (referring to the Zhou state) and the Bai-yue.[26] The most famous example is that of *jiang* 江, which became the proper name of the Yangzi River, but which can be traced to the general word for "river" in several Austro-Asiatic languages.[27] Hypothesizing that this Austro-Asiatic term came into the Chinese vocabulary from the area where the Han River meets the Yangzi River in the South of China, they suggest a southern origin for Austro-Asiatic influences on Chinese.[28]

Norman and Mei further support their linkage between Yue and Austro-Asiatic languages by pointing to early Chinese statements on linguistic differences specifically associated with the Yue peoples. As early as the Han Empire, the famous commentator Zheng Xuan 鄭玄

Taiwan: Genetic, Linguistic and Archaeological Evidence," June 10–13, 2004, Université de Genève, Switzerland, pp. 12–13.

23 *Ibid.*, p. 13.

24 Gérard Diffloth, "The Contribution of Linguistic Palaeontology and Austroasiatic," in Sagart, Blench and Sanchez-Mazas, eds., *The Peopling of East Asia*, pp. 77–80.

25 Tsu-lin Mei and Jerry Norman, "The Austroasiatics in Ancient South China: Some Lexical Evidence," *Monumenta Serica* 32 (1976): 274–301.

26 Mei and Norman, "The Austroasiatics in Ancient South China," p. 276.

27 *Ibid.*, pp. 280–283. 28 *Ibid.*, p. 282.

(127–200 CE) acknowledges a linguistic difference between the Yue language and the Sinitic by highlighting the word "to die," which, he claimed, the Yue people referred to as "*cha*" or "*za* 札."[29] The *Shuo wen* also points to another example: "Nan Yue calls 'dog' **nog-siog* 獀."[30] According to Norman and Mei, such early pronunciations for both "to die" and "dog" can be clearly linked to the Austro-Asiatic linguistic group.[31]

Norman and Mei's theories have created some controversy. A recent refutation by Laurent Sagart contends that it was more likely that the Yue peoples were pre-Austronesian or even Austronesian, rather than Austro-Asiatic.[32] Sagart states: "Their [Norman and Mei's] claim relies on a few Yuè words recorded in late Hàn Chinese texts (1st and 2nd centuries CE), as well as on modern Min (Fújiàn) dialect words viewed by them as substratum words: relics of the old indigenous language in the colloquial layer of the Min dialects."[33] He then continues to discuss four principal pieces of their argument, showing that some of the linguistic connections posited by Norman and Mei linking the so-called "Yue" language with Austro-Asiastic languages were most likely only accidental resemblances or resemblances based on rare and ancient Chinese lexical items, rather than a "putative pre-Chinese Austro-Asiatic substratum."[34] One example in particular is especially convincing: Sagart shows that the recorded Yue term for dog, 獶獀 as cited in the *Shuo wen* just mentioned, actually supports an Austronesian background for the Yue language, rather than an Austro-Asiatic one, as Norman and Mei suggested. Sagart states:

> The pronunciation of this binomial at the time must have been something like *ou-sou* or *ou-ʂou*. This may have transcribed a foreign *oso* or *oʂo*, since in Hàn transcriptions the rhyme /-ou/ frequently served to represent undiphthongized foreign /o/. This disyllable is actually closer in sound to PAN *asu, *u-asu "dog" than to the palatal-initialled Austro-Asiatic monosyllable VN *cho*, Old Mon *clüw*, etc. "dog" to which Norman and Mei compare it.[35]

Regarding the term 札 "to die," Sagart points out that this term is also a well-attested Chinese word that even occurs in contexts unrelated to the

[29] *Ibid.*, p. 277. [30] *Ibid.*, pp. 277–279.

[31] *Ibid.* Chinese words for tiger (*hu* 虎); large tooth (*ya* 牙); crossbow (*nu* 弩); and the ancient Chu word for fly, or gnat (*wei*) are among words deriving from such a linguistic group, though there is no evidence of a connection between these terms and the Yue. Mei and Norman, "The Austroasiatics in Ancient South China," pp. 284–294.

A slightly different claim is that of Stephen O'Harrow, who surmises that archaic Vietnamese might have constituted the lingua franca of the cultures extending from northern Vietnam well into southern China during the Bronze Age. Stephen O'Harrow, "Men of Hu, Men of Han, Men of the Hundred Man: The Biography of Si Nhiep and the Conceptualization of Early Vietnamese Society," *BEFEO* 75 (1986): 249–266.

[32] Sagart, "The Expansion of Setaria Farmers." [33] *Ibid.*, pp. 141–142.

[34] *Ibid.*, p. 142. [35] *Ibid.*, p. 143.

Yue peoples or cultures. It is not unlikely that this word, he claims, which appeared in the Yue language during Han times, could have been borrowed from a Chinese source, or that Zheng Xuan may have unwittingly cited a Chinese language spoken in the Yue regions. For these reasons, Sagart argues, the evidence using this term to conclude an Austro-Asiatic connection is spurious at most.[36]

Many Chinese scholars link the Yue language with an early form of Tai-Kadai. The source they use for such an assertion is an ancient Chinese transcription of a Yue song found in the *Shuo yuan* 說苑 (Garden of Sayings, assembled by Liu Xiang, first c. BCE), titled, "Song of the Yue [Boatwoman] 越歌." The smoking gun for such a connection derives from a 1991 article by Zhengzhang Shangfang 鄭張尚芳 in which he hypothesizes that the language of this Yue song should be early Tai. His interpretation of the song uses Written Thai words and sentence patterns.[37] According to Sagart, such an analysis is problematic and controversial, not least because Thai was not written down before the thirteenth century CE, and because Thai itself cannot be used to represent early Tai, as the former is part of a sub-group of Tai-Kadai known as Kam-Tai: "Proto-Kam-Tai would have sounded significantly different from Written Thai."[38] Despite this critique of Zhengzhang's hypothesis, one must ponder the possible connections between Tai-Kadai languages and the Yue, especially given Sagart's claims about the PAN origins of Tai-Kadai from Taiwan. If it is true that the language represented by the "Song of the Yue Boatwoman" is a language belonging to the Tai-Kadai group, and if Sagart's Tai-Kadai hypothesis were correct, then this would mean that the Yue likely spoke a form of PAN, not AA, as Norman and Mei suggest.

In recent years, some linguists and archaeologists have been converging on an intriguing theory involving prehistoric peoples who settled in the upper reaches of the Yangzi River around 8000 BPE and cultivated rice. First suggested by the linguist and anthropologist Wilhelm Schmidt in his book of 1906, *Die Mon-Khmer Völker*, the "Austric hypothesis" proposes that there are fundamental similarities between AA (which includes languages of eastern and central India, referred to as Munda languages, as well as continental Southeast Asian languages of Mon and Khmer) and AN.[39]

36 *Ibid.*, p. 142.

37 Zhengzhang Shangfang 鄭張尚芳, "Decipherment of Yuè-Rén-Ge," *Cahiers de Linguistique Asie Orientale* 20 (1991): 159–168.

38 Sagart, "The Expansion of Setaria Farmers in East Asia," p. 143.

39 Robert Blust, "Beyond the Austronesian Homeland: The Austric Hypothesis and its Implications for Archaeology," in Ward H. Goodenough, ed., *Prehistoric Settlement of the*

These similarities point to the possible existence of a linguistic macro-family that shared a geographic, cultural, and linguistic homeland. In more recent years, newer formulations of the Austric hypothesis link language to agricultural development (most importantly, rice cultivation), and, importantly, trace the ancestral roots of the so-called "Austric macro-family" to a shared homeland in the upper Yangzi River Valley (southwest China).[40] The implication of this hypothesis is that various sub-groups would later disperse along different rivers (the Salween, Irawaddy, Mekong, and Yangzi, all four of which come within several hundred kilometers of each other in northwest Yunnan), settling in different geographic regions of Austral Asia.

At first, while many scholars found Schmidt's hypothesis to be intriguing, they remained unconvinced. The reasons, as outlined by Robert Blust, were because even though Schmidt demonstrated intriguing similarities regarding the use of infixes in AA and AN languages, he was unable to show conclusively that such similarities were not merely a result of chance or borrowing.[41] More recent work by Lawrence Reid, however, has eliminated the possibility of chance and borrowing as explanations for the presence in AN, Nicobarese, and mainland Mon-Khmer languages of the reflexes of *pa and *ka causatives.[42]

If AA and AN share an origin in an upper Yangzi River culture and macro-family of languages, then it becomes necessary to explain how the early PAN speakers got from an area around Burma and Yunnan down to the Fujian coast and Taiwan. Notably, in his 1996 article, Blust presents an intriguing scenario that suggests a migration into the isolated regions of Fujian not from the coastal South around Guangdong, but from the North; namely, from Zhejiang and farther up to the mouth of the Yangzi River, where the ancient rice-cultivating settlement of Hemudu (c. 5000 BCE) has been uncovered in recent times. Blust arrives at such a hypothesis because millet cultivation in the regions of ancient Fujian,

Pacific (Philadelphia: American Philosophical Society, 1996): 117–140. See also Charles Higham, "Archaeology and Linguistics in Southeast Asia: Implications of the Austric Hypothesis," *Bulletin of the Indo-Pacific Prehistory Association* 14 (1996): 110–118. See also Gérard Diffloth, "The Lexical Evidence for Austric, So Far," *Oceanic Linguistics* 33 (1994): 309–322.

40 Peter Bellwood espouses an overarching theory that connects agriculture and language dispersal (dubbed the "farming/language dispersal hypothesis"). In particular, he links population pressures from farming to language dispersal as new farmers seek out fresh lands, steadily pushing their languages and cultures into wider regions and displacing the foragers who previously inhabited those regions. See Peter Bellwood, "The Origins and Dispersals of Agricultural Communities in Southeast Asia," in I. Glover and P. Bellwood, eds., *Southeast Asia: From Prehistory to History* (London: Routledge Curzon, 2004).

41 Robert Blust, "Beyond the Austronesian Homeland," p. 121.

42 *Ibid.*, pp. 122–123.

which existed in addition to rice cultivation, could not have originated from a southern source, but ultimately from the Yellow Plains region of the North.[43]

The Austric hypothesis provides one way of solving linguists' continued disagreements about which languages were spoken by the ancient peoples of south China. It contends that much of the entire southern frontier of ancient China (generally, south of the Yangzi River) was populated by a diverse range of rice-cultivating Austric peoples whose languages had at some early point diverged and developed into AA and AN language groups. Some Austric groups migrated down the Mekong or dispersed into southwestern China. Such groups were associated with the development of AA languages, which are most prevalent today in continental Southeast Asia. Other Austric groups followed the course of the Yangzi eastward across China to the coast, and were associated with the development of pre-AN languages, which eventually found their way to Fujian and Taiwan (and perhaps back to the coastal Southwest).

A second hypothesis that posits shared early origins for some major language phyla in East Asia has been proposed by Laurent Sagart, which posits an east to west migration of Austronesian instead. He refers to this hypothesis on language origins as "STAN (Sino-Tibetan, Austronesian)," and proposes viewing Sino-Tibetan and AN as two branches of a macro-phylum that had origins in north and northeast China and was driven to expansion (c. 8500 BPE) by the possession of rice and millet (*Oryza sativa japonica* and *Setaria italica*).[44] To refute the Austric hypothesis, Sagart uses basic rice vocabulary in AA and AN to show the independent origins of these two language phyla: "This picture does not support an Austric (AA+AN) rice-driven expansion. If AN and AA had gone through rice domestication as one language, one would expect to find at least traces of a common vocabulary of rice agriculture in them.[45]

The STAN hypothesis is compelling because it argues for a northern origin for AN that is entirely plausible, given archaeological and historical similarities and continuities between the early Shandong coastal regions and the coastal regions farther to the south.[46] Sagart's argument about the separate origins of rice vocabulary in AN and AA also casts doubt on the validity of the view, espoused by the Austric hypothesis, that these two language phyla emerged from the same linguistic origins. While a

[43] *Ibid.*, pp. 126–128.

[44] Laurent Sagart, "The Austro-Asiatics: East to West or West to East?" in N. J. Enfield, ed., *Dynamics of Human Diversity, Pacific Linguistics* (Canberra: Pacific Linguistics, 2011), pp. 345–359, p. 346.

[45] *Ibid.*, p. 348. [46] See the archaeological discussion in Chapter 3 below.

definitive answer as to which is correct is not yet available, both the Austric and STAN hypotheses offer us possible accounts of linguistic origins that may help explain the tight connections between the southern languages of AN and AA on the one hand, and north-south (or, inland-coastal) languages of Sino-Tibetan and AN on the other.[47]

Hmong-Mien (Miao-yao)

One last language phylum associated with southern East Asia and Southeast Asia is worth considering. Hmong-Mien is thought to be a relative latecomer to the linguistic stew of East Asia; one recent estimate gives the date of 2500 BPE as a likely time for proto-Hmong-Mien.[48] Notably, its homeland is associated with the lower and middle Yangzi River areas in southern China and may have been the language spoken by the people of the Chu state in the multi-state Zhou Dynasty interaction sphere.[49] Linguists consider it likely that the peoples who spoke pre-Hmong-Mien were among some of the ancient natives of East Asia.[50] Given that a significant portion of the Hmong-Mien vocabulary is shared with the Sino-Tibetan language group, scholars suspect it developed very closely with this latter group, but convincing evidence for a genetic link has not been forthcoming.[51] With such uncertainty surrounding Hmong-Mien's genetic origins, it is no wonder that many linguists simply add it to the possible mix of Austric, or to the larger macro-phyla of Sino-Tibetan or "pan-Sino-Austronesian" that they propose as mega-categories to help explain relationships among language families.

For our purposes regarding the ancient Yue, it suffices to assume that if Hmong-Mien languages are truly native to the regions around the middle and lower Yangzi regions, and if proto-Hmong-Mien were indeed spoken by those living in the state of Chu, then it is very likely that some indigenes who were being referred to as "Yue" by the Hua-xia (especially those in the "Bai-yue" areas of south-central China) would have spoken proto-Hmong-Mien as well. While the scope of spoken proto-Hmong-Mien during the Warring States and early imperial periods is unknown, we may

[47] While many more hypotheses on possible macro-phyla for East Asian and Southeast Asian languages exist, I have chosen to highlight these two in particular because they seem to represent the poles of a larger debate. Indeed, many hypotheses on linguistic macro-phyla in this part of the world appear to be various shades or less extreme versions of this basic dichotomy. See Sagart *et al.* "Introduction," p. 5.

[48] Sagart, *et al.* "Introduction," pp. 2–3. [49] *Ibid.*

[50] Today, Hmong-Mien languages are spoken in limited areas: mostly in the uplands of southwest China but also among some groups in Laos, Vietnam, and Thailand. See Blench, "Stratification in the Peopling of China," p. 7.

[51] *Ibid.*

assume that its association with the state of Chu would have given it a fairly large spread across the Yangzi regions of south and central China, excepting the southeastern and coastal regions, where Tai-Kadai and pre-/proto-Austronesian were likely to have dominated.

Conclusion

It is impossible to assert with precision who the ancient Chinese meant by the nomenclature, "Yue," and, in particular, which linguistic cultures such a group may have matched up with. But we should not let a mere conceptual conundrum – a deconstructed understanding of Yue and the impossibility of recapturing precise hermeneutical boundaries for any historical identity – impede us from gaining a better understanding of the linguistic landscape of the South in ancient times. Even if we cannot gain more than a crude sense of who the Yue were, we can at least ask whether there may have been some linguistic reasons for ancient Chinese writers to lump peoples from southeast and south China together with southerners of the coastal regions under the rubrics of Yue and Bai-yue.

As this linguistic overview has revealed, the theory of a southern mega-language group – PAN – may in fact turn out to have some merit, especially along coastal spheres. It is likely, however, that the three linguistic phyla – Austronesian (including Tai-Kadai), Austro-Asiatic, and Hmong-Mien – coexisted in various regions in the ancient South and that thousands of different languages belonging to these phyla were spoken among the various peoples in ancient times. Given the predominantly eastern and southeastern locations of the so-called "Yue" peoples, theories that favor a predominantly pre-AN-speaking background for the Yue seem to make sense. But such a speculation does not rule out the possibility that some of the Bai-yue peoples would have spoken AA or proto-Hmong-Mien as well.

I think it likely that the majority of the inhabitants of the ancient state of Yue (centered on the eastern seaboard around Lake Tai, Shanghai, and modern-day Zhejiang, c. fifth century BCE) spoke a pre-AN language that was related to the various Austronesian languages that developed in Taiwan and, quite possibly, southern Fujian. The peoples associated with the term, "Bai-yue," on the other hand, were likely to have been much more mixed linguistically. Hua-xia authors, referring rather indiscriminately to the Bai-yue as peoples of the South, may not have noticed or been aware of significant linguistic differences among groups that inhabited the Southland. Given the rather expansive use of "Bai-yue" in our sources, it would be folly to say that it was only ever used to refer to pre-AN or PAN-speaking peoples.

I have already suggested that the Bai-yue may have seemed like a coherent category to the ancient Chinese because of shared AN linguistic traits among peoples from the southeast areas near Fujian (speaking pre-AN, PAN, or even AN) and the southern areas of Guangdong and Guangxi/Vietnam (speaking Tai-Kadai that may have been PAN). Nonetheless, given the intense diversity of peoples who inhabited areas south of the Yangzi River, it is much more reasonable to conclude that the Bai-Yue languages belonged to a vastly heterogeneous mixture of language families. It is indeed safest at this point to assume that the entire gamut of possible language families that exist and are spoken by peoples in south China, Taiwan, and much of Southeast Asia today were likely not only to have existed in ancient times, but also to have had a much more massive spread across the landscape south of the Yangzi. So, while both the Yue and Bai-yue may have been predominantly pre-AN or PAN-speaking, it is highly likely that AA and proto-Hmong-Mien speakers may have been indicated by the terms "Yue" and "Bai-yue" as well.

3 The archaeological record

Archaeology as a field is often co-opted for nationalistic purposes and the construction of identity. Naturally, then, national pride and a sense of heritage and ownership sometimes undergirds the very scholarship itself. As Diana Lary states: "The beauty of archaeology is that, besides providing incontrovertible evidence, it creates physical sites as visible proof of the past glory of a contemporary people."[1] This statement is true in the People's Republic of China and Vietnam as well as anywhere else. At the same time that archaeologists let breathtaking objects and remains see the light of day, they sometimes seek to understand, categorize, and explain them in light of contemporary ways of thinking and recasting the self vis-à-vis others.

Often, views of Chinese or Vietnamese history are informed by myths of what make the Chinese (Han) or Vietnamese who they are today, which are then projected onto the ethnic history of the past. This problem of nationalistic, ethnic projection is especially current in the archaeological scholarship concerning peoples or cultures that either died out or do not have clear, modern-day counterparts; or concerning peoples who, in the past, were not a part of a given mythology of political, cultural, and ethnic descent. Since the majority of the peoples of the ancient southern frontier – referred to as Yue – both do not exist today (unless one counts Vietnam as a "Yue/Viet" state, which can be problematic, given the vast geographic scope for the Yue in early times) and were clearly ethnically distinct from the Hua-xia in the past, current nationalistic biases as well as ethnic projections can often tint the archaeological study of such an identity.

In addition to nationalism, Chinese archaeologists often participate in a regionalist approach that highlights a region's (or province's) local, distinctive traits while at the same time emphasizing its links to the glorious,

[1] Diana Lary, "The Tomb of the King of Nanyue – The Contemporary Agenda of History," *Modern China* 22.1 (1996): 8.

unified tradition of China.[2] This method, which is basically a function of the demands of such concepts as Chinese national unity, serves the dual purpose of elevating the region's status vis-à-vis the whole of China while feeding into the designs and needs of local tourist economies. Archaeological scholarship that contributes to such a model will no doubt be shaped by contemporary commercial desires and ways of defining a "region" that were not necessarily relevant in the past.

In the past two decades or so, archaeological work on the southeastern and southern regions of the East Asian mainland has progressed at a breakneck pace, yet scholars still often abide in some traditional paradigms that limit the types of archaeological work that are being done and the interpretive possibilities of the data obtained from their work. Francis Allard discusses the largely "descriptive and historical" traits of contemporary Chinese archaeology, which has been slow in accepting recent anthropological theory that might lend nuance to crude models of culture change such as "diffusion" and "evolution."[3] A defining feature of Chinese archaeology is typological analysis – that is, the classification of objects according to physical characteristics. This tends to ignore questions concerning social structure and function, as well as mechanisms for culture change and cross-cultural interactions.[4]

Allard's analysis underscores a larger critique of frontier studies – namely, that archaeologists often assume a model of "simple 'cultural diffusion' between regions (usually from more to less complex centers) without a consideration of how foreign influence or materials are translated and negotiated at the local level."[5] The widespread use of such a model, which essentially espouses a "core-and-periphery" system in which cultural influences spread outward from the Yellow River Valley toward the edges of the mainland, suggests that the concept of sinicization is as alive in archaeological studies as it is in the historical studies of non-Sinitic, non-Yellow Plains regions.[6]

[2] See Francis Allard, "The Archaeology of Dian: Trends and Tradition," *Antiquity* 73.279 (1998): p. 83; and Lothar von Falkenhausen, "The Regionalist Paradigm in Chinese Archaeology," in P. L. Kohl and C. Fawcett, eds., *Nationalism, Politics and the Practice of Archaeology* (Cambridge: Cambridge University Press, 1995), pp. 198–217.

[3] Francis Allard, "Interaction and the Emergence of Complex Societies in Lingnan During the Late Neolithic and Bronze Age." Ph.D. dissertation, University of Pittsburgh, 1995, p. 36. For discussion of archaeological and anthropological models of interregional interaction, see Edward Schortman and Patricia Urban, "The Place of Interaction Studies in Archaeological Thought," in Edward Schortman and Patricia Urban, eds., *Resources, Power, and Interregional Interaction* (New York: Plenum Press, 1992), pp. 3–15.

[4] Allard, "Interregional Interaction," pp. 36–43. [5] *Ibid.*, p. 39.

[6] Core–periphery models often promote an understanding of culture interaction and change in terms of wholesale transfer, unidirectional influence, and an active–passive understanding of give and take, and make little concession to the possibilities of partial

This chapter reviews some of the key archaeological discoveries that shed light on the material history of lacustrine, coastal, and maritime-oriented peoples in the prehistoric South. Since the 1980s, archaeological discussion of the Yue peoples in southern China has flourished to form a massive field known in China as Bai-yue (Hundred Yue) studies.[7] The archaeology of those ancient peoples who inhabited areas that later became the Wu and Yue states of Eastern Zhou China is known under a different name, usually, Yi 夷 studies or Wu-yue 吳越 studies. Archaeology in Vietnam also largely exists as its own, self-contained entity, separate from Bai-yue studies in China. Much archaeological work in Vietnam is state-sponsored, and so Vietnamese archaeologists have made extensive efforts in the past few decades excavating sites to tell a story about glorious civilizations that support the notion of Vietnamese cultural continuity from the remote past to the present.[8]

Given the enormous amount of literature concerning the Bai-yue alone, not to mention other Yue-related areas, it will be quite impossible to address the record adequately in a single chapter, other than to give an overview of the most important material cultures of the South. I organize my inquiry primarily around the geographic regions of modern-day China and northern Vietnam that were linked to the name "Yue" in our ancient texts.[9] These do not necessarily match up with what the Chinese

transfer, mutual influence, and active negotiation and integration of influences at the local level. For a more detailed discussion of the core-and-periphery model, along with challenges to it, in Chinese archaeology, see Allard, "Interregional Interaction," pp. 40–43.

[7] The archaeological Bai-yue mega-culture extends from the Yangzi River to the southern and southeastern coasts of China, down to the Pearl River Delta in Guangzhou, and on into the Red River Delta in northern Vietnam.

[8] Some foreign archaeologists are now working within Vietnam to help chart developments in Vietnamese history while also helping contextualize material data within broader geographical and theoretical frameworks.

[9] Some scholars argue for coherence among coastal East Asian cultures from as far north as the Shandong Peninsula to as far south as Guangxi/Vietnam. As we saw in the previous chapter, Sagart's overall picture of the predominance of Austronesian coastal peoples along the entire coast of mainland East Asia actually locates the pre-Austronesian homeland as far north as the Shandong Peninsula. His scenario of the AN homeland in Shandong (NE coastal) China conflicts with the Austric hypothesis previously discussed, but has resonances with historical sources that sometimes conflate Yi peoples from Shangdong and eastern China with Yue peoples from the South. Luo Chia-li, an archaeologist, recently supports this type of "grand theory of coastal East Asia" as well. She uses archaeological observations to argue for a larger, Neolithic "coastal culture" extending from the Shandong Peninsula down through the far South around Guangdong. Such a coastal culture allegedly shared basic religious beliefs and orientations, as well as geometric stamped pottery. What is striking about Luo's claim is that she argues against viewing the East and South as separate spheres of study – represented in Chinese archaeological circles by so-called "Bai-yue" and "Yi" (or later: "Wu-yue") studies – in favor of an interpretation that sees the entire "coastal cultural sphere" of interaction to constitute a coherent cultural unit. Sagart, "The Expansion of Setaria Farmers in East Asia in East

archaeologists call Bai-yue or what the Vietnamese archaeologists call Vietnam. This is because ancient peoples and contemporary archaeologists necessarily do not think about the category of Yue in the same way.

It is important not to assume that the ancient categories of Yue, Wu-yue, and Bai-yue match up with the archaeological cultures that now go by those names; similarly, we may not assume that just because adjoining groups shared certain aspects of their material culture or reflected some sense of material continuity that they spoke the same language or even belonged to the same ethnic category. As Heather Peters points out, current archaeological or linguistic cultures should by no means be confused with ethnicities: "Widespread similar, or shared, cultural traits need not necessarily mark ethnicity and can easily mask a plethora of diverse ethnic groups and cultures. Some overlapping traits may simply express an ecological response to a shared environment."[10] Others may reflect a shared material culture but not a shared religious, intellectual, social, or political culture. Thus, the Yue that archaeologists refer to cannot, for the most part, be confused with the historical Yue, which, as this book shows, is multivalent and not limited to a single ethnicity or group.

The following review of archaeological scholarship in south China examines what archaeologists say about three particular Yue hotspots so as to ascertain whether there were material continuities that may have influenced Hua-xia perceptions of their southern others. The areas include: 1) those linked to the regions of the Spring and Autumn states of Wu and Yue, 2) those linked to the regions of the Han era states of Min-yue or Eastern Yue, and 3) those linked to the regions of the Han era state of Southern Yue (including parts of northern Vietnam).[11] Such an overview of the material cultures of these regions during prehistory (Neolithic and some Bronze and Iron Age) will serve as a critical counterpoint to the textual assertions during Warring States and Qin-Han China that we encounter later in this book.

Asia: A Linguistic and Archaeological Model," In A. Sanchez-Mazas, R. Blench, M. Ross, I. Peiros, M. Lin, eds., *Past Human Migrations in East Asia: Matching Archaeology, Linguistics and Genetics*, Routledge Studies in the Early History of Asia (London: Routledge, 2008), p. 144 and Luo Chia-li, "Coastal Culture and Religion in Early China: A Study through Comparison with the Central Plain Region," Ph.D. dissertation, 1999, Indiana University, pp. 30–67.

10 Heather Peters, "Tattooed Faces and Stilt Houses: Who Were the Ancient Yue?" *Sino-Platonic Papers* 17 (April 1990): 10.

11 For the most part, I will refer to the states of Wu-yue and not Xu, since the latter – while often associated with the Wu-yue culture – was conquered by the state of Wu relatively early (in 512 BCE) and had joined the Chu state even before that. See Lothar von Falkenhausen, *Chinese Society in the Age of Confucius* (Los Angeles: Cotsen Institute of Archaeology, University of California, 2006), p. 263.

The Yangzi River Basin region: the coastal Neolithic and the ancient Wu-yue

One of the most important discoveries dating to the Neolithic era in southern China is a site around modern-day Yuyao 余姚, Zhejiang (south of Hangzhou Bay), referred to as the Hemudu 河姆渡 culture (c. 5000 BCE). This material culture reflects a strongly coastal lifestyle that may have been ancestral to the Yue – both the peoples who inhabited the areas of the Spring and Autumn period state of Yue, as well as the coastal peoples farther south of such a state. Unearthed in 1976, this excavation reveals the earliest Neolithic strata in the entire southeastern coastal and lower Yangzi Valley areas.[12] Most characteristic of the Hemudu culture are long, stilt houses, rice agriculture, animal domestication (dog, pig, and water buffalo) in conjunction with heavy reliance on seafood and some hunting, the production of lacquer wood, and the production of cord-marked, black pottery painted with plant and geometric designs.[13]

K. C. Chang notes the resemblance of such pottery to the Dapenkeng pottery of Taiwan, suggesting that Hemudu was an early settlement of the later coastal peoples of Fujian and Taiwan.[14] So-called "Yue" archaeological cultures of later times are also associated with stilt houses, a coastal economy, and cord-marked pottery with geometric designs, but due to the considerable difference in time period, it is not possible or advisable to draw firm connections between Hemudu and the Yue material cultures of the first millennium BCE.

At roughly the same time as Hemudu, around the mouth of the Yangzi River and north of Hangzhou Bay, the Majiabang culture (馬家浜) appears for a little over 1000 years, until c. 3900 BCE. This material culture, while distinct archaeologically from that of Hemudu, is contemporaneous with it for at least a millennium before Hemudu settlements were dispersed in the later fifth millennium BCE. Peoples associated with the Majiabang culture engaged in rice farming and hunting, as well as the domestication of animals, focusing more on the use of water buffalo rather than pigs (which were more characteristically used by peoples to the north).[15] Following upon the Majiabang culture is the noteworthy Songze 崧泽 culture (3900–3300 BCE) of the Lake Tai region. The Songze culture reflects an expanded use of jade, which

[12] K. C. Chang, *The Archaeology of Ancient China*, 3rd edn. (New Haven: Yale University Press, 1978).
[13] *Ibid.* [14] *Ibid.* [15] *Ibid.*, 3rd edn., p. 140.

included the production of rings, pendants, bracelets, and mouth plugs.[16]

All of these Neolithic cultures – Hemudu and Majiabang/Songze – are important for our understanding of ancient southern peoples. Since the term "Yue" seems to point to all southern and especially coastal-riverine peoples, it is likely that the southerners of the first millennium inherited the material legacies of both the Hemudu and Majiabang/Songze cultures. In terms of the actual ancestry of the Yue peoples, it is also possible that the people of the Hemudu settlements intermingled and intermarried with peoples whose material cultures were later represented by the Majiabang/Songze cultures, so that there may be some amount of cultural and biological continuity associated with these material cultures.

Besides geographical locations, there are many other similarities between these early material cultures and the later Yue cultures of the late first millennium BCE, such as similarities in pottery design, rice cultivation, and even skeletal remains. As K. C. Chang notes: "physical anthropological studies of Neolithic skeletons from Shantung and northern Kiangsu have shown that the populations in this area (of a slightly later stage than the initial Ch'ing-lien-kang and Ma-chia-pang phases) show a greater morphological resemblance to those further south (especially modern Polynesians) than those in the nuclear area of North China."[17] As discussed above, contemporary Polynesians, whose languages fit into the Austronesian linguistic group, can claim Taiwan and Fujian as their main linguistic homeland. This all suggests that the peoples inhabiting the Hemudu and Majiabang settlements may have been pre-Austronesian peoples who populated and spread out along the entire southeastern coast, including Taiwan.

A significant gap in the data is worth mentioning here. These rather complex Neolithic societies around the lower reaches of the Yangzi River and Hangzhou Bay appear to be rather confined to this region and not spread out farther along the southeastern coast toward Fujian. As Francis Allard points out: "In dramatic contrast to developments in northern Zhejiang at this time, few sites dating to this period [c. 5000–3300 BCE] have so far been identified in the large region extending from central Zhejiang to the southern end of Fujian province."[18] And of the contemporary sites in Fujian that have been excavated, none reveals much social complexity, as is suggested by the finds in the lower Yangzi

16 Francis Allard, "Early Complex Societies in Southern China," Chapter 8 in C. Renfrew and P. Bahn, eds., *The Cambridge World Prehistory, Vol. II* (Cambridge: Cambridge University Press, 2014), pp. 797–823.

17 Chang, *The Archaeology of Ancient China*, pp. 142–143.

18 Francis Allard, "Early Complex Societies," p. 814.

River Delta.[19] Given that the dates are still early (fourth millennium BCE), it is conceivable that the peoples associated with these more complex material cultures to the north had yet to migrate down the coast to either mingle with local peoples in southern Zhejiang/Fujian or transplant them as the pre-AN-speaking groups who likely inhabited these southern Zhejiang/Fujian regions. Or it could be the case that both linguistic and material transfers from the lower Yangzi River Delta seeped southward without any significant changes in migration patterns along the coast. In any case, the gap in the archaeological data between powerful Neolithic societies in the Yangzi Delta and the peoples of southern Zhejiang/Fujian of the same era suggests that there may not have been a close relationship between those Yangzi cultures and the pre-3500, allegedly pre-AN-speaking peoples who migrated over to Taiwan from Fujian. Clearly, more work needs to be done to establish possible connections between ancient Fujian and the ancient Yangzi Delta during this early period.

The late Neolithic, highly stratified culture of Liangzhu 良渚, which is known for its finely constructed, ritual jade pieces, is thought by many scholars to be a more direct ancestral archaeological culture to the Yue of historical times.[20] The dates for the Liangzhu culture are roughly 3300 to 2200 BCE, although remains from a controversial site at Qianshanyang may push the date even farther into the past, to c. 3500 BCE.[21] Its geographic scope covers the region around Lake Tai, eastward to Shanghai and southward to Hangzhou Bay, in northern Zhejiang Province, which is relatively coterminous with the lands of the ancient Yue state.

The Liangzhu culture is noted for its geometric stamped pottery, and its many stilt houses, which were built along shores and rivers. Interestingly, rice farmers who settled into the regions all across Southeast Asia and the

[19] *Ibid.*

[20] Chang, *The Archaeology of Ancient China*, p. 183. Given the sudden and not-well-understood "collapse" of the Liangzhu culture during the third millennium BCE, it is unclear how this culture's use of jade was transmitted to later generations, athough anyone familiar with Chinese culture will have no problem accepting the fact that traditions of exquisite jade carving and decoration continued in a robust fashion up through present times. Jiao Tianlong has recently summarized theories concerning the collapse of Liangzhu culture to argue for a relatively sudden and complete conquest of the Liangzhu by Longshanoid cultures from the northwest. Tianlong Jiao, "The Archaeology of Social Collapse in the Late Prehistoric LowerYangtze River Region," unpublished paper, April 11, 2012, Pennsylvania State University.

[21] Chang, *The Archaeology of Ancient China*, pp. 180–181. See also Anne Underhill and Junko Habu, "Early Communities in East Asia: Economic and Sociopolitical Organization at the Local and Regional Levels," in Miriam T. Stark, ed., *Archaeology of Asia* (Malden, MA: Blackwell Publishing, 2006), pp. 132–133.

Guangdong region of southern China during the third millennium BCE seem to have shared "a novel mortuary ritual and range of artefacts paralleled in the Liangzhu culture of the lower Yangzi region to the north."[22] The spread of such a ritual system across southern China seems to link the Liangzhu with a wide range of other cultures of monsoon Asia (Southeast Asia and south China).

These ties to Southeast Asia notwithstanding, the Liangzhu also likely possessed strong links to the Central Plains cultures. In a provocative discussion of human and animal depictions carved into high-status jade axes (*yue* 鉞) and *cong* 琮 tubes, David Keightley argues that pre-literate codes and symbols of the Liangzhu culture may have contributed to the beginning of writing in Shang China. Keightley shows how these jades "seem to have been written both 'in clear' . . . and 'in code,'" so that only the ritually initiated or educated could properly read the code.[23] While E. G. Pulleyblank has argued against the idea that writing in China started among the so-called Yi in the east in favor of its western origins in firmly Sinitic cultures of the Yellow Plains, he makes no comment on the possibility of influence from the East.[24] Keightley's tantalizing data thus suggest the potentially pivotal role of southeastern archaeological cultures in shaping the very core of Central Plains cultures from Neolithic times.

For the period between Neolithic and historical times, one might mention the Wucheng 吳城 culture of the Southeast (c. 1500 BCE), centered around Lake Boyang 鄱陽湖 on the Gan River 贛江 (Jiangxi Province), and contemporaneous with other Bronze Age cultures (such as the Shang and Sanxingdui 三星堆). K. C. Chang has suggested that this archaeological culture arose through secondary state formation based on Shang influences, but it nonetheless reflects a host of local practices and southern styles stemming from what Chang calls a Geometric Horizon.[25] A large mounded tomb (*tudunmu* 土墩墓) – a form of burial associated with many regions in south China – was discovered in 1989 at Dayangzhou and contained many bronze weapons and tools with distinctive characteristics (such as shamanistic themes, human-animal masks, and tigers on

[22] Charles Higham, "Mainland Southeast Asia From the Neolithic to the Iron Age," in Ian Glover and Peter Bellwood, eds., *Southeast Asia: From Prehistory to History* (London: Routledge Curzon, 2004), p. 46.

[23] David N. Keightley, "Early Writing in Neolithic and Shang China," in Stark, *Archaeology of Asia*, pp. 180–181.

[24] E. G. Pulleyblank, "Zou 鄒 and Lu 魯 and the Sinification of Shandong," in Philip J. Ivanhoe, ed., *Chinese Language, Thought, and Culture: Nivison and his Critics* (Chicago: Open Court, 1996), pp. 52–53.

[25] This refers to the geometric stamped pottery found across the South. Chang, *The Archaeology of Ancient China*, p. 417.

handles).[26] The Wucheng culture and other Bronze Age cultures in surrounding northern Jiangxi and Hunan Provinces provide evidence of the development of early complex societies in the southern reaches of the mainland.[27]

All of these Neolithic and Bronze Age material cultures on the Chinese mainland are likely early predecessors of the material cultures of the states of Wu-yue, mentioned in the literature dating from the mid-Zhou period (c. 500 BCE).[28] Wu-yue Metal Age (Bronze and Iron Age) archaeological cultures are naturally complicated by northern inputs from the Shang-Zhou cultures.[29] But their main influences still appear to be local to the lower Yangzi region. Intriguingly, Wu-yue Metal Age cultures, like their Neolithic forebears, are characterized by the production of geometric stamped pottery, shouldered stone axes, and stepped adzes, as well as coastal, maritime cultures and wet-rice agriculture.[30]

Two elite tombs of significance have been excavated within the past twenty years, giving archaeologists a greater understanding and appreciation of royal burial practices in both Wu and Yue. The tomb at Zhenshan 真山 in Suzhou (Jiangsu Province), which may have been the tomb of a king of Wu during the Spring and Autumn period, is a massive mounded tomb with a sloping ramp in the tomb chamber.[31] Although it had been looted prior to its excavation in 1994–1995, archaeologists were still able to uncover many jades, including the most splendid jade mask with a tiger-shaped pendant. Another massive and quite distinctive mausoleum of a king of Yue, which we will discuss in more detail in the next chapter, was excavated from 1996–1998 at Mount Yin 印山 near the city of

[26] Lu Liancheng and Yan Wenming, "Society during the Three Dynasties," in Sarah Allan, ed., *The Formation of Chinese Civilization* (New Haven: Yale University Press, 2005), pp. 179–180. See also Francis Allard, "Early Complex Societies in Southern China."

[27] Francis Allard, "Early Complex Societies in Southern China," pp. 797–823.

[28] Earlier in the Zhou period, the state of Xu 徐 (conquered by Wu and Chu in the late sixth century BCE) was linked to non-Zhou peoples inhabiting the middle and lower Huai River regions. Textual and archaeological records suggest that the Xu culture gradually penetrated into Wu-yue regions. The discovery in a Spring and Autumn period tomb from Shaoxing (Zhejiang) of a cache of bronzes with inscriptions that confirm they were made in the state of Xu hints at the close connections and influences of Xu on Yue. See Cao Jinyan "曹錦炎, 春秋初期越為徐地說新證" (A New Examination of the Claim "Yue is Xu territory during the early Spring and Autumn Period'), in *Wu-yue lishi yu kaogu luncong* 吳越歷史與考古論叢 (Beijing: Wenwu, 2007), pp. 190–193.

[29] Chang, *Archaeology of Ancient China*, p. 419.

[30] Peters, "Tattooed Faces," p. 3. See also Rao Zongyi, "Wu Yue wen hua," *The Bulletin of the Institute of History and Philology Academica Sinica* 41.4 (1969): 610.

[31] Lu Liancheng, "The Eastern Zhou and the Growth of Regionalism," in Sarah Allan, ed., *The Formation of Chinese Civilization*, (New Haven: Yale University Press, 2005), pp. 245–246.

Shaoxing (Zhejiang Province).[32] It, too, has a long sloping ramp and huge mound, including a defensive moat around the entire mountain.[33] The pointed roof of the tomb – in the shape of a triangle made by leaning large, neatly cut wooden slabs against each other – is reminiscent of an upturned boat, and houses a painted wooden coffin (c. 6 meters long) made from a single log.[34] Although the tomb had been looted throughout the centuries, its remaining contents and forms are suggestive of burial traditions outside of core Zhou areas practiced by people who nonetheless had a high degree of contact with the Zhou. It is through the study of elite burials of this period that we see an intriguing mixture of southern ritual forms and northern, Zhou cultural influences.

Neolithic and Bronze Age southeast China: Min-yue and Eastern Yue

One cannot discuss the background of southern, maritime peoples and cultures without an understanding of the major Neolithic cultures of southern Zhejiang, Fujian, and Taiwan that preceded the historical period. The prehistoric, Neolithic cultures that expanded along the coast of southeastern China seem to have had intensive and extensive connections to Taiwan. Because of the subsequent out-migration of the aboriginal Taiwanese across the Pacific, the history of these Neolithic cultures on the mainland might also be considered, along with the cultures of Taiwan, as the early history of the great Austronesian dispersal.[35] The works of Jiao Tianlong and Wu Chunming provide us with a much more detailed picture of the constant cross-cultural contact between peoples on the islands along coastal Fujian and those in Neolithic Taiwan.[36]

Recent excavations of four distinct Neolithic archaeological cultures in southeast China (Keqiutou, Tanshishan 曇石山, Huanguashan 黄瓜山, Damaoshan 大帽山 cultures) reflect a coastal versus inland pattern of cultural division that corresponds to the geomorphic characteristics of the

[32] Dong Chuping 董楚平, "关于绍兴印山大墓墓主问题的探讨 —兼说绍兴 306 号墓的国属问题" (An Investigation into the Question of Tomb Occupancy at the Great Yinshan Tomb, Along With Some Comments on the State Affiliation of Shaoxing Mausoleum 306), *Journal of Hangzhou Teachers College* 4 (July, 2002): 57–62.

[33] Lu Liancheng, "The Eastern Zhou," p. 246. [34] *Ibid.*

[35] These were likely represented by peoples who spoke a pre-Austronesian (and later, and Austronesian) form of language.

[36] Jiao Tianlong, *The Neolithic of Southeast China: Cultural Transformation and Regional Interaction on the Coast* (Youngstown, NY: Cambria, 2007). See also Wu Chunming 吴春明, 从百越土著到南岛海洋文化 (Maritime Cultural Interactions between the Indigenous Yue in Southern China and Austronesians in Southeast Asia and the Pacific) (Beijing: Wenwu, 2012).

region.[37] Of interest to us is the fact that these Neolithic cultures, while each situated in a specific geographical region and possessing its own distinctive forms of pottery, reveal connections to a larger network of trade and interaction. Stone adzes in the Damaoshan site (on the Dongshan island off the coast of southeastern Fujian) were all made from outside, non-local materials, and similar pottery designs link Damaoshan to other sites such as Keqiutou in Fujian and the Dapenkeng Neolithic on Taiwan.[38] Furthermore, the pottery styles from the younger, inland culture of Huanguashan (southeastern Zhejiang and northeastern Fujian) – painted pottery and pottery with dark slips – are found in certain stratigraphic contexts across many key sites on the southeastern coast, suggesting this culture's extensive reach and confirming the existence of networks of communication during the Neolithic in the entire region.[39]

Despite such extensive material connections, archaeologists are nonetheless able to discern a two-prong development of inland versus coastal Neolithic cultures in the Southeast (c. 2000–3000 BCE). As Jiao Tianlong states: "The Neolithic cultures in these two areas had different adaptation strategies and material inventories, which probably developed from different origins."[40] Most of the coastal sites along the lower reaches

[37] In particular, this refers to the distinctive mountainous region (NE to SW mountain range of more than 1,000 meters in altitude), cut by rivers with narrow bands of land on each side. See Jiao Tianlong, "The Neolithic Cultures in Southeast China and the Search for the Austronesian Homeland," in Victor Paz, ed., *Southeast Asian Archaeology* (Quezon City: University of Philippines Press, 2004), p. 567.

[38] *Ibid.*, p. 577. The Dapenkeng (Tapenkeng, TPK) culture on Taiwan was prevalent on the island before 2500 BCE. It is characterized by pottery made with cord-marked and incised impressions (and hence, also referred to as the "Corded Ware Culture"), and it is clearly the oldest Neolithic cultural horizon discovered in Taiwan. The Dapenkeng peoples engaged in subsistence farming, and had fish, deer, pigs, and dogs in their diet. The discovery of millet in addition to carbonized rice was of great significance because it suggests the migration of millet-producing knowledge and technologies from the Yellow River areas farther north.

Some scholars have linked the Dapenkeng material cultures to PAN-speaking populations in Taiwan and the southeast coast of China. New evidence from sites at Nanguanli (2002) near Tainan (c. 3000 BCE) supports views that Taiwanese Neolithic cultures were closely linked to Neolithic cultures in Hong Kong and the Pearl River Delta (Guangdong Province). Intriguingly, there are possible affinities between the Dapenkeng culture and that of the Jomon of Japan, south China (Xianrendong and other sites), and insular Southeast Asia (the Kalanay complex in the Philippines).

See Tsang, Cheng-hwa, "Recent Discoveries at the Tapenkeng Culture Sites in Taiwan: Implications for the Problem of Austronesian Origins," in L. Sagart, R. Blench, and A. Sanchez-Mazas, eds, *The Peopling of East Asia: Putting Together Archaeology, Linguistics and Genetics* (London: Routledge Curzon, 2005), pp. 63–71. See also K. C. Chang, *Fengpitou, Tapenkeng and the Prehistory of Taiwan* (New Haven: Yale University Press, 1969).

[39] Jiao Tianlong, "The Neolithic Cultures in Southeast China," pp. 575–576.

[40] Ibid., p. 580.

of the Min River and coast are shell midden sites of low social complexity containing materials such as animal bones, shells, ceramics, and tools made from stone, bone, and shell.[41] Inland sites, on the other hand, show signs of greater social complexity and even contact with the Liangzhu culture to the north, as seen through the presence of jades in many burials.[42] Such fine-grained studies of the material cultures of the Min-yue and Eastern Yue regions easily refute the notion of a single, monolithic ethnic culture of the Yue in ancient times. This evidence underscores the intensive diversity among peoples in the South, calling into question claims that the peoples of this region were all genetically or ethnically related, or that they all spoke a language deriving from a single language family.

K. C. Chang, who theorized for decades about such a connection, argued in favor of linking the cord-marked pottery cultures of the coastal Neolithic in Taiwan (specifically, the Dapenkeng culture) with archaeological cultures from these mainland regions.[43] He states:

> Thus, although the coastal assemblages of Fujian and Guangdong dating to the fifth millennium B.C. are not identical with Taiwan's Dapenkeng, a systematic comparison of both pottery and lithic inventories from the sites in Taiwan and the southeastern coastal areas of mainland China shows enough similarity to allow us to regard them as representing regional manifestations of a single cultural tradition.[44]

A word of caution is warranted concerning Chang's archaeological hypothesis of "regional manifestations of a single tradition." Even though the idea of a single ethnicity may seem enticing – after all, it would seem to fit well with the linguistic data concerning the relatively dominant use of pre-Austronesian and PAN languages in the ancient regions of Fujian/Taiwan, Guangdong and Guangxi/Vietnam – one simply cannot conflate Chang's concept of a single archaeological tradition with a lived culture or ethnicity. This does not preclude the existence of a biological link among peoples along the Zhejiang/Fujian–Taiwan corridor. In fact, recent phylogenetic analysis using mitochondrial DNA suggests a direct link between peoples in southeastern, coastal China (near the Yangzi Valley Delta, Zhejiang) and aboriginals on Taiwan who seem to have migrated from northern to southern Taiwan and then to the rest of island Southeast

[41] Francis Allard, "Early Complex Societies," p. 816. [42] *Ibid.*

[43] See Chang's discussion of the Dapenkeng culture of Taiwan and its related mainland correspondents in Chang, *The Archaeology of Ancient China*, pp. 228–233.

[44] K. C. Chang and Ward H. Goodenough, "Archaeology of Southeastern Coastal China and its Bearing on the Austronesian Homeland," in Ward H. Goodenough, ed., *Prehistoric Settlement of the Pacific* (Philadelphia: American Philosophical Society: 1996), pp. 36–56.

Asia and Oceania.[45] But whether the material, linguistic, and biological data all match up to provide evidence for a single ethnic group in this region is doubtful, and we should not interpret Chang's reference to "a single tradition" in such a light.

By the Western Zhou (c. ninth–eighth centuries BCE), Bronze Age developments farther north had already begun to influence the Central Min (River) and coastal regions of Fujian, where the later state of Min-yue would be situated. The two archaeological styles of the region are referred to as the Tieshan 鐵山 and Fubin 浮滨 (c. 1500–1000 BCE) styles, and the latter style extends along the coast, with a probable center near the border between Guangdong and Fujian Provinces.[46] Many of the bronze objects from these cultures include vessels of all types that reveal a northern influence (Shang/Zhou and Wu-yue styles), distinguished by localized forms of decorations and details.[47] Also during the early Zhou period, Wu-yue types of axes, halberds, knives, and agricultural tools started to be produced locally, although the absence of tools such as the plow and hoe still suggest simpler, smaller-scale forms of agricultural production at the time.[48] Changes in the construction of buildings and luxury objects (such as decorative or ritual stone adzes found at Nan-an 南安) began to reveal the budding of ritual influence from farther north on local elites, as well as an increased stratification of society.[49]

By the Warring States period, the increased diversity and number of iron agricultural tools and weapons in the region around Wuyi Mountain 武夷山 (Fujian) attest to the growing influence of iron technologies from farther north, although articles for daily use still reveal the prevalence of local styles of stamped and corded ware.[50] Notably, the fact that representative northern-style tripods were absent in this area through the end of Warring States period also suggests the continuation of local rituals in

[45] Albert Ko, Chung-yu Chen, *et. al.*, "Early Austronesians: Into and Out of Taiwan," *The American Journal of Human Genetics* 94 (March 6, 2014): 426–436; especially pages 426 and 430–431. Specifically, the researchers focus on a comparison of mtDNA data from "Liangdao Man" (c. 8,000-year-old skeleton found on an island between the Fujian coast and Taiwan) and 550 mtDNA sequences from various aboriginal Formosan groups. The comparison reveals that the Liangdao Man carries an ancestral haplogroup E sequence that evolved from haplogroup M9 (distributed along coastal China), strongly connecting Liangdao Man with contemporary Formosan aboriginals, as well as with descendants in island Southeast Asia and Oceania.

[46] Wu Chunming, 从百越土著到南岛海洋文化 (*Maritime Cultural Interactions*), pp. 112–113.

[47] *Ibid.*, p. 113. [48] *Ibid.* [49] *Ibid.*, pp. 113–114.

[50] The remains of an important Han era palace, which some scholars think suggest the regional significance of Wuyi Mountain as a possible center for a native "Min-yue" state before the imperial era, can be found at this site and will be discussed in more detail in Chapter 4. *Ibid.*, pp. 114–115.

daily life.[51] So even before early imperial times, some ritual imports and iron technologies from the North can be found in the Min-yue areas, but only amid a sea of local objects and styles.

Neolithic and Bronze Age south China: Nan-yue and Luo-yue/Ou-yue

The material mega-culture associated with the southeastern seaboard from Zhejiang through Fujian extends into eastern Guangdong as well. In fact, some archaeologists like K. C. Chang lump most of Guangdong (Canton Province) into the same Geometric Horizon as those southeastern coastal cultures already examined, and speak of a "highly homogenous style of artifacts brought into a large area by a rapid or even explosive expansion."[52] This archaeological horizon corresponds with the main material features usually attached to the Yue archaeological cultures of later periods: geometric stamped pottery and stone inventories (with the stepped adze being the most characteristic), an agricultural (predominantly rice-growing) economy with heavy inputs from the sea, and a habitation pattern of dwellings on mounds or wooden piles.[53]

More fine-grained studies, however, reveal an astonishing diversity and a multiplicity of networks of varying scope from within the all-encompassing archaeological framework of the Geometric Horizon. Francis Allard has done extensive work on the archaeology of Lingnan, a name referring to the region south of the Nanling 南岭 mountain range in Guangdong Province. Of particular interest is the Neolithic site of Shixia 石峡, located in the northern parts of Guangdong, where many locally produced jade and non-utilitarian artifacts have been uncovered from elite burials.[54] Many of these jade artifacts have "clear counterparts north of Lingnan" – in particular, in the Liangzhu culture, some 1,000 kilometers to the northeast of Shixia. As Allard suggests, these connections "clearly attest to an association between status, craft specialization, and access to – and control of – exotic forms and ideas of non-local origin."[55]

In addition to links between Lingnan and material cultures farther north, intriguing networks of material exchange reveal inland Lingnan to have been a core, non-coastal area of exchange. Small-scale societies in southern Guangxi produced elaborately carved stone shovels during the second millennium BCE.[56] Allard, who has mapped the distribution of these shovels in the region, points out that it follows a fall-off pattern that

[51] *Ibid.*, p. 117. [52] Chang, *The Archaeology of Ancient China*, p. 412. [53] *Ibid.*, p. 414.
[54] Francis Allard, "Early Complex Societies," pp. 817–818. [55] *Ibid.*, p. 818.
[56] Private conversation, 9/17/2014.

suggests short-distance exchange systems along rivers and streams, many of which made their way to inland Lingnan as well as to Hainan island and northern Vietnam. Such work suggests the importance of overland and inland, riverine routes in conjunction with coastal trade, even in coastal areas of the South. It also suggests a clear trade link between the Guangxi and Vietnam regions during the Neolithic.

With the establishment of bronze metallurgy in the Lingnan region by 1000 BCE, social complexity increased considerably, as evidenced from cemetery sites such as Yuanlongpo 元龍坡 in southern Guangxi, Henglingshan 横岭山 in Guangdong, and sites associated with the Fubin coastal culture (mentioned in the Min-yue section above) connecting regions in Guangdong with Fujian. A case for an established system of social differentiation can be ascertained through a collection of data concerning burial artifacts drawn from graves associated with the Fubin culture in Guangdong. Such burial artifacts reveal "a loose (but nevertheless statistically significant) association between the number of glazed vessels, serving vessels, the presence of incised symbols, and the number of stone *ge* halberds."[57]

In China, Guangdong is often included in the Geometric Horizon that links it to a southeastern archaeological mega-culture containing geometric stamped pottery since Neolithic times. However, it is important to note a considerable distinction between eastern Guangdong and its western parts that border on Guangxi and continue farther west into the Yunnan–Guizhou Plateau. As Alice Yao states:

> Contrary to Rispoli's (2007) characterization of a regionally "shared" Neolithic tradition extending from southern China to Southeast Asia and southwestern China, archaeological data from the Yunnan–Guizhou Plateau do not show a continuous distribution of rice agriculture, animal husbandry, pile dwellings, impressed pottery, and polished stone tools, all hallmark features of the Neolithic cultural package. Instead, the data reveal considerable interregional diversity, defined by a highland–lowland dichotomy.[58]

While such interregional diversity may be true of the southwest region of the Yunnan–Guizhou Plateau during the Neolithic, southwestern coastal areas in the subsequent era suggest important continuities. The spread of metallurgy during the subsequent Bronze Age from the Wucheng culture in Jiangxi (c. 1500 BCE) down the coast of Fujian (c. 1200 BCE), and farther along the coast of Guangdong, Guangxi, and northern Vietnam (c. 1200–1100 BCE) supports a theory of the

57 *Ibid.*

58 Alice Yao, "Recent Developments in the Archaeology of Southwestern China," *Journal of Archaeological Research* 18 (2010): 209.

transfer of technical knowledge and styles far and wide along the coast.[59] Clearly, the coastline was a highway for relatively rapid transmission of cultural and material goods that could cut across ethnicities. Such a route served as predecessor for a great interregional trade network that facilitated the movement and exchange of bronze prestige items throughout coastal southern and southwestern China, northern Vietnam, and Southeast Asia that existed prior to the Qin-Han period.[60]

To consider the southwest regions (i.e., Guizhou, Yunnan) as distinct from southern, southeastern China, and northern Vietnam is not new or surprising, and it is interesting that in ancient texts, Hua-xia authors considered the coastal regions in western Guangdong, Guangxi, and northern Vietnam to be distinct from other, southwestern regions.[61] These latter regions were also Bai-yue areas – in particular, regions inhabited by the Luo-yue or Ou-yue (groups allegedly centered around modern-day Guangxi and northern Vietnam). The fact that authors went out of their way to refer to these groups in the far South as "Bai-yue" suggests that they thought of the Luo-yue and Ou-yue as sharing certain similarities with the Yue from the Southeast. So far, we have seen that the data suggest possible linguistic and material connections along the coast. However, while such material and linguistic connections may have been partly responsible for the Hua-xia perception of similarity among so-called Yue groups, one cannot jump to the conclusion that these groups were in fact related culturally or ethnically during the periods under examination.

Having outlined some key archaeological characteristics and developments associated with the main geographical regions implicated by the ancient term "Yue," we may now ask ourselves about the relationship between such a term and ancient, northern Vietnam. The archaeology of the Red River Delta reveals an extensive set of connections between

[59] The relatively close dates appear to reflect a rapid transfer facilitated by coastal trade networks. Clearly, there would have been other, slower ways for such transfers to have taken place, such as along inland routes from Jiangxi to Guangdong (over mountain passes north of Shixia in northern Guangdong), and so the main direction of the transfer remains unconfirmed. Allard subscribes to the coastal transfer theory. Private conversation, 09/24/2014.

[60] Miriam Stark, "Early Mainland Southeast Asian Landscapes in the First Millennium AD," *Annual Review of Anthropology* 35 (2006): 407–432.

[61] The ancients distinguished clearly between the Yue, centered around the Southeast and South, and other southwestern, non-Yue regions such as Ba and Shu (centered around the southwest in current-day Sichuan). By Han times, records of southwestern places were even more extensive, and settlements such as Dian (in and around modern-day Yunnan Province), Yelang (east of Dian, around Yunnan and Guizhou Provinces), Qiongdu 邛都 (around Sichuan and the Sichuan–Yunnan border), and other non-Yue southwestern place names abound in the literature. These are mentioned in all of the Han histories, starting with the *Shi ji*.

Southeast Asia and China as well as the rise of complexity and an independent centralized Metal Age state in the region just north of Hanoi. During Neolithic times (before the first millennium BCE), links among regions in Guangdong, Guangxi, and Yunnan are suggested by the presence of a cord-marked, ceramic bird (or chicken) vessel.[62] This does not necessarily point to shared origins but at the very least to communications among these various regions. The Neolithic pottery prevalent in northern Vietnam is, notably, also incised, cord-marked pottery that is typical of some Neolithic wares in the southwestern regions, although such wares are distinct from the geometric stamped pottery that entered into the Guangdong region around 2500 BCE.[63]

Further links between Yunnan (especially its southeastern, south-central, and northeastern parts) and northern Vietnam can be found during the Bronze Age through a set of shared bronze objects, including boot and *yue*-shaped (鉞) axe heads and giant, lavishly decorated bronze drums depicting warriors, captives, boats, and ceremonial rituals (sometimes referred to as the Dong son bronze drums).[64] One of the most spectacular archaeological finds in the Southwest – the Dong Son bronze drums – links the Red River Delta of northern Vietnam to a corridor of northeastern Yunnan.[65] While the presence of these drums is far-flung across southwest China, coastal southern China, and mainland and island Southeast Asia, their primary spatial concentration (when considering drums of known provenance) is limited to two zones: the Hanoi Basin and the Lake Dian 滇池 and Fuxian Basins in the northeastern corridor of Yunnan. Alice Yao explains the phenomenon in terms of "two separate but interconnected regions," differentiating between the

[62] Ho, Chui-mei, "Pottery in South China: River Xijiang and Upper Red River Basins," *World Archaeology* 15.3 (February, 1984): 294–325; and Sarah Allan, ed., *The Formation of Chinese Civilization: An Archaeological* Perspective (New Haven: Yale University Press, 2005). For the bird-shaped pottery, see Ho, Chui-mei, "Pottery in South China," p. 305.

[63] Minh Huyen Pham, "The Metal Age in the North of Vietnam," in Ian Glover and Peter Bellwood, eds., *Southeast Asia: From Prehistory to History* (New York: Routledge Curzon, 2004): pp. 200–201; and Ho, Chui-mei, "Pottery in South China," pp. 304–305.

[64] The indigenous Bronze Age culture of the Dong Son (c. 600 BCE–200 CE), centered around the Red River Delta, is most renowned for these drums, although other elaborately decorated bronze vessels form a part of the excavated Dong son culture, including drum-like containers with a lid (*thap* in Vietnamese) and large bronze vessels that were possibly spittoons. Minh Huyen Pham, "The Metal Age in the North of Vietnam," p. 200. See also Ho, Chui-mei, "Pottery in South China," p. 305; and Robert E., Murowchick, "The Interplay of Bronze and Ritual in Ancient Southwest China," *JOM* 42.2 (1990): 44–47.

[65] Given the archaeological data, one cannot link the drums with the entire portion of the southern frontier that associated with the Yue. Instead, they appear to be material achievements specific to the Dong son (of northern Vietnam) and other ancient cultures of Yunnan.

pre-Han centralizing state of Co Loa 古螺 in the Red River Delta (near modern-day Hanoi) and a Dian polity in the Lake Dian and Fuxian Basin region of the Yunnan–Guizhou Plateau.[66]

Recent work by Nam Kim, Lai Van Toi, and Trinh Hoang Hiep examines data from an abandoned fortified settlement at Co Loa, just north of Hanoi, to argue for the existence of a large, pre-Qin (c. fourth–third centuries BCE), centralized polity that developed somewhat independently from the polities farther north in China. The massive earthen ramparts and fortifications, including moats and ditches, mounds and towers, exterior ditches, and three walls (inner, middle, and outer) shed light on defensive structures that required considerable labor to construct and maintain.[67] Using radiocarbon determinations of artifacts or charcoal samples found in the various stratigraphic layers of the ramparts, Nam *et al.* were able date and delineate different periods and phases of construction, starting from the fourth century BCE and gaining momentum after the third century BCE.[68] Notably, one charcoal sample drawn from a trash pit of an arrow head-producing kiln appears to represent some of the earliest remains, and dates to 2190+−35 BPE (or 180 BCE +−35), which is right around the time when King Zhao Tuo of Southern Yue was expanding the reach of his empire and appropriating the northern term *Di* Emperor 帝 for himself.[69] Regardless of whether the polity at Co Loa formed as a result of contact or pressures from the north, or whether it evolved independently from indigenous forces, the defensive remnants at Co Loa attest to the extensive development of society and a large population of indigenous peoples inhabiting the Red River Delta before and during the Qin-Han and Southern Yue periods of the third–second centuries BCE.[70]

66 Alice Yao, "Dian and Dongson Cultures," unpublished article and private conversation, 7/24/2014.

67 Nam *et al.* "Co Loa: An Investigation of Vietnam's Ancient Capital," *Antiquity* 84 (2010): 1013–1014.

68 Using a wide array of radiocarbon data, Nam and his team estimate that the ground was likely cleared for construction of the ramparts as early as the fourth century BCE, and that "the Period 2 rampart may have commenced sometime in or after the third century BC, and that it continued in existence until its disuse, probably in the early years of the first millennium AD." *Ibid.*, pp. 1017 and 1023.

69 We will discuss some of the finds associated with the Han period kingdom of Southern Yue in later chapters. Nam's article was published in 2010; I am not privy to the date the radiocarbon measurement was taken. *Ibid.*, p. 1015.

70 Nam discusses whether Co Loa reflects secondary state formation (based on influences from the North) or independent evolution, stating:

> Overall, the combination of artefacts, contrasting building techniques and radiocarbon dates currently suggest that the majority of the middle wall rampart was constructed by a local and indigenous society prior to the first century AD solidification of Han colonial

Conclusion

At only the most general level, intriguing linguistic and archaeological continuities in the South can be found, and our discussion of social science research in the last two chapters points to at least two main networks of interaction dating from the Neolithic period. One consists in a southern China/mainland Southeast Asian complex that primarily involved inland material/linguistic transfers or migrations from the upper Yangzi River region to southwestern parts of China (Sichuan, Yunnan, Guizhou) and mainland Southeast Asia. This mega-group generally does not seem to have been implicated in the notion of "Yue" in our ancient texts. The other network of interaction consists in an island/coastal southern China and Southeast Asian complex that involved coastal peoples – with respect to the East Asian mainland and its close islands only – who transferred knowledge, materials, and language from areas around modern-day Shanghai all the way down the coast to areas in Fujian/Taiwan, Guangdong, and possibly even Hainan, Guangxi, and northern Vietnam. It is this coastal complex (note: not a single ethnicity) that may be more justifiably linked to historical references to the Yue: to the ancient states of Wu-yue near Lake Tai and the Hangzhou Bay area, to the Min-yue regions of southern Zhejiang and Fujian, and to the Southern Yue regions of Guangdong, Guangxi, and ancient northern Vietnam.

At least by Bronze and Iron Age times, if not earlier, there is evidence of broad, interregional trade and interaction across the entire coastal area as far as northern Vietnam, connecting the Red River Delta with areas of Yunnan as well as Guangdong/Guangxi Provinces. The presence of mounded tombs, which first appear in areas near Zhejiang around 1500 BCE, appears to link the Yue archaeological cultures associated with the states of Wu and Yue from c. 600 to 300 BCE to areas in southern Zhejiang, eastern Jiangxi, and Fujian.[71] Intriguingly, in this lower Yangzi region, even when the type of tomb diverges from the mounded

control. Given the timing of construction, it is possible that turmoil in China during the Warring States period may have played some role in motivating fortification.

Ibid., p. 1023

[71] Archaeologists have located the core area of such tombs in northern Zhejiang and Jiangsu, but some such tombs intriguingly extend down the southeastern coast of Zhejiang and into the mountainous areas of southern Zhejiang and northwestern Fujian. Also, there are different types of mounded tombs: simple earthen ones with a rather wide distribution across lower Yangzi regions, and stone-chamber mounds, which are found only in the Lake Tai and Zhejiang areas. Lothar von Falkenhausen, "The Waning of the Bronze Age: Material Culture and Social Developments, 770–481 B.C.," in Edward Shaughnessy and Michael Loewe, eds., *Cambridge History of Ancient China: From the Origins of Civilization to 221 B.C.* (Cambridge: Cambridge University Press, 1999), p. 527.

type, the funerary assemblages in each type are comparable with those contained in mounded tombs.[72] Boat-shaped coffins are a special feature in many of these tombs, underscoring the importance of marine activity in the lives of the inhabitants.

Bronze Age mounded tombs of the South reflect distinctive burial cultures – and, hence, local, regional forms of religious belief – that seem to map onto the core geographic regions typically referred to by the ancient Chinese as Yue. Given that famous tombs of Yue kings of the fifth to third centuries BCE were mounded – such as the royal mausoleum at Yinshan (near Shaoxing, mentioned above), which is shaped like an upturned boat and allegedly houses the son or grandson of King Goujian of Yue himself – it is likely that the Bronze Age material culture in the Hangzhou Bay area, which is often dubbed "Yue" by archaeologists, corresponds to the reference "Yue" in our textual sources.[73] The boat-shaped wooden coffins found in the cliff-cave tombs of the Wuyi Mountains (eastern Jiangxi and northern Fujian) also suggest a more generalized ritual culture that may have been shared between the regions of the so-called Wu-yue and Min-yue cultures, as identified in the textual tradition.[74]

Our inquiry has focused more on connections and continuities and said less about the material diversity of the cultures in the regions, especially that associated with the ancient term, "Bai-yue." This is because we were evaluating whether, from an archaeological perspective, the ancients were justified in using the term, Yue, to group peoples together. To be sure, a fuller material understanding of the cultures of these regions would reveal immense differences at the local, micro-level. Such distinctions and differences are not reflected in any unifying notion such as the ancient term, "Yue," the modern archaeological culture of "Yue," or a rubric such as "Geometric Horizon" or "proto-Austronesian-speaking group." If anything, micro-level analysis sheds light on the hundreds (*bai* 百), if not thousands, of different cultures and ethnicities that were encompassed by the term, "Bai-yue."[75]

[72] Lothar von Falkenhausen mentions two other distinctive types of tombs in the region: megalithic chamber tombs (coastal southern Zhejiang) and cliff-cave tombs that contain boat-shaped wooden coffins (Wuyi Mountains of eastern Jiangxi/northern Fujian). *Ibid.*, pp. 527–528.

[73] See Dong Chuping, "Tomb Occupancy at the Great Yinshan Mausoleum," pp. 57–62.

[74] Contrary to this claim, some archaeologists suggest that the absence of mounded tombs along the Fujian coast reflects an important divergence among these southeastern coastal cultures. According to Allard, "Except for a few sites located at its northernmost end (e.g. Guangjiu), it [Fujian] did not participate in the mounded tomb tradition." Allard, "Early Complex Societies."

[75] In his survey on complexity in southern China, Francis Allard discusses the South in terms of three main sub-regions and goes on to underscore the significant level of variations even within these sub-regions. Allard, "Early Complex Societies."

Part II

Timelines and political histories of the Yue state and Han period Yue kingdoms, c. 500–110 BCE

4 Political histories of the Yue state and Han period Yue kingdoms, c. 500–110 BCE

There is not much about the pre-imperial and early imperial history of various Yue states in East Asia that intrinsically ties them together. Aside from the fact that many contained "Yue," in their name, these kingdoms were as motley as the landscape and peoples who inhabited the southern regions. While some of the political elite in each of the groups may have been related to each other culturally and/or biologically, it is difficult to know the extent to which both the ancient population and elite may have identified with or would have been categorized as "Yue" by insiders and outsiders alike. Because of the tenuous links among various Yue states of different eras and geographical locations, we must proceed with caution, keeping in mind that the histories of these states and their leaders provide only a thin slice of Yue history, especially if we take "Yue" to be an ethnonym and not merely limited to the political sphere. In what follows, I provide the basic political background for key states of the early period that were associated with Yue peoples and cultures: 1) the Spring and Autumn states of Wu and Yue, 2) the Bai-yue and the state of Nan-yue in the South, and 3) the early imperial history of the Han period south-eastern kingdoms of Min-yue, Ou-yue, and Eastern Yue. My abiding question concerns the extent to which we see a cross-cultural, cross-ethnic type of interaction between local Yue personalities or leaders and the non-local, Hua-xia.

Wu-yue history: King Fuchai of Wu and King Goujian of Yue

The ancient kingdom or state of Yue was deeply intertwined with its non-Zhou and also non-Central State neighbor, the state of Wu, the boundaries of which correspond roughly to the region from southern Anhui through Jiangxi to its southernmost point.[1] Yue, on the other hand,

[1] The core region of Wu seems to have been around the Lake Tai area near present-day Wuxi, and its ancient capital was at the city of Wu, which is presently Suzhou. See Lothar von

Table 4.1 *Political timeline of the state of Yue*[a]

510 BCE	King Helü of Wu 吳王闔閭 invades Yue, setting off a series of wars between the two states for control over land and fertile agricultural regions
514–496 BCE	King Helü reigns in state of Wu; employed Wu Zixu 伍子胥 and Sunzi 孫子 as advisors
?–497 BCE	King Yunchang 越王允常 reigns in state of Yue
496–465 BCE	King Goujian 越王勾踐, Yunchang's son, reigns in state of Yue
495–474 BCE	King Fuchai 吳王夫差, Helü's son, reigns in state of Wu
482 BCE	King Fuchai of Wu conquers Yue and goes on to win the status of Protector General (*ba* 霸) over the interstate community
473 BCE	King Goujian battles Wu for three years, eventually conquering and annexing it
c. 470 BCE	King Goujian wins status of Protector General over the interstate community
464–459 BCE	Wang Shiyu 王鼫與 (Goujian's son, also called Zhezhiyuci 者旨于賜), reigns in state of Yue
333 BCE	King Wei of Chu 楚威王 conquers and annexes Yue (during the reign of King Wujiang of Yue 越王無彊)
333–223 BCE	Royals and aristocrats of conquered Yue regions disperse southward, some becoming rulers of their own principalities and attending court in the state of Chu
223 BCE	State of Qin conquers Chu and creates the Commandery of Kuiji, with capital at Wu, located in the former lands of Yue

[a] I am indebted to Eric Henry's king list and discussion for the names of many of the kings appearing in this timeline. Henry, "Submerged History of Yuè," Sino-Platonic Papers 176 (2007): 10–16.

occupied the territories south and east of Wu, from the region around Lake Tai (which was probably contested and occupied by both Wu and Yue at various times) to the coast and down to the Hangzhou Bay region in Zhejiang Province (see Map 1).[2] Despite the separation of the polities of Wu and Yue, and despite the historic rivalry between them, the history

Falkenhausen, "The Waning of the Bronze Age: Material Culture and Social Developments, 770–481 B.C.," in Edward Shaughnessy and Michael Loewe, eds., *Cambridge History of Ancient China: From the Origins of Civilization to 221 B.C.* (Cambridge: Cambridge University Press, 1999), p. 526. For a detailed discussion of the similar origins of the Wu and Yue states, and their relationship to Chu, see Rao, "Wu Yue wen hua 吳越文化," *The Bulletin of the Institute of History and Philology Academica Sinica* 41.4 (1969): 609. Rao cites Sima Qian to show that the Wu-yue regions were originally known as the "Jing man 荊蠻" or "Chu man 楚蠻" regions, in reference to the Man 蠻 (also Min 閩) peoples. Rao goes further to claim that these terms seem to be taken from the customary names for these peoples. See Rao, "Wu Yue wen hua," p. 609 and notes 1 and 2, p. 628.

[2] Given that the early ancient Yue capital of Kuaiji 會稽 was located near modern-day Shaoxing, and also that one of the major tombs of a king of Yue was located just outside of Shaoxing, it was likely that this region was the traditional center of Yue territory.

of the state of Wu is also usually considered to be a history of Yue peoples. This is because both states were thought to share the same general culture, which is reflected in archaeological and historical sources as the "Wu-yue" culture.

Even though Wu and Yue were ostensibly established as states during the Spring and Autumn period (770–476 BCE), it is not until the early Warring States period (476–221 BCE) that Wu and Yue are truly featured and acknowledged as states of some importance. Lothar von Falkenhausen writes: "Yue . . . is an almost unknown entity during the Spring and Autumn Period."[3] Indeed, most textual references to the Yue occur only late in the *Spring and Autumn Annals*, which were named after this period, recording political and military events that took place from about the mid-sixth century to 470 BCE.[4] The bloody rivalry between the two states began when Wu invaded Yue in 510 BCE and set off a series of battles involving control over the rice-growing land in the Yangzi Delta.[5] By 482 BCE King Fuchai of Wu 吳王夫差 (r. 495–474 BCE) had not only conquered Yue but had also turned his military exploits toward the north to compete for and win the status of Protector General (*ba* 霸) – a type of supreme, hegemonic ruler – over the interstate community.[6] The tide quickly turned against King Fuchai, however, for in 473 BCE, under the leadership of King Goujian of Yue 越王句踐 (r. 496–465 BCE), Yue engaged in a victorious, three-year conquest of Wu.[7] Shortly thereafter, Goujian proclaimed himself Protector General of the interstate community, marking the zenith of Yue power in the history of the Zhou period.[8]

At this point it is worth mentioning an important archaeological site that attests to the immense power of the Yue state around the time of King Goujian. Just southeast of modern-day Shaoxing, there is a tomb of a Yue king – now referred to simply as the "Yinshan Mausoleum" because of the uncertainty surrounding the identity of the tomb's occupant.[9] A report from the archaeological team of the journal *Wenwu* 文物 from 1999

[3] Falkenhausen, "The Waning of the Bronze Age," p. 526.

[4] While the term "Yue" occurs in the text of the *Zuo zhuan* for years that precede this period, it only occurs about six times in the entries dating from 601 to 510 BCE. See Eric Henry, "The Submerged History of Yuè," *Sino-Platonic Papers* 176 (May, 2007): 8.

[5] Hsu, Cho-yun, "The Spring and Autumn Period," in Edward Shaughnessy and Michael Loewe, eds., *Cambridge History of Ancient China: From the Origins of Civilization to 221 B.C.* (Cambridge: Cambridge University Press, 1999), p. 564.

[6] *Ibid.* [7] Von Falkenhausen, "The Waning of the Bronze Age," p. 526.

[8] Yang Bojun, *Zuo zhuan* 12.20 and 12.24 ("Duke Ai"), pp. 1715–1717, 1722–1724. Cited in Hsu, Cho-yun, "The Spring and Autumn Period," p. 564.

[9] See Dong Chuping 董楚平, "關於紹興印山大墓墓主問題的探討—兼說紹興 306 號墓的國屬問題 (An Investigation into the Question of Tomb Occupancy at the Great Yingshan Mausoleum, Along with Some Comments on the State Affiliation of Shaoxing Tomb 306)," *Journal of Hangzhou Teachers College (Social Sciences Edition)* 4 (July, 2002): 57–62.

claims that the location of the tomb should correspond to what the Han text, the *Yuejue shu*, refers to as the Great Mounded Tomb of Mt. Muke (木客大冢), which belonged to King Yunchang of the Yue 越王允常.[10] King Yunchang, who died in 497 BCE, was Goujian's father. There is some controversy surrounding this identification.[11]

The burial mound, excavated from 1996 to 1998, is a unique monument that conveys the distinctive religious culture of the Yue. Consisting of a massive tumulus covering an area of over 1,000 square meters, the mausoleum complex includes a 14-meter-long rectangular shaft pit containing a tomb in the shape of a giant wooden boat along with a 46-meter passageway leading outside (see Figure 4.1). It is surrounded by a moat 20 meters wide and 3 meters deep in the shape of an "L."[12] The boat or triangular-shaped tomb, formed by propping up many wooden beams against each other and laying even larger beams along the ground as cross-beams, has three chambers: front, main, and rear. It is in the main chamber that one finds the distinctive, 6-meter outer coffin made from the trunk of a single tree and forming the shape of a dugout canoe. The canoe has since collapsed in on itself and lies at present on the ground, but archaeologists have deduced that it had originally been suspended in mid-air from the top (see Figure 4.2).[13]

[10] Zhejiang Wenwu Archaeological Research Group 浙江省文物考古研究所, "绍兴县文物保护管理所. 浙江绍兴印山大墓发掘简報 (Report on the Great Tomb of Yinshan Excavated in Shaoxing)," *Wenwu* 文物11 (1999).

[11] Dong Chuping has since challenged this belief by arguing that the types and number of tomb artifacts, as well as the particular designs on the pottery, suggest that the tomb was constructed after Yue's protracted military engagements with the state of Wu – in other words, after Yue's subsequent meteoric rise to power and access to resources. Dong argues that such a technological and massive achievement could only have been constructed at the heyday of Yue power – therefore, not before King Goujian; and he argues that the tomb's occupant was Zhezhiyuci (者旨于賜; this is his name according to bronze inscriptions, Shiyu in the *Shi ji*), Guojian's son, who ruled for a mere six years from 464 to 459 BCE. Dong also argues that the political turmoil at the Yue court starting in the year 376 BCE probably made such lavish tomb constructions obsolete, so that the dating of the Yingshan tomb should be somewhere between the death of Goujian (who was said to have been buried in Langye) and 376 BCE. Dong Chuping, "An Investigation into the Question of Tomb Occupancy," pp. 57–59.

[12] Eric Henry, "The Submerged History of Yuè," p. 5.

[13] Eric Henry provides further detail:

"Extraordinary antiseptic measures were used to protect the corpse from decay; the crypt was enveloped by a thick layer of white clay, a layer of charcoal one meter thick, and a layer of tree bark. Like other burial mound tombs it has inward leaning wooden posts on either side, resulting in a structure 5 meters high with a long apex. These posts, most unusually, have survived; the structure is essentially intact . . . The coffin was coated with black lacquer. Though the site was looted in the late Warring States era, more than 40 objects were found in the tomb, including a wooden pestle, a bronze bell, a jade arrow head, a jade dragon's head, and various Warring States grave-looters' tools. With the exception of a tomb near Baoji in Shanxi province . . . no other tomb in pre-Qin China matches this one in scale."

Ibid.

Figure 4.1: Boat-shaped tomb, Yinshan Tomb of the king of the Yue kingdom

This tomb is phenomenal not only because it is the largest of its type (a few other similar tombs have been discovered in areas throughout Guangdong Province),[14] but because it at once suggests the grandiose power of the Yue state while also pointing to stark cultural differences between it and the other Central States farther north. Archaeologists in China almost unanimously take this to represent traditional Yue burial practices – although the sheer massiveness of the tomb, along with the fact that it consists in a pyramid-like tumulus with a rectangular shaft, may actually reflect a desire on the part of the occupant to project Central States-like power through his burial. Regardless of the level of Central States influence in the Yinshan Mausoleum, it is fair to say that this site offers a concrete example of the stellar rise to power of the Yue at the beginning of the fifth century BCE.

After King Goujian's installation as Protector General, the record is fairly silent about the state of Yue until 333 BCE, when the state of Chu

[14] Of course there are the boat-coffins that "take flight" in the cliff faces of ancient Fujian, which we have briefly mentioned in Chapter 1.

Figure 4.2: Dugout canoe coffin, Yinshan Tomb of the king of the Yue kingdom

decisively defeated Yue, bringing about its end as a formal state. As Sima Qian writes, King Wei of Chu 楚威王 (r. 339–328 BCE) defeated and killed King Wujiang of Yue 越王無疆, "completely overtaking the old Wu lands up to Zhejiang, and, in the north, destroying [those parts of] Qi up to Xuzhou 盡取笔吳地至浙江，北破齊於徐州."[15] Sima Qian continues: "And as a result of this, the Yue [ruling class] dispersed. The sons of many clans vied for positions, some becoming kings and others rulers. They banked south of the Yangzi along the coast and attended court in the state of Chu 而越以此散，諸族子爭立，或為王，或為君，濱於江南海上，服朝於楚."[16] Sima suggests a shattering of the rather large and powerful Yue state into many kingdoms and principalities farther south along the coast, ruled over by dispersed members of the Yue ruling class. Significantly, the Yue princes who became the leaders of these kingdoms and principalities were compelled to pay homage to the Chu royal court so that all of Yue leadership was nominally subordinated to Chu from that time to the end of the Chu state in 223 BCE. After Qin conquered the state of Chu in 223 BCE, they created the commandery of Kuaiji 會稽, with its capital at Wu, in the former lands of the Yue.[17]

Sima's account is the first piece of information concerning the Yue ruling class in the aftermath of the Chu defeat, and it is the source for much scholarly debate about the date of establishing kingdoms farther to the south in Fujian, such as Min-yue. Not everyone accepts this account, however. Eric Henry claims that while most scholars suppose that the state of Yue ceased to exist "as a strong, single, independent entity after this date," there is evidence to suggest the contrary – that the Yue state did have a strong presence in the political landscape of the late Warring States. Drawing upon a bronze inscription written on a vessel dating to c. 300 BCE and unearthed in 1977, as well as textual support from various texts such as the *Zhanguo ce, Yuejue shu*, and *Han feizi* 韓非子, all of which speak of the continued existence of Yue or the annexation of Yue land near Langye (a northern center of power that Yue had attained during its heyday in the fifth century) by Chu, Henry casts doubt upon the

15 Sima Qian, *Shi ji* 41 ("Yue Wang Gou Jian Shi jia 越王句踐世家"), (Beijing: Zhonghua shu ju, 1992), p. 1751. I adopt the precise date from Keith Taylor, *The Birth of Vietnam* (Berkeley: University of California Press, 1983), p. 16.

16 *Shi ji*, 41.1751. In this passage, commentators point out that the region referred to corresponds to the Nanjing–Suzhou area in contemporary China.

17 Rafe de Crespigny, *Generals of the South: The Foundation and Early History of the Three Kingdoms State of Wu* (Canberra: Australian National University, Faculty of Asian Studies, 1990), Chapter 1.

extent to which the Chu conquest of Yue in 333 was really a clear loss of statehood for Yue.[18] For if Yue had been decisively defeated by Chu in 333 BCE, Henry contends, then why would the *Zhanguo ce* speak of Yue as having been a constant menace to the state of Chu and Qin throughout the third century BCE?[19] Similarly, the *Yuejue shu* maintains that Chu annexed Yue at Langye sometime between 262 and 238 BCE, suggesting that the Yue had at some point after the conquest of Chu in 333 BCE regained their land around Langye and were still a viable power in that area.[20]

I find Henry's arguments for the continued existence of a strong, independent polity of Yue in the post-Chu conquest years plausible and intriguing, but I wonder if it might not be the case that post-333 Yue was something of a "rogue state." In such a scenario, the remaining Yue royalty and elite maintained power and authority over certain smaller regions in their erstwhile territory, but they would have had to pay lip service to Chu in an official capacity, and therefore did not warrant the label "kingdom." Regardless, it is nonetheless noteworthy that the segment of history post-dating the Chu defeat of Yue sees the creation of a new category of Yue, which was not affixed uniquely to a single state or region, but to what seems to have been a larger, possibly ethnic, grouping: the Bai-yue.

Bai-yue and Southern Yue (Nan-yue) history

The term "Bai-yue" represents a Chinese shorthand for these many dispersed and variegated groups thought somehow to be related to the peoples and cultures of the erstwhile state of Yue.[21] Our sources unfortunately do not provide solid clues regarding a perceived ethnic relationship between "Yue" and the Bai-yue. The only information we might glean consists in references to the general geographic region of the "Bai-yue," which may have overlapped with the regions where the dispersed Yue elite fled after the conquest of Chu. The *Lüshi chunqiu* of the third century BCE states that the regions of the Bai-yue are delimited by the areas south of the Yang and Han Rivers 揚漢之南，百越之際 (in general: the Southeast).[22]

[18] Henry, "The Submerged History of Yuè," pp. 13–14. [19] *Ibid.*, p. 13.

[20] *Ibid.*, p. 14.

[21] There are no existing references to the Bai-yue that pre-date the dissolution of the state of Yue, the earliest found in the *Lüshi chunqiu*, dating to c. 239 BCE. Rao explains that people referred to the Yue as "hundred Yue" because the ruling classes of Yue themselves possessed mixed surnames. Rao, "Wu Yue wen hua," p. 609.

[22] Chen Qiyou 陳奇猷, *Lüshi chunqiu jiaoshi* 吕氏春秋校釋 (Shanghai: Xuelin Publishing, 1984), 20.1322. The ancient region of Yangzhou 楊州 is known as Yang among commentators, referring to an ancient reference for the Nine Province of Yu the Great associated with the southeastern part of the known world during Warring States times. See Zhang Shoujie's Tang Dynasty comments in *Shi ji*, 113.2968, #4.

Table 4.2 *Political timeline of Southern Yue*[a]

c. 204 BCE	Zhao Tuo established the kingdom of Southern Yue 南越 (Nan Yue/ Nam Viet); extending from modern-day Canton Province to northern Vietnam; took title, King Wu of Southern Yue 南越武王; kingdom thrived for ninety-three years until conquered by Han imperial forces
196 BCE accepted	Zhao Tuo position as feudal king under the Han (Lu Jia 陸賈 was Han emissary)
183 BCE	Empress Lü 呂太后 placed economic sanctions on Southern Yue; Zhao Tuo assumed title, Emperor Wu of Southern Yue 南越武帝
181–180 BCE	Zhao Tuo attacked border towns of Changsha; Empress Lü sent Han forces to attack Southern Yue; Han army succumbed to illness and hardship; troops were recalled in 180 BCE; Zhao Tuo expanded territory into regions of Min-yue, Western Ou, and Luo-luo.
c. 180 BCE	Lu Jia was sent again as Han emissary under Emperor Wen 漢文帝 to gain submission of Zhao Tuo; Zhao Tuo formally relinquished use of imperial designations and prerogatives vis-à-vis the Han, but continued to use them in internal matters of Southern Yue
137 BCE	Zhao Tuo died; grandson Zhao Hu (Zhao Mo) 趙胡/趙昧 succeeded him as king of Southern Yue
137–122 BCE	Zhao Hu (Mo) retained use of imperial designations and prerogatives in internal affairs of Southern Yue; outwardly remained a loyal vassal to Han; sent his son, crown prince Zhao Yingqi 趙嬰齊, to Chang'an to serve as an attendant
122 BCE	Zhao Hu (Mo) died; was posthumously conferred the title, King Wen 文王; Zhao Yingqi ruled Southern Yue; was married to a wife from the Central States
113 BCE	Zhao Yingqi died and was posthumously conferred the title, King Ming 明王; crown prince Zhao Xing 趙興 ascended the throne; Queen Dowager resumed an affair with an old lover from the Han court, Anguo Shaoji 安國少季, who was sent to Southern Yue as a Han envoy
113–112 BCE	Southern Yue Prime Minister Lü Jia 呂嘉 committed regicide, killed Queen Dowager, and wiped out 2,000 Han troops sent to punish him
111 BCE	Han regime conquered Southern Yue; divided it up into seven commanderies from Canton to northern Vietnam

[a] Based on accounts of Southern Yue in *Shi ji*, 113 and Ban Gu, *Han shu* (Beijing: Zhonghua, 1995), p. 95.

Later texts expand the location of the Bai-yue, shifting it even farther south and southwest. In one example from the *Shi ji*, the Bai-yue refer to groups south of Chu that were conquered by the Chu minister Wu Qi 吳起 during the reign of the king Dao Wang of Chu 楚悼王

(r. 328–298 BCE).[23] This would approximately mean areas south of the Yangzi spanning at least the length of modern-day Guangdong Province. Another example from the same text refers to the Bai-yue in relationship to the areas around modern-day Guangdong, Guizhou, and Guangxi.[24] From these references, we gain a sense that the geographical location of the Bai-yue may have shifted from the Southeast to cover the entire South, and that the expanded notion of Bai-yue may not have been a mere shorthand for the broken-up principalities of the previous state of Yue. Indeed, it seems to have become a shorthand for something much larger.

References to the geographical scope and periphery of the Bai-yue occur somewhat later in the textual record. The *Han shu* provides an example in which the "lands of Yue" span a distance from the regions of Kuaiji to Jiaozhi 交阯; or, as one commentator quantifies it, about 7,000–8,000 *li* (approximately 3,200 kilometers).[25] Of course, one must allow for the likelihood that reference points for the Bai-yue during the first century CE when the *Han shu* was written had already changed dramatically since the late Warring States and early Han. Nonetheless, it is clear that by the first century CE the lands of Yue were thought to cover extremely great areas. This suggests that, with the emergence of the concept of Bai-yue, the general category of Yue had become something

[23] *Shi ji*, 65.2168. Heather Peters, "Tattooed Faces and Stilt Houses: Who Were the Ancient Yue?" *Sino-Platonic Papers* 17 (April 1990): 3. As Peters points out, this story is repeated in the *Hou Han shu* 後漢書 (fourth century CE), where the authors use the reference "Southern Yue," and not "Bai-yue," perhaps because they interpreted Sima's vague reference to be located approximately around the regions of the early Han kingdom of Southern Yue. We do not know whether or not "Southern Yue" existed as a kingdom in the Canton region before Zhao Tuo in the late third century BCE, or sometime after the Chu conquest of Yue in 333 BCE. In *Zhuangzi* there is a reference to the kingdom of Southern Yue, occurring in a passage that most likely post-dates the Qin Dynasty. Zhuangzi, annot. Guo Qingfan 郭慶藩, *Zhuangzi ji shi* 莊子集釋 (Taipei: Wan juan lou, 1993), 20.671.

[24] *Shi ji*, 113.2967.

[25] Guiji is also pronounced, "Kuaiji," but "Guiji" seems to be the preferred pronunciation for the ancient capital. Also noteworthy is the fact that the *Han Shu* does not technically use the term "hundred Yue" here. The phrase is merely, "the lands of the Yue 粵地." Note the different character used here for Yue. This character comes to refer to the areas around modern-day Guangdong and Guangxi in general. Ban Gu, *Han Shu* (Beijing: Zhonghua shuju, 1995), p. 1669. It is the Jin Dynasty commentator, Chen Zan 臣瓚, who substitutes "hundred Yue" for Yue in commentary to this passage. I cannot ascertain from the sources just when the name "hundred Yue" became synonymous with "Yue" in common usage.

This expanse corresponds roughly to the area between the mouth of the Yangzi near Shanghai and the Red River Valley near Vietnam. See Taylor on the origins of the name Jiaozhi and its general location as a prefecture in the Red (Hong) River plain. Taylor, *The Birth of Vietnam*, p. 26.

more than the specific reference to the ancient kingdom of Yue. It had become a relevant marker for peoples and places situated most anywhere in the entire southern portion of modern-day China, including northern Vietnam.

The early imperial period helps clarify the fuzzy nature of the political situation in the South, since it witnesses the creation of actual political entities that are better defined (at least, in our Chinese sources) than the Bai-yue. The First Emperor of Qin (r. 221–210 BCE) was responsible for opening up the lands of the Bai-yue to more extensive northern influence and influx. Sima Qian's history tells us that he sent 500,000 troops southward to attack the Bai-yue and set up Qin commanderies in the Far South. After successfully attacking the Min-yue, Qin troops set up the Minzhong Commandery in southeastern China. In order to facilitate the takeover of the South, the First Emperor ordered the construction of what became known as the Lingqu Canal 靈渠, a canal that connected the Xiang 湘 and Li 漓 Rivers and allowed Qin troops to more easily supply their various companies waging war on the Bai-yue.

The attack on the Bai-yue of the Lingnan region proved more difficult at first. After their leader, Yi Xusong 譯籲宋, was killed by the Qin, the Western Ou 西甌 (also 嘔) peoples retreated into the jungle, refusing to submit.[26] From there, they continued to raid the Qin, and, in one attack at night, they successfully killed the Qin leader, Du Sui 屠睢, and devastated Qin troops.[27] In 214 BCE, the First Emperor had the military commanders Ren Xiao 任囂 and Zhao Tuo lead a massive and decisive campaign against the Western Ou. The result was the latter's defeat, and the colonization of the Lingnan area by Qin administrators. The three commanderies of Nanhai 南海 (South Sea), Guilin 桂林, and Xiang 象 were established at that point.

The history of the various Bai-yue kingdoms during the Han Dynasty is one of Han imperial conquest and incorporation, as well as the gradual trickling in of cultural and political influences in these regions. A very important entity in this history was the kingdom of Southern Yue, due to its massive size (in name, it covered a distance roughly from Canton Province through the northern reaches of contemporary Vietnam), its incorporation of a variety of different political units, and its strategic location at the southern, maritime edge of the Han Empire. The Southern Yue lasted for ninety-three years before it was conquered by

26 Liu Wendian 劉文典, *Huainan honglie jijie* 淮南鴻烈集解 (Beijing: Zhonghua Publishing, 1989), 18.617.

27 *Ibid.* The text says that hundreds of thousands of people were killed.

Figure 4.3: Miniature model, Southern Yue royal palace site remains

Han troops and subsequently incorporated more fully into the administrative control of the Han.

Beginning as early as the fall of the Qin Empire, Zhao Tuo became the military commander of Nanhai and conquered the surrounding lands to create the kingdom of Southern Yue in 204 BCE. Of these surrounding lands, Zhao Tuo conquered and united two erstwhile Qin commanderies of Guilin and Xiang, joining them with Nanhai, home to the capital city of Panyu, which became Tuo's central headquarters and the capital of his newly formed kingdom, the Southern Yue (see Figures 4.3, 4.4, 4.5). Tuo then renamed himself the Martial King of Southern Yue (Nanyue wuwang 南越武王). When the first Han Emperor Gaozu (r. 202–195 BCE) sent emissary Lu Jia 陸賈 to Southern Yue to obtain Zhao Tuo's formal submission to the Han, the latter conceded, but over the years, his submission and loyalty to the Han court was to prove dubious and superficial at best.

The reign of Empress Lü (188–180 BCE) was a particularly tense time for Han–Yue relations. As the story in the *Shi ji* goes, Empress Lü had listened to false accusations against Zhao Tuo by ministers at her court, possibly stemming from the king of Changsha, who may have had plans to

Figure 4.4: Royal garden with crooked stone brook (poster view), Southern Yue royal palace site remains

acquire the kingdom of Southern Yue as his own.[28] Whatever the true reasons, Empress Lü acted belligerently toward Southern Yue by blocking off much critical trade with it from the North. Zhao Tuo responded by invading the areas around Changsha, and the Empress sent troops down to attack Southern Yue. Fortunately for Zhao Tuo, the Han troops fell ill before being able to cross into Southern Yue. They withdrew, and the

[28] See Zhang Rongfang 張榮芳 and Huang Miaozhang 黃淼章, *Nanyueguo shi* 南越國史 (History of the Kingdom of Nan-yue) (Guangzhou City: Guangdong Renmin Publishing, 1995), pp. 70–71 for more details on the Southern Yue border with Changsha. Note that the king of Changsha at the time, Wu Ruo 吳若 (also known as "The Absolute King of Changsha" 長沙共王, r. 188–178 BCE), was a descendant of Wu Rui 吳芮 (d. 202 BCE). Wu Rui had allegedly been promised authority over the regions of Nanhai, Xiang, and Guilin by Han Emperor Gaozu at the beginning of the latter's reign. Scholars still dispute the northern extent of the Southern Yue border, especially since an early map from the founding of the Han (excavated in the 1972 Mawangdui finds) suggests at least three counties in the region were designated as belonging to Changsha. Such an unclear northern border no doubt seeded disputes over this territory, as witnessed by the struggle during Empress Lü's reign. *Shi ji*, 113.2969.

Figure 4.5: Qin period shipyard (surface reconstruction), Southern Yue royal palace site remains

kingdom of Southern Yue was able to avoid a costly military engagement with the Han at this time.[29]

Han Emperor Wendi (r. 180–157 BCE) adopted a conciliatory approach toward Southern Yue. Sima Qian tells us that he not only sent Han representatives to Zhao Tuo's hometown in northern China, Zhending 真定, to pay respects to Zhao Tuo's ancestors and maintain the ancestral graves, but he also sent Lu Jia as an emissary back to Southern Yue. Zhao Tuo had been proclaiming himself "Emperor of Southern Yue" ever since Empress Lü's actions against him. Lu Jia skillfully got Zhao Tuo to submit to the Han again, and to formally renounce the title of "Emperor" for himself. Even though Zhao Tuo accepted submission, thereby once again lowering the position of Southern Yue to that of a dependent kingdom of the Han, his continued practices within Southern Yue suggest that these changes were in name only. Indeed, as we will analyze in more detail later in the book, when not dealing directly with the Han (which was most of the time), Zhao Tuo continued to act and be

[29] *Shi ji*, 113.2969.

treated as emperor within his own kingdom. He died in 137 BCE and bequeathed the kingdom to his grandson, Zhao Hu (also thought to be Zhao Mo 趙胡/趙眜, the occupant of the magnificent tomb unearthed in Guangzhou).[30]

When King Zou Ying 騶郢 of Min-yue attacked the border regions of Southern Yue in 135 BCE, Zhao Hu appealed to the Han court for military aid. Han Emperor Wudi (r. 141–87 BCE) responded promptly by sending down two generals to attack Min-yue with their armies. Before any battle took place, the younger brother of King Zou Ying, Zou Yushan 騶餘善, killed the latter and surrendered to the Han. After this incident, Zhao Hu promised the Han that he would pay a visit to the Han court. In addition, he sent his son, Zhao Yingqi 趙嬰齊, to the court to serve as an attendant in the Emperor's palace. Zhao Hu never kept his promise to visit in person, feigning illness instead, perhaps out of fear that leaving his base in Southern Yue would provide the Han with an easy means of usurping his power at home. From tomb remains, we know that Zhao Hu had also used the title "Emperor" for himself: in the world of the Southern Yue, he was "Emperor Wen 文帝," the Civilizing Emperor – not, "King Wen 文王," the "Civilizing King," a title which Han Emperor Wudi had bestowed upon him posthumously, as a result of Southern Yue's cooperation with the Han against Min-yue.

Upon the death of Zhao Hu in 122 BCE, his son, Zhao Yingqi, who had been residing in Chang'an, took power in Southern Yue. Like his father and Zhao Tuo, Yingqi carried on the tradition of flouting Han laws and letting slide relationships with the larger empire to its north. Sima Qian notes that he had murderous tendencies and reigned according to an unrestrained pursuit of his own passions, and that he refused to visit the Han capital for fear that he would be punished under Han law for his excesses. Sima's narrative clearly suggests that Yingqi's reign was the beginning of the end for the Southern Yue. After Yingqi's death in 113, his son Zhao Xing 趙興 (a son with a wife from the Central States – the now Queen Dowager of Southern Yue) ascended the throne. Xing was young, and so, much of the state administration was controlled by the powerful prime minister of Southern Yue, Lü Jia 呂嘉. But Queen

[30] In addition to the breathtaking archaeological finds associated with the tomb of Zhao Hu/Mo of the Nan-yue kingdom, other recent, scintillating excavations of the imperial palace at the ancient capital of Panyu (c. 203–111 BCE) are furthering our understanding of the importance and the status of Nan-yue as a commercial hub of the ancient world. The old town of the city of Panyu is square with a five-kilometer circumference. The remains of the palace, a large pond (85 x 65 meters), and its gardens and famous "Crooked, windy stream" – a long channel with a stone bed that meandered through the palace garden – are featured in a new museum complex, The Southern Yue Royal Palace Museum, in the inner city of Guangzhou. See Figs. 4.3, 4.4, and 4.5.

Dowager was still able to have Zhao Xing send a memorial to Han Emperor Wudi requesting Southern Yue's renewed submission to Han administrative control as a dependent state. While we will discuss the meaning of such an act in Chapter 8, suffice it to say that this was the decisive step in bringing on the demise of Southern Yue, just two years later.

Prime Minister Lü Jia opposed the submission of Southern Yue to Han and decided to rebel against his own king and Queen Dowager to save the kingdom. After an alleged attack on his life by the Queen Dowager at a palace banquet, Lü gathered his forces and staged a coup, assassinating the young king, Zhao Xing, along with his mother the Queen Dowager and all the Han emissaries at court. He then set up Zhao Jiande 趙建德, a son of Zhao Yingqi with a native Yue mother, who was also the step-brother of Zhao Xing, as king. By then, the Han Emperor had been duly warned about the unrest and dissent in Southern Yue, and he sent 2,000 troops to the region to keep the peace. The pro-Yue people who inhabited towns along the roads leading to Panyu contributed to Lü's cause in a vital way. They tricked advancing Han troops into thinking they were friendly by opening up the roads and supplying them with food. Lured into a trap, the Han troops were then conquered by Lü's forces, which ambushed and destroyed them when they were but 40 *li* from Panyu. This incident elicited the wrath of the Han imperial court, which declared war upon Southern Yue, leading to the defeat of this kingdom in 111 BCE.

Of the approximately 100,000 Han troops dispatched to conquer Southern Yue (after the initial "peace-keeping" troops had failed), many did not in fact come from the Central Plains region. The troops advanced from five different directions and traveled much of the way by river. The "Lord who swiftly assumes duty 馳義侯" (a reference to a native from Yue who has chosen to side with the Han), for example, leads into battle an army comprised of prisoners from the southwestern regions of Ba and Shu who had been pardoned by Han Emperor Wudi.[31] Surrounding the city of Panyu, Yang Pu 楊僕, another general, set the city afire and Yue soldiers and people started to defect to the Han side. Panyu was taken, and Lü Jia and the Zhao king fled in boats toward the west. The Han gave chase, and Zhao Jiande was captured first, then Lü Jia later. This famous military defeat of a great Southern kingdom marked a major victory in the history of Chinese colonization of the region. Soon after the Han defeat, Han administrators were sent down and nine commanderies were established (Dan'er 儋耳, Zhuya 珠崖, Nanhai 南海, Cangwu 蒼梧, Yulin 鬱林, Hepu 合浦, Jiaozhi 交阯, Jiuzhen 九真, and Rinan 日南), and

[31] *Shi ji*, 114.2975.

the erstwhile regions of Southern Yue served under colonial rule for the rest of the Han period.[32]

The kingdoms of Eastern Yue (Min-yue, Eastern Sea/Eastern Ou)

Most of the information that we have concerning the regions around modern-day Fujian associated with Yue peoples during the early Han period comes from the *Shi ji* 114, "The Account of Eastern Yue." This chapter is dedicated to the brief history of the states of Min-yue, Eastern Ou, and Eastern Yue, as they were called at various times during the Western Han period. Two polities appear to have pre-existed the Qin conquest of the Fujian region, just to the east of Southern Yue: Min-yue and Donghai (Eastern Sea). As mentioned above, the kings of both states – Zou Wuzhu 騶無諸 in Min-yue and Zou Yao 騶搖 in Eastern Sea – were descendants of King Goujian, which means that they were likely part of the royal elite that allegedly spread out to rule over the "Bai-yue" after the conquest of Yue by Chu in 333 BCE.

We know virtually nothing from our texts about the founding of these two kingdoms before Qin-Han times. Many archaeologists believe that the material record in the Fujian region strongly suggests the pre-Qin existence of a relatively powerful state, which they call "Min-yue."[33] The *Shi ji* confirms the fact that there were at least two pre-Qin states of significance by telling us that the Qin were able to oust the two regional kings (Zou Wuzhu and Zou Yao 搖), turn their polities into a single commandery called Min-zhong 閩中(Central Min), and grant these former kings a new status under the Qin as chieftains (*jun zhang* 君長).[34]

After the fall of the Qin, in 202, Emperor Gaozu of the Han re-established the kingdom of Min-yue from what had been Min-zhong, and named only Zou Wuzhu king. He presided over the capital of Eastern Ye 東冶. After a decade, it became apparent that the erstwhile King of Eastern Sea (Donghai 東海), Zou Yao, was also in need of official, Han recognition. In 192 BCE, no doubt apprehending an impending conflict

32 *Han shu*, 95.3859. The exception to this was Dan'er and Zhuya commanderies, on Hainan island, which were withdrawn as commanderies in 82 and 42 BCE.

33 Jiao Tianlong 焦天龍 and Fan Xuechun 范雪春, 福建與南島語族 (Fujian and the Austronesians) (Beijing: Zhonghua shuju, 2010), pp. 127–144. While archaeologists have clearly established that there was a noteworthy distinction between the material cultures of inland and coastal Fujian during Neolithic times, such an inland–coastal distinction appears to have dissolved by the late Warring States, further suggesting the unification of the region by a significant power (that archaeologists call "Min-yue"). See Jiao and Fan, *Fujian and the Austronesians*, p. 132.

34 *Shi ji*, 114.2979.

Table 4.3 *Political timeline of Min-yue, Eastern Ou, and Eastern Yue*[a]

Before c. 221 BCE	Zou Wuzhu 騶無諸 rules as king of Min-yue 閩越 in the Yue region of Min. Zou Yao 騶搖 rules as king of the Yue of East Sea 越東海, in a nearby region
221–210 BCE	The First Emperor of Qin transforms the kingdom of Min-Yue into the Commandery of Min-zhong 閩中 and the two kings become Chief Administrators in the commandery
210–202 BCE	Zou Wuzhu and Zou Yao aid Wu Rui 吳芮 in helping overthrow the Qin Empire. Later, they side with the Han against the rebel and contender for the throne, Xiang Yu 項籍
202 BCE	Han Gaozu 漢高祖 reinstates Zou Wuzhu as king of Min-Yue, ruling over the erstwhile Qin Commandery of Min-zhong, with his capital at Eastern Ye 東冶
192 BCE	Emperor Hui 漢惠帝 sets up Zou Yao as king of Eastern Sea 東海, with his capital at Dong-ou 東甌. He was informally known as the king of Eastern Ou 東甌王
154 BCE	Yao, king of Eastern Ou, joins feudal rebellion led by Liu Pi 劉濞, king of Wu, against the Han central court. Eastern Ou accepts a Han bribe to kill Pi, succeeds. Men of Eastern Ou are spared and return home safely
138 BCE	Min-Yue lays siege to Eastern Ou. Han intercedes and Min-yue withdraws troops. (Portions of) Eastern Ou population out-migrate to the regions between the Yangzi and Huai Rivers
135 BCE	King Zou Ying 騶郢 of Min-Yue attacks Southern Yue. Zou Yushan 騶餘善 commits fratricide, deposes Zou Ying. Zou Chou 騶丑 is named new king of Yue-yao 越繇王. Han Emperor Wudi 漢武帝 later declares Yushan to be king of Eastern Yue, ruling alongside Zou Chou, the king of Yue-yao
112 BCE	Han attacks Southern Yue. King Yushan of Eastern Yue requests to aid the Han in the attack but stalls
111–110 BCE	King Yushan revolts against Han troops and is killed. Eastern Yue surrenders to Han rule. Zou Jugu 騶居股 (son of Chou) is enfeoffed as Marquis of Eastern Yue. Emperor Wudi orders the mass migration of the people of Eastern Yue to the Central States region between the Yangzi and Huai Rivers

[a] Based on accounts of Eastern Yue in *Shi ji*, 114 and *Han shu*.

of leadership in the region, Emperor Hui of the Han (r. 195–188 BCE) formally acknowledged Zou Yao as king of Eastern Sea, with a capital at Eastern Ou (henceforth his kingdom was also known by "Eastern Ou" 東甌). The *Shi ji* justifies this Han appointment by stating that Yao was a "ruler of Min 閩君," and that "his people were loyal [to him] 其民便附."[35] This all suggests that pockets of pre-existing regional power in

[35] *Ibid.*

Min-yue (southern Zhejiang/Fujian) were still in effect and continued to create power struggles in the area. Additionally, local chieftains and leaders could clearly still be de facto rulers without having to be officially recognized by the Han court, although recognition by the court seems to have been desirable and sought after.

In 154 BCE, during the Revolt of the Feudatories, the king of Wu persuaded several rulers to rebel against the Han. Of the two Min kingdoms, only Eastern Sea (also referred to as "Eastern Ou," after the capital city) conceded to join the rebellion. When it was clear that the Han would prevail, "Eastern Ou" (here, Sima Qian likely refers to the then-king and his highest generals) accepted a Han bribe to kill the king of Wu and thereby remained unharmed.[36] Having fulfilled such a bribe, the men of Eastern Ou returned safely to their kingdom, but their actions incurred the wrath of Liu Ziju 劉子駒, the son of the king of Wu, who had fled into hiding in the kingdom of Min-yue. Sima Qian cites the revenge of Liu Ziju as the reason that the kingdom of Min-yue laid siege to Eastern Ou in 138 BCE, surrounding the capital city (Eastern Ou) and exhausting its resources. As the story goes, the king of Eastern Ou begged the Han court to send aid, which it did by dispatching a naval fleet from the city of Kuaiji to Eastern Ou. By the time it arrived, the kingdom of Min-yue had already withdrawn its troops. Although Sima Qian gives no explanation for this, one might assume that it was because Min-yue wished to avoid an encounter with Han naval forces. This interpretation is strengthened by the fact that after Min-yue's withdrawal of troops, the Eastern Ou still felt threatened and vulnerable, so much that its king asked to "be allowed to move the kingdom to the Central States 請舉國徙中國."[37] Presumably, even though Sima Qian indicates that "masses of people眾" then migrated out of Eastern Ou to settle in the region between the Yangzi and Huai Rivers, moving the entire kingdom referred primarily to a mass migration of the elite members of the court, not the entire population.[38]

The kingdom of Min-yue continued in its aggressive stance toward its neighbors. In the year 135 BCE, King Zou Ying 騶郢 of Min-yue attacked Southern Yue. We are not provided any reason for this action, but there are hints in Sima Qian's record that it had to do with the aggressive, expansionist policies of a single, Min-yue king, King Zou Ying, who likely

[36] Note that Sima Qian often fails to name the reigning kings of these regions, most likely because he did know the names. As Yang Cong surmises, the royal lines of the Min-yue, Yao, and Eastern Yue kings were likely very complicated, and not just the "Three generations in ninety-two years" that scholars sometimes assume to be the case. Yang Cong 楊琮. *Minyueguo Wenhua* 閩越國文化 (The Culture of the Kingdom of Min-yue) (Fuzhou: Fujian Renmin Chubanshe, 1998), pp. 17–18.

[37] *Shi ji*, 114.2980. [38] *Shi ji*, 114.2980.

wished to secure Min-yue independence and consolidate his power over a larger portion of the maritime South. Zou family rivalries and disagreements seem to have been as fierce as those at the Han court, and ostensibly not everyone at the Min-yue court thought the king's actions wise. After the Han responded to the attack by sending out troops to help Southern Yue, Zou Ying's younger brother, Zou Yushan 騶餘善, who may have feared that the king's actions against Southern Yue would doom the state and put his own life, power, and resources at risk, committed fratricide and deposed Zou Ying. Zou Yushan thereby staved off an impending battle between Han forces and the state of Min-yue.

Instead of rewarding Zou Yushan, however, Emperor Han Wudi set up Zou Chou 騶丑 (erstwhile Chief of [a region called] Yao 繇 and grandson of Zhou Wuzhu) as the new "King of Yue-yao 越繇王" [alternatively, "the King of Yao in Yue"], granting Chou the right to carry on ancestral sacrifices to the Min-yue ancestors. This signaled that there was to be a single, main authority in Min-yue, one which possessed sole rights over the religious act of sacrifice to the royal ancestors of the Yue. No doubt a political move to diminish Min-yue power and increase its allegiance to the Han, the artificial act of setting Zou Chou up as the Han puppet backfired against the Han. Zou Yushan had in the meantime secretly declared himself king, depriving Chou of a certain amount of authority. Han Emperor Wudi, like Huidi before him, was forced to deal with the situation in some way. Instead of a military solution, Wudi declared Yushan – who, after all, had helped the Han by committing fratricide – to be "King of Eastern Yue 東越王," and the latter ruled alongside Han Wudi's erstwhile puppet, now referred to as the "King of Yao 與繇王并處."[39] In such a manner, the precarious situation in this Yue region was temporarily settled, although one may argue that having two official rulers lead simultaneously was by no means an adequate way of ensuring stability in the region.

During the Han attack on the Southern Yue in 112 BCE, King Yushan of Eastern Yue offered to aid the Han. Yushan and his troops made it as far as Jieyang 揭揚 (in what is now eastern Guangdong Province) but advanced no further, citing inclement weather at sea as an excuse. Sima Qian notes that the king actually maintained communications with both Southern Yue and Han forces, and he makes it clear that the Han were made cognizant of Yushan's duplicity but were too depleted from the war on Southern Yue to launch an immediate attack against Eastern Yue.[40]

By 111 BCE, after the Han had defeated Southern Yue and had time to regroup its forces, King Yushan must have sensed that a Han attack on

[39] *Shi ji*, 114.2981–2982. [40] *Shi ji*, 114.2982.

Eastern Yue was imminent. He revolted against Han troops at his borders, conferring upon his generals such titles as "Generals Who Swallow the Han 吞漢將軍."[41] After killing three commanders in various strategic locations, Yushan began carving imperial seals for himself, usurping the title "Emperor" (specifically, "Emperor Wu 武帝"). Sima Qian's tale of the Han attack against Eastern Yue is long and complicated, outlining the names, ranks, and sometimes even the backgrounds (whether they were originally from "Yue" or not) of the various generals who had been sent to attack the kingdom on at least four fronts.[42] In the end, the Han made use of local Yue chieftains or Yue leaders who were loyal to the Han. Three local Yue leaders plotted against Yushan, killing him and forcing his troops to surrender to the Han. In 110 BCE, ninety-two years after the naming of the Min-yue state as a loyal kingdom of the Han, local non-Han leadership in the region was dealt a great blow and the state of Eastern Yue came to an end.

Zou Jugu 騶居股 (son of Chou), the king of Yao and one of the local leaders who helped assassinate Yushan, was subsequently enfeoffed as marquis of Eastern Yue and the area was carved up and divvied out as marquisates to those who had fought bravely for the Han. But unlike the kingdom of Southern Yue, which was promptly divided into commanderies, Han Emperor Wudi allegedly deemed the area of Eastern Yue unsuitable for continued administration. In an act that resembled the mass migration of Eastern Ou people in 138 BCE, Emperor Wudi issued a decree ordering the Han army and its officials to move the people of Eastern Yue into the (Central States) region between the Yangzi and Huai Rivers. Sima Qian ends thus his incredible account with the simple statement: "The lands of Eastern Yue were thereupon emptied."[43]

Rafe de Crespigny contends that only the royal and noble families of Eastern Yue were likely to have been forcibly moved by the Han: "Their departure removed the cultural and political leadership of the native people, and the county settlements maintained thereafter by the Han empire were sufficient to prevent any future development of renewed political independence."[44] But if such were the case, why did the Han divvy out marquisates to local chieftains after the war? Surely Han loyalists such as Zou Jugu, who had just been enfeoffed, did not leave his newly acquired territory? Indeed, though the textual record makes a bold

[41] *Ibid.*

[42] The attacks were to be launched from the cities of Juzhang 句章, Wulin 武林, Ruoye 若邪, and Baisha 白沙. Given the hilly and riverine landscape of Fujian, an attack by land was virtually impossible. These were presumably all coastal cities, although I am unsure of the exact whereabouts of each.

[43] *Shi ji*, 114.2984.

[44] De Crespigny, *Generals of the South*, Chapter 1.

conclusion concerning the emptying out of these lands, we can read between the lines to see that the forced migration may not even have included all Yue nobility, and that local, indigenous government may have continued uninterrupted for the entire Han period.

The defeat of the entire Yue Southland (represented by the kingdoms of Southern Yue and Eastern Yue) by 110 BCE marks the beginning of more intensified Han influence in the political, administrative, and cultural sphere of the southern peoples. While many original rulers continued to maintain control over their localities, these leaders had to pay allegiance to the Han and sometimes share control with immigrant Han administrators whose efforts were focused on overseeing commerce and ensuring the security and maintenance of trade networks.[45] It seems likely, then, that the Han loyalists who had acquired Yue territory in the aftermath of the Han conquest remained in their regions to rule as the local aristocracy. That the Han did not bother to set up its own administrative commandery in the region of Eastern Yue for some while therefore represents a comment on Han involvement in the region, not the entire lack of inhabitants or the lack of local leadership during the post-conquest period.

The material record provides us with tantalizing hints of a vibrant regional culture with various capital cities in the areas around Fujian during the early imperial period, corresponding in time to the Qin and early Han periods. Evidence of what appear to be at least two capital cities – one inland on a tributary (Yang River陽溪) that feeds into the Min River 閩江 in Wuyi Mountain 武夷山 County (at a site in Chengcun 城村 – formerly the early town of Chong'an 崇安), and the other in modern-day Fuzhou City at the delta of the Min River – might serve as material support for Sima Qian's reference to the two distinct, capital cities of Eastern Ye 東冶 (of the Min-yue) and Eastern Ou (of the Kingdom of Eastern Sea). Field archaeologists of the ancient city of Xindian 新店古城 site in Fuzhou City believe it to be the ancient capital city of Min-yue: EasternYe.[46] Others, including some renowned scholars of Fujian archaeology, do not think the evidence warrants such a conclusion, and some go so far as to say that the central palace of Eastern Ye actually lies at a site in the northwestern section of Ye Mountain 冶山 in Fuzhou City, called Pingshan 屏山.[47] Still others locate the capital city of Min-yue farther inland, at the Wuyi Mountain site. Dating to around the

[45] Taylor, *The Birth of Vietnam*, p. 29.
[46] Jiao and Fan, *Fujian and the Austronesians*, p. 142.
[47] Fan Xuechun and Wu Chunming subscribe to this view. *Ibid.*

Figure 4.6: Miniature model, Min-yue Han Dynasty city uncovered at Wuyishan

second century BCE, this excavated city is both the best-preserved city in south China as well as the largest Han period settlement in Fujian.[48]

Archaeologists have excavated the foundations of a massive city wall of rammed earth, five city gates – three of which were water gates – and clear remnants of a palace with an elaborate pipeline system, an indoor bath, and still-functioning well.[49] All scholars agree that this latter site, referred to as "Han City [near the village of] Chengcun at Wuyi Mountain 武夷山城村漢城," was without a doubt a capital city during the early imperial

48 Michele Pirazzoli-t'Serstevens, "Urbanism," in Michael Nylan and Michael Loewe, eds., *China's Early Empires: A Reappraisal* (Cambridge: Cambridge University Press, 2010), p. 183.

49 As Pirazzoli-t'Serstevens notes, the wall "surrounds a vast, irregular rectangle, has a circumference of almost three kilometres and a width of between fifteen and twenty-one metres at its base." *Ibid.* Fujian Bowuyuan 福建博物院 and Fujian Minyue Wangcheng Bowuguan 福建閩越王城博物館, eds., *Wuyishan Chengcun Hancheng yizhi fajue baogao 1980–1996* 武夷山城村漢城遺址發掘報告 (Excavation Report on the Site Remains of the Chengcun Han City at Wuyishan, 1980–1996) (Fuzhou: Fujian renmin chubanshe, 2004).

Figure 4.7: Remains of a palace foundation, Min-yue Han Dynasty city uncovered at Wuyishan

period (see figures 4.6, 4.7).[50] They disagree, however, about which capital city it was, as well as the dates during which it was functioning as an administrative headquarters of some kind. In both Wuyi Mountain and the Pingshan area to the north of Fuzhou City, tile remnants with the imperial inscriptions, *wansui weiyang* (萬歲未央); *wansui* (萬歲); *changle wansui* (常樂萬歲) etc. – which are all highly formulaic blessings for lasting happiness and prolonged longevity – suggest the imperial use and high quality of the buildings in these regions.

[50] Some of the possibilities proposed by Chinese field archaeologists for when the Wuyi Mountain palace site and city was an active administrative seat include the following: 1) From the mid- to late Western Han (135–9 CE). According to this proposal the capital at Wuyi Mountain served as the capital of the so-called "Yue-yao" kingdom, which was initially ruled by Zou Chou (a Han puppet), and then simultaneously by Chou and Zou Yushan. 2) From after the Western Han through the Eastern Han. If this were the case, then it was where Yue troops serving the Han (after collapse of Eastern Yue) were stationed, or where the troops for the Eastern Division of the Capital Commandant (*du wei* 都尉) were stationed. Or 3) from the late Qin through early Eastern Han. In this case, it was the capital of Min-yue, Eastern Ye, and later where the Han set up Ye Commandery City 冶縣城. Fujian Bowuyuan and Fujian Minyue Wangcheng Bowuguan, *Wuyishan Chengcun Hancheng yizhi fajue baogao 1980–1996*, pp. 373–5.

Based on clues from Sima Qian's account in combination with archaeological data, it is possible to entertain a few possible scenarios of what the geopolitical landscape of the region looked like. The main question vexing archaeologists today is whether or not there were two separate capitals of the Min-yue: one at Wuyi Mountain and one near modern-day Fuzhou. We know from the record that there were at least two kings ruling simultaneously in the region at a couple of points in the history of this southeastern region. First, we know that since before Qin times the name of the kingdom, "Eastern Sea," was distinct from the kingdom of Min-yue. Just as "Southern Sea" was a coastal region surrounding the Pearl River Delta, and its capital of Panyu was located relatively close to the coast, the name "Eastern Sea" suggests that this kingdom was also coastal. It was likely located at the easternmost border of the mainland in southeastern Zhejiang Province (the Ou River 甌江 flows through this region). Archaeologists are beginning to suspect that the capital of Eastern Sea, Eastern Ou, was likely situated in modern-day Taizhou, where archaeologists have found a city site with some large tombs, all dating to the early Western Han period.

The second simultaneous reign of two kings occurred when Han Emperor Wudi granted the local leader of the erstwhile kingdom of "Yao," Zou Chou, the title, "King of Yue-yao 越繇王" in 135 BCE. Shortly thereafter, Wudi acknowledged the power of King Zou Yushan and named him "King of Eastern Yue 東越王," to rule alongside Zou Chou, now referred to as the "King of Yao 與繇王并處." Perhaps the erstwhile kingdom of Yao was located inland at Wuyi Mountain, and that it became a capital of Min-yue in 135 BCE when Chou was first anointed "King of Yue-yao" by the Han Emperor. It is therefore conceivable that the palace at Wuyi Mountain may have been built to reflect the newly invested, Han-style king.[51]

[51] Given that the remains for only a single palace have been found in the ancient city at Wuyi Mountain, it may not have been feasible for the two kings, Chou and Yushan, to rule together there. Even if only one of them was doing the de facto governing, they each would have needed separate palaces to live in and inhabit. If Chou had remained in the Wuyi Mountain region, then it would seem natural that King Yushan might have ruled from a different capital region, perhaps in the Fuzhou region (the location of the Min-yue capital of "Eastern Ye"). Naturally, it is also conceivable that the two kings both ruled from different palaces in Fuzhou City, but they would have needed different palaces. If this latter scenario were the case, it may explain why there is a controversy among archaeologists about which remains – the Pingshan or Xindian – represent the remains of a capital city.

Another possibility is that it was strategically desirable for there to have been two headquarters for the kingdom of Min-yue that were in different geographic locations: Wuyi Mountain and Fuzhou. Given the difficulty of passing overland through the hilly terrain of Fujian, leaders in the region may have deemed it strategically essential to have both a coastal and inland base. The palace at Wuyi Mountain may have been an inland

In his 1959 study of the colonization of Fujian in early Chinese history, Hans Bielenstein posits that the area was basically a political vacuum until at least the end of the Han Empire, around 200 CE.[52] Moreover, "since no Chinese cities were founded in Fukien and no colonists penetrated into the region, the Chinese commandery existed in name only."[53] Bielenstein claims that the region was not easily reached by military troops; there were no easy waterways leading there, whereas major rivers ran through other areas of the South (such as Jiangxi and Guangdong, Hunan, and Guangxi), giving colonial troops from the north easier access to cities and ports in Southern Yue or more western reaches of the Yue (Luo-yue).[54]

Given what we now know from archaeological excavations in Fujian, including the excavation of the Han capital city of Wuyi Mountain and other sites in Fuzhou City such as the Pingshan and Xindian sites, such claims are simply not sustainable. First, the port city of modern-day Fuzhou City (which may have been ancient Eastern Ye) could be accessed relatively easily via coastal routes, and water travel up the Min River to the Wuyi Mountain capital may not have been as difficult as Bielenstein suggests. The layout of the capital at Wuyi Mountain shows how the city was primarily reached by boats through three water gates (see Figure 4.6). In the future, scholars should pay more attention to the relatively easy access that ancient southern peoples and foreigners may have had to Min-yue via maritime routes. To think about the historical evolution of the ancient Min-yue region only in terms of a Sinitic migration from the north – essentially, Bielenstein's approach – seems to be missing a crucial aspect of its history as a vibrant, coastal region of great significance and an entrepot for maritime inputs of all kinds.

summer palace and/or site for strategic planning and defense. The ruler at Wuyi Mountain would have been right in the vicinity of the border with Southern Yue and in a good position to want to defend his turf or acquire a greater buffer around it.

I thank Jiao Tianlong for keeping me abreast of and helping me think through the current archaeological data on these ancient capitals. Private conversation, 06/30/2013.

52 Hans Bielenstein, "The Chinese Colonization of Fukien Until the End of T'ang," in Soren Egerod and Else Glahn, eds., *Studia Serica Bernhard Kargren Dedicata* (Copenhagen: Ejnar Munksgaard, 1959), p. 98.

Bielenstein may have been right about a few things. For one, his claim that the colonization of Fujian by Hua-xia northerners did not occur as a sudden, violent conquest or takeover, but as a gradual, peaceful influx of migrants who settled there in increasing numbers after the Han period seems sound. Using the few census figures available for the region, Bielenstein concludes that the only significant migration of Sinitic peoples into the region occurred after 140 CE and before 609 CE, when the province numbered 12,000–13,000 households. Moreover, the claim that this region was the least populated of the southern regions until after the Han period may also be correct. See *ibid.*, p. 99.

53 *Ibid.* 54 *Ibid.*

We now also know that the Min-yue/Eastern Sea region likely continued during the Han to have political representation, as objects dating from the Eastern Han also appear in the inventory from the various sites around Fuzhou City and Wuyi Mountain.[55] So Bielenstein's claim that the commandery existed in name only is incorrect. Moreover, the palaces excavated in these regions reveal a very strong imperial Han influence – or, more specifically, an attempt to mimic imperial power – demonstrating how local lords made use of imperial symbols of power to make an impression upon their local populations.[56]

[55] Jiao and Fan, *Fujian and the Austronesians*, pp. 131–144.
[56] Jiao and Fan, *Fujian and the Austronesians*, p. 142.

Part III

Performing Hua-xia, inscribing Yue: rhetoric, rites, and tags

5 The rhetoric of cultural superiority and conceptualizations of ethnicity

Having introduced "Yue" as a concept and explored its problems and geographical scope, as well as some of the historical polities and social science research on the various peoples of the ancient South, I now turn to the Chinese texts to see what they reveal about perceptions and identities. "Part III: Performing Hua-Xia, Inscribing Yue: Rhetoric, Rites, and Tags" looks more closely at the language of the Hua-xia self – ways of writing, composing arguments, and using rhetoric, lineage taxonomies (categories of descent), geographic imprinting, and tropes – that helps create various manifestations of Hua-xia and Yue identity. Since the perspectives of these texts change with author and era, I try whenever possible to provide contextual background and highlight developments or important changes in the way authors expressed themselves and thought about identity and the southern other.

This chapter examines rhetorical strategies and conceptual structures used by ancient elites to depict the Yue other in Warring States and early Han texts. The dating of the texts I use in this chapter goes back primarily to the late Zhou period of the Warring States (c. fifth–third centuries BCE), but some date even later, to the Qin and early Han Empires, roughly from 220 to 100 BCE. I analyze three different spheres in which writers compared their own norms, practices, and identities – mostly stemming from Central Plains' culture – to that of the Yue state, its rulers and people, and its cultures. These areas concern the ethnic, political, and cultural representation of the Yue other.

The ancient textual tradition and its biases

Before we begin to analyze the ancient texts in greater detail, it will help to outline the general scope and nature of our early sources on the Yue. While early Chinese historical literature may provide us with our first historiographical glimpse of the Yue regions of what is now southern China and Southeast Asia, it is in no way completely reliable. Warring States period authors speak rather often of the historical events involving the state of Yue and its precipitous climb to the top, as hegemonic state over the entire Central States sphere in the early fifth century BCE, but while they discuss key political actors and their active military, strategic, and political engagements, they reveal much less about the actual peoples and cultures referred to as "Yue." As we will demonstrate in Part III, we are left with tropes and brief descriptions that provide a general, stylized, and most assuredly biased impression of who these people were and how they may have lived their lives.

In addition to distortions stemming from the biases and lack of adequate information of Central Plains elite authors, there are huge gaps in the sources as well. These occur not only as gaps in chronological time between sources, but they occur spatially as well, insofar as scattered comments might be spread over vast, diverse regions that reflect different intellectual micro-cultures and senses of identity. Another major bias in the historical sources is ideological and concerns the overarching rubric of sinicization and the predominance of the Hua-xia self. For example, Sima Qian's *Records of the Historian* (100 BCE), one of the first histories in China and a major early source for knowledge about the Yue, presents a perspective that reveals little about Yue and Yue identity outside of its relationship to the Han imperium. Tantalizing hints of more autonomous Yue states and cultures can be found here and there. Still, the central approach depicts Yue as actors in a largely Han drama.

Other histories and historical romances from the later Han era, such as the *Han History* (*Han shu* 漢書), *The Glory of Yue* (*Yuejue shu* 越絕書), and *Spring and Autumn Annals of the States of Wu and Yue* (*Wuyue chunqiu* 吳越春秋) are also limited in the information they offer and the ways in which they offer it. Later during the Eastern Han, the *Han shu* accounts of Yue usually copy from the *Shi ji*, sometimes adding spurious information that was not in the original and may have been motivated by authorial desires to invent dialog and stories that were concordant with late Han attitudes toward the Yue other.

While the *Yuejue shu* is perhaps the best source for a more local perspective on ancient Wu-yue cultures and the physical sites of historical events, it was most likely written by elites of Hua-xia ancestry living in the Wu-yue region during the Eastern Han, and therefore reflects attitudes that are slightly later than the bulk of what we examine in this book.[1] The

[1] See Olivia Milburn, *The Glory of Yue: An Annotated Translation of the Yuejue shu* (Leiden: Brill, 2010). Milburn provides a discussion of the likely authorship and dating of this text on pp. 37–52. She thinks it likely that the text was compiled from a variety of sources at the end of Wang Mang's Xin Dynasty (9–23 CE) by two Eastern Han scholars, Yuan Kang 袁康 and Wu Ping 吳平. There are hints in the text itself that Yuan Kang may have been a native of Kuaiji.

Wuyue chunqiu is a historical novel written during the later Han about the ancient rivalry and struggle for dominance between the states of Wu and Yue from the seventh to fifth centuries BCE.[2] Given that this text largely revolves around political events and presents elite, Wu-yue royalty as though they were one and the same as elites from the Central States, it offers limited insights into earlier conceptualizations of Hua-xia and Yue identity. Indeed, the focus of both the *Yuejue shu* and the *Wuyue chunqiu* on the rivalry between Wu and Yue and the political events leading up to the rise of Yue as hegemon over the Central States in the fifth century BCE renders these works into historical romances that fit the mold of Hua-xia identity, as though these states and their main actors had been fully integrated into the Hua-xia belief system. Because such texts in and of themselves warrant an in-depth study that would go well beyond the scope of this book, we will only discuss them briefly at the end of this chapter.

Ancient thinkers who leaned in the direction of strong traditionalist Ru values and norms sometimes spoke of cultural interactions in terms of purely one-way civilizing projects – through the concept of "educational reform" (*jiao hua* 教化), which basically translates into "sinicization" – and goals. The more ideological treatises of the Ru, such as those by Mencius孟子, Xunzi 荀子, Han Feizi 韓非子, Jia Yi 賈誼, and Wang Chong's 王充 (27–100 CE) *Measured Essays* (*Lun Heng* 論衡), likely provide the most distorted presentation of the Yue other and Hua-xia relationships to it.[3] As the current analysis will reveal, perhaps the most unbiased information relating to the Yue come from non-Ru writers who wished for some reason or another to highlight or endorse a more culturally relativistic view of the other. Such writers, for example Mozi and Zhuangzi, provide at times seemingly more objective descriptions of the Yue other, but even theirs is nonetheless a biased perspective coming from limited knowledge and interest in the other – one that still presumes upon a sense of the Hua-xia self.

What were the rhetorical strategies, conceptual structures, and techniques of categorization used by ancient writers and thinkers to depict the Yue "other"? To answer such questions, we might more closely analyze ancient textual passages in which Hua-xia writers compared their own norms, practices, and identities to those of the Yue state and its peoples

[2] The compiler of the *Wuyue chunqiu*, Zhao Ye 趙曄 (c. 40–100 CE), also hailed from Kuaiji, the erstwhile capital of the state of Yue, and served some time there as a government official. James Hargett, "會稽: Guaiji? Guiji? Huiji? Kuaiji? Some Remarks on an Ancient Chinese Place-Name," *Sino-Platonic Papers* 234 (March, 2013): 30.

[3] This having been said, one should note that Wang Chong was a native of Kuaiji at the heart of the territory of the ancient Yue state.

and cultures. Ancient texts often present the self and other in terms of ethnic, political, and/or cultural criteria. Usually, but not always, they do so in ways that reveal a dominant–subordinate relationship. In analyzing the following passages, therefore, it is fruitful to notice not just the ways in which authors were representing the self and other, but also the level to which they sometimes exaggerated or diminished the role and agency of the self in relationship to the Yue.

Given the patchwork nature of remnant sources and texts for understanding Warring States and early imperial periods, it is difficult to ascertain the degree to which the attitudes toward southern others that one encounters in our sources are fully representative of the entire Central States region. Because I work mainly with anecdotal evidence, evidence that does not constitute a statistically substantial sample, I do not aim to construct a far-reaching, definitive argument concerning the overarching or even most prevalent attitudes at the time, but, rather, simply to demonstrate the types and even prevalence of rhetoric – along with how such rhetoric may have changed over time – present in the textual sources available to us. Thus, while the analysis that follows may shed light upon certain historical trends, at the very least it imparts a striking glimpse of certain attitudes as they were recorded at various points and places in early China.

Hua-xia/Zhu-xia as an early ethnicity

In almost every text of ancient China, one can find explicit formulations or implicit visions of self and other. To my mind, however, the concept of the Chinese self as Hua-xia or "various Xia (Zhu-xia)" as an ethnic one, and not merely an indication of political affiliation or clan lineage, is most clearly and elaborately expressed in one text, which contains passages dating to a rather early period (the late fifth and early fourth century BCE): the *Analects* 論語. We might justifiably consider this text – a text attributed to Confucius but most certainly not written by him – as a relic providing some of the earliest formulations of the "Chinese" self conceived as an ethnicity, not just as a dynastic house or royal lineage such as the Shang or Zhou.

Certain passages in the *Analects* contrast the "various Xia" with the notorious "Yi-di" 夷狄 groups, who, "even with a ruler are not the equal of the 'various Xia' without a ruler 夷狄之有君, 不如諸夏之亡也."[4] Here, one senses that political order is not the only factor that distinguishes the "various Xia" from their alien neighbors to the east. According to this

[4] *Lun yu*, 3.5, see Yang Bojun 楊伯峻, *Lunyu yizhu* (Hong Kong: Zhonghua shuju, 1984).

perspective, culture, as *wen* 文 patterns or forms, was transmitted exclusively through Zhou traditions since the time of King Wen. This is especially clear in the following two statements: "Zhou looks back to the two previous dynasties [of Xia and Shang]. How resplendent is its culture! I support the Zhou 周監於二代, 郁郁乎文哉 吾從周,"[5] and, "With King Wen, already gone, is not culture present with me 文王既沒, 文不在茲乎?"[6]

By declaring his admiration for the refined patterns of Zhou, Confucius stresses their transmission through the Zhou as well as their origins in the two previous dynasties. He intimates that cultural achievements are goods that are passed down and enriched from one civilization and one great person to the next. Thus, Confucius advocates not a myth of family or biologically inherited ancestry, but a myth of cultural descent from the time of Xia through the Shang to the present Zhou. This most precisely accords with our definition of ethnicity outlined in the Introduction.

The ethnicity of the "various Xia" and "Zhou" also appears to be associated with a specific territory in the *Analects*.[7] For example, the Nine Yi 九夷 peoples whom Confucius considers to be non-Zhou and, hence, not descendants of the patterned and civilized cultures from Xia through Zhou, reside in the eastern reaches of the more central Zhou states such as Lu 魯, Song 宋, Wei, Zheng 鄭, Deng 鄧, and Jin 晉. Although it is unclear from the *Analects* exactly what the territorial boundaries of the "various Xia" might have been for Confucius and his disciples, or whether they considered the states of Qin and Chu to have been part of this cultural sphere, the Zhou states certainly do appear to have been clustered together in one more-or-less contiguous region around the Yellow and Wei River Valleys.[8]

An important aspect of Confucius' sense of ethnicity is that it can be acquired and that it has more to do with culture than with genetic heritage. Those who were unfortunate to have been born into baser (*lou* 陋) civilizations can, through the moral example of the gentleman, learn to behold and transmit the patterns of the civilized Zhou. In one example, Confucius argues that the gentleman is capable of transforming the

5 *Ibid.*, 3.14. 6 *Ibid.*, 9.5.

7 Although the distinction between these two names is unclear in the text, one might speculate that they refer to the same group of people. The term "Zhou" perhaps serves as a more direct way to reference the dynasty and people who have carried on the traditions of Xia, while "various Xia" highlights their cultural origins.

8 It is commonly understood that Confucius did not think much of the customs and political practices associated with the state of Chu, as seen in his comments in 13.6 and 13.7.

baseness of the Nine Yi peoples simply by residing among them (君子居之，何陋之有).[9] In another passage, a boy of the alien location of Hu Xiang 互鄉 is accepted into Confucius' pedagogical care on the basis of his ritual purification, and, presumably, his potential for change – not on the basis of his past connections to a sullied location.[10] All of these examples provide a picture of an early Ru concept of ethnicity as an acquired marker of distinction among different groups of peoples.

The above statements attributed to Confucius go beyond merely linking members of the larger Zhou polity with the culture of Zhou. They equate so-called Zhou peoples with the peoples and cultures that can claim cultural ancestry in the Xia: the Hua-xia peoples. In such a fashion, Confucius invokes an ethnonym to refer to something more than living culture or biology; he uses Hua-xia to delineate an assumed lineage of peoples related not by blood but by inherited cultural patterns, cultural patterns that must at all costs be perpetuated and transmitted to future generations. This view constitutes an early articulation of a shared myth of descent for the Hua-xia, or what would later become known as the "Chinese" people. It satisfies our three criteria, outlined in the Introduction for what constitutes an ethnicity: a shared myth of descent (Xia cultural descent), shared association with a specific territory (Central Plains regions occupied by the Zhou), and a shared sense of culture (Zhou, stemming from Xia, then Shang).

We may thus conclude that Confucius and his disciples promoted a conception of ethnicity that distinguished between the culturally dispossessed other and the self as heir of civilized cultural patterns. This concept of ethnicity proclaims the superiority of Zhou cultural traditions and the people who possess them, whether such possession is acquired or inherited, over all other alien traditions and peoples. By definition, then, people practicing non-Zhou rituals remain unworthy until they are civilized by Zhou customs. And the terms "Hua-xia" and "Zhu-xia" serve as ethnonyms that define a *people* who inherit, acquire, embrace, maintain, and transmit such a culture.

Ecliptical rhetoric in political and diplomatic contexts

In his discussion of more recent, European depictions of the Chinese in Western literature and the imagination, Eric Hayot co-opts the astronomical term, the "ecliptical," or "ecliptic," to describe how the universal "is imagined from a particular perspective, one whose locality is named

[9] *Lun yu*, 9.14. [10] *Ibid.*, 7.29.

and defined by the universal it declares."[11] In other words, the ecliptical refers to the construction of the universal "in relation to a false sense of centrality rather than the universal as such."[12] This type of formulation is especially relevant, I think, to the way the ancients depicted the peripheral others as political actors in the world. Below, I show how "ecliptical rhetoric" casts the Yue other as a universal partner at the extreme periphery of the known world. Though they may not always demean the Yue other directly, some authors use this rhetoric to implicitly carve out their own centrality by means of their universalizing depictions of the other.

In a few early texts, dating approximately to the middle Warring States period (fourth century BCE), most textual instances of "Yue" involve uses of the term not primarily as an ethnonym representing a cultural or ethnic other but as a powerful political state that lay on the periphery of the known, civilized world. The rhetoric associated with Yue in such instances is interesting not so much for what it reveals about cultural bias and senses of ethnic or cultural superiority, but for its lack of interest in such matters. While the number of sources we have from this period is few, the instances in which the Yue are mentioned are quite numerous, and so it is possible to glean some information about certain Central States perspectives on the Yue as a political entity.

The Yue as political actors were often clearly differentiated from the authorial self, but instead of being a lesser or odious "other" (aka "barbarian"), they often served in varying roles as an exaggerated reflection of the self or instantiation of human existence at the remote corners of both the world and individual psyche. Especially in contexts that do not provide a strong articulation of the notion of Hua-xia cultures and polities, the Yue other appears to be a foil used to critique or shed light on the nature of the localized self. And in some instances, the Yue serve as an important ingredient in helping to define the "universal" through an ecliptical perspective; in other words, through a perspective that claims universality through an implicit specification of the self as center.

Many of the examples of the Yue as an exaggeration of the self occur in the Mohist corpus. When reading through the text, one is struck by the rather consistent image of the Yue king, Goujian, and his people as potent actors capable of successful political machinations and overwhelming military force. Take, for example, an anecdote in the early chapters of the *Mozi* 墨子 (c. 350 BCE), which illuminates King Goujian's personal

[11] Eric Hayot, *The Hypothetical Mandarin: Sympathy, Modernity, and Chinese Pain* (Oxford: Oxford University Press, 2009), p. 11.

[12] *Ibid.*

taste for bravery.[13] To test the bravery of his *shi*-warriors, King Goujian personally requests that his own ships be burned:

"The treasures of Yue are in there!" he yelled to his warriors, and personally drummed them to progress. Upon the sound of the drum, the warriors were goaded on into a chaotic frenzy [to recover the treasure from the boats]. More than a hundred of the surrounding men found their deaths by leaping into the fire.

試其士曰:「越國之寶盡在此 ！」越王親自鼓其士而進之, (曰)〔其〕士聞鼓音, 破碎亂行、蹈火而死者 左 右 百 人 有 餘.[14]

This anecdote, which occurs in two of the three early Mohist chapters called "Universal Caring," points to problems associated with the partialities of rulers. King Goujian's tastes and his men's desires to pander to them give rise to the chaotic and uncontrollable behavior of his warriors. The author points to the Yue as one of many (including the cases of King Ling of Chu 楚靈王 and Duke Wen of Jin 晉文公 – both also possibly considered to be on the edges of Central States cultures) that might demonstrate how humans from all over are both partial (King Goujian) and poised to please and curry favor with those in power (Yue warriors). What is noteworthy is the fact that King Goujian and his followers serve as an extreme example of a particular type of universal human behavior. As such, the Mohist author exploits their distance and difference to strengthen his point about how power functions universally upon human desires. The fact that the Yue state lies on the periphery of contemporary political interactions, moreover, proves to be a significant rhetorical choice: it allows the author to depict faraway peoples not just as equally vulnerable to the pitfalls of political disorder, but also as extreme cases on the fringes of the known world. The use of the rhetoric of extreme cases – whether in geographical or moral terms – serves to cover all areas of the spectrum, suggesting that everything else in-between remains subject to the same universal rules.[15]

Just as Yue was located on the extreme periphery of the Zhou cultural and political sphere, it seems to have been associated with the extremity of common ideals, especially political ones and those related to diplomacy

[13] For more information about the so-called "early" chapters of the Mohist corpus, see A. C. Graham, *Divisions in Early Mohism Reflected in the Core Chapters of Mo-tzu* (Singapore: Institute of East Asian Philosophies, 1985).

[14] Sun Yirang 孫詒讓, *Mozi jian gu* 墨子閒詁 (Taipei: Huaqu shuju, 1987), 15.97–98. This story also found in *ibid.* with more details, and in *Han feizi*, "Nei Zhu Shuo, Shang 內諸說上," see Zhong Zhe 鐘哲, *Han feizi jijie* 韓非子集解 (Beijing: Zhonghua shuju, 1998).

[15] This is similar to the linguistic schema in classical Chinese, "If even X, then how much more so Y!" Or, "X 何況 Y!"

and warfare. In one of three early Mohist treatises against warfare, the author states that Qi, Jin, Chu, and Yue are fondest of warfare.[16] In the *Guanzi* 管子 as well, Yue is clearly a superior power in comparison with those of the Central States.

Duke Huan [of Qi (r. 685–643 BCE)] said: "there is no state in the world that is as powerful as Yue. Now I would like to launch an attack against Guzhu and Lizhi in the north. I fear that Yue will arrive here [to invade us]. Is there anything we can do about this?"

桓公曰：天下之國莫彊於越。今寡人欲北舉事孤竹離枝。恐越人之至。為此有道乎?[17]

This statement is interesting because it presents us with an anachronistically strong Yue of the seventh century BCE, suggesting an imaginative distortion of the region and its political prowess.[18] The story lacks historical accuracy and is probably better understood as a comment on the relative strength or importance of Yue in the author's own time and cultural memory. It can also be read as the author's exaggerated sense of a dangerous potency that lurks in distant, fringe regions. Since the author stresses difference in terms of extremes, the real difference between Yue and the other Central States in this passage seems to be one of degree and not of kind.

Other passages in the *Mozi* support this ecliptical presentation of the Yue, establishing what is universal by depicting the latter as distant, peripheral, extreme cases of what is morally and physically possible or desirable. In one example, the king of Yue sends a Mohist disciple to invite the latter's master, Mozi, to serve as his own personal teacher. For Mozi's services, the king offers him an apportionment of the old state of Wu as a fief. Mozi's reply reveals what might have been a typical, Central States impression of Yue's distance from what matters:

If the King of Yue does not listen to my words and make use of my Dao but I go nonetheless, then I allow justice to be enticed. To be lured and caught, this I can do in the Central States. Why should I need to go to Yue for it?

[16] *Mozi jian gu*, 19.134. Of these four states, the only state that does not lie on the periphery of the Zhou sphere and maintain somewhat questionable Zhou status is Jin.

[17] Yan Changyao 顏昌嶢, *Guanzi jiaoshi* 管子校釋 (Changsha: Yuelu shushe, 1996), 80.596. Slightly altered from W. Allyn Rickett, trans. *Guanzi: Political, Economic, and Philosophical Essays from Early China, Vol. II* (Princeton: Princeton University Press, 1998), p. 454. The component chapters of the *Guanzi* might be dated from the middle of the Warring States through the early Han Empire.

[18] The military and perhaps even economic power of Yue is not attested until the fifth century BCE when the state of Yue overtakes Wu, allowing Yue's ruler, Goujian, to become Protector General of the interstate regions.

抑越（王）不聽吾言,不用吾道, 而我往焉, 則是我以義糶也。 鈞之糶, 亦於中國耳, 何必於越哉?[19]

This excerpt underscores the fact that Yue was not considered to be a part of the Central States, but that it participated in interstate diplomacies and exchanges. It makes clear that while corrupt practices and diplomatic activity might equally occur in the Central States as anywhere, the Central States are still more desirable than Yue when it comes to moral depravity. Better to associate with a local scoundrel than a distant one.

While most of the passages discussed so far derive from the *Mozi*, the use of the Yue as a model of the extreme, fringe case that establishes a so-called "universal" is certainly not isolated to that text. In a particularly poignant example from the *Mencius* 孟子, we have the person of Yue serving as the ancient counterpart to what Eric Hayot refers to as "Balzac's hypothetical mandarin," so distant is he from the everyday that one does not care about killing him:[20]

There is a person here. If (he is) from Yue and (someone) stretched a bow and shot at him, you could retell the incident in a jovial and casual manner. There is no other reason for this than the fact that he is distant. If it were your own older brother and (someone) stretched a bow and shot at him, then you would be bawling while retelling the incident. There is no other reason for this than the fact that he is your close relation.[21]

有人於此, 越人關弓而射之, 則已談笑 而道 之; 無他, 疏之也。其兄關弓而射之, 則己垂涕泣而道之; 無他, 戚之也。

Just as China and Chinese people were considered to be just beyond the pale of moral relevancy by eighteenth- and early nineteenth-century Europeans, the Yue were beyond the moral concern of the typical person from the more "central" regions of Warring States China. Mencius' hypothetical Yue person proves effective in this thought-experiment precisely because it is through such a person that one might detect discrepancies in one's hierarchy of moral concern. "Yue" here signifies the peripheral and unrelated other that helps define the "universal" and, hence, what it means to be close and related to someone. It is the necessary abstract and rhetorical complement to all that is central, local, worthy, and valuable to the self.

19 *Mozi jian gu*, 49.436.

20 Hayot, *The Hypothetical Mandarin*, pp. 4–5. Hayot also notes the famous thought-experiment, mentioned by Adam Smith in *The Theory of Moral Sentiments*, concerning an average European person's reaction to the news of a massive earthquake suddenly destroying the "great empire of China." See pp. 3–4.

21 *Mencius*, annot. Yang Bojun 楊伯峻, *Mengzi yizhu* 孟子譯注 (Hong Kong: Zhonghua shuju, 1988), 6B3.278.

Even a passage from the later chapters of the *Zhuangzi* 莊子 stresses this sense of the Yue hovering along the physical, cultural, and emotional periphery. It mentions the condition of people exiled to Yue who, upon seeing any rare stranger who might recognizably be from their homelands, immediately feel affinity to them.[22] Admittedly, the mere fact that people from the Central States could be exiled to Yue reveals the Central States' perception of Yue as an undesirable backwater far away from the center of civilization. That there might have been clearly identifiable physical differences between the peoples of Wei in the North, where the anecdote is situated, and those of Yue in the South also suggests distance and distinction, not closeness and solidarity. All of these clues show that the Yue occupied a clear spot in the imagination of Warring States authors as the distant that defines what is close, the unfamiliar that gives meaning to the familiar, and the unworthy that gives value to the worthy.

In these examples, the state of Yue – though it formally did not belong to the geopolitical category of "Central States," is presented as a full contender for power in interstate politics of the later Zhou period. Not only is its inclusion as a legitimate player confirmed through these statements, but, furthermore, its ranking as most aggressive, or most powerful among contenders is striking, and is generally not historically accurate, especially not by the fourth century BCE when many of these texts were likely written down.[23] The distortion of Yue's power can be explained in terms of identity and its role in shaping historical memory: to many fourth-century Warring States authors, Yue had been a threatening power at the fringes of the known world whose very existence at the extremes challenged the sense of centrality and a secure core identified with the self.

Perceptions of geographic extremity could easily be translated into a sense of cultural extremity, loss of control, and, hence, danger. Yue's reputation as a daunting political and military power that threatened interstate order thus can be linked to its place in the Central States' imagination just beyond the edge of the familiar, which helped complete the fashioning of an ecliptical sense of the universal. As a quintessential marker of the fringes of the known world and psyche, the Yue other takes on a useful role as an extreme, or often complementary, version of the self.

[22] *Zhuangzi*, 24.822.

[23] The Yue were perhaps all of these things a century earlier, during the period of King Goujian, in the early fifth century BCE.

Cultural and ethnic rhetoric

As seen above, a rather clearly defined concept of ethnic identity can be found in the sayings of Confucius in the *Analects*. The relevant ethnic marker in that text is the Zhu-xia, which is essentially the same as the ethnonym, Hua-xia, which I primarily use in this book. Intriguingly, this ethnicity is not defined along biological, hereditary lines: it can be acquired and passed on through culture. Linked tightly to the Zhou 周 dynastic house but going beyond the Zhou to incorporate its cultural forebears, this ethnicity demands the acquisition of certain cultural trappings – ritual traditions, family values, and ethics – which were considered to be defining aspects of a civilized culture. Below, I gauge the extent to which this general sense of Hua-xia ethnicity affected the ways in which authors spoke of the Yue in cultural and ethnic terms. I highlight certain types of rhetorical methods and devices that assert Hua-xia superiority over the Yue or use the assumption of such superiority to turn cultural mores on their head.

Cultural slurs against the peoples of the periphery occur quite frequently in the textual tradition. This has often resulted in contemporary scholars using the term "barbarian" to describe anyone outside the Central States or Hua-xia sphere. Such a translation is not always accurate or appropriate, however, especially when the term "barbarian" is used as a translation for more specific place-related or directional ethnonyms in classical Chinese, many of which describe ancient polities or tribal names that do not in and of themselves highlight or even suggest cultural inferiority.[24] Rather than indiscriminately applying the term "barbarian" to every cultural or ethnic other outside the Hua-xia or Central States sphere, I prefer to translate the proper names for each group as they exist in the classical Chinese and delve into the language of cultural or ethnic bias on an individual basis. Therefore, in what follows, I only focus on textual evidence for the two terms most relevant for peoples or cultures that appear to be of the southern, cultural or ethnic type: the Yue and Man-yi 蠻夷 (as they relate to the Yue).

In some texts from the Ru tradition, the Yue are contrasted with local persons of more cultural refinement and moral cultivation. This implies that they are not considered to be members of the Hua-xia ethnic sphere outlined by Confucius in the *Analects* and are disparaged implicitly. Take, for example, a passage from the *Xunzi* 荀子: "The people of Yue take their

[24] Terms such as *yi* 夷, *di* 狄, *rong* 戎, *man* 蠻, Yue, Wu 吳, Ba 巴, Shu 蜀, Xiongnu 匈奴, and many more are all often lumped together and translated into English as "barbarians" when in fact some of them possess their own specific connotations of place, ethnicity, polity, and culture.

abode in Yue; the people of Chu take their abode in Chu; and the gentleman takes his abode in refinement 譬之越人安越，楚人安楚，君子安雅."[25] Here, the Yue join the Chu as peoples who inhabit the southern frontier. The point of the passage is simply to draw an analogy about and play with what it means to inhabit, or "take one's abode" somewhere. In the cases of Yue and Chu, the reader or audience is supposed to understand the phrase in a literal way. In the case of the gentleman, however, Xunzi challenges one to understand the phrase in a metaphorical sense that grows out of the physical act of residing or inhabiting a place. Such rhetoric is effective in its moral point because it uses the act of physical residence to reinforce notions of how one should commit to moral self-cultivation. But what does it reveal about the perception of Yue (and Chu) at the time?

While one may argue that the use of "Yue" and "Chu" are arbitrary in this instance, I suggest they are not. They enhance the effectiveness of Xunzi's point about moral self-cultivation precisely because the chosen regions are fringe, non-Hua-xia areas whose peoples would not usually be considered morally uplifted gentlemen. In other words, precisely because of who they are, where they are located, and the relative moral degeneracy of their cultures vis-à-vis that of the Hua-xia, they serve as an effective foil to the image of the refined gentleman. If, for example, Xunzi had chosen the state of Lu – the center of Ru moral values, ritual refinement, and education – the contrast would have not been as apparent, and Xunzi's point would not have been as clear. This is because his audience would likely have not been associating the person who resides in Yue or Chu with moral self-cultivation, as they would have the person from Lu. Thus, thanks to the implicit understanding that southern cultures are morally inferior, it is easier for Xunzi's audience to perceive of the contrast between physical uses of the phrase, "take abode in" and figurative uses of it.

There are some cases in which authors who do not rally for a specifically Ru cause may at times also reveal a disdain for the Yue or southerners associated with the Yue.[26] In the *Lüshi chunqiu*, for example, one author depicts the majority of Bai-yue peoples from South of the Yang and Han

[25] Xiong Gongzhe 熊公哲, *Xunzi jinzhu jinyi* 荀子今註今譯 (Taipei: Shangwu Publishing, 1990), "Rong Ru Pian 榮辱篇."

[26] The nature of "Confucianism" during Warring States times is indeterminate, and many questions arise when using the term to label modes of thinking at the time. Certainly, there were lineages that taught and transmitted Confucius' teachings and identified themselves as "Ru 儒." However, as these teachings influenced and were influenced by other ways of thinking during the Zhou, it becomes difficult to apply the label "Confucian" without oversimplifying the matter considerably.

Rivers as bestial and "having no ruler 揚漢之南，百越之際多無君."[27] Such peoples, this author contends, lack sages and a moral order that constrains the violent and powerful from taking advantage of the peaceful and meek:

Their peoples are like deer, birds, and beasts. The young order about their elders; the elderly fear the able-bodied; the strong are considered to be worthy; and the violent and proud are honored. Day and night they destroy each other, so that one finds not a moment of rest. In this manner they exhaust their own kind.

其民麋鹿禽獸，少者使長，長者畏壯，有力者賢，暴傲者尊，日夜相殘，無時休息，以盡其類.[28]

Although it is questionable whether the author is referring directly to the Yue peoples or to the many groups surrounding the Yue, there should be no doubt that he denigrates the cultural and moral values of those on the periphery of the known world. The values associated with the morally central or balanced self correspond to the ritual norms and values inhering in the Zhou ways. Conversely, the traits associated with the southern savages are bestial and off-kilter: not only do such savages look like deer, birds, and beasts, but also they resemble such animals in their moral depravity, lack of filial respect for elders, and topsy-turvy values. Comparing peripheral peoples to destructive, amoral beasts is the *coup de grâce* in the process of denigrating the other to underscore the civilized nature of the self.

One should distinguish between the conception of culture as *wen*-patterns and Zhou traditions, defined through the *Analects*, and "culture" as we often define it through such contemporary criteria as local customs, habits, mores, and language. By now it should be clear that the Ru prided themselves as Hua-xia because of their acquisition, preservation, and transmission of *wen*-cultural traditions (which included a sense of the moral Dao). But when we examine statements about culture in the broader, more contemporary, Western sense, it becomes less clear that all early Chinese authors considered themselves superior to foreign others. I now turn to passages in which ostensibly non-Ru authors from the Warring States actually refute the value-laden dichotomy between superior and inferior, refined and unrefined, described above. These authors approach the issue in different ways: some choose to draw simple comparisons among the habits and customs of various peoples, without

[27] Chen Qiyou 陳奇猷, *Lüshi chunqiu jiaoshi* 呂氏春秋校釋 (Shanghai: Xuelin Publishing, 1995), 20.1322.

[28] Ibid. Translation adapted from John Knoblock and Jeffrey Riegel, *The Annals of Lü Buwei (Lü Shi Chun Qiu): A Complete Translation and Study* (Stanford: Stanford University Press, 2000), p. 512.

focusing on the merits or demerits of whole traditions and lines of descent; others choose to refute the supremacy of Hua-xia cultural and moral refinement by lauding certain idealized traits of others and implicitly mocking the self. These varied tactical approaches to the question of Yue alterity reveal how traditional values and conceptions of superiority were contested and overturned in ironic, self-aware, and critical ways. Nonetheless, the very nature of the criticism in these approaches buttresses the notion that the rhetoric of Hua-xia centrality, cultural refinement, and moral propriety held dominance at the time.

One example from the *Zhuangzi* (fourth century BCE) illustrates how the text proposes the equalization of cultural norms: "A man of Song who sold ceremonial hats took them to Yue. The Yue people, however, wore their hair short and tattooed their bodies, so they had no use for them 宋人資章甫而適諸越，越人斷髮文身，無所用之."[29] This passage depicts the Yue as an outside group that abides by different systems of behavior and methods of calculating utility and necessity. In typical Zhuangzian style, cultural difference is not evaluated but relativized, and evocation of the alien other helps Zhuangzi poke fun at entrenched assumptions and perspectives on the self while relegating conventional practice to a relative position of value. Thus, for Zhuangzi, the habits and values of Yue are in themselves not of greater or lesser value than those of Song.

In the passage above, Zhuangzi noticeably does not appeal to the traditions of Zhou to differentiate between a larger ethnic "us" and "them," but, rather, he refers specifically to the people of the states of Song and Yue. His non-judgmental style conveys no sense of cultural superiority. While he does expect his audience to identify with the man from Song and to assume that using ceremonial paraphernalia is the norm, Zhuangzi's focus on geopolitical units steers the reader away from a hierarchy of value between ethnic identities such as the Hua-xia and the barbarians.

In a later chapter of the *Zhuangzi* (third–second century BCE) the author goes so far as to liken the Dao to the ways of a people in a far-off city in Southern Yue (dating to the Western Han, c. 204–111 BCE):

In Southern Yue there is a city by the name of The Land of Establishing Power. Its people are dumb and simple; they lessen their personal needs and have few desires. They know how to construct but not how to save; they give without expecting anything in return. They do not know what fits with propriety, nor do they know how to conform with ritual. Uncouth, uncaring, they move recklessly – and in this way they tread the path of the Great Space. They are able to rejoice their newly born just as they are able to mourn their dead. I urge you to discard

[29] *Zhuangzi*, 1.31.

your state, break away from its customs, and, travel there with the Way as your support.

南越有邑焉，名為建德之國。其民愚而朴，少私而寡欲；知作而不知藏，與而不求其報；不知義之所適，不知禮之所將；猖狂妄行，乃蹈乎大方；其生可樂，其死可葬。吾願君去國捐俗，與道相輔而行.[30]

Here is a description of a Daoist utopia in the far South – an early romanticization of the primitive and pre-civilized. Living in blissful harmony with Dao, the people of this world do not follow mores, customs, and conventions, and especially not Zhou rituals or concepts of propriety. The peripheral location of the Southern Yue kingdom provides this author with distance enough to grant his description a fairy-tale like quality, while at the same time positing its real existence in the known world. At the brink of physical geography and the edge of the imagination, this wondrous place occupies a world of its own, much like the islands of the immortals outlined in other passages and texts.

There are yet other writings besides the *Zhuangzi* that do not endorse the stark civilized–barbarian dichotomy between the Hua-xia self and Yue other. The late Warring States, early Han text, *Zhanguo ce*, records an anonymous letter sent to the King of Yan, stating:

The Hu and the Yue peoples cannot understand one another's language and cannot communicate their ideas and intents, but when mountainous waves arise about the boat they share, they go as far as to rescue each other as though they were one and the same. Nowadays, as for the allies of Shandong,[31] if Qin troops were to arrive while they were sharing a boat across a river, they would not rescue each other as though they were one and the same. Indeed, their wisdom cannot even match that of the Hu and Yue peoples.

胡與越人，言語不相知，志意不相通，同舟而凌波，至其相救助如一也.今山東之相與也，如同舟而濟，秦之兵至，不能相救助如一，智又不如胡、越之人矣.[32]

Throughout this passage, we see how alien cultural practices are used as a foil to critique the self. The author openly commends the wisdom, loyalty, and cooperation of the Hu and Yue peoples, especially their ability to recognize the importance of uniting against a common enemy (Qin troops). Yet such praise clearly has its limits. It is founded on an

30 *Zhuangzi*, 20.671. Translation adapted from Burton Watson, trans., *The Complete Works of Chuang Tzu* (New York: Columbia University Press, 1968), p. 211.

31 Not referring to modern-day Shandong, but to an area east of the Taihang Mountains 太行山.

32 He Jianzhang 何建章, *Zhanguoce zhushi* 戰國策注釋 (Beijing: Zhonghua shuju, 1990), 30.1110. Translation adapted from J. I. Crump, *Legends of the Warring States: Persuasions, Romances, and Stories from Chan-kuo ts'e* (Ann Arbor: Center for Chinese Studies, The University of Michigan, 1998), p. 516.

assumption that the Hu and Yue are usually considered to be of lesser worth than the author's audience (presumably, the allies of Shandong), for it is only by recognizing that one is not even able to surpass such peoples that one is to realize the folly of one's self and be motivated to change.

In this example from *Zhanguo ce*, the author does not try to overturn attitudes and values toward the Yue other, as in the *Zhuangzi*. Nonetheless, such blatant praise of the other demonstrates a certain level of awareness of their humanity, so that it becomes difficult to claim that people who may have identified with the perspective from the center invariably viewed their southern or northern neighbors with disdain. It is examples like these that show the complex attitudes toward and rhetorical uses of the Yue in mainstream, Central States writings, which are almost invariably focused on the self. In many cases, the Yue are neither full-fledged barbarians nor full-fledged civilized sophisticates, but somewhere in-between.

For Confucius, his followers, and many other educated Central States elite, the cultural traditions of Zhou serve as bonafide markers of ethnic identity that set what is civilized apart from what is not. This view is echoed in writings that have no specific link to strict Confucian lineages of thought as well as in Confucian texts. However, not everyone shared in the belief in Hua-xia superiority, and not everyone interpreted Yue differences along ethnic lines. Zhuangzi, for example, tried to push beyond simple hierarchical distinctions between Hua-xia and other, civilized and base, promoting instead a relative sphere of customs of equal value – or, more aptly, no value at all. Zhuangzi depicted many, variegated customs, and often distinguished among them according to geopolitical boundaries rather than polarized ethnic lines. Other authors go even further to assume a self-consciously critical stance toward the self. They do this by various means: a later author of the *Zhuangzi* exhorts readers to transcend one's own flawed culture – indeed, to transcend the notion of "culture" itself, while another author humbles his readers by highlighting Hu and Yue virtues at battle. Both authors use the Yue other to argue against unquestioned celebration of the superiority of one's own culture.

The creation of ancestral and environment-based ethnicities

Writings that date from the Han Dynasty (202 BCE–220 CE) reveal changing frameworks within which authors represented themselves and the Yue peoples. Unlike those of earlier writings from the Warring States, the authors of these texts do not primarily focus on political and cultural criteria in differentiating themselves from others. They begin to discuss the Yue in terms of other standards: physical environment and ancestor-based ethnicity. In what follows, I highlight new ways of writing about the self and southern other through the creation of lineage taxonomies and geographic imprinting. Each of these methods of inscribing and thinking about the Yue other creates a more systematic way of thinking about both self and other, one that involves the drawing of a line of descent or the boxing of people into a particular geographic space, one which was primarily characterized by climate and natural environment. The use of these methods results in particularly interesting forms of kinship-based or environmental determinism, which can be distinguished from more simplistic claims for cultural difference. The former locate group difference neither in an acquired cultural good nor an acquired social habitus, but in more fixed, natural environments.

Sima Qian in particular uses clan affiliation as well as geography and environment to invoke a kinship and environmentally based sense of Yue ethnicity. In his accounts of the Southern and Eastern Yue kingdoms during the Qin and early Han, he sometimes associates the natural geography and/or climates of the South with the cultural attributes and/or worth of its peoples. A faint sense of this association can be seen in the following quote attributed to King Zhao Tuo of Southern Yue:

> Of the Man and Yi peoples in the low and damp regions of the South, thousands of the Eastern Min-yue people call me "king," and those of the Western Ou and Luo-luo kingdoms also call me "king."
>
> 且南方卑溼, 蠻夷中閒, 其東閩 越千人眾號稱王, 其西甌駱裸 國亦稱王.[33]

This passage links geographical, climatic, and physical attributes of the land with a fixed set of peoples who reside there. Though Sima Qian establishes no causal connection between environment and people, the very juxtaposition of the two is revealing. It implies a one-to-one correlation; a fixedness of category; and an ineluctable sense that these physical attributes of the environment play a role in defining these people.

Other examples in the *Shi ji* provide possible causal connections between environment and people, representing a simple form of environmental determinism. In 111 BCE, Emperor Wudi of the Han issued an order for the military officials to resettle the people of Eastern Yue to the area between the Yangzi and Huai Rivers, thereby emptying the lands and allegedly withdrawing Han administration from the region.[34] A look at the stated rationale behind this large-scale operation is revealing. Emperor Wudi allegedly states: "the lands of Eastern Yue are narrow

[33] *Shi ji*, 113.2970. [34] *Shi ji*, 114, p. 2984.

and full of obstructions, and people of Min-yue are fierce and have shifted their allegiance on numerous occasions 閩越悍，數反覆."[35] Wudi's remarks about the lay of the land in Min-yue may have been based on political exigencies linking geography with human behavior: narrow passes and obstructions make it easier for a people to defend themselves and maintain autonomy in deciding on political allies. Another possible interpretation, however, highlights a causal link between geography and the character of the people: "Because the lands of Eastern Yue are narrow and full of obstructions, the people of Min-yue are fierce and have shifted their allegiance on numerous occasions." According to such a reading, environmental factors such as physical terrain and climate are directly accountable for people's behavior. Hence, Wudi may be blaming the effects of the natural habitat upon its people. But because of the ambiguity of Emperor Wudi's statements, it is not possible to confirm the existence of a belief in environmental determinism from this passage.

Records linked to the Han Dynasty statesman, Chao Cuo 晁錯 (d. 154 BCE), go further to provide a causal link between characteristics of a people with their environment: "The Yang and the Yue [peoples] have little *yin* and much *yang*. Their people have a thin skin, their birds and animals have thin furs, and their nature is to withstand heat."[36] Here, the entire animal realm associated with the Yang and Yue peoples (Yang-yue is also another way of referring simply to "Yue," or a sub-set of the Yue peoples) is causally linked to the hot atmosphere in which the *yang* force is in ascendance over the *yin* force. Yang-yue peoples possess environmentally determined, and quite possibly inborn, characteristics that come to define them as distinct others.[37]

Another example of this kind of environmental determinism can be found in the "Water and Earth" chapter of the *Guanzi*, whose date, though unknown, most likely falls within the early imperial period (Qin and Han).[38] "The water in Yue is muddy, heavy, and easily floods; therefore, its people are stupid, sickly, and filthy 越之水濁重而洎，故其民愚疾而垢."[39] This passage appears among a list of connections

[35] *Ibid.*

[36] *Chao Cuo ji zhu shi* (Shanghai: Renmin, 1976), cited in Nicola Di Cosmo, *Ancient China and its Enemies: The Rise of Nomadic Power in East Asian History* (Cambridge, Cambridge University Press, 2002), p. 296.

[37] While the exact date of this passage is not known, I find it difficult to believe that these were Chao Cuo's actual statements. The passage seems like later Han thinking attributed to Chao.

[38] W. Allyn Rickett believes the work might stem from the scholars at the court of Liu An 劉安 (180–122 BCE) in the early Han Dynasty. Rickett, *Guanzi*, p. 100.

[39] *Guanzi*, 39.352.

between the peoples of various states and the descriptions of their local water. While the author limits the scope of his determinism to the quality of water, he nonetheless views human difference as directly fixed and correlated to the environment and region one lives in.

So far I have given examples that suggest an emergent Han Dynasty association between fixed environments and behaviors, cultural characteristics, or even inborn physical human and animal traits. I do so in order to highlight what appears to be something new in early imperial writings on the Yue peoples: an environmentally linked or determined conception of the other. In previous representations of the Yue, authors tended not to be as interested in identifying fixed, determined, or innate traits, but in showing how the power of culture might influence its peoples. I also have pointed out how some Han authors began to characterize and label the other in a different manner, by seeking out one-to-one correspondences between geography and human nature. This type of activity is recognizable not as a kind of rhetoric but as a mode of inscribing the other through systematic efforts in taxonomy. It reveals a process of compartmentalizing knowledge of the self and other by assigning fixed traits to rather fixed geographies or climates. The mapping out of self and other, which I refer to as "geographic imprinting," differs from less systematic representations of the Yue that we have examined in the previous section, which tended to be more dialogical and performative, rather than spatial and fixed.

With the development of notions of geographic imprinting or environmental determinism, authors show an interest in pinning down fixed connections between environment or geography and peoples. The fact that these texts date to the early imperial period suggests that authors were seeking a more systematic way of explaining the manifest diversity of the shrinking world they lived in. Their carving out of the known world and its horizons was likely part of a colonial attempt to gain control by securing geographical categories and devising fixed formulas for understanding the other.

What do such environmentally determined views say about Yue as an ethnicity? Was geographic imprinting a means of separating peoples according to ethnic criteria as well as geographic criteria? Unfortunately, the scant information provided in the passages above does not allow us to make such a determination. From Sima Qian's own hand, however, we find another type of deterministic view that clearly constitutes an ethnic identity. Notably, Sima Qian underscores a notion of an ethnicity based on ancestral lineage, and not through a "myth of cultural descent," as was the case for certain writers of the Warring States period. An ethnicity based on ancestral lineage differs is mythical as well, however, insofar as it links an entire group of people, ostensibly unrelated, to a single kinship line.[40]

Sima Qian places Yue people in a direct lineage with the great ancestor, Yu the Great 大禹 – the founder of the Xia Dynasty – who also happens to be the ancestor of the Zhou peoples (hence, the name, "various Xia").[41] This is stated in his account of the great Yue king, Goujian:

Gou Jian, the king of Yue, was the descendant of Yu and the grandson of Shao Kang of the Xia. He was enfeoffed at Guiji and maintained ancestral sacrifices to Yu. [The Yue] tattooed their bodies, cut their hair short, and cleared out weeds and brambles to set up small fiefs.

越王句踐, 其先禹之苗裔, 而夏后帝少康之庶子也. 封於會稽, 以奉守禹之祀。文身斷髮, 披草萊而邑焉.[42]

In this statement Sima strongly associates "Yue," defined through habits and customs on the one hand, with "Yue," defined through inherited descent on the other. This type of ethnic conceptualization is distinct from Confucius' cultural perspectives on ethnicity, in which shared descent was based on cultural transmission and acquisition, and not exclusively on ancestry.[43] In addition, Sima Qian's method of defining the Yue constitutes a lineage taxonomy that applies to groups other than the Yue, as well as the Hua-xia self. As much as Confucius was interested in defining a myth of cultural descent for the Hua-xia, he did not share in Sima's zeal in categorizing – in a universalizing way – all sorts of ethnicities according to lines of descent.

Sima Qian underscores this ancestor-based ethnic identity in his postscript to the accounts of the Eastern Yue peoples. He states: "Although the Yue are considered to be southern barbarians (Man-yi 蠻夷), is it not

[40] That is, the people of such a group share ancestral founders; they do not share the same immediate relatives.

[41] As Wang Mingke points out, it was common from as early as the Spring and Autumn periods for the noble elites of civilizations on the peripheries of the Hua-xia to fabricate claims of their own Hua-xia ancestry. See Wang Mingke, *Hua-Xia bianyuan: Lishi jiyi yu zuqun rentong* 華夏邊緣歷史記憶與族群認同 (Frontiers of the Hua-xia: Historical Memory and Ethnic Identity) (Taipei: Yunchen wenhua, 1997), pp. 272–284.

I have not found any evidence that the reference "various Xia" includes the people of Yue, even though the Yue come to be associated with a Xia ancestry. In fact, the exclusion of Yue from the more geopolitical identity of "Central States," which appears to be loosely associated with the concept of "various Xia," suggests to the contrary that though the Yue might have claimed such a lineage, they were not actually considered by others to be a part of the "various Xia" ethnicity.

[42] *Shi ji*, 41.1739.

[43] Arguably, the phrase, "Zhu Xia" implies kinship-based ethnicity that identifies one's original ancestors in the Xia Dynasty. Since, however, Confucius does not exclusively define it as such, it is best not to refer to it as kinship-based ethnicity.

true that their ancestors had once benefited the people with their great merit and virtue 越雖蠻夷, 其先豈嘗有大功德於民哉?"[44]

Given Sima's generally broad usage of the term, "Yue," in his history, it does not seem likely that he is confining the Yue merely to one clan here – that of the ruling house. The merit and virtue of past ancestors lend value to the current peoples of the entire state, thus defining a sort of group lineage. Such a relationship goes further than demonstrating shared, cultural descent that might be acquired through intellectual transmission or guided, studied acquisition.[45] It posits an inborn ethnicity that defines descent in terms of ancestral lineage. As such, this vision compares nicely to Han Dynasty visions of the other, which also tend to associate group identity with inborn or environmentally determined traits – traits that are not entirely within an individual's power to change.

Despite Sima's use of the term "Man-yi," which imparts at the very least a mild sense of derogation, he nonetheless explicitly praises certain Yue individuals and their ancestry. In the chapter on King Goujian, Sima presents his leading Yue protagonists, King Goujian and his minister, Fan Li 范蠡, as great men deserving of praise.[46] Sima's final statements on the Eastern Yue, as well, do not demonize them as a ruling class, or, implicitly, as a people. Like many of the examples shown above, he wishes to highlight their strengths, praise their virtues, and, in this case, even remind his readers of their esteemed ancestry. In such a manner, Sima Qian imparts a more nuanced judgment upon the ethnic other: though they might not always demonstrate it, Yue peoples at least have the potential to act in a civilized manner. Unlike the one we found in the *Analects*, this view contends that the Yue do not need to transform themselves into members of Zhou civilization in order to serve as legitimate custodians of

[44] *Shiji*, 114.2984. It is likely Sima Qian speaks here of the Yue ruling class. Since we cannot assume a direct correlation between the ancestry of the ruling class and that of their subjects, it is impossible to know much about the people of Yue from these statements. One would surmise that over the course of centuries of Yue rule, this aristocratic lineage would have come to adopt certain customs and traits of the peoples of that region. They also would have helped populate the areas with descendants of their own who likely had interbred with the original leading clans of the region. Over time the interrelationships between the ruling elite and a certain portion of their subject population would have become quite deep and extensive, so that we might indeed be justified in speaking about a Yue group of considerable size.

[45] The Yue ancestors' great merit and virtue of which Sima Qian speaks in this passage cannot manifest itself without the aid of proper and continuous ritual sacrifices on the part of the descendants. Identity is therefore not innate in a biological sense. It is partially realized through the commitment of whole communities and families to the ritual practices that fulfill their ancestors' merit and virtue.

[46] *Shi ji*, 41.1739–1747.

power; they can act civilized in their own right, by virtue of their ethnic ancestry.

The romances of the later Han

Later historical romances dating from the Han period, such as the *Spring and Autumn Annals* and *The Glory of Yue* provide novelistic accounts of the epic battles, plotting, and revenge that make up what audiences since Han times have known as the stories of Kings Fuchai and Goujian.[47] However, given their dating in the later Han period, these two accounts do not reveal as much about Hua-xia depictions of the Yue other as they do about a Hua-xia interest in identifying with underdogs who express virtues (such as hard work and patience), and who vindicate their lots in life by transforming personal humiliation into undeniable, global success.[48] Aside from an emphasis on political events and battles, these texts focus as well on apocryphal discussions between ministers and their lords concerning state-related matters and decisions concerning battles, resources and aid, women, economic theory, etc.

When the authors do dramatize events, they do so in a fashion that incorporates the king of Yue (specifically, King Goujian) more as part of the Hua-xia self than a Yue other. In other words, the alterity of the king of Yue is still one that Hua-xia readers could identify with, especially when he is disenfranchised and wronged, because he is presented as someone who fundamentally belongs to the unified self (qua Han Empire). In light of the latter's ability to undergo hardship and humiliation while plotting his revenge against Fuchai, King Goujian emerges as a particular favorite for ages to come. This is one of many great ironies in the history of Chinese identity: it took but a few centuries for a non-Hua-xia, Yue king to become a central figure in the imagination of the Chinese. Such turnabout – the movement from outsider to insider and foreign to

[47] Axel Schüssler was the first to discuss the *Yuejue shu* as a source of history in Axel Schüssler, "Das Yüeh-chüeh shu als Hanzeitlicher Quelle zur Geschichte der Chan-kuo-Zeit,: Ph.D. dissertation, University of Munich, 1969. For a recent translation and commentary to the *Yuejue shu*, see Milburn, *The Glory of Yue*. For a partial translation of the *Wuyue chunqiu*, see John Lagerwey, "A Translation of *The Annals of Wu and Yue*, Part I, with a Study of its Sources," Ph.D. dissertation, Harvard University, 1975.

[48] Parts of the stories they contain appear in ancient texts dating from the Warring States period, such as the *Zuo zhuan, Guoyu*, and *Lüshi chunqiu*, as well as the Han texts, *Wuyue chunqiu* and *Yuejue shu*. Mentions of King Goujian occur throughout the textual record, beginning in Warring States times. Modern accounts of the story abound, including Yang Shangqun 楊善群, *Woxin changdan: Yuewang Goujian xin zhuan* 臥薪嚐膽：越王勾踐新傳 (Sleeping on Twigs and Tasting Gall: A New Biography of the Yue King Goujian) (Taipei: Yunlong chubanshe, 1991), and Paul Cohen, *Speaking to History: The Story of King Goujian in Twentieth-Century China* (Berkeley: University of California Press, 2009).

native – mimics the history of the Chinese South, whose later history in the second millennium CE features areas in the South (cities such as Kaifeng and Hangzhou especially) as the center of Hua-xia culture and tradition. Indeed, the most salient issue that comes across in these texts is not the king's quality of essential otherness, but his suffering and heroic comeback in the face of defeat.

That an erstwhile Yue king should be assimilated in such a fashion makes sense because the legacy of the ancient state of Yue and its general territories around Lake Tai and Zhejiang Province were co-opted and integrated into Han territory fairly early in the imperial period (since 154 BCE after the quelling of the Revolt of the Feudatories). These stories were compiled more than 150 years later. Perhaps it is through these stories that the process of assimilating Yue-otherness is partially fulfilled in Han times.

Conclusion

Much secondary scholarship dealing with the relationship between self and other in Chinese history assumes a simple bifurcation between civilized Chinese or Han peoples and the barbarian other. While it is perhaps undeniable that many of our texts – especially prominent in texts with a Ru leaning – may assume a kind of Hua-xia superiority, the extreme Ru position of cultural superiority is not usually present with such vehemence or force in the extant tradition. Milder, more moderate, or complicated positions are abundant. This analysis of elite writings of Warring States and early imperial China shows that the simple and value-laden dichotomy of civilized and barbarian did not always exist, and that some early authors differentiated between themselves and others in much more complicated manners, and according to a host of motives.

While there are indeed instances in the early textual tradition when the language of "civilized versus barbarian" can be justified, much of the time authors refer to the Yue (sometimes even praising them) as a means of criticizing the self. I have shown that this strategy can be read with an eye to what makes the self-criticism powerful in the first place. Sometimes, it is the very belief that Hua-xia culture should be superior that underlies the critical reference to the Yue.

The theory of Chinese cultural dominance assumes that writers made overtly ethnocentric claims that posited their own superiority vis-à-vis another. Though my analysis essentially reveals a Hua-xia bias and sense of superiority, it shows that extreme, overt forms of ethnocentrism are limited in scope to certain positions, perhaps associated with the Ru lineages of thought, which held Hua-xia, Zhou cultural traditions as a premium signature of civilization. Some elite writers reveal bias in a mild, rather subtle way. Their writings, however, and are usually so concerned with using the Yue to criticize the self that they end up saying little about the Yue and more about the general ignorance or lack of concern about who the Yue were.

In terms of politics, we found that authors often spoke of the Yue state as an equal yet distant political player in an interactive multi-state sphere of the late Zhou period. I have employed the term "ecliptical rhetoric" to point to a particular way of constructing universal claims that reflects a central self in relationship to an extreme other along the periphery. The very act of including or speaking about the Yue other in such a manner reveals a certain devaluation of them in terms of an ontological hierarchy of "local," "central," and "familiar" on the one hand, and "distant," "peripheral," and "unfamiliar" on the other. Hence, even in what seem to be neutral discussions of Yue as a political entity of some consequence, we see that its status as extreme other serves to set up an ecliptic universal with the self situated at the center.

Statements concerning the political status of Yue are interesting not because of their specific formulation of ethnicity, for they are not identifiably ethnic in orientation, but because they reveal an attitude toward this distant other that complicates the notion that the Yue are outright barbarians. In an effort to ascribe universal traits to all human beings, authors revealed their beliefs concerning just who fits into the category of "human." They accepted the Yue as humans like everyone else – weaknesses and all. Sometimes they depicted the Yue as more extreme or powerful than the self, and so the Yue were perceived to be a potential threat that needed to be overcome. Or they demonstrated a nonchalant moral attitude toward the humanity of those on the periphery of their world – as was the case when the Yue other became a hypothetical figure in a moral thought-experiment.

We also saw how some authors such as Zhuangzi convincingly relativized the cultural differences of the other, including the Yue. By humanizing outside groups, Zhuangzi suggests that they possessed equally valid epistemologies and modes of behavior. He depicts others such as the Yue not in terms of the Confucian conception of culture – wrapped up so tightly with ethnic identity – but in terms of habits and customs, and even state affiliation. All of these techniques help Zhuangzi steer his reader away from customary categorizations toward a more level playing ground of value.

By Han times authors seem to have developed different ways of viewing and talking about the Yue other. References to the Yue changed to include more explicitly innate or environmentally determined conceptions of the other. Sima Qian's creation of lineage taxonomies or clear lines of descent linked the Yue back to specific, esteemed ancestors and provided them with a sense of ancestor-based ethnicity that parallels the Hua-xia model. In other Han texts as well, authors defined the Yue other according to geographic coordinates and environmentally determined factors that characterized the foreign other in terms of a larger system of traits, often highly deterministic in nature.

Certain passages in Han texts hint at a new awareness of how natural environments influence and sometimes determine the characteristics of their peoples. This points to new techniques of writing about self and other, which possess a more totalizing, systematic, and inscriptional character than previous techniques. Such approaches attempt to map out a geography and environment that imprints itself indelibly upon its people. This mapping of the other may take the form of a grid-like, spatial understanding of environment and influence, or a timeline of ancestors and their various descendants. Regardless, it is interesting that both of these methods – spatial and lineage-based – attempt to account for the differences in cultures based not on cultural factors, as did the Warring States Ruist authors, but on things that are more physical or biological, such as natural environment and ancestry. This inscriptional style, along with the practice of mapping or categorizing human beings, may indeed be linked to the imperial aims of writers during the Han period.

6 Tropes of the savage: physical markers of Yue identity

O soul, come back! In the South you cannot stay.
There the people have tattooed faces and blackened teeth;
They sacrifice flesh of men and pound their bones for meat paste.
There the venomous cobra abounds, and the great fox that can run a hundred leagues,
And the great nine-headed serpent, who darts swiftly this way and that,
And swallows men as a sweet relish.
O soul, come back! In the south you may not linger.
魂兮歸來！南方不可以止些。
雕題黑齒, 得人肉以祀, 以其骨為醢些。
蝮蛇蓁蓁, 封狐千里些。
雄虺九首, 往來倏忽, 吞人以益其心些。
歸來兮！不可久淫些。[1]

Physical appearance can often be read in terms of one's personal identity or as a marker and statement of social norms, cultural values, or responses to one's environment. In ancient China, a society especially attuned to ritual regulations that served as the backbone to its ethical system, one's physical appearance and comportment were an integral part of educated discourse. In fact, in certain circles such as those of the Ru, discourse on ritual was dominant, especially as it implicated moral values, norms, and behaviors. As seen in the last chapter, Ru intellectuals of the Warring States period often revealed in their writings an awareness that Hua-xia and Zhou-related customs were superior to those of outlying peoples, and perhaps that is the reason they compared themselves relatively infrequently with those outsiders.

In the writings of cultural iconoclasts such as Zhuangzi or authors of the *Huainanzi*, we find attempts to relativize one's own cultural norms in light of alien practices. For example, according to an author in the *Huainanzi*, signs of the Central Plains people included "Leather caps and jade belt ornaments, and the postures of bowing and bending 皮弁搢笏之服,

[1] *Chuci*, translated by David Hawkes, *The Songs of the South: An Ancient Chinese Anthology of Poems by Qu Yuan and Other Poets* (London: Penguin, 1985), p. 224.

拘罷拒折之容."[2] Unlike the lengthy discussions of ritual comportment, attitude, and costume that may be found in Ru treatises, we have here an oversimplified, generic objectification of the self – one that verges on caricature.

While there is no such thing as a purely unbiased, objective representation of the self, the variety of visual and textual sources available to us suggests that the above description of elite standards for dress and comportment, while simplistic, is believable. That is, even though this text recounts an idealized standard (wearing leather and jade; bowing and bending), we have so many representations of Zhou peoples and culture that we can often confirm whether or not a given description is generally within credible bounds. But what happens when we turn our focus to the Yue in the East and South, who no doubt possessed elaborate rituals and norms themselves? What can we glean from the texts about the level of veracity or bias in the sparse descriptions about them? And what do such descriptions of the other say about how the Hua-xia wished to see and present themselves?

This chapter attempts to uncover the main meanings of a few stock phrases and descriptions of bodily physique and customs used in the textual repertoire to depict ethnic outsiders, in particular, those of Wu-yue and Bai-yue cultural origins. Since these descriptions all stem from the perspective of the Hua-xia outsider, I examine them in order to highlight their deeper meanings from within the Hua-xia ecumenical world. In particular, I tease out possible meanings and motivations for presenting the Yue in certain ways, and I do so with an eye to how such representations reflect back on the Hua-xia self. In addition, I ask the extent to which certain cultural markers such as hair, clothing, and manners may have been stereotypes, exaggerations, and/or stock expressions used more broadly to discuss all types of foreigners. This latter analysis will provide a metric for understanding the particular type of identity created through Hua-xia engagement with the southern other, as well as the level of actual knowledge and experience authors may have had with the Yue.

Layers of meaning: hairstyle and Yue identity

Hairstyle signaled a variety of social distinctions and was rife with cultural meaning. Mark Lewis, in following the work of anthropologists such as Edmund R. Leach and Gananath Obeyesekere, has persuasively

[2] *Huainan honglie jijie*, 1.355. In this passage, notably, the description of the Hua-Xia self is mentioned in relationship to the Yue king, Goujian, who did not do any of these things, cutting his hair and tattooing his body instead.

demonstrated how hair "is a key social marker and symbol in most cultures, indicating gender, class, age, character, social role, and degree of civilization."[3] In Zhou culture, adults bound their hair, and ceremonies that were held to mark adulthood incorporated changing one's hairstyle in accordance with the transition to this stage of life. For men, there was a capping ceremony, and, for women, there was a similar ceremony for pinning the hair.[4] It comes as no surprise, then, that the hairstyles of alien others were an area that did not go unnoticed in the textual record.

This section examines meanings associated with three hairstyles depicting ethnic outsiders, in particular, those of Wu-yue or Bai-yue cultural origins: unbound hair, sheared hair, and the mallet-shaped bun.

Letting it loose: "unbound hair" (pi fa 被髮)

Two related markers – that of "unbound hair" (*bei* 被 read as *pi* 披; "exposed," "opened," or loose hair) and "sheared hair" (*duan fa* 斷髮) – are associated with the Yi and Yue peoples of the East and South. Based on connotations and early uses of the word *pi* 被, to wear, unbound hair may have implied that the hair hung down over the neck and shoulders, as one would wear a robe or cape. This would have been quite different from the latter formulation, sheared hair, which presumably described hair that did not extend beyond the neck.[5] Even though the two phrases differ from each other, the custom of cutting off one's hair appears to be linked to wearing it loose or unbound, and, often, the two phrases are used interchangeably in stock descriptions of certain Yue peoples. We will first examine each of these two hairstyles separately, and only later will we ask what it means for these two styles to be so closely enmeshed.

What were the connotations of keeping one's hair loose, or unbound, in Zhou culture? In the *Analects*, Confucius famously discusses Guan Zhong 管仲, a seventh-century BCE minister to the then-overlord of the Zhou regions, Duke Huan of Qi 齊桓公, saying that "if it were not for Guan Zhong, we would all be leaving our hair unbound and fastening our garments on the left 微管仲, 吾其被髮左衽矣."[6] While this quote likely refers to Qi's successful exploits against northwestern, non-Zhou others (sometimes referred to as the "Rong 戎"), Confucius' sentiment –

3 Mark Lewis, *The Construction of Space in Early China* (Albany: State University of New York Press, 2006), pp. 69–71. See also, Alf Hiltebeitel and Barbara Miller, eds., *Hair: Its Power and Meaning in Asian Cultures* (Albany: State University of New York, 1998).

4 Lewis, *The Construction of Space*, p. 70.

5 I am thankful to Gopal Suku for this suggestion. Informal conversation, Columbia University Seminar, 05/12/12.

6 *Lun yu* 論語 (Analects), 14.17.

namely, that Guan Zhong saved them from such unseemly, barbaric habits – rings clear. Here, ethnic otherness, along with a concomitant sense of the cultural superiority of the self and one's own ways, is partly expressed through unbound hair.

In the *Liji* 禮記 (Book of Rites) we have confirmation that both western and eastern (Yi) tribes could each be characterized as having "unbound hair":

The peoples of the five directions, including those from the Central States, Rong and Yi, all have their natures, which they cannot be pushed to alter. In the east they are called the Yi. They wear their hair unbound and tattoo their bodies. There are some who eat food that has not been cooked. In the south they are called the Man.[7] They carve into their foreheads and are pigeon-toed. There are some who also eat food that has not been cooked. In the west they are called the Rong. They wear their hair unbound and dress in skins. There are some who do not eat grains. In the north they are called the Di. They wear animal and bird skins and dwell in caves. There are some who also do not eat grains.

中國戎夷, 五方之民, 皆有其性也, 不可推移。東方曰夷, 被髮文身, 有不火食者矣。南方曰蠻, 雕題交趾, 有不火食者矣。西方曰戎, 被髮衣皮, 有不粒食者矣。北方曰狄, 衣羽毛穴居, 有不粒食者矣。[8]

Here, keeping one's hair unbound, in and of itself, was not a trait that could identify a person from Yue, as opposed to a person from the Rong tribes. However, when the two traits of unbound hair and tattooing the body were combined, this was indisputably thought to be a signature of the Yue peoples. Notably, the only time hair is mentioned as a marker of identification in this entire passage is when it is "unbound"; no other hairstyle seems to elicit comment or consideration. This suggests the transgressive, non-normative nature of "unbound hair," as opposed to hair that is fixed in a different style from that of the people from the Central States (or Hua-xia). It appears that what mattered most was the act of doing something to one's hair, which implies extra work, attention, effort, and artifice, as opposed to letting it hang loose in its natural state.

References to loose and unbound hair do not only appear as ethnic markers. Not infrequently, they represent transgression and everything that seems to go with the act of going beyond or breaking through cultural norms. As Mark Lewis puts it, wearing one's hair unbound "invariably denotes figures outside the human community: barbarians, madmen,

[7] It is noteworthy that in this passage, the Man – who may very well have been considered to be a type of Yue by some – are not noted for their hairstyle.

[8] Sun Xidan 孫希旦, ed., *Liji jijie* 禮記集解 (Collected Explanations of the *Liji*) (Beijing: Zhonghua shuju, 1989), Wangzhi 王制, p. 359.

ghosts, and immortals."[9] The transgressive connotations of unbound hair are clearly linked to perceptions of the Yue other throughout Warring States literature. In stories about the legendary figure of Wu Zixu 伍子胥, this occurs quite frequently.[10] Authors often discuss the time when Wu escapes from Chu to the state of Wu, where he "unbound his hair and begged for food in Wu 被髮乞食於吳."[11] This reference makes clear use of the widespread knowledge that the Wu-yue peoples kept their hair unbound, and points to hairstyle in order to quickly denote how Wu Zixu had crossed over into a foreign culture as well as social class (that of a beggar). It imparts a poignant portrayal of a man down-and-out on his luck, who not only enters new geographic space, but also engages in a physical transition of the body. In his new form, Wu must embrace an odd, perhaps humiliating custom just as he must accept poverty. Indeed, the image is powerful because it points to a double transformation at both the cultural and social levels. Intriguingly, it does not point to a degradation of his moral fiber, so, in one sense, the normative values of honesty and righteousness were preserved in the process.

A passage in the *Mencius* drives home the opposite point: that to keep one's hair unbound was considered not only unseemly, but morally depraved as well:

> Now, if people in the same room with you are fighting, you should stop them. If you do so while wearing but a cap tied over your unbound hair, it is permissible. However, if others are fighting in the village or vicinity, and you went to stop them while wearing but a cap tied over your unbound hair, you would be misguided. In such a case, shutting your door [and not going out to help] would even be allowable.
>
> 今有同室之人鬬者，救之，雖被髮纓冠而救之，可也。鄉鄰有鬬者，被髮纓冠而往救之，則惑也，雖閉戶可也.[12]

According to Mencius, it is only acceptable to appear publicly with unbound hair – and a simple cap over it – if there is an emergency directly in front of your person and your aid is required. Any other situation dictates that you hide yourself and your unbound hair, and that you do not provide aid, even if the fighting is occurring outside your house. In short, sporting unbound hair was not merely a serious social faux pas; it

[9] Mark Lewis, *The Flood Myths of Early China* (Albany: State University of New York Press, 2006), p. 89.

[10] Wu Zixu (d. c. 484 BCE) was a noble and famous advisor in the state of Wu who vowed to take vengeance on the state of Chu for wrongly executing his father. His story was immortalized in many different accounts in early Chinese history.

[11] *Shuo yuan* 說苑 (Garden of Sayings), Juan 12, Fengshi 奉使.

[12] Yang Bojun 楊伯峻, ed., *Mengzi yizhu* (Translation and Commentary to the *Mencius*) (Hong Kong: Zhonghua shuju Hong Kong branch, 1984), Lilou xia 離婁下, 8.29, p. 199.

signified an utter breach of ritual comportment and so, in a sense, a lack of moral integrity.

As Lewis has already noted about hairstyle in ancient China, "The binding of one's hair marked membership in civilized society, and variations in style indicated differences in status."[13] Any glimpse of the hundreds of different styles of hair worn by the terracotta soldiers found in the tomb of Qin Shihuang, the First Emperor of Qin, attests to the ways in which such markers could indicate difference in rank and culture of origin. To my knowledge, there is not a single terracotta soldier with unbound hair, even though it has been argued that the many hairstyles of the soldiers represent the diversity of peoples over whom the First Emperor ruled.[14] Presumably, the First Emperor would have expected the soldiers of his army to conform to a minimal standard of hair dressing while active on duty. While, certainly, military rules of personal upkeep were likely to have been different than civilian protocols, the lack of any soldier with unkempt, unbounded hair may still support the general notion that this hairstyle marked disorder and transgression in the Zhou context.

It does not take a great leap of the imagination to link unbound hair with an unbounded mind. Many usages of the phrase "unbounded hair" occur in stories about the legendary figure Jizi 箕子, the grand tutor of Zhou 紂, who was the last king of the Shang Dynasty. In order to avoid execution, Jizi allegedly "wore unbounded hair and pretended to be crazy 被髮而佯狂."[15] In the Han text, *Wuyue chunqiu*, the same statement is made about Wu Zixu, and in the *Yuejue shu*, about the Yue minister, Fan Li 范蠡.[16] Phrases such as "wore unbounded hair and sang crazily 被髮而狂歌" occur in the literature to alert one to the transgressive behavior of lunatics.[17]

[13] Lewis, *The Flood Myths of Early China*, p. 89.

[14] To this date, there is no complete catalog of all the terracotta figures excavated thus far, so I have been unable to confirm this. I thank Lukas Nickel for this information.

[15] *Shuo yuan*, "Zunxian 尊賢," chap. 8 (also in *Hanshi waizhuan* 韓詩外傳 [Commentary to the Han Version of the Odes], chap. 7, *Dadai Li ji* 大戴禮記 (Book of Rites by Dai the Senior), Bao fu 保傅 and *Chuci* [Songs of Chu], Xishi 惜誓.

[16] *Wuyue chunqiu* 吳越春秋 (Spring and Autumn Annals of the States of Wu and Yue), "Wangliaoshi gongziguange zhuan" 王僚使公自光傳. Contrast this with the depiction in the *Yuejue shu* 越絕書 (The Glory of the Yue) of Wu Zixu going to Wu and "walking barefoot and wearing his hair unbound 徒跣被髮, 乞於吳市." *Yuejue shu*, Jingping wang neizhuan 荊平王內傳. For Fan Li wearing unbound hair and feigning madness, see *Yuejue shu*, Waizhuan Ji Fanbo 外傳記范伯, and *Yuejue shu*, Pianxu Waizhuan ji 篇敘外傳記.

[17] John Makeham, *Balanced Discourses: A Bilingual Edition* (New Haven: Yale University Press, 2002), Yaoshou夭壽, p. 202.

The figure of the crazy man is not always a negative one in ancient China. The very act of leaving one's hair unbound, in fact, has special resonance in early Daoist texts, such as the *Laozi* 老子 (also known as the *Daodejing* 道德經), *Zhuangzi*, and *Huainanzi*. In such contexts, it is the crazy man who is also a wise and complete, attained human – a free spirit, so to speak – who follows what is natural without any articulation of artifice. Other examples of a link between loose hair and natural sprites or ghosts abound in the literature. For instance, a man with unbound hair who appears in a dream turns out to be a divine tortoise.[18] Or an apparition with "unbound hair reaching the ground 被髮及地" manifests itself in a dream.[19] A few examples from the most fantastical chapters of the *Shanhaijing* 山海經 (Classic of Mountains and Seas) even attribute unbound hair to the mythical peoples and creatures living outside the familiar regions.[20]

Since in Zhou culture young boys or girls did not gain access to the ritual prerogatives of adults until their capping ceremonies, it stands to reason that pre-pubescent boys and girls may have worn their hair loose, and that this marker represented innocence and youth as well as social status. There is one instance in the *Shi ji* in which a "young boy with unbound hair 被髮童子" reveals himself to have sage-like abilities regarding the practice of divination.[21] While this passage is reminiscent of depictions of the sages or crazed persons found in Daoist texts mentioned above, it is noteworthy that the connotations of both youth and extrasensory, sage-like wisdom are combined here. One may argue that merely the figure of the young boy is enough to suggest sagehood, as the primordial *qi* of youth is venerated in Daoist strands of thought. Nonetheless, the element of loose hair enhances such an image, adding an additional layer of meaning. The lad possesses both pristine youth and an unhinged – and hence, unlimited – state of consciousness.[22]

[18] *Zhuangzi jishi*, 26.933.

[19] *Zuo zhuan* 左傳 (The Zuo Commentary on the *Spring and Autumn Annals*), Cheng Gong 成公, year 10. Another apparition with unbound hair appears in a story featured in Ai Gong 哀公, year 17.

[20] In particular, see *Shanhaijing* 山海經 (Classic of Mountains and Seas), Haiwai xijing 海外西經.

[21] *Shi ji*, 127.3217.

[22] One may even argue from other contexts that unbound hair signified the primal and primitive, before the overlays of culture encapsulated by Zhou ritual. This is evident in a passage from the *Wenzi*, where people who live in an idyllic, primitive past – before humans had been corrupted by culture – "wear their hair unbound." See *Wenzi* 文子, Shangli 上禮. For a detailed account of the received *Wenzi* and the newly excavated version of it, see Paul van Els, "The *Wenzi*: Creation and Manipulation of a Chinese Philosophical Text," Ph.D. dissertation, Leiden University, 2006.

And lastly, there are certain figures in the historical tradition who are associated with wearing their hair unbound on occasion so as to symbolize the abandonment not just of public decorum, but of responsibility to others as well. We have already mentioned the minister Wu Zixu and how letting his hair down symbolized his shift of allegiance over to the state of Wu (and hence, Wu-yue cultural mores). The seventh-century BCE overlord Duke Huan of Qi also famously let his hair go unbound at certain times. In two passages from the *Han feizi*, we hear how the duke let the two famous men under his charge take care of affairs of the state while he "wore his hair unbound and drove around with his wife in a carriage 被髮而御婦人."[23] Clearly, this transgression is associated with the relinquishing of one's official duties and responsibilities. The duke's unbound hair connotes a state of being derelict and lacking any sense of moral obligation to the greater social good.

From these examples, we see that not only were upright ministers (such as Wu Zixu), paranormal humans, spirits, youth, and idealized primitive peoples depicted in such a way, so were those selfish, immoral men who considered themselves above the law. Many of these layers of meaning were no doubt embedded in the ancient description of the unbound hair of the Wu-yue and Hundred Yue peoples.

*Sheared hair (*duan fa 斷髮*)*

The phrase *duan fa*, or "sheared hair," is also a stereotypical marker of Yue identity in ancient texts. The specific phrase "sheared hair, tattooed body (*duan fa wenshen* 斷髮文身)" appears in Warring States texts such as the *Zhuangzi, Zuo zhuan*, and *Han feizi*, as well as some Han texts, to refer to the Yi in the East, or, sometimes, more specifically to the peoples of Wu and Yue in the Jiangsu–Zhejiang–Fujian areas, depending on the text. Before we discuss the reasons why both sheared hair and unbound hair are associated with the ancient Yue peoples, let us first briefly consider the breadth of usage and scope of meaning for *duan fa* in the textual record.

A particularly noteworthy example of sheared hair in association with Yue peoples can be found in the first chapter (likely an earlier part) of the *Zhuangzi*: "A man from the state of Song, who traded in ceremonial caps, went to Yue, but the people of Yue sheared their hair and tattooed their bodies, and had no use for them 宋人資章甫適諸越, 越人斷髮文身, 無所用之."[24] The manner in which the author uses the phrase "sheared

[23] Wang Xianshen 王先慎, *Han feizi jijie* 韓非子集解 (Collected Explanations of the *Han feizi*) (Beijing: Zhonghua shu ju, 1998), 37.363.

[24] Guo Qingfan, *Zhuangzi* jishi, 1.31. A very similar type of anecdote appears in the *Han feizi*, Shuolin shang 說林上, in which a shoe and hat maker (husband–wife pair) moved to

hair and tattooed bodies" is casual, as though such knowledge was familiar to every educated reader. This suggests that from fairly early in the literary record, the phrase served as a quick shorthand to distinguish Yue peoples from the Zhou through easily identifiable, physical markers. Though we cannot know for certain, it seems likely that despite the caricatured usage of such a phrase, there was some factual basis for such a distinction. Visual evidence from the period, which we will discuss shortly, certainly confirms that some people in the Southeast engaged in such physical practices, so that it was not just some imagined trope of the savage.

Unlike *pi fa*, the phrase, *duan fa*, seems to be used more frequently in association with the Yue peoples. Whereas *pi fa* could be used to describe a host of supernatural beings or ethnic groups, "sheared hair" is used mostly in conjunction with "tattooing the body," and is closely linked to the Wu-yue or "Eastern Yi 東夷" cultures. For example, a reference in the Han period text, *Huainanzi*, depicts the mighty Yue king, Goujian, as having cut his hair and tattooed his body:

King Goujian of Yue cut his hair and tattooed his body; he did not have leather caps or jade belt ornaments; [he lacked] the postures of bowing and bending. Even so he defeated Fuchai at Five Lakes; facing south he was hegemon of the world.

越王勾踐劗髮文身，無皮弁搢笏之服，拘罷拒折之容，然而勝夫差於五湖，南面而霸天下.[25]

Since this passage is part of a larger argument for accepting the rituals and customs of various peoples of the world and placing them on par with each other, the author is careful not to proclaim a superior attitude toward King Goujian's appearance. Rather, farther down in the same passage, he delimits and relativizes even Hua-xia norms by specifying a bounded region where Hua-xia rites and customs flourish: in the "states of Zou and Lu 鄒魯."[26] In this instance, then, having cut hair, while a marker

the state of Yue and became poor, since people went barefoot and "wore their hair unbound (*pi fa*)." Indeed, nobody had any need for hats or shoes.

25 Although the exact phrase used here, *zuanfa wenshen* 劗髮文身, differs slightly from what we have been analyzing so far, most commentators believe the verb *zuan* 劗 to be but another (perhaps southern) way of saying "to cut." *Huainan honglie jijie*, 11.355. Translation adapted from John S. Major *et al.*, *The Huainanzi: A Guide to the Theory and Practice of Government in Early Han China* (New York: Columbia University Press, 2010), p. 407. Note that the translators of this latter text interpret *zuanfa* 劗髮 as "to shave the head," but I have found no evidence from the commentaries mentioned in the *Hanyü dacidian* 漢語大詞典 (Comprehensive Chinese Dictionary) (Shanghai: Hanyü dacidian Publishing, 1995) that this is the case. Indeed, it also makes more sense with the historical record (all the citations of "sheared hair" in association with Yue) if we imagined short-haired Yue people, rather than bald ones. *Hanyü dacidian*, vol. II, p. 758.

26 *Huainan honglie jijie*, pp. 355–356. Translation from Major *et al.*, *The Huainanzi*, p. 407.

associated with Yue practice, helps the author argue for the equality of customs throughout the lands occupied by the great Han imperium.

Other legends speak of "shearing the hair and tattooing the body" instead of keeping the hair unbound and tattooing the body, as found in the legend of Wu Zixu. The story of the founding of the state of Wu by Wu Taibo 吳太伯, eldest son of Ji Gugong Danfu 姬古公亶甫, the grandfather of King Wen of the Zhou, depicts Taibo and his second brother's move to Wu in terms of their act of "shearing their hair, tattooing their bodies, and putting on the dress of the Yi-di peoples 斷髮文身，為夷狄之服."[27] This description, which dates to the Han, contradicts a passage in the *Zuo zhuan* in which Taibo adhered to Zhou rituals while Zhongyong 仲雍, his younger brother and successor, adopted the Wu-yue custom of shearing the hair, tattooing the body, and "using the naked body as decoration 贏以為飾."[28] Regardless of whether Taibo himself engaged in such native practices, it is clear from both stories that the practice of shearing the hair and tattooing one's naked body go together as a physical package denoting Wu-yue custom and the lack of Zhou ritual.

In some contexts, sheared hair not only signifies Yue customs and peoples, but an entirely different religious complex that commands its own logic. Sheared hair and tattooing, some early authors claim, were apotropaic, ritualistic measures of warding off illness or harm. We see such attempts at explaining the practice in relatively late passages dating to the Han, such as the following in the *Han shu*: "Ziyun, the son of Emperor Shaokang by a concubine, was enfeoffed at Guiji. He tattooed his body and sheared his hair so as to ward off harm from flood dragons 帝少康之庶子云，封於會稽，文身斷髮，以避蛟龍之害."[29] Here, the author justifies the cultural practice of tattooing and shearing the hair in terms of local religious belief, associated with the Yue region of Guiji, around current-day Shaoxing, Zhejiang. We do not know whether the apotropaic justification for such practices is based on fact, but it suggests that authors were going beyond surface appearances to try to explain an

27 *Wuyue chunqiu*, Wu Taibo zhuan 吳太伯傳. The reference to Yi di 夷狄 peoples seems to be a general reference to Yi barbarians. Since the text dates to the Han period, it is likely that the distinctions between the Yi and Di peoples – originally two distinct groups from two different directions, East and North – were collapsed, and that such a term referred more generally to barbarians.

28 *Zuo zhuan*, Ai Gong, year 7, p. 1641.

29 Ban Gu 班固, *Han shu* 漢書 (History of the Han), chap. 28 (Beijing: Zhonghua Publishing, 1995), p. 1669. I am taking *jiaolong* 蛟龍 as a compound referring to one type of dragon, not two. Hugh Clark has pointed out that the reference to *jiao* 蛟 (or *jiaolong*) unlike the *long* 龍 (dragon) was always considered to be maleficent, and that it was usually associated with the far South. At least by later times (Tang and Song), the *jiao* is used in conjunction with the crocodile, so that it may actually have referred to the crocodile in early times as well. Private communication with Hugh Clark, August 9, 2012.

alternative worldview linked to a different culture, rather than merely differentiating oneself from the other based on physical appearance alone.

What is interesting about the bulk of references to shearing hair and tattooing the body in the received literature is that, unlike the more general and multivalent signifier of "unbound hair," these references describe an ethnic, and possibly religious, practice that is rather confined to a certain people and region. In addition, the appearances of the term "sheared hair," and the variant "cut hair" (*zuan fa*), are much fewer than the appearances of "unbound hair" in the received literature.[30] Aside from a single reference each in the *Zuozhuan* and *Zhuangzi*, "sheared hair" occurs in texts that date from the Han period on. And the latter practice is more commonly associated with tattooing. In addition, when sheared hair is combined with tattooing, it provides a ready reference to the Yue, and not some other indication, for example being a ghost, idealized human, primitive being. Recalling the *Zhuangzi* passage above, we note that it was not necessary for Zhuangzi to mention the practice of tattooing to make a point about how the Yue people do not need hats. His gratuitous use of tattooing suggests that when one wished to depict the Yue peoples, one needed only to conjure up the double description of tattooing and shearing one's hair, and one's point would be clear.

Given the real physical differences between sheared hair and unbound hair, why did authors sometimes use "sheared hair" and others use "unbound hair" to describe the Yue? We may be able to explain such a discrepancy by considering that most Hua-xia authors of the Warring States and early imperial period may not have ever had firsthand experience with a person from Yue or the Hundred Yue, and that their use of either one of the hairstyle descriptions was simply a matter of picking up on popular clichés of the Yue other. Or perhaps, even if some of these authors had had personal experience with Yue people, they may only have known about one particular branch or sub-group of what might have been accepted as Yue at the time. It is not unthinkable that some Yue groups would have kept their hair unbound while others cut it short. A last explanation may be that Yue hair was both unbound and short. If the Yue had cut their hair only in the front, leaving the back "unbound" and "worn" – like a cape draping over one's shoulders – then it would not be incorrect to describe Yue hair in at least two ways.

[30] The phrase *zuanfa* only occurs about twice in the entire pre-Qin and Han corpus: once in the *Huainanzi*, as mentioned here, and once in the *Han shu*, each with reference to the Yue. The verb *zuan* is rare and occurs only four times total in my search through the pre-Qin and Han corpus. Three of those occurrences are from the *Huainanzi*, where it refers to cutting hair or fur.

This leads us to the third type of hairstyle associated with Yue peoples and cultures: the mallet-shaped bun. The fact that this last style is also associated with the Yue almost seems to render the literary record incomprehensible. For one thing, a bun or knot of any sort on the head blatantly contradicts leaving one's hair loose, or unbound. Again, before we ponder the reasons why three seemingly incompatible descriptions of hairstyle are used to typify the Yue, let us at least come to grips with the basic scope of uses and meanings concerning the mallet-shaped bun.

*Mallet-shaped bun (*chuijie 椎髻/魋結*)*

The mallet-shaped bun, *chuijie* 椎髻 (sometimes written using *chui* 魋 for 椎 and *jie* 結 for 髻), is interesting in that it occurs in spite of the other textual references, discussed above, to the Yue as having sheared or unbound hair.[31] Like the references to sheared hair, mentions of the mallet-shaped bun also appear to have been later, dating from the Han period on. The mallet-shaped hairdo is usually associated with the Yue or Hundred Yue as Southerners, but it is not limited to descriptions of the Yue. As with unbound hair, it could describe foreign peoples of numerous other geographic regions: the Northwest, the far Southwest, and the Shandong coastal areas and beyond, including the Korean Peninsula and even tribes in Honshu, Japan.[32] It is worth exploring the spatial range of this description so that we might better gauge its usefulness as an apt one for the Yue peoples.

The first ruler of Chaoxian (a region on the Korean Peninsula), Wei Man 衛滿 (Korean, Wiman), is described in both the *Shi ji* and *Han shu* as having, during a period of chaos and revolt, gathered together a force of over 1,000 followers who "[adopted] the mallet-shaped bun and clothing of the Man Yi peoples 魋結蠻夷服" and crossed over the then-Han border of the Yalu River to create a settlement.[33] In the *Nihon shoki* (Chronicles of Japan), there are two instances in which the mallet-shaped bun is mentioned to describe local or native customs: the first occurs in a

31 *Chui* 魋 appears to be a phonetic loan for 椎. It means "bear." *Chui* 椎, on the other hand, refers to a hammer, mallet, or even vertebra. To my mind, none of the translators who use the phrase "mallet-shaped" to describe this hairstyle can confirm with any certainty that the shape is indeed that of a mallet. It may have pointed to braids that resembled the vertebra or spine of animals. Given our inability to match up this hairstyle with a confirmed pictorial representation, I will use the phrase "mallet-shaped" as a convenient translation.

32 I am grateful to Jonathan Best for taking interest in this hairstyle and pointing out various instances in which the phrase "mallet-shaped topknot" was used to describe natives of the Yalu River region and Honshu, Japan. I mention those instances below.

33 *Shi ji*, 115.2985, and *Han shu*, 95.3863.

description of a fierce people living in the eastern part of Honshu, dated (probably anachronistically) to Keikō 27:2 or 97 CE. In such a location, the "males and females both wore mallet-shaped buns and tattooed their bodies."[34] Intriguingly, this fits descriptions of the Yue peoples most precisely, and one wonders whether the *Nihon shoki* was borrowing useful clichés from early Chinese histories to depict its own local natives, or whether there really were fierce peoples on Honshu who adopted some of the same physical habits of the Yue.[35] The second account, dating to Jingū 1:3 or 201 CE, a date that covers a historically unverified period of Japanese history, narrates a story of subterfuge by a Yamoto general who was able to convene a so-called "peace parley" of local, rebellious tribes. The mallet-shaped hairstyle (椎結) figures prominently in this story because the general's troops allegedly hid their bow strings in their own mallet-shaped buns, while everyone else attended in peace with unstrung bows. The natives were thus tricked and slaughtered.[36] Yet another interesting passage from the *Shi ji* tells of a certain refugee from Shandong, Cheng Zheng 程鄭, who "smelted iron and sold it to the people with mallet-shaped buns 亦冶鑄, 賈椎髻之民."[37]

Not only are peoples from the Shandong, Korean, and Japanese (Honshu) regions described in early texts as wearing the mallet-shaped hairdo, starting from the Han, this coiffure is sometimes linked explicitly with the Western Di of the northwestern regions. In the following statement appearing in the Han text, *Shuo yuan*, the speaker – a certain Lin Ji 林既 – tells Duke Jing of Qi 齊景公 (d. 490 BCE) that famous ministers emerged from peripheral regions, despite their ostensibly backward or uncivilized customs:

In Yue, they tattoo their bodies and cut their hair short, yet the Minister Fan Li and Grandee Zhong came from there. The Western Di fasten their clothing on the left and wear mallet-shaped buns, yet You Yu came from there.

越文身剪髮, 范蠡大夫種出焉; 西戎左衽而椎結, 由余亦出焉.[38]

[34] See *Nihon shoki* 日本書紀 (Chronicles of Japan), 7.297 行18, in Sakamoto Tarō *et al.*, comp., *Nihon koten bungaku taikei* 日本古典文學大系 (Compendium of Classical Japanese Literature) (Tokyo: Iwanami Shoten, 1965–67), and also William G. Aston, trans., *Nihongi: Chronicles of Japan from the Earliest Times to AD 697*, vol. I (London: George Allen and Unwin, 1896), p. 200. I am grateful to Jonathan Best for providing these citations involving Korea and Japan.

[35] As Jonathan Best points out, the eighteenth-century scholar Motoori Norinaga was unsettled by the way in which the *Nihon shoki* seemed to borrow descriptive passages from Chinese historical accounts and apply them to things Japanese. Personal communication, April 6, 2012.

[36] See *Nihon shoki* 9.347 行14, and Aston, *Nihongi*, pp. 239.

[37] *Shi ji*, 129.3278.

[38] *Shuo yuan*, Juan 11, Shanshuo 善說.

This particular example is confounding because it seems to suggest that the Western Di, and specifically not the Yue, wore mallet-shaped buns. There seems to be a discrepancy in our sources about who might claim the mallet-shaped coiffure.

Since this is the first explicit mention of the Western Di wearing these buns, one might suspect that the author of the *Shuo yuan* passage is merely spouting cultural stereotypes without taking care to link them more accurately to reality. After all, the main purpose of this passage is not to convey vital or strategic information about peoples on the periphery, but to show that good ministers can emerge from any cultural background. However, there may be some truth to the notion that the Di fastened their garments on the left. In a passage from the *Analects*, mentioned above, Prime Minister Guan Zhong, through his victorious exploits against the Di, is said to have saved the Hua-xia from having to wear their hair loose and button up on the left.[39] But notice that in the *Analects* passage the Di wear their hair loose, not in the mallet style, as in the *Shuo yuan* passage.

The *Shi ji* and *Han shu* also mention two other regions outside of the South in which the mallet-shaped bun was used: among the Xiongnu in the North, and in a so-called kingdom of Qiongdu 邛都 in the Southwest, just north of the major kingdom of Dian 滇. In this latter location, the people all "wore mallet-shaped buns, engaged in agriculture, and gathered in settlements 此皆魋結, 耕田, 有邑聚."[40] In addition, an Eastern Han scholar, Wang Chong, provides a list of places in the South and Southwest where people practice wearing such a coiffure, the content of which is consistent with the fact that so-called "Yue" peoples, among many others, may have sported such styles:

> [The Great Yu] of the Xia entered the state of Wu naked. Taibo gathered medicinal herbs, cut his hair, and tattooed his body. At the limits of the world of Emperors [Tang] Yao and [Yu] Shun, the Wu peoples wore uncultivated clothing and the Yue were members of the Nine Yi Tribes, who wore felt garments and closed headgear [helmets?]. Now, they all dress like the Xia [peoples], wearing fine clothing and footwear. In Zhou times, peoples in the following regions *sheared their hair and wore a mallet-shaped bun*: Ba, Shu, Yuexi, Yulin, Rinan, Liaodong, and Yuelang.[41] Now, they don the leather, conical cap.[42]

[39] *Lun yu*, 14.17.

[40] *Shi ji*, 116.2991. For mention of the practice among Xiongnu, see *Han shu*, 54.1458, where the statement reads: "the two people, dressed in the costume of the Hu and wearing mallet-shaped buns 兩人皆胡服椎結."

[41] Italics mine. All of these locations, with the exception of Liaodong (near the Korean Peninsula), are situated in the far southwest of the mainland, including areas in modern-day Vietnam, and areas in Yunnan, Sichuan, Guizhou, and Guangxi provinces.

[42] A type of cap worn during Zhou times

During the Zhou, one had to communicate by repeating and translating. Now, they all recite the *Odes* and *Documents*.

夏禹倮入吳國。太伯採藥, 斷髮文身。唐、虞國界, 吳為荒服, 越在九夷, 罽衣關頭, 今皆夏服, 褒衣履舄。巴、蜀、越嶲、鬱林、日南、遼東, 樂浪, 周時被髮椎髻, 今戴皮弁; 周時重譯, 今吟詩書.[43]

This passage is astonishing in more than one way. Not only does Wang Chong's statement link up Southerners and those from the Southwest (including Rinan, an area in what is now north-central Vietnam) with those from the Northeast (Liaodong), but it also connects the practice of "sheared hair" in the same breath with the practice of the "mallet-shaped bun." If Wang Chong is correct, then he helps us partly solve the riddle of the mallet-shaped bun: by Han times, both sheared hair and the mallet-shaped bun were hairstyles associated with the South and Southwestern Yue, Ba, and Shu peoples as well as the natives inhabiting the northeastern region of the mainland.

By far the most commonly mentioned story involving the mallet-shaped bun is linked to a familiar figure: King Zhao Tuo of the Southern Yue, whom we will discuss at length later in the book. The *locus classicus* for the story about the king's meeting with the Han envoy, Lu Jia, at the beginning of the Han period, appears to be the *Shi ji*. In this famous story, Tuo greets his esteemed Han guest wearing the mallet-shaped bun and squatting or sitting in the "dustpan style."[44] This story, repeated in texts from Han times on, comes to signify the act of "going native." One may note that passages that mention the mallet-shaped hairstyle generally do not combine such a hairstyle with the practice of tattooing the body (except for the example provided by the *Nihon shoki*, above).

That the mallet-style bun should be implicated in such an act makes sense in light of its ubiquitous proliferation as a descriptive marker of wild, native, otherness. This is confirmed in a slightly later story, appearing in the *Lienü zhuan* 列女傳 (Biographies of Exemplary Women), about the wife of Liang Hong 梁鴻妻. Liang Hong, a recluse of the Eastern Han period, after having refused numerous marriage proposals from powerful clans, finally chooses to marry a woman who presents herself to him "in course clothing, wearing a mallet-shaped bun 乃更麄衣, 椎髻而前."[45] Even though we may assume that Liang and his wife are of Hua-xia

[43] Huang Hui 黄暉, ed., *Lun heng jiaoshi* 論衡校釋 (Edited interpretations on the *Lun heng*, or *Critical Essays*, by Wang Chong 王充), "Hui guo恢國 [Restoring the State]," pp. 832.
[44] *Shi ji*, "Li Sheng, Lu Jia Liezhuan 酈生陸賈列傳," pp. 2697.
[45] *Lienü zhuan jiaozhu* 列女傳校注 (Collected Commentaries on the Collected Life Stories of Women), "Liang Hong Qi" 梁鴻妻.

descent, the wearing of the mallet-shaped bun on the part of the future wife signals their unified wish to live in the wild as recluses.

Recently, the Chinese scholar, Peng Nian, has demonstrated that the mallet-shaped hairdo was not original to the Yue peoples, but that the ancestors of the Hua-xia peoples also sported such a coiffure.[46] If so, then one might note the irony of the fact that by the time of the Han Empire this type of hairstyle had not only become uncommon among Hua-xia peoples, but, furthermore, it had been transformed into a marker of foreign, primitive status, especially as a "Man Yi 蠻夷," but also as a Northerner or native of the Southwest. Given that the mallet-shaped bun was used to describe Man-, Yi-, and Di-type peoples, it seems less useful as a defining trait of the Yue, and more useful as a clichéd trope for anyone who has not adopted the refined, civilized ways of the Hua-xia and Zhou cultures.

At this point we may question the reason why three seemingly different types of hairstyles were all used as a common shorthand for describing the Yue. Our analysis suggests that early Chinese authors may have mixed and matched their cultural stereotypes in an impressionistic way. If they were indeed employing a common trope with the sole purpose of designating "otherness," they would not need to pay heed to ethnographic reality. It is likely that many of our authors referred to the Yue with such an intent. However, given the distinctive nature of the physical marker of tattooing the body, which often accompanied the phrase, "sheared hair," I find it likely that such indicators were based on some sort of ethnographic reality. It thus behooves us to consider alternative possibilities for why Central States authors could describe Yue hairstyles so differently.

Another explanation is that Central States authors properly described the alien Yue that was known to them but, by using the term "Yue," they encountered certain problems. No doubt, the ethnonym "Yue" pointed to a vast diversity of individual cultural and ethnic groups, each with its own practices and histories. Perhaps some of the Yue peoples were related linguistically, genetically, or in terms of material culture, but this does not preclude the fact that each sub-group may have had its own practices and religions, as reflected in such markers as hairstyle. Central States authors, by pointing to but a single sub-group's habits as typical of the Yue, may have thought that they were accurately describing all Yue when in fact they were only speaking about a certain type or sub-group of them. Thus, different authors, writing at different times and potentially denoting substantially different groups of Yue, are likely to have described the Yue in

[46] Peng Nian 彭年, "'Shufa chuiji' fei Nanyue zhi su – jianlun shufa zhi su de qiyuan ji qita 束髮椎髻非南越之俗 – 兼論束髮之俗的起源及其他," *Zhong yang min zu da xue xue bao* 中央民族大學學報 (2001): 6.

different ways. According to this logic, then, perhaps not all the Yue wore their hair loose; perhaps some of them cut it short, while still others adopted the mallet-shaped bun. Given the large gaps in chronology in our sources, it is also likely that different Yue groups altered their hairstyles at certain points in history, confusing the matter even further.

A recent encounter with an ancient image of a so-called "Yue" person at the Zhejiang Provincial Museum allowed me to realize that Wang Chong's seeming conflation of sheared hair and the mallet-shaped bun may have been correct, and that a single hairstyle may be described in both ways. In Figure 6.1, we see a kneeling man, supposedly from Yue, with tattoos all over his body. From this frontal view, the bangs are neatly cut, parted in the middle, and combed out of the face. Figure 6.2, the view from the side, shows us how the bottom layer of hair is cut short while the rest is pulled back into what seems to be a bun of some sort. Perhaps these depictions of the Yue are what authors had in mind when they specifically linked the Yue people to "sheared hair and tattooed bodies," as well as "sheared hair and mallet-shaped buns."

We may ask what all these textual discrepancies and ways of denoting difference through hairstyle mean. In the case of the so-called Yue marker of "loose hair," we learn of the many cultural meanings associated with keeping one's hair unbound, such as the suggestion of numinosity, insanity, youth, purity of the spirit, or proximity to nature or truth. By placing unbound hair into a broader cultural context of meaning, we see how notions of the Yue other might be informed by the above-mentioned values in addition to a sense of alterity, baseness, and that which is uncivilized and primitive.

Some of the hairstyles that are allegedly unique to the Yue turn out not to be so unique at all. The mallet-shaped hairstyle, in particular, seems to have provided authors with a pervasive and easy marker of one's position as an alien outsider, and therefore it serves nicely as an example of the trope of the savage. Its appearance in the Zhao Tuo story from the *Shi ji*, therefore, compels us to reconsider Sima Qian's (or the narrator's) connection to the Yue peoples of the South, shedding light on the fictional nature of a story that later comes to epitomize what it means for a northerner to have "gone native" in Yue style.

The inconsistencies and stereotypical ways in which the Yue are described all suggest that Central States authors may not have possessed very good or accurate knowledge about the Yue other. Alternatively, regardless of whether Warring States and early imperial authors possessed accurate information of the other, they may have had other motivations in mind when invoking the Yue and were simply not interested in outlining Yue difference in any detail beyond the simplistic stereotypes concerning

Figure 6.1: Front view of tattooed, seated figure of a person from Yue.

hair and tattooing. This latter explanation does not preclude the fact that while Central States authors may have been ethnographically accurate in their simplistic descriptions of the Yue, their lack of any kind of deep and sustained encounter with them would have rendered them incapable of or uninterested in penetrating beyond the superficial layers of appearance to understand more minute differences among various sub-groups, or the reasons and beliefs that underlay certain practices.

Figure 6.2: Side view of tattooed, seated figure of a person from Yue.

Sitting in an uncouth manner (*ji ju* 箕踞/倨)

As comportment was one of the defining signifiers of ritual knowledge and expertise, sitting was an act that was carefully observed. In Song period China, when sitting on a mat on the floor was no longer customary, the thinker Zhang Zai 張載 (1020–1077) reminds his readers of what was at stake when sitting in ancient times: "That the ancients did not employ chairs and tables is not because they were lacking in intelligence; how could the sages [of antiquity] be our inferiors? It was instead because they expressed reverence by sitting on mats, which allowed for bowing and kneeling."[47] Indeed, judging from statements in Warring States and early imperial period literature, sitting styles allowed for attitudes of reverence, humility, and respect to take proper forms in Zhou culture. Sitting styles that deviated from ritual protocol were often viewed not merely as offensive and disrespectful, but as a sign of cultural deviance and the lack of civilization as well.

In this section I explore the meanings behind the dustpan sitting style (*ji ju* 箕踞/倨), which I have translated as such because it may have involved sitting, with buttocks on the ground and the legs bent or spread out wide, like the mouth of a bamboo dustpan.[48] The term *ji* is also important because it conjures up the image of garbage and refuse, as such a sitting style no doubt made Hua-xia people think about baseness and lowliness when they encountered it. That this style was associated with the Yi other (夷) can be found in a later chapter of the *Analects*, no less. According to this story, a certain Yuan Rang waited for Confucius with legs sprawled out.[49] Intriguingly, the phrase, *yi si* 夷俟, or literally, "waiting as an Yi-alien," is translated and understood by later commentators as corresponding to *ji ju*. Whether or not this is a correct interpretation of *yi si*, one cannot be sure. Given that in the story Confucius tries to correct Yuan Rang's comportment by whacking him on the shin with a rod, it seems likely that the phrase points to some form of squatting or sitting. What is important for us, however, is not what the true meaning of *yi si* is, but, rather, the fact that later scholars, most likely influenced by Zheng Xuan 鄭玄 (127–200 CE) or He Yan 何晏 (190–249) of the later Han period – readily associated the Yi style of sitting with *ji ju*.

One will recall the famous story about King Zhao Tuo of the Southern Yue, who, when greeting a well-respected Han envoy, Lu Jia, "wears a

47 *Zhang Zai ji* 張載集 (Beijing: Zhonghua shuju, 1988), p. 265, as quoted in John Kieschnick, *The Impact of Buddhism on Chinese Material Culture* (Princeton: Princeton University Press, 2003), p. 233.

48 The Northern Wei statesman Cui Hao 崔浩 (d. 450 CE) provides a gloss on this sitting style in the *Shi ji*, claiming that it involved "sitting with one's knees bent so as to resemble the shape of a dustpan." See *Shi ji*, 89, note 2, p. 2583. As far as I can tell, the main criterion for dustpan sitting was that the buttocks touched the ground. Whether the knees were bent or straight appears to be disputed, although most commentators suggest that the legs are spread wide like a dustpan, either way. Donald Harper discusses this type of sitting, which he refers to as "winnowing basket sitting," as a prophylactic measure against ghosts in Donald Harper, "A Chinese Demonography of the Third Century B. C.," *Harvard Journal of Asiatic Studies* 45.2 (1985): 459–498.

49 *Lun yu*, 14.43, p. 159.

mallet-shaped bun and sitting in the dustpan position 魋結箕倨."[50] Lu Jia responds with an appropriately winning speech that not only persuades the poor figure of King Zhao Tuo of his wrongdoing and threatens him with military action, but also provides the reader with an example of a high-sounding rhetoric of Han legitimation and authority. The text goes on to highlight Zhao Tuo's response to Lu's speech:

Upon [hearing this], Wei Tuo clumsily rose from his seated position, and, thanking Envoy Lu, stated: "I have been living among the Man-yi for a long time and my sense of ritual and propriety has been lost."

於是尉他乃蹶然起坐, 謝陸生曰: 「居蠻夷中久, 殊失禮義.[51]

Zhao Tuo's physique and manner are supposed to have been "Man-yi." This is interesting because, as Hans van Ess points out, the episode of Zhao Tuo's meeting with Lu Jia occurs in the same chapter of the *Shi ji* as a parallel story in which the Scholar Li (酈生; Li Yiji 酈食其) meets with the First Emperor (Gaozu) of the Han, only to find the latter greet him in the dustpan style. Van Ess believes that Sima Qian includes the Zhao Tuo incident in the same chapter in order to deftly and indirectly criticize the former Han Emperor as acting like a barbarian, since Zhao Tuo himself admits to having acted like a Man-yi in such a passage.[52]

In another Han period description of uncouth sitting, we see the Northerners, and not just the Man-yi, sitting in the dustpan style: "In the countries of the Hu, Mo, and Xiongnu, [people] leave their limbs unwrapped and their hair combed out; they sit in the dustpan style and talk back [to their superiors] 胡、貉、匈奴之國, 縱體拖發, 箕倨反言."[53] We thus begin to wonder whether this style of uncouth sitting was ubiquitous in all other non-Zhou cultures, not just the Yue. Indeed, as Li Ji 李濟 notes, by Zhou times, the dustpan style of sitting was denigrated not merely because it was associated with the Yi-di 夷狄 aliens of the East, but because it did not conform to the civilized form demanded in most public occasions by Zhou ritual protocol.[54] The traditional Zhou style of

[50] *Shi ji*, 37.2697–2698. [51] *Shi ji*, 97.2698.

[52] Hans van Ess, *Politik und Geschichtsschreibung im alten China* (Wiesbaden: Harrassowitz, 2014), pp. 75–76, 338–339.

[53] *Huainanzi*, 11.7 (Integrating Customs, trans. p. 407). I adapt the translation from Major *et al.*, *The Huainanzi*, p. 407, as they translate this passage in terms of aliens with "hair unbound" who "sit cross-legged." I am not convinced with the translators' description of the hairstyle, which I do not believe should be conflated with the phrase *pi fa* described above. Instead, it appears that *tuo fa* 拖發 may have something to do with dragging or brushing the hair out, leaving it long. But this may have been different from the wild, unbound hair used to reference Southerners above. Also, I have not found any evidence for translating *ji ju* as "sitting cross-legged."

[54] Li Ji 李濟, "Gui zuo, dun ju, yu ji ju 跪坐蹲居與箕踞," *Zhongyang yanjiuyuan lishi yuyan yanjiusuo jikan* 中央研究院歷史語言研究所集刊 24 (1953): 283–301.

respectful sitting, *gui zuo* 跪坐, was highly formalized kneeling with the buttocks resting lightly on the ankles, much like the kind of kneeling still practiced in Japan today.[55] To the Hua-xia, such a kneeling posture was likely thought to have struck the proper balance between alertness and humility.[56] In such a context, one can imagine that sitting with one's buttocks to the ground may have evoked comfort, casualness, and carelessness, and it would have been considered an easy way to spot people unversed in Zhou manners.[57]

If we look to other contexts in which this phrase is found, we see that this style occurs even from within the Zhou culture. In a later chapter of the *Zhuangzi*, even the master of flouting Zhou ritual – Zhuangzi himself – is featured in this pose: "When Zhuangzi's wife died and Huizi went to mourn her, Zhuangzi was just sitting in the dustpan style, drumming on a basin, and singing 莊子妻死, 惠子弔之, 莊子則方箕踞鼓盆而歌."[58] In this instance, everything about Zhuangzi and his actions expresses a grievous disrespect for traditional Zhou ritual protocol. Not only is Zhuangzi not sad and dour in the time after his beloved wife's passing, he is joyously celebrating in a low-tech, ad hoc, and casual way. While it is difficult to disambiguate the phrase "dustpan style" from the rest of the meanings clustered in this image of Zhuangzi, we see clearly in this context that it is associated with all that is anti-ritual, casual, and, quite possibly, utterly barbarous.

Apart from – but certainly related to – its signification as the antithesis of Zhou ritual customs, this sort of sitting style was read as a sign of disrespect. This is conveyed in two memorable stories from the *Shi ji*. The first story features Jing Ke's 荊軻 unsuccessful assassination attempt on the king of Qin (later to become the First Emperor). Jing Ke after realizing he has failed at his mission and is about to be killed by the king's guards, spends his last moments "leaning on a column, laughing, and dropping down to the seated dustpan style, cursing [his Majesty] . . . 倚柱而笑, 箕踞以罵."[59] Jing Ke's movements and words, which follow upon this description, serve as an example of the pinnacle of disrespect for another human

[55] See *Lun yu*, 10.24, which suggests that there were formal styles of sitting for ritual occasions and hosting guests, and more casual styles for lounging (likely, squatting) around home. *Ibid.*, p. 107.

[56] For a visual account of this style, see Anthony Barbieri-Low's description of the kneeling woman featured in the Changxin Palace lamp, discovered in 1968 at the Han imperial tombs at Mancheng. Anthony Barbieri-Low, *Artisans in Early Imperial China* (Seattle: University of Washington Press, 2007), pp. 10–12.

[57] In fact, according to Li Ji, squatting and dustpan sitting may have been the predominant sitting styles of pre-Shang times. The art of kneeling for certain religious occasions appears to be an invention begun sometime during the Shang. Li Ji, "Gui zuo," pp. 298–299.

[58] *Zhuangzi*, "Zhi Yue至樂."

[59] *Shi ji*, 86.2535.

being. Cursing appears to be the verbal equivalent of sitting in this manner, appropriate not just for uncivilized aliens but for assassins as well.

The other story features a certain man of integrity, a so-called "knight errant," from the Central States and is worth discussing here:

Whenever Guo Xie [郭解] came or went, people were careful to get out of his way. Once, however, there was a man who, instead of moving aside, merely sat in the dustpan style and stared back at Xie. Xie sent someone to ask the man's name. Xie's retainers wanted to kill the man on the spot, but Xie told them, "If I am not respected in the village where I live, it must be that my virtue is insufficient to command respect. What fault has this man committed?"

解出入, 人皆避之。有一人獨箕倨視之, 解遣人問其名姓。客欲殺之。解曰: "居邑屋至不見敬, 是吾德不修也, 彼何罪.[60]

While we are not given the origins of the man in the village, we are nonetheless duly alerted to the fact that in some situations the dustpan style of sitting was taken as an affront punishable by death. That the hero, Guo Xie, does not punish this man, but, on the contrary, relieves him of military service so that the latter returns to Xie, bared of clothes, and begging forgiveness for his wrongdoing (*routan xiezui* 肉袒謝罪), signals the unusual virtue of Xie.[61] Like a noble gentleman, rather than blame the offender, Xie looks within to find his own potential culpability.

Zhuangzi and Guo Xie were not the only men of repute in the Central States cultural sphere to have sat in this manner. In early Han times, the First Emperor of the Han, Gaozu, is also said to have "sat in the dustpan style and cursed out 高祖箕踞詈" the king of Zhao, who demonstrated a grave lack of ritual protocol when the new Emperor was passing through his kingdom.[62] Given that the Emperor himself could embody this pose when he wished to humiliate another, it seems clear that the style had meanings of its own within the sphere of Zhou cultural norms, and that such meanings may have paralleled indications of "barbarian manners" as suggested elsewhere. Whatever the origins of the style, it is clear that anyone of any culture or status could embrace it to send a message of disgust, disrespect, and anger.

To the peoples of the Central States, the dustpan style represented a drastic difference of culture and departure from Zhou protocol, but not

[60] *Shi ji*, 124.3186. Translation adapted from Burton Watson, *Records of the Grand Historian of China*, Vol. II, *The Age of Emperor Wu 140 to Circa 100 B.C.* (New York: Columbia University Press, 1961), pp. 414–415. Watson describes this sitting style as sitting "sprawled by the road," p. 414.

[61] *Routan* is a phrase used to express the Hua-xia custom of stripping one's clothes to ask for forgiveness or, in certain situations, to worship at an altar. *Shi ji*, 124.3186.

[62] *Shi ji*, 89.2583.

anything specific to Yue. Among its many meanings, this sitting style signaled a certain state of mind: rudeness, lack of respect, disgust, and a desire to humiliate the viewer. Except for the story of Zhao Tuo meeting with Lu Jia, there is no mention in any of the accounts of Yue people in association with the dustpan sitting style. It would seem, then, that the dustpan style may not even have been a particular habit of the Yue. Anyone who initially doubted the veracity in the *Shi ji* of the description of Zhao Tuo as someone who had become just like the local Yue people certainly now has even more reason to be doubtful of it.

Tattooing the body and engraving the forehead (*wen shen* 文身, *diao ti* 雕題)

Some scholars have linked certain cultural practices, like tattooing, with Austronesian-speaking peoples and have argued for the diffusion of these practices according to a specific historical trajectory across island Southeast Asia and the Pacific.[63] Indeed, one may have good reason to link what the ancient Chinese called the "Eastern Yi" and Yue peoples to the Austronesians of later times. In ancient China, references to Eastern Yi and Yue peoples tattooing their bodies abound in the early and medieval literature regarding the South.

Whether the reference is short and vague or part of a long description of the other, the fact of tattooing the body is almost invariably mentioned and associated with the aliens of the East and Southeast, usually referred to as "Jing Man 荊蠻," "Dong Yi 東夷," "Wu-yue 吳越," "Wu 吳," "Yue 越," or "Ou-yue 甌越." Given the pervasive and relatively consistent mentioning of tattooing the body in connection with either "loose" or "sheared" hair, it seems likely that this particular trope of the savage was based on real cultural habits. Unlike the reference to hairstyles, which conjured up images that went well beyond the savage, or ethnic other, such as that of the unhinged sage, the ghostly or spiritual being, or uncontaminated youth, references to tattooing the body or branding certain parts of it, especially the forehead, seem to have been specific to types of peoples and their cultural habits. For this reason, it is worth paying attention to the regions and ethnonyms employed in association with these practices, as they are likely to have some ethnographic value, especially in relationship to the Yue cultures under consideration here.

[63] Peter Bellwood, "The Origins and Dispersals of Agricultural Communities in Southeast Asia," in I. Glover and P. Bellwood, eds., *Southeast Asia: From Prehistory to History* (London: Routledge Curzon, 2004), pp. 21–40.

A reference in the *Li ji*, mentioned earlier, distinguishes between *Yi* 夷 peoples from the East who wear their hair loose and tattoo their bodies, and Man 蠻peoples from the South who carve on their foreheads and walk pigeon-footed.[64] In the *Shuo yuan*, those who cut their hair and tattoo their bodies are in fact the Yue of the erstwhile kingdom of Yue, to the south and east of Wu.[65] This is similar to the story in the *Zuo zhuan* (repeated in Wang Fu's 王符 *Qianfulun* 潛夫論), mentioned above, in which Taibo of Wu followed Zhou custom while his successor, Zhongyong, followed the local habit of wearing his hair loose and tattooing his body.[66] In Wang Chong's 王充 *Lunheng* 論衡 as well, references to both Wu and Yue stress their similar habits of going naked, cutting the hair, and tattooing the body (禹時吳為裸國, 斷髮文身).[67] The description is slightly different in another section of the same text, where the Wu peoples are said to "pick medicinal herbs," as well as cut their hair and tattoo their bodies.[68] All of these references, primarily from the Han period but dating as far back as the *Zuo zhuan*, share in associating peoples of the Wu-yue cultures with the ethnonym "Yi" and with the custom of cutting the hair and tattooing the body.

One of the most interesting aspects of the trope of the savage is how authors try to justify or explain so-called primitive habits in light of arguments that Hua-xia peoples might easily accept or understand. In the *Shuo yuan*, for instance, we find a beautiful story about a man named Zhu Fa 諸發 from Yue who insisted on maintaining his culture's habits, namely, to cut the hair and tattoo the body, so as to colorfully appear like a dragon and thereby avoid trouble from the water spirits (是以剪髮文身, 爛然成章以像龍子者, 將避水神也).[69] A similar story is found in Han Ying's 韓嬰 *Hanshi waizhuan* 韓詩外傳, which attributes even more extreme habits to the Yue people, such as cutting off the nose and branding one's face, tattooing the body, and cutting the hair short (劓墨文身翦髮). Lian Ji replied: "As for Yue, it is also an outer territory of the Zhou. It is not located near the great kingdoms, and is situated instead on the banks of the Yangzi and Seas. Its peoples take the various fishes and turtles as company, and so they must tattoo their bodies and keep their

64 *Li ji jijie*, 王制. A similar passage can be found in Baihutong 白虎通 (also 白虎通義) (Discourses from the White Tiger Hall), "Rites and Music" 禮樂.

65 *Shuo yuan*, 善說. 66 *Qianfu lun*, "Zhi shi xing" 志氏姓.

67 *Lun heng*, "Shu xu" 書虛.

68 Additional embellishments to this core description may have been true, but they are too few to confirm. At the very least, details like "going naked" or "picking medicinal herbs" help evoke a sense of the savage, primitive, and native aspects of the Wu-yue other. Certainly, one would expect that if people were tattooing their bodies, then at least those tattooed portions would often be exposed and naked. *Lun heng*, 四諱.

69 *Shuo yuan*, 奉使.

hair short in order to be able to live among them" (夫越、亦周室之列封也，不得處於大國，而處江海之陂，與魭鱣魚鱉為伍，文身翦髮，而後處焉).[70]

In the first example from the *Shuo yuan*, the Yue tattoo their bodies for religious reasons, as a talismanic protection against evil water spirits. Their colorful bodies, in resembling the dragon – which may have been thought of as a lord of the water – protected them, and so the practice is rationalized and justified in utilitarian, religious terms. In the second story from the *Hanshi waizhuan*, the Yue people are also justified in tattooing themselves, but for different reasons. This time, the explanation invokes a utopian land in which people need to live in complete harmony with the aquatic fauna surrounding them. In this latter case, it is necessary for the people to appear like the sea creatures with whom they carry on. This not only primitivizes the Yue but does so by exhorting the Hua-xia reader to embrace a radically different cultural reality by literally imagining what it must be like to inhabit the shores and peripheries of human culture. Tattooing, here, is a manifestation of an amphibian lifestyle that challenges what it means to be fully human.[71]

In the *Huainanzi*, the people "south of the Nine Passes" wear their hair loose and tattoo their bodies for amphibian reasons as well, but not because they consort with sea creatures:

> To the south of the Nine Passes, tasks on dry land are few, while tasks on water are many. So the people cut their hair and tattoo their bodies in order to resemble scaly creatures. They wear short pants, not long trousers, in order to make swimming easier. And they have short sleeves in order to make poling their boats easier. In doing this, they are adapting [to their natural environment].
>
> 九疑之南，陸事寡而水事眾，於是民人被發文身，以像鱗蟲；短綣不絝，以便涉遊；短袂攘卷，以便刺舟；因之也.[72]

In order to make an argument for human adaptation to different natural environments, this author discusses traits typically associated with Yue peoples – such as cutting the hair short, tattooing one's body – in terms of the logical consequences of one's living in a certain climatological zone. These Southerners are no longer peripheral bodies living among sea creatures. They are resourceful humans who know how to fit in and make the best of an aquatic environment. Here, the humanization of the other serves an important rhetorical goal: to make a convincing point

[70] *Hanshi Waizhuan*, 卷八.

[71] Sima Qian himself uses such descriptions of the Yue other in his "Self-preface." Yi-Man 夷蠻 peoples of the likes of King Gou jian and Shaokang's descendants, after all, "tattooed their bodies, sheared their hair, and lived among the giant turtles and eels" 文身斷發，黿鱓與處.

[72] *Huainan honglie jijie*, 1.19. Translation adapted from Major *et al.*, *The Huainanzi*, p. 57.

about the adaptability of all humans, regardless of their strange customs. This is entirely fitting with the types of critical, rhetorical uses of the other mentioned in Chapter 5.

Another form of body decoration is the act of engraving the forehead (*diao ti* 雕題). This latter description is more specifically associated with certain Yue peoples, and is less likely to be found as a blanket term for all Yue. We find the following description in Jia Yi's *Xin shu* 新書: "Thus, Emperor Yao was able to spread civilization to the peoples of Shu and Yue who engraved their foreheads, to pacify Jiaozhi 是故堯教化及雕題蜀越, 撫交趾."[73] A passage from the *Shi ji* associates the practice of engraving the forehead with the Wu-yue cultures of the East, thereby showing that such a practice may not have been limited to the southwest and southern regions of Shu and Jiaozhi:

> As for cutting the hair and tattooing the body, piercing the arms and buttoning lapels on the left, these [are the practices of the] Ou-yue people (of the Southwest).[74] Blackening the teeth, engraving the forehead, wearing a fish cap, and weaving with glutinous rice stalks: these [are the practices of the] peoples of the Great Wu kingdom.
>
> 夫翦發文身, 錯臂左衽, 甌越之民也。黑齒雕題, 卻冠秫絀, 大吳之國也.[75]

Previously, we encountered passages that described the Wu-yue peoples in no uncertain terms as engaging in the practice of tattooing. Why, then, do some passages, like the *Shi ji* one above, link tattooing with the peoples farther south, and forehead engraving with the Wu-yue peoples? One could imagine that the practice of engraving the forehead may also have been understood by Hua-xia peoples as a form of tattooing the body,

[73] Jia Yi, *Xin shu* 新書, "Words on Cultivating Government, Upper *Xiuzheng yushang* 脩政語上." It is unclear from this passage whether it is the Shu, the Yue, the Yue of the Shu areas, or both Yue and Shu peoples who engraved their foreheads. The passage may also be read as pointing to the "Engraved Foreheads" as a people unto themselves, distinct from the Shu, Yue, and even those of Jiaozhi. Such a reading would not be unorthodox. For a similar usage, see *Guanzi*, 80.596 where the author refers to quite a number of kingdoms in the Wu-yue regions in terms of the practices of their inhabitants, not specific names or ethnonyms: "[In the South, I arrived at the] kingdoms of Wu, Yue, Ba, Zangge, Gua (an unattested graph), Bu-yu [No Granaries], Engraved Foreheads, Black-toothed, and Thorny Yi 南至吳, 越, 巴, 牂牁, 㶚, 不庾, 雕題, 黑齒, 荊夷之國."

[74] Sima Zhen's 司馬貞 (679–732) commentary to the *Shi ji*, the *Shiji Suoyin* 史記索隱, suggests that the reference to *cuo bei* 錯臂 means tattooing the arms using red and green colors. To my knowledge, there is no evidence that this was the case, and since tattooing was just mentioned, it seems unlikely that the author is referring to the same practice. The verb *cuo* 錯 may in fact suggest poking or piercing in some way.

[75] *Shi ji*, "Zhao Shijia, 趙世家," p. 1809. A similar passage occurs in the *Zhanguo ce*, "Wuling Wang Pinghua Jianju 武靈王平晝間居," p. 657. There, the phrase *que guan* 卻冠 is written as *ti guan* 鯷冠, "anchovy cap," suggesting that the cap was somehow made from marine life.

and that one author's tattooing was another's forehead engraving. After all, it is not unthinkable that people unfamiliar with practices of body art might confuse the different types or merely consider all forms to be the same. Even though I translate *wen shen* 文身 here as "tattooing," it more literally refers to "body decoration," or "making the body ornate." Many authors may in fact have used *wen shen* to point to a wide variety of bodily decorative practices, such as branding; carving, engraving, or chiseling using a knife-like object; piercing, tattooing, etc., all of which may have existed among the diverse tribes and peoples of the South, Southwest, and Southeast at the time.[76]

Nonetheless, it is worth considering the possibility that the practice of engraving the forehead was not the same as tattooing the body, and that very different groups were associated with each practice. The *Chuci* poem, "Zhao hun," quoted at the beginning of the chapter, reveals that the deep South is linked to practices often associated with the Yue, such as "engraving the forehead and blackening the teeth," as well as human sacrifice and cannibalism (雕題黑齒，得人肉以祀，以其骨為醢些).[77] Often, texts will mention groups that "tattoo their bodies" and others that "engrave their foreheads," in the same passage, reflecting an awareness that two distinct groups and types of practices are being observed. But, intriguingly, there does not seem to be any fixed geographic location – other than a generalized "South" – associated with either practice.

The phrase, "engraving the forehead" (*diao ti*) appears much less frequently than *wen shen* in the textual record – a mere ten to fifteen times in Han and pre-Han literature – and yet it is associated with peoples ranging from the Wu-yue in the East and Southeast to the people of Jiaozhi in the deep South, and even peoples in the West.[78] *Wen shen* has a range even more vast, even though it is primarily associated with the Yue and the South. Given such geographical discrepancies and imprecision, it appears that there is no way of using the textual record to ascertain clear-cut or definitive boundaries for such practices. At most, we are provided with an impressionistic image of a wide range of non-Hua-xia peoples in the South who engaged in various forms of body art.

[76] The Maori of New Zealand, for example, were known for carving into the skin and injecting the dye to make a bumpy, three-dimensional surface, rather than piercing the body to apply decoration smoothly.

[77] *Chuci*, Hawkes, trans., *The Songs of the South*, p. 224. It is also worth noting that the Museum of the Tomb of the king of Southern Yue in Canton City explicitly discusses the use of human sacrifice in the tomb as a residual local practice. There is also copious evidence that many indigenous Austronesian-speaking societies on Taiwan and the Chinese mainland were cannibalistic.

[78] The one mention of this practice in the West occurs in the *Yizhou shu* 逸周書, "Wang Hui Commentary 王會解."

"The land of the pigeon-toed": Jiaozhi 交趾 and the Commandery of Jiaozhi 交阯

Another description of certain Yue peoples of the far South concerns turning the feet inward, or being "pigeon-toed 交趾." Intriguingly, this phrase was an alternative, less common way of writing the name of a specific region – and, later, a commandery – in the far South: Jiaozhi 交阯 (Vietnamese: Giao Chỉ; literally, "Intersecting Site"). This commandery was located in the so-called Ou-yue (Au Lac) regions of the Southern Yue kingdom, in modern-day southwestern Guangxi and northern Vietnam (what has also been referred to as "Tonkin," and extending over the Red River Delta region). Just south of it was the Han Commandery of Jiuzhen (Vietnamese: Cửu Chân, 九真, associated with the Thanh-hoa region of modern-day Vietnam), which, combined with Jiaozhi, contained the erstwhile region of the kingdom of Ou-yue.[79] Below, I will explore the potential connection between the bodily description and the place name.

While the connection between the description and the place name may seem obvious, especially given the fact that authors sometimes referred to kingdoms by such descriptive markers as "Blackened Teeth," "Engraved Foreheads," we cannot take the connection for granted. For one thing, the two graphs for *zhi* 趾 ("toed") and *zhi* 阯 ("site") do differ slightly, and they mean very different things when paired with *jiao* "intersecting." The fact that each of the two compounds is meaningful on its own suggests that this is not necessarily a case of using either *zhi* as a loan word for the other. (Often, in classical writing, one graph will clearly be a loan for another, especially if that particular graph makes no sense on its own in the context.) I have also not found an explanation in the sources that explicitly links the two, although this does not exclude the possibility that they are connected.

Jiaozhi as a region came to represent a faraway place in the deep South, linked to the five directions, just as Youdu 幽都 was associated with the North. In early imperial accounts, legendary ancient sage Emperors and rulers, Yao 堯, Yu 禹 (also known as Yu the Great , Shun 舜, and Zhuan Xu 顓頊 are said to have pacified and ruled at various times over the five directions of peoples. In each of these accounts, Jiaozhi is the region that denotes the directional South.[80] For example, in the *Li ji*'s description of

[79] The Province of Jiaozhou 交州 came officially into existence in 203 CE. B. J. Mansvelt Beck, *The Treatises of Later Han: Their Author, Sources, Contents and Place in Chinese Historiography* (Leiden: E. J. Brill, 1990).

[80] See stories in the *Shuo yuan, Dadai Li ji, Bohu tong, Xin shu, Kongzi Jiayu, Han feizi, Huainanzi*, and *Yantie lun*, which refer to Jiaozhi in relationship to the conquests and pacification projects of the legendary emperors.

the peoples of the five directions, cited above, the southern Man 蠻 people "engrave their foreheads and are pigeon-toed. There are some who also eat food that has not been cooked 雕題交趾, 有不火食者矣."[81] Similarly, in one of the core chapters of the Mohists, the legendary Emperor Yao ruled over a vast expanse of land that extended into the Southland: "[Yao] pacified Jiaozhi in the South, obtained the surrender of Youdu in the North, and East to West, from where the sun rises to where it sets, there was nobody who did not submit 南撫交阯北降幽都, 東西至日所出入, 莫不賓服."[82]

This latter passage, perhaps written as early as the fourth century BCE, demonstrates that the name for the far South, Jiaozhi, like the place name for the far North, Youdu, has an early history in the geographical minds of Central States authors. Such a place name may actually have preceded the association between certain groups of Southerners and being pigeon-toed, so that any alleged link between the Jiaozhi the place and *jiaozhi* the description of pigeon-toed people in the South would likely have been coincidental, or an intentional slur (in slightly later texts) based on a pun between the compound graphs.

The following passage from the *Lüshi chunqiu*, this time concerning Yu the Great, also describes the peoples and environments in four distinct directions. For the East and South, we have a few descriptions that are reminiscent of certain Yue groups; namely, in the East, "the kingdoms of the black teeth people 黑齒之國," along with a statement about the region "South to Jiaozhi," which speaks of "the areas of the feathered people and naked inhabitants 羽人、裸民之處."[83] While here it seems as though Jiaozhi is the name of a place rather than a description of its people, one wonders the extent to which, because of the homophonic relationship between Jiaozhi 交阯 and *jiaozhi* 交趾 (pigeon-toed), people started randomly attaching the physical image to the inhabitants of the region (with whom they likely had never had any personal contact).

Perhaps this random linguistic connection – a felicitous pun on an old geographic name and a funny characteristic of people – was exploited by later authors to paint the fringes of the known world as they would imagine them to be: strange, murky, abnormal, and utterly fantastical. The following reference from the *Lüshi chunqiu* certainly seems to suggest this: "[Emperor Yao] teaches the fertile people of the West, reaches the Black Teeth [Kingdom] in the East, pacifies the Dark City (Youdu) in the North, and leads the "Pigeon-toed [Kingdom] in the South"

81 *Li ji jijie*, "Wang Zhi." 82 *Mozi jiangu*, "Jie yong 節用中," p. 150.
83 *Lüshi chunqiu*, "Qiu Ren 求人."

西教沃民，東至黑齒，北撫幽都，南道交趾.[84] Here, Jiaozhi is written with the character *jiaozhi* 交趾, as in "pigeon-toed," and not "intersecting site 交阯." It is as though the author wished for his readers to imagine these four locations in terms of the vivid descriptions of peoples and environments that their names evoke.

The move to associate peoples on the periphery with strange or fearsome traits hints at how Central States authors centered themselves by decentering others. They imagined the unknown regions of the periphery to be precisely what such descriptions suggest: off-kilter, off-balance, and off-center. Just as the *Classic of Mountains and Seas* (*Shanhaijing*) describes ever more fanciful humans and human-like creatures the farther one wanders from the center, place names such as Jiaozhi connoted difference and deviation from the norm, which betrayed the fear, loathing, disgust, and excitement the Hua-xia peoples must have felt when imagining the peoples dwelling in the far corners of the world.

In short, given its long history in Warring States discussions of the ancient sage kings, it is likely that the place name Jiaozhi came first, and the description of Yue peoples as pigeon-toed, based on homophonic links with the name "Jiaozhi," thereupon followed. If this is true, we see how some stereotypical descriptions of the other tend to lack a basis in any reality. There likely was never an entire kingdom of pigeon-toed people. Rather, there were people who inhabited a region whose name sounded a bit like "pigeon-toed" in Chinese, and so authors from the Central States regions began to play upon the homophonic possibilities between the two phrases to further denigrate and highlight their centrality and distinction from the other.

[84] *Lüshi chunqiu*, "Xiuwu xun 脩務訓." It is important to note that although such stories are legends, the places mentioned do not seem to be mythical regions. Blackening one's teeth, as we have already seen in many of the descriptions discussed, is a custom that was associated with various Yue groups who also engraved their foreheads, as the two descriptors are paired together a few times in the various Warring States and Han texts. Cultures found throughout South China, Southeast Asia, Japan, and Taiwan are associated with teeth-blackening. In Chinese literature more generally, peoples with black teeth are mentioned in relationship to the South. Often the practice was attributed to chewing betel nut (associated at times with the Yue peoples), but it was also linked to lacquering the teeth. In Japan, the practice was called *ohaguro*, and was widespread for many centuries through the late Meiji period, outlasting most places on the Asian mainland. Thanks to Sean Marsh and Megan Bryson for tips on finding instances of teeth-blackening in later Chinese texts.

7 Savage landscapes and magical objects

Hua-xia remarks on Yue-style oddities and savagery are not limited to the body but incorporate the entire landscape of the Yue other. Because the list of savage markers is long and cannot be exhausted by a discussion of a few bodily indications, we now extend our inquiry to things external to the body such as landscape and objects/possessions. A consideration of the various meanings associated with identifying markers of the Yue, along with an evaluation of the extent to which such markers may have adequately described reality, will provide us with further insight into how the Hua-xia imagined themselves through their depictions of others.

The core of the following analysis involves spatial dimensions relating to identity construction; in particular, how the spatial elements of these tropes cast the self and other in a clearly hierarchical relationship defined most fundamentally by inside–outside and center–periphery polarities. Such spatial elements help explain the logic of Hua-xia centrality that appears to ground the entire concept of early Chinese ethnicity and the self. The varied topics of water and marine life, amphibian creatures, disease, and swords and knives each help in affirming the centrality and primary nature of Hua-xia identity, which stands in opposition to the murky, fluid contours of Yue identity, receding in the background. Nonetheless, just as a background is necessary for the creation of a foreground, so too is it necessary that Yue serve as a secondary, subliminal phenomenon foregrounding the paramount position of the Hua-xia self.

The landscape of the South is comprised of difficult mountainous terrain dotted everywhere by riverine valleys and narrow passes. By Han times the areas to the far south or southwest, including the Yue and Bashu regions, were used as places of exile for Han officials or banishment for criminals and prisoners of war. As Rafe de Crespigny describes it:

> During the Tang period, the Gate of Ghosts, a narrow gap between crags on the West River, still embellished by a stele ascribed to the great general Ma Yuan of Later Han, was viewed as the entrance to a land of strange and deadly air, and a popular saying claimed that for every ten men who went out only nine would

return. Under Han, the same conditions applied, and Hepu was used as a place of banishment for criminals and their associates.[1]

Such a pristine, savage landscape – one associated with the liminal world of ghosts, criminals, and outcasts – conjures up feelings of fear and uncertainty as well as distance and externality. These emotions are expressed well in the link between the Yue peoples and water or marine life, since an economy based on aquatic activities is one that differs essentially from land-based, agricultural enterprises more commonly associated with the Central Plains regions. In the following section, we gain insights into the ways in which a marine-based, liquid perception of the South helped contribute to the sense of Yue as designating fundamentally different types of cultures and peoples.

Water, swimming, boats, and marine life: the Yue as creatures of the sea

In Warring States times, the peoples of the Wu-yue cultures were praised for their swimming abilities and naval prowess, and, at the very least, authors seem to take it for granted that the Wu-yue were aquatic cultures. King Goujian's troops are often depicted on boats, as in the example provided in the *Mozi*, in which the king tests the bravery of his warriors by setting his ships on fire and then sending more than a hundred of his own troops on a suicidal mission into the burning flames to recover the alleged Yue treasures inside.[2] In another example in the *Zhuangzi*, a battle between the states of Wu and Yue is described as a naval battle (*shui zhan* 水戰).[3] And in the *Guanzi*, we are presented with an unlikely victory by the state of Qi against the Yue, who were known to be naval experts:

When it comes to being on water, the people of Qi cannot hide from the people of Wu or Yue. Duke Huan made a northern attack at Guzhu and Lizhi. When the Yue people finally arrived, they hid themselves at Quqiang so as to gain access to Qi by water. Guanzi had 50,000 support cavalry ready waiting to fight [the Yue] at Quqiang. The Yue suffered great losses. This is called "naval readiness."

齊民之游水，不避吳越。桓公終北舉事於孤竹離枝，越人果至，隱曲蔷以水齊，管子有扶身之士五萬人，以待戰於曲蔷，大敗越人，此之謂水豫.[4]

[1] Rafe de Crespigny, *Generals of the South: The Foundation and Early History of the Three Kingdoms State of Wu* (Canberra: Australian National University, Faculty of Asian Studies, 1990), Chapter 1.

[2] *Mozi*, 15 ("Jian Ai, Zhong 兼愛中"), pp. 97–98. This story also found in *Mozi*, "Jian Ai, Xia 兼愛下" with more details, and in *Han feizi*, "Nei Zhu Shuo, Shang 內 諸 說上."

[3] Guo Qingfan 郭慶藩, *Zhuangzi ji shi* 莊子集釋 (Taipei: Wan juan lou, 1993), 20.671.

[4] *Guanzi*, 80.596.

The moral of this last tale is that it is possible to beat the odds when one prepares correctly for an occasion. It fits into a larger philosophical message, found in a variety of ideological books by ancient Chinese intellectual elites, that it does not matter how good one is at a certain skill, one can always be outwitted by those who persist or plan accordingly, or that one's very strength may ironically be one's downfall.[5] In order to properly understand this lesson and fathom the greatness of Guanzi's tactics, however, the reader must assume that the Yue had a formidable naval force that was generally unbeatable by others from the Central States. Aside from the fact that the author clearly wishes to highlight Guanzi's exceptional talent as a military tactician, there is little other reason why the author would need to exaggerate his claims concerning Yue naval capabilities. I therefore see no reason why we should not accept at face value the notion that the Yue other was likely a culture that paid lots of attention to water and their ability to move about on it.

Han Feizi also uses analogies concerning Yue swimmers to make a point about the importance of applying talent where it is needed, not where it might be squandered or not applicable:

> [It is like] waiting for the Yue swimmer who is adept at swimming at sea to save a person drowning in the Central States. Even though the person from Yue is a good swimmer, the drowning person will not be saved.
>
> 夫待越人之善海遊者以救中國之溺人, 越人善游矣, 而溺者不濟矣.[6]

Here, the point is not to praise Yue swimmers and their abilities to save people from drowning, although such a meaning emerges from the remark's basic premise; it is to show that sometimes underlying structural difficulties must be considered instead of raw talent (a Yue person swimming in Yue cannot save someone who is currently drowning in a distant location). In each of these types of examples involving either Yue swimmers or Yue naval force, readers are presented with what appears to have been a well-known fact of the day: the Yue people invested their time and resources in aquatic activities of a variety of sorts, and their naval and swimming abilities were famous and admired throughout the land.

While there are more examples in the literature of the notion that Yue was an aquatic, maritime culture, most of them make little of such a fact and hardly consider it worth belaboring. The rhetorical use of such a marker, therefore, lay in its universal acceptance as fact, which allowed

[5] See *Guanzi* 樞言 and *Huainanzi* 原道訓 for passages claiming that it is often the best swimmers who die in the water.

[6] *Han feizi*, "Nan shi 難勢," p. 393. A similar message appears in "Shuo lin shang 說林上."

authors to quickly move beyond such a given to prove a larger, often educational, point about tactics, logic, usefulness, and the likes.

To what extent was this characterization of marine facility based on a reality concerning the Yue? Comments such as the ones found in passages cited above do not give much room for debate; the very basis of the moral point being made relies heavily on the perceived verity of the association between Yue and swimming/water/naval forces. This is not to say that every mention of the Yue and water or marine activity was true, and that such an image was not a stereotype, but at the very least one can imagine that it was a stereotype based on what Hua-xia authors felt were predominant characteristics of the Yue other in comparison to the relatively land-locked culture of the Zhou.

While the authors of the examples above seem to stand in awe of Yue marine facility, they also sometimes imply that such technical abilities are of limited scope and use. Indeed, Hua-xia authors seem to have dealt with their fear of Yue areas of superior ability by writing about or coming to terms with the ways in which such ability might be overcome by superior and tactical planning. The stereotype of Yue aquatic superiority was thus helpful rhetorically to Central States authors precisely because it made use of a universally accepted fact to highlight larger points about overcoming foes (dangerous, powerful ones from the periphery) with a winning approach involving superior planning, practice, and preparation.

Southern Chinese serpent affinities: snakes and dragons

Related to the idea that the Yue were creatures of the sea is the notion that such peoples were linked to reptiles in some significant way. The link between the Yue and certain serpents may not have been totally imagined by the Hua-xia. As we will see below, there is much data in the visual record to suggest that snakes may have possessed a totemic function in certain cultures of the ancient South. Unfortunately, there is not much in early records that discusses the relationship between the Yue and their religious practices. Aside from a mention in the *Shi ji* of Han Emperor Wudi supporting a southern practitioner of chicken-bone divination and giving official sanction of the practice more broadly, we only have glimpses of what seems to have been a vast panorama of religious customs, techniques, and beliefs.[7] When mentioning the practice of tattooing, we recall, some authors make an effort to note the likely apotropaic

[7] *Shi ji*, 10.478.

function of the tattoos, but beyond that, we learn very little about the content of those beliefs.

By later Han times, there is textual data linking the Southern Man with snake totems or divinities. The Han etymological index, the *Shuo wen jiezi*, characteristically makes use of a graphic element in the written word for "Man 蠻" to attribute a general characteristic to the people to whom such a graph is applied: "南蠻, 蛇種."[8] Such a folk etymology need not be taken as solid evidence for the relationship between the Southern Man and snakes, although the fact that the *Shuo wen* mentions snakes in particular (and not merely any pest or creepy-crawly creature, as the radical *chong* 虫 suggests) seems to demonstrate that by later Han times, authors were beginning to see these peoples as possessing some sort of ritual affinity with this animal.

Archaeology, on the other hand, has yielded much information about the religious practices and possible conceptual underpinnings of ancient southern religious cultures. Snake-pattern decorations appear on Neolithic and Bronze Age artifacts from the entire southern region. Wu Chunming has provided a sweeping overview of Neolithic and Bronze Age artifacts from various southern regions including Hunan and Jiangsu, and as far southwest as Yunnan, to show the striking use of snake patterns and even shapes in early pottery, bronze drums, swords, adzes, and daggers.[9] Similarly, modern anthropologists have noted the appearance of snake ancestors and divinities in ethnographic origin stories from several of the southern minority groups.[10] Wu cites the existence of stone statues in modern-day Wuming 武鳴 and Tengxian 藤縣 counties (both in Guangxi Province) of what is believed to be a Snake Mother or Snake Ancestor divinity worshipped by locals.[11] Along with evidence of snake-patterned tattoos, artifacts, and house decorations from other geographical hotbeds of ancient Yue culture (such as in Hainan, Fujian, and among aboriginals in Taiwan), we have good reason to believe that snake worship was a widely held practice among many groups across southeastern and southwestern China.

While the snake image was commonly used in ancient southern China, it is not entirely clear why this object was depicted in the material cultures

[8] Duan Yucai 段玉裁, ed., *Shuo wen jie zi zhu* 說文解字注 (Shanghai: Shanghai Publishing, 1992), p. 673.

[9] See Wu Chunming, "The Change of Snake Divinity Worship of Aboriginals and Han Cultural Assimilation in Southern China," conference paper presented at Pennsylvania State University, April 10, 2013; pp. 4–6.

[10] *Ibid.*, p. 5. The minority groups in question include the Li 黎, Dong 侗, Dai 傣, Zhuang 壯, and Taiwan aboriginals, among others.

[11] *Ibid.*

of the day – was it a spirit or totem of specific clans, a talisman of spiritual power, an integral part of ancestral mythology, or something else? Similarly unclear is whether such an image marks a unique cultural or religious trait of the Yue or some sub-group of them, or whether it was incorporated by dozens of drastically different ethnic groups in the region. Certainly, if one accepts the argument put forward in this book that the "Yue" likely consisted of many different ethnic communities dotting the eastern and southern landscape in ancient China/Southeast Asia, then there is no inconsistency in saying that the image of the snake seems to have been associated with the Yue peoples.

Hugh Clark has provided an overview of a post-Han engagement with snakes in the Fujian region that corresponds to what Wu Chunming thinks of as the "suppression of the snake" by Sinitic immigrants to the region.[12] One famous account, featured in the fourth-century CE *Soushen ji* 搜神記, tells of a local practice of human sacrifice – the repeated, annual sacrifice of live, female virgins – to a fearsome snake in the Eastern Yue region (i.e., Min River Valley).[13] By the tenth sacrifice, Girl Number 10 outsmarted the snake and killed it.[14] Whether this story should be read as a fable of the Sinitic colonization of parts of Fujian during the Middle period, or more literally in terms of the actual fear among local peoples associated with snakes in the region, is hard to know. In any case, it is clear that in the post-Han record, there are more stories featuring human–snake interactions in the South than during the period under scrutiny. It is certainly interesting, given the widespread prevalence of snake patterns on artifacts associated with the ancient Yue, that our Warring States and early imperial textual sources do not make a big deal out of it, barely mentioning the connection between the two. This surprising omission in the early textual record attests once more to the contrived, rhetorical nature of the literature being written at the time and the type of interest the Hua-xia had in the Yue other.

As for dragons, much has already been written on the ancient Vietnamese or otherwise Southern myths that link dragons to the origins

[12] *Ibid.*, p. 6. Clark also writes intriguingly of a particular serpent associated with Fujian in later times, a crocodile-like animal called the *jiao* 蛟 or *jiaochi* 蛟螭 in later texts. Jiao in early (pre-imperial and Han texts) is often paired with "dragon," to form the compound, *jiaolong*, or "scaly dragon." To date I have found no evidence in the textual record that this particular mythological figure is linked to Southerners; it seems to be a generic term for a type of magnificent dragon, often referred to as such in Han texts.

[13] Hugh R. Clark, *Portrait of a Community*: Society, Culture, and the Structures of Kinship in the Mulan River Valley (Fujian) from the Late Tang through the Song (Hong Kong: The Chinese University Press, 2007), p. 172.

[14] *Soushen ji*, 19:1a–2a. Kenneth DeWoskin and J. T. Crump, Jr., *In Search of the Supernatural: The Written Record* (Stanford: Stanford University Press, 1996), pp. 230–231.

of a people and the beginning of genealogies.[15] It is therefore superfluous for me to repeat this material here. The dragon, also a symbol of the Hua-xia peoples, is often shared with peoples on the margins through elaborate retellings of creation myths, dating from at least as early as the late Warring States period. This attests to a desire on the part of authors and certain groups of people to connect lineally with the Hua-xia from the North through the concept of a shared origin. We have already seen how the historian Sima Qian links the Yue royal lineage to the legendary Yu the Great, who was also ancestral to the Hua-xia peoples. Such a connection to Yu the Great implies a connection to dragons, too, as there seems to have been an early link between Yu the Great and dragons. This is borne out in the following passage from Guo Pu's (郭璞, 276–324 CE) commentary to the *Shanhaijing* 山海經: "After Gun [Yu's father] died, his body did not rot for three years. When cut open with a Wu knife, it transformed into a Yellow Dragon 鯀死，三歲不腐。剖之以吳刀，化為黃龍."[16] In other words, the corpse of Yu's father changes into a Yellow Dragon, which – as readers are supposed to apprehend – turns out to be Yu the Great. Hence, the same ancestral claims of the Hua-xia to Yu the Great and dragons also connect the Yue peoples to these legendary figures/creatures as well.

The South as a disease-ridden and noxious no man's land

A general description of the South is "low-lying and wet (*bei shi* 卑溼) [*shi* also appears as 濕]," a phrase used frequently during the Han period to talk about entire regions and specific kingdoms such as "the South (*nan fang* 南方)," "the kingdom of Changsha 長沙," "the Jiangnan region 江南," and even "India (*Shen du* 身毒)."[17] This notion of the South as a low-lying, wet region that adversely affected the quality of life for its inhabitants helped spawn perceptions of it as a diseased wasteland.

[15] See Edward Schafer, *The Vermilion Bird: T'ang Images of the South* (Berkeley: University of California Press, 1967), pp. 87–114 and 206–248; and Keith Taylor, *The Birth of Vietnam* (Berkeley: University of California Press, 1983), p. 1, concerning the dragon origins of the alleged Hung kings.

[16] Hao Yixing 郝懿行, *Shanhaijing jian shu* 山海經箋疏 (Taipei: Zhonghua shuju, 1966), p. 479. In this section, Guo is quoting the "Kaishi 開筮" hexagram of the ancient divination manual, the *Gui cang* 龜藏. The "Tianwen" in the *Chuci*, dating to the Warring States period, confirms that Yu emerges from Gun's belly. "Tianwen" 天問 in *Chuci buzhu* 楚辭補注 (Taipei: Zhongwen, 1979), pp. 150–152. Translation by David Hawkes, *The Songs of the South: An Anthology of Ancient Chinese Poems by Qu Yuan and Other Poets* (Middlesex, England: Penguin, 1985), p. 128.

[17] These references to 卑溼 appear to be limited to the *Shi ji* and *Han shu*.

To us, low-lying and wet regions certainly suggest the presence of mosquitoes, and, hence, the presence of tropical diseases such as malaria and dengue fever. Yet to the ancients, the connection between the climate and illness was not always assumed. While we have many accounts in later histories of China describing the disease-ridden and toxic lands of the South, it is notable that this particular association may not have been commonly used in the textual record until later times, forming during the early imperial period and becoming much more prevalent thereafter. Perhaps this is a clue that Warring States authors had not lived in the Southland themselves and, thus, were not quite attuned to the link between sub-tropical or tropical environments and malarial epidemics. Nonetheless, there are a few passages dating from the third century BCE that discuss large-scale illnesses among foreigners, soldiers, or immigrants to the South, and it is worth trying to figure out both when these stories became part of the common perception of the South and why the trope of southern miasma became prevalent in the literature later on.

In only one pre-Qin instance do we find the phrase, "low-lying and wet," and it is used to describe the humors of southern people, not the land. Such an instance occurs in a passage in the *Xunzi*, which discusses how "blood and *qi*" characteristics help define human mood, temperament, and intent: "If [one's blood and *qi*] are too shallow and wet, laggard, and covetous of gain, then one should oppose this [condition] with high intent 卑溼重遲貪利，則抗之以高志."[18] Here, while Xunzi's laggard and unbalanced individuals are not ill per se, they certainly are not paragons of health, balance, or moral wellbeing.

In the *Guanzi* chapter on water, cited in the Chapter 5, we find an indictment of the Yue region and its peoples in terms of illness: "The water in Yue is muddy, heavy, and easily floods; therefore, its people are stupid, sickly, and filthy 越之水濁重而洎，故其民愚疾而垢."[19] This description does not specifically target southern waters as being more noxious than others, as the passage contains recriminations of several other regions, their waters, and peoples that rival this: peoples of the northern regions around the state of Yan are also stupid, "look lightly upon illness and die easily 輕疾而易死"; those from the erstwhile state of Jin profit-seeking and deceitful; in Chu they are like thieves; and in Qin they are greedy, among other traits.[20] Aside from the people of Yan "looking lightly upon illness," of all the descriptions, only the description of the Yue mentions a causal, physical connection between land and

[18] Xiong Gongzhe 熊公哲, *Xunzi jinzhu jinyi* 荀子今註今譯 (Taipei: Shangwu Yingshuguan, 1990), 2.22.
[19] *Guanzi*, 39.352. [20] *Ibid.*

illness. Perhaps this passage in the *Guanzi*, then, is one of the first mentions of the Southland in association with noxious illnesses due to the environment.

In Chapter 5, we saw that the Han Dynasty statesman, Chao Cuo, comments on the abundance of *yang qi* in the bodies of the Yue people. Intriguingly, the result of this imbalance was not illness but an adaptive response to the environment in which the people grow thin skin and can withstand heat.[21] Such a description of the link between climate and people does not discuss the land in terms of noxious vapors or illness-producing toxins, as some Han descriptions of the South almost invariably would do. It merely links a preponderance of *yang qi* with a people's appropriate physical response to it, focusing not on illness but on providing a reason for differences among peoples of the world.

With the more massive influx of foreigners into the South via incursions and colonization during the early imperial periods, Han Empire authors seem to become more aware of the connection between the damp region and illness. In some Han period texts, we find the connection between the vapors of the land and the humors of the people to quite specific. Instead of focusing on moral character or the quality of one's energy, some authors link the land to illness and death. Indeed, this is born out in the various descriptions that accompany the fact of the "low-lying and wet" Southland: one will die young, one's life expectancy will be lowered significantly (*zhangfu zaoyao* 丈夫早夭, or *shou bude chang* 壽不得長), or one will be sickly and pestilence will abound.[22]

The widespread illness among Empress Lü's troops during their failed attempt at invading Lingnan from 181 to 180 BCE was, in the words of Sima Qian, due to the "heat and dampness" of the region (*shu shi* 暑溼).[23] In another instance in the *Han shu*, the Southland are mentioned in terms of inhospitable environment and illness. This latter passage follows a paragraph-long discussion of Yue military capabilities along the southern frontier. It is one of the few discussions in which the reader senses that the author actually speaks from experience or a perspective of greater knowledge about the region and its peoples:

> The South is hot and wet, when summer approaches it gets bitterly hot. One is violently exposed [to the elements] and must live on water. There are vipers and snakes, and everything is fermented (?). Illnesses and pestilences abound, and soldiers die by the scores of disease without having to be killed by the blade. Even

[21] *Han shu*, 49.2284.

[22] Such comments are found in the "Huozhi 貨殖列傳" and "Qu Yuan, Jia Sheng 屈原賈生列傳" sections of the *Shi ji*.

[23] *Shi ji*, 113.2969.

though one overtakes the Yue kingdoms and makes the people slaves, nothing can repay one's losses.

南方暑溼，近夏癉熱，暴露水居，蝮蛇蠚生，疾癘多作，兵未血刃而病死者什二三，雖舉越國而虜之，不足以償所亡。[24]

From our discussion above, it seems as though the trope of the South as a miasmic no man's land was not too prevalent in the literature of the pre-imperial period. One might speculate that the relatively sparse usage of this trope in Warring States literature suggests that the majority of the writers before and during the Han were still relying mostly on imagination rather than eyewitness accounts from travelers, merchants, soldiers, settlers, and migrants. Fact-based connections between land and illness seem only to occur in but a few instances, mostly appearing in passages from the *Shi ji* and *Han shu* that may have been drawn from on-the-ground reports of what happened to troops sent down to fight in Yue regions. When writing about military encounters, some Han authors reveal knowledge that the Southland were not merely inhospitable in a geographic sense, but that they were deadly from the point of view of pathology as well.

Other early imperial writers, however, merely stick to general Five Phases concepts regarding the South and its relationship to *yang qi*. Their comments about the effects of the southern landscape on humans are usually much more unrealistic, and they hint at a lack of awareness of the disease-causing capacity of the humid climates of the South. This suggests that such authors, usually of philosophical treatises, relied on home-grown philosophical explanations and theories of the other rather than empirical knowledge from firsthand accounts and experience in the South. The South was, for such authors, still a part of the larger Hua-xia imagination – one that fit into a Five Phases cosmological vision of the world – and not a significant part of their reality. As such, the South served the more rhetorical and theoretical purpose of occupying an off-center space in the conceptual mapping of peoples and cosmic forces in the world – a role that fulfilled the compartmentalization of knowledge about the self and other as expressed through center–periphery geography and the spiritual landscape of the cosmos.

Land of swords and magical knives

Another trait associated with Yue cultures is their ability to produce swords of excellent caliber, as well as the existence of talismanic knives

[24] *Han shu*, 64a.2781.

that are linked to the birth of dragons and other amphibious creatures. This Yue link to technological expertise is similar to the trope concerning naval and aquatic superiority and abilities. Unlike the trope of aquatic superiority, however, the Yue association with swords does not underscore radical cultural or environmental differences or modes of existence. Also, given that technological expertise is at issue, this link suggests a kind of parity in the degree of civilization between Hua-xia and Yue.

Like other descriptions of regions and their various specialties, Hua-xia admiration of Yue swords is partly a compliment. Such admiration is rooted in an appreciation of the superior materials and craftsmanship of swords linked to the peoples, cultures, and regions of Yue. For this reason, although swords do connote violence and danger, and the wielder of swords was linked to dangerous elements, this motif may not possess quite the stigma of savagery carried by some of the others discussed so far. Indeed, at some level, the Hua-xia considered the Yue to be capable and talented enough to produce objects of high quality and value, objects that fit into a conceptual schematization of the world and its commercial objectification. According to such a schema, each diverse region of the world had a commercial specialty that could lend value to the whole, and, especially, the center.[25]

Yue swords had been valued since at least the latter part of the Warring States period. An "Outer Chapter" of the *Zhuangzi*, dating to some time after the third century BCE, clearly proclaims the value of swords made in the Yue region: "Now, if you possess a sword from Gan-yue,[26] you will box it away and store it, and not dare to use it, as it is an exquisite treasure 夫有干越之劍者, 柙而藏之, 不敢用也, 寶之至也."[27] By the Han period, not only did the Yue possess a reputation for fine swords, but they were

[25] Perhaps this mode of "world-making" is one effect of the intensifying trade relations between Center and South, which likely helped counter frictions in cross-cultural exchanges as the central, Greater Yellow River cultures came into contact with the Greater Yangzi River and coastal cultures of the Southeast and South.

[26] I am not certain why the term "Gan 干" precedes Yue here, although the appearance of the phrase "Gan-yue 干越" occurs several times in the textual record and seems to be read together as a single place name. It may be a mistake for Yu-yue 于越 (sometimes written 於越), an ancient name for Yue, mentioned in the *Zhushu jinian* under the fourteenth year of King Wu of Zhou. (Yu was a pre-syllable in Yue languages associated with place names.) I am grateful to Axel Schüssler for sharing a draft article of his on an ancient Yue languages that mentions this.

In *Mozi*, "Jian Ai, Center," Gan-yue is used along with the reference to the state of Chu as "Jing-chu 荊楚." Since we know that this latter phrase is redundant; that, in fact, *jing* refers to *chu* and vice versa, then we might also conclude that the term "Gan" may have been a way of referencing the local Yue state as well. In the *Shi ji*, "Account of Trade," Gan-yue is paired with Min-zhong, a known region in the Min-yue area of Fujian.

[27] *Zhuangzi*, "Ke Yi 刻意," p. 544.

praised for their swordsmanship as well. One particular story in the *Wuyue chunqiu* mentions the phrase "the Sword [Technique] of the Lady of Yue," to indicate a particular style of sword-fighting associated with a young woman from Nanlin in Yue. In this intriguing story, no doubt apocryphal, King Goujian is introduced to a female sword-fighter who divulges to him her secrets of success and mastery of the art. Upon witnessing the excellence of her technique, King Goujian

was so greatly pleased that he gave the style a feminine appellation, "Lady of Yue." He then ordered the troop leaders of the five offices and those of highest talent to practice it, so as to be able to teach their troops. Ever since this time, all have been calling it the "Sword [Technique] of the Lady of Yue."

越王大悅,即加女號,號曰「越女。」乃命五校之隊長、高才習之,以教軍士。當此之時皆稱越女之劍.[28]

The passage preceding this statement describes for the reader the Lady of Yue's technique. While it reads as though it were plucked from a cosmological treatise on the ways of yin-yang, closer inspection reveals some insights into distinctive attitudes toward both the Yue and women. For example, the Lady of Yue allegedly states:

In general, in the arts of hand-to-hand combat, one must fully embody the energy and spirit on the inside while manifesting calm and composure on the outside. What one expresses outwardly resembles a "good wife," and what one hides inwardly is a terrified tiger . . .

凡手戰之道, 內實精神, 外示安儀, 見之似好婦, 奪之似懼虎 . . .[29]

The reference to both the "good wife" and "terrified tiger" is a most excellent way of describing the divergence between reality and appearance on the one hand, and Zhou ritual expectations and wild savagery on the other. In terms of reality versus appearance, the passage leads us to consider a person's hidden, inner reality, which is drastically different than the outer one and might at any point be unleashed into the external world. Unlike traditional Zhou or Ruist morality tales, the goal is not to render one's inner reality the same as one's outward appearance. Moral cultivation and the evening out of one's inner and outer appearance is in fact unnecessary. Rather, it is precisely the disjuncture between outward appearance and inner reality that lends power to the technique.

Does the fact that this woman is from Yue make a difference in the meaning of this passage? Her association with Yue may not have been a coincidence. Certainly, the story could be narrating what really

[28] *Wuyue chunqiu*, "Gou Jian yinmou waizhuan, 勾踐陰謀外傳," chap. 13. [29] *Ibid.*

happened, documenting the amazing existence of a female master of swordsmanship from Yue. Yet it is difficult to imagine that any dialog between a female swordsman and King Goujian would have ever been recorded at the time. Indeed, the contrived, elegant nature of the explanation makes one wonder at the extent to which it is not merely an anecdote created *ex post facto* to explain why people refer to the arts of swordsmanship as "Sword [Technique] of the Lady of Yue." That techniques of the sword should be named after a woman from outside the margins of Hua-xia culture seems understandable, too. We have already examined how the margins were imbued with a special power – a power that inheres in extremity. What better way to signify extremity than with a sharp, cutting sword and a culturally anomalous female swordsman to wield it?

The images associated with the sword of the Lady of Yue are at once fitting and inappropriate, shocking and mundane, meaningful and trivial. Inappropriate, shocking, and meaningful because not only were women in civilized society supposed to behave like "good wives," but, furthermore, they were not supposed to fight or know about the arts of the sword, let alone fight men with their art. Moreover, the reference to "the Lady of Yue" could in other contexts be referring to great female beauties such as Xi Shi 西施, who came from Yue. The image of great female beauty juxtaposed with that of a female master at fighting certainly would have evoked a shocking conceptual contrast.

Yet the passage is also fitting, mundane, and trivial, because while Hua-xia women were supposed to behave like "good wives," this woman was from Yue, so it would have been perhaps easier to accept her transgression of those boundaries so as to behave like a tiger poised to pounce and rip apart its foe. Furthermore, the Yue peoples possessed only the finest swords, so it is appropriate that they should also have people who know how to wield such swords properly.

At the same time, the figure of this "terrified tiger" from Yue may be understood as the inner savage of all. It is something dreadful but potentially very valuable that should be tamed, controlled, and successfully harnessed – and only unleashed upon the world at the perfect time. Thus, the parable of the "sword of the Lady of Yue" is not just one of Hua-xia fear and awe of the Yue other, but one that sings the importance of controlling and exploiting the ferocious savage that lies within everyone.

Naming a fencing technique after a woman from the margins of civilization is an act of irony that creates a cognitive dissonance from unexpected opposites: woman/sword; "good wife"/"terrified tiger," great female beauty/fierce female tiger; Hua-xia/Yue, and Zhou ritual values/ alien forms of savage power. The Yue strength for swords is transposed into a story about female transgression and ferocity on the margins of society and self. At the same time, cultural associations with ultimate female beauty (from Yue) are transformed into a fearsome portrait of a cunning female fighter. In such ways, the somewhat violent connotations of the Yue facility with swords and mastery over the craft of making them are deployed not merely to depict and contrast self and other, but also to challenge the self to manage, tame, and deal with the superiority, ferocity, craftiness, and power of the southern other.

Conclusion

While there are still more tropes of the savage and other descriptions of the southern or Yue peoples and their strange habits and appearances, habitats and associated objects, the ones discussed in the last two chapters constitute a handful of the most frequent and important ones in the early textual record. Scholars often take textual descriptions of the Yue other at face value, without approaching them critically in an attempt to reveal their biases. The foregoing analysis has tried to tease out potential motivations or underlying assumptions that may have influenced the creation of rhetoric, fantasy, or bias and error in descriptions of the Yue. Through such an exercise, I have highlighted the ways in which the Hua-xia self used simplified but poignant images of the other to center and create a fixed, unified sense of self on the one hand, or, on the other to destabilize its sense of superiority by relativizing diverse cultural habits and mores vis-à-vis a central self. These formulations of self and other are windows onto certain Hua-xia visions, representations, and admonitions of the self.

By exploring the broader interpretive contexts in which a given trope appears, we gain a deeper understanding of the ways in which the southern other served to complete both a critical and self-congratulatory presentation of the self. In the case of the so-called Yue marker of "loose hair," we learn of the many (Hua-xia) cultural meanings associated with keeping one's hair unbound, such as the suggestion of numinosity, insanity, youth, purity of the spirit, or proximity to nature or truth. The broader cultural context of unbound hair showed us that notions of the Yue other were likely colored by the above-mentioned values, all of which helped accentuate and lend a specific flavor to certain qualities of Yue alterity: including baseness, power, or a state of being unsophisticated, unrefined, and uncivilized.

The textual record reveals many inconsistencies and contradictions in its descriptions of the Yue other. Some of the hairstyles that were allegedly unique to the Yue turn out not to be so unique at all. The mallet-shaped hairstyle, in particular, seems to have provided many authors with a pervasive and easy marker of one's position as an alien outsider, and therefore it serves nicely as an example of the trope of the savage. Its appearance in the Zhao Tuo story from the *Shi ji*, is noteworthy, especially since there is little indication in the archaeological or textual tradition that the Southern Yue peoples who surrounded Zhao Tuo wore their hair in that fashion. Its appearance in the story, therefore, compels us to reconsider Sima Qian's (or the narrator's) connection to the Yue peoples of the South, shedding doubt upon a common interpretation of the story: that a northerner had "gone native" by embracing Yue styles and behavior. In addition, the reference to the Far South in association to the phrase "pigeon-toed" is interesting and perplexing. This may be a case in which a fantastical or exaggerated description of faraway peoples turned into a place name, or, as I suspect, a place name later being confused phonetically and conflated with a homophonic phrase that seems to describe human beings. It shows us how many of the tropes associated with peoples on the fringes were imagined or randomly created so as to fulfill the imperative of Hua-xia centrality, clarity, and normalcy.

We have also seen how certain, so-called markers of Yue culture could serve simultaneously as generic markers for Central States people of lower classes, people in casual settings, or people who flouted Zhou ritual. This was true of the dustpan style of sitting, which held a special resonance in light of the traditional Zhou ritual forms of sitting and kneeling, used especially when greeting another or attending ceremonies or performances. The appearance of this marker in reference to the Yue, therefore, does not provide much that is culturally specific to the Yue. Rather, we should recognize it as a Central States shorthand for denoting an uncouth or uncivilized person, or even a person who wishes to insult another or express a certain defiance for Zhou cultural practices.

In our discussion of landscapes and environments of the South, we also often encountered what seemed to be imagined geographies rather than real ones. Again, these spatial tropes associated with the Yue are better understood in terms of a logic of Hua-xia centrality that attempts to assimilate difference through categories of the center and periphery. The savagery of the South is expressed through its distance to the center – through a liminal space whose uncertainty increases with distance from the central self. Drastically different conditions for life are projected onto southern landscapes, and actual features of the landscape are taken as markers that define – sometimes in a wholly deterministic way – the lives and the people of the region. In such a light, we see that images of the South as mysterious and serpentine, as well as disease-ridden and filled with noxious *qi* attempt both to express certain realities about tropical regions while also betraying dream-like, Hua-xia perceptions and fears of the distant unknown.

Despite an underlying sense of awe for Yue achievements and aquatic abilities, Central States authors consistently maintain the structural logic of self-in-center and other-at-periphery in their writings. This psycho-spatial logic of self–other relies on an intrinsic evaluation of what is central as safe, normative, identifiable, and even healthy, while what is off-center is dangerous, abnormal, obscure, and unhealthy. The externalization of the other in psychic terms is therefore literally played out in the mapping of the other according to a "center–periphery" landscape that at once lends mystique and fear to that which is farther away.

The specific connection between southern environments and deadly disease may have matured only after the early imperial period, especially in records of military engagements in the South. We have seen that some authors used the hot, humid climate of the South to draw up a schematic account of the natives and their attributes, while others – usually in military contexts – described how alien forces from the Central States were decimated by illness and pestilence. Philosophical speculation seems to have sometimes relied on purely imagined sources; at other times, it may have based itself in on-the-ground descriptions of reality among troops and visitors to the Southland. Nonetheless, such speculation often was so entwined with its overarching goals – attempting to organize the world into neatly defined geographic compartments, each with its defined, normative traits – that it likely departed substantially from reality.

The link between the ancient Yue state and both sword manufacturing and swordsmanship exemplifies a Hua-xia appreciation for certain technological and artistic achievements associated with the southern periphery. Our discussion of the "Lady of Yue" fencing technique explored the nature of a Hua-xia fascination with an exotic female art, showing why the values of "Yue" and "female" provided a particularly felicitous combination of mystique, shock, and awe that authors or promoters of such a technique would be seeking to elicit in their viewers.

Last but not least: snakes and dragons. Warring States and early imperial sources do not go into great detail concerning specific religious orientations related to the Yue peoples. We are provided tantalizing hints at alternative forms of divination (chicken-bone), the apotropaic effects of tattooing, and the totemic beliefs of the Yue in serpentine creatures such as snakes and dragons. Even these hints suffice in providing a sense that the cultures of the South were considered to be drastically different from those of the Central Plains regions. Similarly, the religious cultures of the South were thought to be liminal, watery, and steeped in ways that were utterly exotic and esoteric to the Hua-xia peoples.

If one takes a sweeping look at the ways in which Sinitic authors describe outsiders throughout Chinese history, one might generally state that as authors came into increased contact with others on the periphery, their descriptions of the other were more likely to be accurate or contain elements of reality, even though cultural biases and rhetorical or stylistic practices would always affect their representations of self and other. In the Yue tropes examined here, the inconsistencies and stereotypical ways in which the Yue are described all suggest that Hua-xia authors of the Warring States and early imperial period may not have possessed very good or accurate knowledge about the Yue other.[30] Alternatively, and also likely, it may have been the case that some authors possessed some accurate information of the other, but that they were still not interested in outlining Yue difference in any detail beyond the simplistic stereotypes concerning hair, tattooing, water, swords, etc. This latter explanation does not preclude the fact that while Central States authors may have been accurate in some of their simplistic descriptions of the Yue, their lack of any kind of deep and sustained encounter with them would have rendered them incapable of penetrating beyond the superficial layers of appearance to understand more minute differences among various sub-groups, or the reasons and beliefs that underlay certain practices. And lastly, we cannot overlook the possibility that many Central States authors were simply not interested in writing up realistic portrayals of the other – that the very reason they invoked the Yue other was to serve a larger purpose in the project of presenting and framing the self.

Given the lack of extensive and meaningful ethnographic writings on the Yue other, it is likely that cross-cultural encounters and communications between the majority of the Central States elite and the Yue other were few and far between. We should therefore approach passages that describe the Yue during this period with a skeptical eye, accepting the fact that much of what is written contains fantasy, hearsay, and imaginative

[30] Sima Qian is perhaps an exception to this rule because of the special access he had to a massive archive of political and historical documents concerning Central States engagements with others. But even Sima Qian was unable to give a detailed list of the names of basic kings in the Min-yue region during the Han, and the names he gives are at times at odds with the archaeological recordFor example, the name he gives to the grandson of Zhao Tuo in Southern Yue, Zhao Hu, differs from the (likely more local) name that same figure is called in the Southern Yue tomb discovered in modern-day Guangzhou (Zhao Mo). Such omissions and discrepancies suggest that even the knowledge of the Great Office of Archives (*tai shih* 太史) during Han Emperor Wu's reign had limited access to information about the southern peoples, especially ethnographic knowledge about their cultures as opposed to knowledge concerning political and military events and interactions.

bias rather than deep knowledge and understanding of the Yue. This does not mean that the literary record is useless, for, as these chapters show, its lack of depth betrays vital information about Hua-xia views of and modes of representing the self and other, as well as the level of Central States and Yue contact among the literary elite classes.

Part IV

Performing Yue: political drama, intrigue, and armed resistance

8 Yue identity as political masquerade and ritual modeling

In Part IV, "Performing Yue: Political Drama, Intrigue, and Armed Resistance," we conclude our analysis of ethnicity and perceptions of identity with a discussion of Yue resistance to the Han imperium. By shining the spotlight on historical figures who helped carve out a specific type of Yue identity in the creation and maintenance of states, as well as in moments of political rebellion or defiance, we can gain insight into the ways in which locals appropriated and used the term "Yue" for their own purposes, goals, and power. Indeed, it is often the case that when one attempts to differentiate oneself and establish a sense or degree of autonomy, one is compelled to articulate aspects of identity more clearly than at other times. The justifications for rebellion, along with the defiant actions and words of Han detractors, form a fertile arena for studying and coming to terms with the history of Yue identity in the making.

This chapter presents a case study of political modes of formulating Yue identity by the Zhao 趙 ruling clan of the kingdom of Southern Yue (Nan Yue 南越). Drawing primarily from the *Shi ji* and *Han shu* accounts of Southern Yue, I recount a period ranging from the beginning years of the Han around 200 BCE to the period of increased Han expansionism under Emperor Wu in the 120s BCE. I enhance such accounts with information from the tomb of the king of Southern Yue, as well as information on the economic and political ties between Han and Southern Yue.[1]

While not much is known about Yue identity during this period, and while the main figures examined – King/Emperor Zhao Tuo and King/Emperor Zhao Hu (or Zhao Mo as an alternative name) – do not and cannot represent common Yue individuals of the day, this analysis will nonetheless reveal some of what we can know about the ways in which Yue identity was invoked, formulated, and strengthened through a type of

[1] Note that the *Han shu* accounts are often virtually identical to those found in the *Shi ji*, with some extra information at times. When there are differences meriting comment, I shall duly note them.

ritual modeling of external, imperial authority. I do this by linking, when possible, specific representations of Yue culture and identity to the concrete historical and political motivations underlying the actions of individual Yue elites.

Scholars might at first glance think that the most reliable evidence for culture change would be found among the "pristine" commoners who must somehow come to grips with a new, colonizing identity in their midst. Elites, on the other hand, might be considered to have been tainted by the colonizing culture – that is, to have been more familiar from the beginning with it, or themselves to have stemmed from it or a mixed cultural zone in which they interacted and intermarried with other elites. Contrary to such a presumption, the act of examining elites and elite cultures can be a most effective means of understanding cross-cultural contact and the mixing of identities. As new archaeological studies show, far from being mere puppets of their Han overlords, elite, aristocratic people on the frontier were pioneers of social and cultural change.[2] Furthermore, these elites demonstrated an agency that neither wholly accepted nor resisted the Han, but which attempted to create original, mixed identities and responses to Han influence and pressures for their own benefit.[3]

The lineage and royal figures of the Southern Yue to be examined in this chapter represent some of the pioneers of culture change along the southern frontier. The Zhao lineage in Southern Yue was originally from the Central States, yet its members demonstrated attempts to co-opt and adopt Yue culture and identity in interesting ways. In my analysis of such culturally liminal figures, I reveal various types of cross-cultural conflict, negotiation, and expressions of identity between figures from the Western Han court and the leadership of the Southern Yue kingdom. Most importantly, I underscore the notion that in order to meet their own needs and/or gain benefit and advantage for themselves, their lineage, kingdom, and its supporters, aristocratic figures in Southern Yue eagerly adopted and adapted Han imperial tools of control, using them for their own purposes. Coming to terms with their activities and possible motivations for action, we gain insights into the innovative ways these elites presented their identities to themselves and others.

[2] See Gil Stein, *Archaeology of Colonial Encounters* (Santa Fe: SAR Press, 2005). For China, see especially Alice Yao's recent archaeological study of cultural contact along the southwestern Han frontier, where she argues that culture change and new, mixed responses to imperial contact are most pronounced in individuals from the highest strata of society. Alice Yao, "Culture Contact and Social Change Along China's Ancient Southwestern Frontier, 900 B.C.–100 A.D.," Ph.D. dissertation, University of Michigan, 2008, pp. 259–278.

[3] Yao, "Culture Contact," pp. 259–278.

In trying to uncover the modes that these elite men used to formulate Yue identity, I encounter certain difficulties. The Han texts I analyze do not shed much light upon what one might call the personal or cultural identities of these men, that is, as such identities may stand apart from their political identities as rulers and ministers of kingdoms. My analysis, therefore, must perforce take into account the heightened public and political nature of identity construction for these men. Because whatever personal, cultural identities these men may have possessed are basically indistinguishable from their public personas as given in our sources, we must settle for an account that highlights political contingencies and power struggles. The so-called cultural identity of these figures thus often collapses into what we might wish to view as political representation and status. While we examine how certain ruling elites chose to portray themselves to both their subjects and the imperial Han court, we must also ask what were the possible reasons or political benefits for representing themselves in such a manner. In other words, our analysis must necessarily link processes of identity construction to specific local, historical, political, and economic contingencies. Indeed, it will often be impossible for us to discern what is "Yue" from a particular political identity or construct.

Zhao Tuo, emperor and king of Southern Yue

Our inquiry into modes of identity construction begins with Zhao Tuo 趙佗 (230–137 BCE), also sometimes referred to as "Commandant Zhao Tuo 趙尉佗," who was not a native of Yue and who founded the kingdom of Southern Yue after the fall of the Qin Empire.[4] Tuo – a king and emperor – was a pivotal figure in the brief history of Southern Yue (est. 204 BCE), which lasted for ninety-three years, ending in 111 BCE when Emperor Wu of the Han successfully invaded and either killed members of the ruling elite or forced them to submit completely to the Han. Indeed, the story of Tuo and his royal descendants provides us with an excellent account of how Yue and Central States identities were intertwined, confused, and used as tokens of political value during the period of Han imperial domination, encroachment, and then, finally, conquest of the ancient Yue kingdoms.

Zhao Tuo was originally from Zhending 真定, in the present-day northern province of Hebei. A military general under the Qin, he was

[4] Because I will be addressing many different members of the same Zhao clan, I conveniently refer to each member not by the surname Zhao but by his individual name. For Zhao Tuo, I follow the *Shi ji* practice of simplifying his name to "Tuo."

appointed magistrate of Dragon River, in the Qin province of South Seas (Nanhai 南海). This province occupied a large area on the southern and southeastern tip of the Chinese mainland, including areas in modern-day Canton Province. We know that this region was considered to be inhabited by the Yue, as Sima Qian states that the Qin settled the region of the "Yang-yue 楊越."[5] After the fall of the Qin (c. 210 BCE), Tuo took up arms, eliminated all the remaining Qin officials in the region, consolidated his own power by appointing his own men to important posts, and founded the kingdom of Southern Yue, which covered an enormous geographic cross-section of southern China – roughly, the area of three former Qin Provinces: South Seas, Guilin 桂林 (encompassing large portions of Hunan and Guangxi Provinces), and Xiang 象 (encompassing most of Guangxi Province, parts of Yunnan Province, and the northern reaches of Vietnam).[6] Tuo then proclaimed himself the "Martial King of Southern Yue," setting up his capital at Panyu (番禺, modern-day Guangzhou).[7] While he would remain a sovereign for the rest of his life, Tuo's various political identities changed, depending on the time and context. First he was a king of an independent southern kingdom, next a king in a dependent relationship to the Han Emperor, then a rogue emperor, and, finally, an amphibian "Emperor/King" whose relationship to the Han was uncertain at best.[8]

After the first Han Emperor, Gaozu, emerged victorious and set up court at Chang'an, he sent Lu Jia 陸賈 in 196 BCE to Southern Yue to present to Zhao the "split tallies marking a lord–vassal relationship 剖符通使."[9] Zhao accepted this gesture no doubt so as to avoid conflict with a superior military power. The *Shi ji* account of this event describes how Gaozu ordered Zhao to "collect together in harmony the Hundred Yue so

[5] *Shi ji*, 113.2967. Commentators speak of "Yang" as referring to the ancient region of Yang 楊州, but the geographic location of this region is disputed. It is usually associated with the Southeast, but may refer to southern parts of Guangdong as well.

[6] Yü Tianchi 余天熾 *et al.*, *Gu Nan Yue Guo shi* 古南越國史 (Nanning: Guangxi renmin Press, 1988), p. 31. See also the map of Yue regions in Chen Guoqiang *et al.*, *Bai Yue minzu shi* 百越民族史 (Beijing: Zhongguo shehui kexue, 1988), p. iii. These maps of the ancient abodes of the Yue are not completely reliable, since many do not include current-day Vietnam. For example, in this latter book, the southern boundaries for the ancient Yue coincide neatly – and falsely – with the contemporary border between the People's Republic and Vietnam.

[7] *Shi ji*, 113.2967.

[8] A brief overview of this history and that of the southeastern kingdoms can be found in Yü Ying-shih, "Han Foreign Relations," in Denis Twitchett and Michael Loewe, eds., *The Cambridge History of China, vol. I: The Ch'in and Han Empires, 221 B.C.–A.D. 220* (Cambridge: Cambridge University Press, 1986), pp. 453–457. For an overview in Chinese, see Fang Tie 方鐵, "Nanyueguo de nei-wai guanxi ji qi zhengce" 南越國的內外關系及其政策, *Journal of Wenshan Teachers College* 19.2 (2006): 1–7.

[9] *Shi ji*, 113.2967.

as not to cause trouble and upheaval along the southern border 和集百越，毋為南邊患害."[10] In other words, the Han used its superior military strength to threaten Zhao Tuo into formal submission as protector of the borders of Han. Of course, Zhao Tuo and his successors would also have been enticed by the perceived benefits of easier relations with the Han Empire: the consistent exchange of envoys to and from the Han and Southern Yue courts, better trade relations, and military aid. For example, Zhao Tuo's son, Zhao Hu, wrote Emperor Wu directly to ask for military aid against the invading kingdom of Min-yue. Indeed, good relations with the Han would have been necessary, given Southern Yue's precarious location surrounded by rival kingdoms in the west (Ba-shu 巴蜀, Yelang 夜郎), east (Min-yue 閩越), and north (*Changsha* 長沙).[11] As a dependent king to the Han, Tuo and his heirs officially ruled from around 196 to 111 BCE, or eighty-five years.

Such an official status, however, did not reflect the complexities of an ever-changing situation, especially if viewed from the perspective of the Zhao clan, and not that of the Han court. Tuo's avowed concession – or rather, submission – to the Han was from the beginning fraught with problems. First, Sima Qian mentions that Gaozu might have executed Tuo for his disobedience in setting up his own kingdom. The Emperor decided against it, exonerating Tuo instead because – as Sima Qian claims – Han forces were at the time too depleted to expend further energy on such a matter.[12] This suggests that Gaozu, faced with the question of whether Tuo was to be indicted as a rebel or recovered as a potential ally, made an expedient decision for the latter based on his own relative weakness at the time. Such a decision would have been a great concession, given Gaozu's famed practice of appointing only kin of the Liu family as kings of vassal kingdoms. Certainly, there were reasons for thinking that Tuo might be coaxed to comply. He was, after all, not a Yue native himself, had originally been a loyal official to the Qin, and his credentials and personal background all suggested an understanding of what would be expected of a distant, dependent kingdom under a centralized regime. But could Tuo really act as a dependent king to the Han?

The evidence suggests that Zhao Tuo had empire-building aspirations of his own, and upon provocation from his Han neighbor, such ambitions became obvious to all. While Tuo renewed his status as Han subject after Gaozu's death by sending tribute to the new Emperor, Hui 惠, in 192 BCE,

[10] *Shi ji*, 113.2967–68.
[11] See Lü Liedan 呂烈丹, *Nanyue wang mu yu Nanyue wang guo* 南越王墓與南越王國 (Guangzhou: Guangzhou wenhua, 1990), pp. 145–146.
[12] *Shi ji*, 113.2967.

he would soon revolt and make a nuisance of himself to the Han.[13] During the reign of Empress Lü, the Han placed a ban on the export of metal and iron, agricultural tools, and certain domesticated animals from the Han Empire into the Southern Yue (in particular, horses, oxen, and sheep).[14] Clearly, Empress Lü desired to deprive Southern Yue of their self-sufficiency in military affairs, agricultural production, and livestock. Some scholars think that Empress Lü proceeded so aggressively toward Southern Yue because she was hoping to weaken it, thereby allowing the king of Changsha, Wu Rui 吳芮, to invade and "reclaim" the three regions of Southern Yue (Nanhai, Guilin, and Xiang) that he had been hollowly given by Gaozu.[15]

In response to such open hostility, Tuo sent emissaries to the central court to clarify the situation and beg his forgiveness for not keeping up with his ancestral graves back in the homeland, Zhending.[16] When his emissaries did not return, and he got wind of a rumor that his parents' tombs had been dug up and desecrated and his siblings murdered, Tuo rebelled, attacking the borders of the kingdom of Changsha to the north and referring to himself as the Martial Emperor – not merely king – of Southern Yue.[17] The *Han shu* dates these events for us by claiming that Tuo began calling himself "Emperor" during the spring of 183 BCE, and only in the fall of 181 BCE did Tuo attack the Changsha region.[18]

That Tuo was able to successfully establish himself within Southern Yue as emperor lay no doubt in his military might, but also in part in the distance of his kingdom from the imperial court and the difficulty imperial troops had traversing southern territories just to arrive at Yue. A case in point is the fact that Empress Lü's attempts to quell Zhao Tuo's rebellion were halted because the southern climate induced the deaths of most of her troops from an epidemic (probably of malaria, but the source just attributes it to the heat and dampness of the region).[19]

Tuo's self-identification as "Martial Emperor of Southern Yue" (Nanyue Wudi 南越武帝) is interesting on several levels. First, as the term *Di* 帝 had by that time been used most prominently by the Qin Emperors and

[13] *Han shu*, 2.89.

[14] *Shi ji*, 113.2969. *Han shu*, 95.3848. Empress Lü qualified such a ban by stating, "If one is to export [such animals], then one is to export the male, and not the female." *Han shu*, 95.3851.

[15] See Zhang Rongfang 張榮芳 and Huang Miaozhang 黄淼章, *Nanyueguo shi* 南越國史 (History of the Kingdom of Nan-yue) (Guangdong: Guangdong renmin, 1995), pp. 168–169. *Han shu*, 1.53.

[16] The explanation concerning ancestral graves is provided exclusively in the account from *Han shu*, 95.3851.

[17] *Shi ji*, 113.2970. *Han shu*, 95.3851.

[18] *Han shu*, 3.99–100.

[19] *Shi ji*, 113.2969. *Han shu*, 95.3848.

Gaozu of the Han before him, Tuo was modeling himself after a relatively recent, northern vision of universal rulership in which the *Di* or supreme ruler was not native to the lands over which he ruled. Its associations with the divine realm – in particular, the High God (or Gods) of the Shang – as well as its linkages to cultural sages of antiquity would also have conferred an aura on its beholder that transcended more local interpretations of time and place.

Tuo might also have been aware of previous attempts during the late Warring States period (notably, in 288 BCE) of kings in the states of Qi and Qin at adopting the title "*Di* of the East" and "*Di* of the West" respectively.[20] Such historical usages of the title demonstrated that powerful monarchs could lay claim to large swaths of land associated with a particular cardinal direction, thereby carving out a space for trans-local and supreme rulership with ties to the astral realm and independent of any royal lineage such as the Zhou. Thus, by adopting the title *Di* for himself, Tuo would have been trying to impress upon the many Yue elites his universalistic intents, celestial authority, and trans-local interests, as well as his independence from the Han. In his use of such a non-native title, Tuo was in some ways admitting to his non-local status while still asserting his authority over them as their supreme *Di*.

An interesting case for comparison is that of the king of Huainan 淮南, Liu Chang 劉長, who, though he allegedly usurped the ritual prerogatives of the Emperor for himself, did not actually refer to himself as *Di* within his own kingdom. Of royal lineage, such an overt move of rebellion would have brought about immediate punishment from the Han court. Furthermore, as far as we know, Liu Chang's actions date to Emperor Wen's reign, so that Zhao Tuo would have been the first in the Han kingdoms to stake such a claim.[21]

That Zhao Tuo claimed the title "Emperor" (*Di*) for himself is also interesting in other ways. *Di* could confer upon its holder a liminal status of both insider and outsider. As the highest deity (deities) of the Shang, *Di* was associated with the greatest ancestors of the royal clan. As such, a *Di* could have been understood to be an original member of a lineage, which would have inspired people to think of him as a native par excellence of a particular region. So while the very deification of *Di* wedged a divide of time and space between him and the common people, it also presented him as the perfect specimen of one of themselves. For Zhao Tuo, the title *Di* might therefore have served as both a link to Yue identity and a wedge between him (in particular, his royal family) and both Yue elites and common people.

[20] Twitchett and Loewe, *Cambridge History of China*, 53–54. [21] See *Shi ji*, 58.3076–77.

Zhao Tuo's relative freedom from the Han state is suggested by the fact that even when the next Han Emperor, Wendi, pressured him into renouncing the title of *Di* and resuming the title of "minister" (*chen* 臣) to the Han – thereby acknowledging Han superiority over Southern Yue as a dependent kingdom (*shu guo* 屬國) – Tuo continued to have the people and ministers of Yue refer to him as *Di* behind the Han Emperor's back. Though he sent a biannual tribute to the Han court and referred to himself in such contexts as a minister, he openly continued to adopt the imperial terminology for his own rule in Southern Yue.

Even by calling himself "minister" in his direct relations with the Han, however, Tuo was not necessarily conceding that Southern Yue was a completely dependent kingdom of the Han. Many early Southern Yue kings did not uphold the tributary regulations required of foreign kingdoms that had submitted formally to the Han. For instance, often by feigning illness, they repeatedly refused to pay visit in person to the imperial court.[22] Moreover, the economic and diplomatic relationships between the early Han and its outermost frontier kingdoms were emergent and complicated, changing frequently with the reign of new Han Emperors as well as leaders of outside regions. Yü Ying-shih has explored Han-foreign economic and political relations, including the tributary system in general and the cases of outer versus inner or submitted aliens (*nei shu* 內屬). He mentions how the Lingqu Canal 靈渠 of southwestern China (linking the Li River with the Xiang River) served as a major water route between the Southern Yue capital of Panyu and the Yangzi River region, bringing foreign goods arriving in Southern Yue closer to the Han heartland.[23] This supports the notion that the Southern Yue served as a vital link between Han and other key areas in South and East Asia, much as Venice served the rest of Europe as portal to the Middle and Far Eastern trades. Since Southern Yue held a certain degree of leverage against its Han neighbor, this would have affected how Tuo's status as "minister" or Southern Yue's status as "dependent kingdom" would have been understood in reality.

[22] See the chapter on "Surrendered Barbarians and Their Treatment," Yü Ying-shi, *Trade and Expansion: A Study in the Structure of Sino-Barbarian Economic Relations (Berkeley: University of California Press, 1967)*, pp. 65–91, and *Shi Ji* , 113.2971. For a good discussion of the rather independent political status of Southern Yue in relationship to the Han court, see Liu Rui 劉瑞, "Nanyueguo fei Han zhi zhuhouguo lun 南越國非漢之諸候國論," in Zhongshan Daxue lishi xi, ed., *Nanyueguo shiji yan tao hui* (Beijing: Wenwu Publishing, 2005), pp. 9–22. A discussion of tributary expectations, in the form of homage and tribute from Southern Yue to Han in return for imperial gifts, see Zhang Rongfang 張榮芳, "Han chao zhili Nanyueguo mou shi tan yuan 漢朝治理南越國謀式探源," in *Nanyueguo shiji yan tao hui*, pp. 1–8.

[23] Yü, *Trade and Expansion*, p. 29.

Using the title *Di* for himself allowed Tuo to draw upon and compete with the prestige of the Han court, as is evidenced in his own explanation of his offense in retrospect:

My officials together debated [the matter of Empress Lü's mistreatment of Southern Yue], stating: "At present our kingdom does not receive [economic] support from the Han, and outside our kingdom there is nobody who might claim greater distinction [than our king]." I therefore changed my title to *Di* and served as *Di* [only] over my own kingdom. I did not dare wish harm upon the rest of the world.

吏相與議曰:『今內不得振於漢, 外亡以自高異。』故更號為帝, 自帝其國, 非敢有害於天下也。[24]

Tuo's submission to the Han after Han Emperor Wen confronted him on the matter appears to have been a pragmatic move to avoid hassles with the more powerful, yet distant, imperial neighbor. Most likely for Tuo, submitting to the Han through ritual means constituted a nominal act of allegiance and small price to pay for relative freedom and substantial economic benefits. After all, in the days of the early Han, there was a relatively low risk that the Han would take successful military action against him, as Empress Lü's unsuccessful military mission shows. By paying lip service to the Han imperial court, Tuo could enjoy the economic and trade benefits of good relations with the Han without having to sacrifice too much of his own political authority at home.[25]

In order to drive home this point, it is necessary that we first understand a bit about the economic power of the Southern Yue and what it stood to gain from good trade relations with the Han. The region of Southern Yue, referred to by some scholars as Lingnan 岭南 (South of the Nanling mountains, see Map 1), was part of a much larger network of maritime trade. The goods it received from foreign, non-Chinese ships included

[24] *Han shu*, 95.3851.

[25] Semi-autonomous or autonomous states on the peripheries of various Chinese empires often chose to submit themselves politically or culturally in specific ways to the superiority of the Chinese. Such a relationship was usually complicated, and not necessarily defined by pure submission. For various reasons, foreign states often willingly conformed to certain nominal forms and demands from Han China in the hopes of gaining various economic, political, and cultural benefits. For an example of Korea's use of "marquis" status in conducting state sacrificial rites and music, see Robert Provine, "State Sacrificial Music and Korean Identity," in Evelyn Rawski, Bell Yung, and Rubie Watson, eds., *Harmony and Counterpoint: Ritual Music in Chinese Context* (Stanford: Stanford University Press, 1996), pp. 54, 71–75. The Xiongnu of Han times, as well, agreed in 53 and 51 BCE to tributary relations with the Han after an extended period of a Han policy of appeasement through annual payments. For more on this change of power in favor of the Han, see Yü, *Trade and Expansion*, pp. 36–51.

exotic products that were coveted by the Han, so that the latter would have served as an important buyer and Southern Yue a critical middleman in such exchanges. For example, the *Shi ji* mentions the city of Panyu's trade in pearls, rhinoceros horns, striped-tortoise shells (*dai mao* 玳瑁), fruits (such as longan and lychee), and textiles.[26] That Panyu served as an important ancient center for trade has been confirmed by archaeological finds, including precious materials likely imported from the South Sea, such as glass, amber, and agate.[27] Not only was Panyu important as a nexus for maritime trade among various foreign locations and the Han, it was also important in conducting trade with other areas along the Han frontier, as exemplified in the trade of *ju* 枸 (berry) sauce, native to Sichuan, between Yelang in the Southwest and Southern Yue.[28]

It may also have been the case that Zhao Tuo was more positively predisposed to Emperor Wen of the Han because the latter treated him with respect. Accounts reveal that even though Tuo had been living the better part of his life in the deep South, he still possessed living relatives and ties back in the old country, where his ancestral tombs were being maintained. Emperor Wen of Han was said to have capitalized on Zhao Tuo's ties to the erstwhile Central States regions by making sure that Tuo's ancestral graves were properly worshipped and by lavishing official posts and favorable treatment onto the latter's siblings.[29] Such actions, if true, would have ingratiated the Han to Tuo, so that the latter could save face and more easily abandon the title *Di* vis-à-vis the Han.

So far, we have depicted a power-hungry yet politically astute ruler, not anyone that might be identified as either "Yue" or "Han." Indeed, if Tuo identified himself as anything, it seems to have been with a more rarefied category of deified sovereign than with members of the Han or Yue elite. We have also seen how the imperial court of Han tried to tame Tuo's wayward proclamations of imperial identity by trying to hold him to the proper ritual protocol demanded of a subordinate king, not an independent sovereign. The result was Tuo's construction and use of two different identities – one used infrequently for interactions with Han envoys and the Han imperial court, and the other used on a daily basis within the boundaries and contexts of the Yue court. Both identities might be

[26] Nancy Lee Swann, *Food and Money in Ancient China* (Princeton: Princeton University Press, 1950), p. 446. See also Francis Allard, "Frontiers and Boundaries: The Han Empire from Its Southern Periphery," in M. Stark, ed., *Archaeology of Asia* (Malden: Blackwell Publishers, 2005), pp. 236–237.

[27] Yü, *Trade and Expansion*, pp. 178–180.

[28] Yü, *Trade and Expansion*, p. 94. For more on trade among the frontier kingdoms, see Lü, *Nanyue wang mu*, pp. 151–159.

[29] *Shiji*, 113.2970. We are provided the full text of Emperor Wen's letter to Zhao Tuo in the *Han shu*, which confirms the Emperor's efforts in this regard. *Han shu*, 95.3849.

viewed as politically expedient, public, and only marginally "Yue," insofar as a leader of the Yue might be considered "Yue."

We may never know the extent to which someone like Zhao Tuo identified himself personally with the Yue. No doubt he was an outsider to Yue in more ways than just place of origin. Yet from our sources it is possible to discern ways in which Zhao Tuo used Yue identity to best serve his imperial aspirations. It appears that he tailored Yue, southern, or Man-yi identity and culture to fit the specific situation at hand: sometimes it was useful for him to stress his independence from Han and accentuate the so-called "Yue" elements of his identity; other times it was useful to appear detached from the Yue and not entirely "one of them."

Tuo at times identified himself fully as a sovereign of the Yue, taking pains to present himself to outsiders as such. According to Francis Allard, Tuo "is said to have adopted Yue customs, married a Yue woman, encouraged Han men to do the same, and appointed Yue generals and officers."[30] As discussed in Chapter 6, when the Han envoy, Lu Jia, was sent on his first mission to convince Tuo to submit to Han, for example, our sources describe Tuo as greeting Lu in Yue style: with a mallet-shaped hairdo and sitting on the ground with both legs splayed out in the dustpan style.[31] As mentioned above, such a description seems apocryphal and appears to fulfill the literary and moral aims of the storyteller rather than serve as a faithful record of what happened. If true, however, it suggests that Zhao Tuo wished to present himself as ruler of the Yue rather than lackey to the Han. It would suggest that Tuo, defiantly, was signaling to Lu that the latter should interact with him on his own terms, according to the ritual prerogatives dictated by Yue customs, and not those of the Central States.

There are other instances in which Tuo identifies only weakly with the southern peoples. In a letter to the throne, Tuo explains his reasons for usurping the title, *Di*, by speaking diminutively of the Man-yi peoples and identifying with them only as their "old man":

Moreover, the Southlands are low and wet. Of the Man-yi 蠻夷 in the Central West there are the [peoples of] the Western-ou 西甌. More than half of the

[30] Allard, "Frontiers and Boundaries," p. 235.

[31] *Shi ji*, 97.2697–98, *Han shu*, 43.2111–12. The two versions concerning Lu's encounter with Tuo in the *Shi ji* and *Han shu* are virtually identical. Some commentators believe the sitting style to have resembled a dustpan – legs are spread wide at the end and narrow closer to the body. *Han shu*, 43.2111. Peng Nian argues that the mallet-shaped hairdo was not original to the Yue peoples but to the ancestors of the Hua-xia peoples of the Central Plains regions. This would demonstrate how fluid such "cultural markers" can be. Peng Nian 彭年, "'Shu fa chui ji' fei Nanyue zhi su – jian lun shu fa zhi su de qi yuan ji qi ta 束髮椎髻非南越之俗—兼論束髮之俗的起源及其他," *Zhong yang min zu da xue xue bao* 中央民族大學學報(2001): 6.

population is feeble, and yet I face south and rule over them as king. In the East there is Min-yue, where the population consists of [a mere] few thousand people, and yet I rule over them as king. In the Northwest there is Changsha, where half the population is Man-yi, and yet I rule over them as king. For this reason, this old man [i.e., "I"] absurdly and furtively dared to use the title *Di*, merely in attempt to amuse myself.

且南方卑溼，蠻夷中西有西甌，其眾半羸，南面稱王；東有閩粵，其眾數千人，亦稱王；西北有長沙，其半蠻夷，亦稱王。老夫故敢妄竊帝號，聊以自娛.[32]

This letter is full of attempts to humble himself and play down the gross, ritual violation of using the title *Di* in light of Tuo's formal submission to Han. Of the Man-yi, Zhao Tuo speaks dismissively, as though they were of lesser worth than other Han subjects. This seems to be the case in Tuo's reference to the largely "feeble" (*lei* 羸) population of Man-yi in Western Ou as well as in his reference to the large Man-yi population of Changsha. As ruler, Tuo is clearly distinct from the populations of Man-yi themselves. Nonetheless, because the Man-yi are insignificant and feeble, Tuo – as king or even *Di* of such peoples – cannot be considered to be a powerful rival to the Han. By devaluing the peoples over whom he rules and using Han-style rhetoric to ingratiate himself with the Han imperial court, Tuo presents his leadership as mere child's play in comparison to that of the Han.

In trying to further unpack the statement attributed to Zhao Tuo above, it is worthwhile to note the way in which Man-yi peoples likely interacted with people from the Central States during the early imperial period. Man-yi peoples, after all, were not the ethnic minorities of the region, living in the hillsides and mountains and sidelined in the more inhospitable geographic zones, as James C. Scott's nomenclature "Zomia" would suggest.[33] On the contrary, the so-called Man-yi peoples were in the majority. They lived among transplants from the Central States in the larger cities of the South. In addition, there were many separate and homogeneous Man-yi units dispersed throughout the countryside that were not under the direct control of the local court. Sensitive border regions, inhabited primarily by aliens, were known as "marches" along the northern frontier.[34] In the South, however, alien tribes dispersed

[32] *Han shu*, 95.3851–52.

[33] James C. Scott, *The Art of Not Being Governed: An Anarchist History of Upland Southeast Asia* (New Haven: Yale University Press, 2009).

[34] On marches, see Hans Bielenstein, *The Bureaucracy of Han Times* (Cambridge: Cambridge University Press, 1980), pp. 99–100. The fact that many tribal peoples still lived in homogeneous settlements separate from more Han or mixed settlements is confirmed throughout the archaeological record. For the case of the Qujing Province in Yunnan, see Yao, "Culture Contact and Social Change," pp. 259–278.

throughout the countryside constituted no special administrative unit, perhaps because they were ubiquitous and that was the norm.

In a separate attempt to explain his usurpation of the title *Di*, we see Tuo representing himself again as leader of the Man-yi, this time identifying himself even more with such peoples. In such a passage, he complains that Empress Dowager Lü's actions revealed prejudice against his people – and, by extension, against himself, as both his court and kingdom were suffering from her embargos.[35] Again, he belittles himself as the "Old Chieftain of the Man-yi, Minister Tuo 蠻夷大長老夫臣佗."[36] As "leader of the Man-yi," rather than *Di*, Tuo identifies himself with explicit reference to his alien population, just as he allegedly did through his dress and behavior, as described in the *Han shu* encounter with Lu Jia. Here, by complaining about bias against the Man-yi, Tuo demonstrates both concern about their wellbeing and a desire to be their representative.

Such instances might be construed as Tuo identifying with – not identifying as – the southern peoples of his sprawling kingdom. Whether just rhetoric imagined by our authors or an accurate citation of Tuo's own words, the passage as a whole conveys an authorial intent to depict Tuo as a representative of Yue interest. In such a manner, it provides a challenge to the ways of the Hua-xia – a challenge that underscores Hua-xia weaknesses, limitations, or boundaries by accentuating the differences of the southern other. It also depicts a wily Tuo who is able to use such differences to attempt to gain leverage, power, or control over the situation. Again, whether this was really Tuo or just the author's (we assume: Sima Qian's) imagined depiction of him, it demonstrates an understanding that the act of assuming alterity (rhetorically through Sima's depiction, or in reality through Tuo's actions and words) was a means of harnessing the power of the remote and humble other to challenge normative power and ways. We are familiar with this type of challenge from the rhetorical uses of Yue found in the more philosophical texts of the Warring States period, discussed in Chapter 5.

There are other stories in the *Shi ji* that paint a picture of a formidable Han and a weak, backward Zhao Tuo of the Southern Yue kingdom. The following, lengthy passage from the "Account of Li Sheng and Lu Jia 酈生陸賈列傳" depicts Han emissary Lu Jia as a haughty and firm official who has no qualms about putting Tuo in his place. The scene occurs at an

[35] It is worth noting that Burton Watson translates, and, hence, understands this passage in a different way, depicting Zhao Tuo as saying, "[Empress Lü] is discriminating against me, treating me as one of the barbarians." Burton Watson, *Records of the Grand Historian of China, vol. II: The Age of Emperor Wu 140 to Circa 100 B.C.* (New York: Columbia University Press, 1961), p. 240. *Shi ji*, 113.2969.

[36] *Shi ji*, 113.2970.

initial meeting of the two in Southern Yue, in 196 BCE when Zhao Tuo accepts his position as subject king under the Han, but only after greeting Lu Jia like a native (sitting in the dustpan style and with his hair in a mallet-shaped bun), being reprimanded by the following words, and changing his mind because of the reprimand. This passage is intriguing on many counts, but especially as an example of the "taming the other" genre. It starts with Lu Jia's words – no doubt an imagined fiction – which reveal an arrogant disregard for the power and prestige of anything associated with the Yue:

> "Your majesty is a man of the Central States; your kin and brothers are all buried in Zhending. Now, your majesty goes against the nature that Heaven has given you and abandons the cap and belt.[37] If you desire with this far-flung land of Yue to rival the Han and become an enemy state, then you will meet with disaster . . .
>
> It would be appropriate for Your Majesty to welcome me in the suburbs and face north to announce your submission as a subject. Yet, here you wish to tempt your fate with this newly created and scattered kingdom of Yue. If the Han gets word of this, they will dig up and burn your ancestors' graves, laying to waste the remains of your lineage temple. The Han would but need to call upon a single general to gather up a force of 100,000 troops and face them against Yue, and the Yue people would commit regicide and surrender to the Han. This would be as easy as flipping one's hand."

> 足下中國人,親戚昆弟墳在真定。 今足下反天性,棄冠帶,欲以區區之越與天子抗衡為敵國,禍且及身矣 . . . 君王宜郊迎,北面稱臣,乃欲以新造未集之越,屈彊於此。漢誠聞之,掘燒王先人冢,夷 滅宗族,使一偏將將十萬眾臨越,則越殺王降漢,如反覆手耳.[38]

The passage tells us that the Han emissary, Lu Jia, is not impressed by Zhao Tuo's alleged adoption of Yue customs and lack of "Central States" (i.e., Hua-xia) ritual propriety. Intriguingly, it is neither Zhao Tuo's hairstyle nor the dustpan sitting style per se that angers Lu Jia; it is the fact that the former is consciously adopting alien customs in an attempt to flout the ritual norms of his own homeland, thereby signaling – through the process of cultural distancing – Tuo's intentions to maintain independence and distance from the newly formed Han Empire to his north. Having Zhao Tuo flout Zhou ritual norms is tantamount to an invitation for military punishment, which is forthcoming in Lu Jia's response.

What seems to be most abhorrent in Lu Jia's eyes is Zhao Tuo's disloyalty to his homeland and the fact that he is clearly flouting Zhou ritual norms. This type of rebellious presentation of one's identity is therefore not so much focused on a disapproval of the Yue other as it is

[37] The "cap and belt" represent appropriate Zhou paraphernalia worn by elite men.
[38] *Shi ji*, 97.2697.

a disapproval of the act of rejecting the self. Posing as the Yue other is not merely a signal of disloyalty; it is the flagrant rejection of one's homeland and ritual propriety, an open rejection of the self and its values.[39]

Readers may look at this passage and see a strongly skewed Han bias, packaged in terms of military threats and a cultural battle in which the inferior ways of the Yue should be abandoned in favor of the superior ways of the Hua-xia. Indeed, Lu Jia's response provides an effective justification for Zhao Tuo's complete and immediate turnaround from wayward renegade and to submissive and humbled former "man of the Central States." The story effectively reclaims the importance and power of Zhou religious beliefs vis-à-vis alien cultural mores.

It is likely that the account of Lu Jia might be more of a Han fantasy and tale of the victory of moral suasion over alien values. A few passages on, our suspicions of the story's rhetorical aims are confirmed when Zhao Tuo admits that he actually does not like living among the Yue barbarians: "In the midst of the Yue there is no one worth talking to. Ever since you have come, you have made me hear something new every day 越中無足與語, 至生來, 令我日聞所不聞!"[40] King Zhao Tuo's concession of boredom by Yue ignorance reveals the utter success Lu Jia had as a diplomat. Not only was the latter able to extract the desired goal of the king's political and ritual submission to the Han throne, but he was also able to allow Zhao Tuo to make an inner revelation concerning the inferiority of his life among the Yue people. This marks success of the highest order, one that is compatible with Ru goals of inner realization and transformation rather than outward compliance.

What is interesting about this entire passage is that we know from King Zhao Tuo's later actions that he must not have felt so humbled by his existence among the Yue. After all, he continued to defy the Han and act as an emperor throughout his later reign. The depiction of King Zhao Tuo's inner realization of Hua-xia cultural superiority and his humility is indeed humorous and quite unbelievable when we consider the reality of Zhao Tuo's prodigious political ambitions among the Yue, as described in part in Chapter 4.

Some passages of the *Shi ji*, especially those that contain dialog that allegedly took place in faraway places, should be viewed with suspicion and understood with an eye to their rhetorical and fictional qualities. Stories like the encounter between Lu Jia and Zhao Tuo are most likely complete fantasies that reveal more about the construction of a vision of

[39] As we have discussed in Chapter 6, the author of this dialog may have mixed up his "barbarian customs" by depicting a mallet-shaped bun, which was not necessarily associated with the Yue of the South.

[40] *Shi ji*, 97.2698.

the Hua-xia self as arbiter and ambassador of moral power than about any reality concerning the Yue other. The depictions of identity in such stories therefore help us see how Yue identity is mainly a function of the Hua-xia presentation of the self, not something constructed or presented independently from it.

In the *Shi ji*, the figure of Zhao Tuo is, at its most believable, a distant and not-well-understood political figure with great ambitions who challenged the superiority of Han rule from within his own kingdom. At other times, the record reveals him as a stock renegade figure, testing the limits of Han authority and the superiority of Hua-xia culture just as a toddler would test a parent. Such morality tales do not hesitate to slap Zhao Tuo on the wrists for his misguided behavior and rejection of core Hua-xia values. Their mode of narrating the psychological transformation of a lost and wayward figure serves as one of the Hua-xia strategies for reifying core concepts of the self and its proper development vis-à-vis outside challenges to the system.

Zhao Hu (Mo 眛), Zhao Yingqi, and the continuation of an imperial line

For the next Zhao ruler of Southern Yue, Zhao Hu 趙 胡, we witness a continuation of Tuo's rather independent attitude as sovereign over the Yue or Man-yi. Archaeological remains corroborate our textual data, providing new information about the extended use of the term *Di* for Southern Yue rulers. Zhao Hu was a grandson of Tuo, ruling over Southern Yue from 137 BCE to 122 BCE. Most scholars believe the occupant of the tomb at Xianggang Hill to be Zhao Hu (a seal found in the tomb refers to Zhao Mo, who is generally taken to be Hu), though they are not certain of it.[41] Here, I follow the dominant view that Hu was the tomb occupant, and I refer to him by the name provided by Sima Qian in the *Shi ji*, Zhao Hu, not the name provided by the tomb, Zhao Mo.

[41] Presuming the tomb occupant is Hu, then some controversy ensues, as archaeological sources suggest the occupant was called Mo 眛, rather than Hu. The three main explanations for the discrepancy between the textual and archaeological sources are as follows: 1) "Hu" was a clerical error in the received texts, and should have been "Mo" instead; 2) "Hu" was the king's Han name, while "Mo" was his local, Yue name; and 3) "Hu" and "Mo" were both his names, and constituted one of many possible names for any given individual according to Yue custom, which might have had even more complicated methods of naming people than the customary *ming* 名 (name), *zi* 字 (style-name), and *hao* 號 (honorific-name) of the Central States region. See Guangzhou shi wenwu guanli weiyuanhui, *Xi-Han Nanyue wang mu* 西漢南越王墓, 2 vols. (Beijing: Wenwu, 1991), p. 322. For a skeptic who claims the occupant to be Zhao Hu's father (and Zhao Tuo's son), Zhao Mei 趙眛, see Wu Haigui 吳海貴, "Xianggang Nanyue wang mu zhu xin kao 象崗南越王墓主新考," *Kaogu Wenwu* 考古輿文物 (2000): 3.

Like Tuo, Hu was especially savvy in his interactions with the Han, at one point sending his own son, Yingqi 嬰齊, to the Han court – ostensibly to act as a palace attendant (not a hostage) with civil duties to the Emperor.[42] As the *Shi ji* account relays, the state of Min-yue 閩粵 attacked the border towns of Southern Yue in 135 BCE. Zhao Hu sent a letter to the Han Emperor Wu asking for military aid, invoking the prohibition against calling out one's own troops without formal permission from the Han court. Emperor Wu responded with military aid, which had the favorable result of encouraging royalty in the state of Min-yue to kill their rebellious king and surrender to the Han, thereby staunching their attack on Southern Yue.

As a result of his peaceful and relatively cooperative relationship with the Han imperial court, Zhao Hu was given the posthumous title, "Civil King (Wen Wang)." Yet, the *Shi ji* account casts doubt upon Zhao Hu's actual consideration of himself as a subordinate king of the Han. For instance, while Hu sent his son, Yingqi, to attend the Emperor at court, he himself stayed behind and pleaded ill rather than visit the capital and pay ritual respect to the Son of Heaven. It is interesting to note that many medicinals were included in the tomb for King Hu of Southern Yue, possibly supporting the view that he had been prone to illness in life.[43] Just as Zhao Tuo had never visited the Han court in person, only sending envoys, tribute, and labor services when required, his successor Hu did the same, suggesting that he, too, only maintained minimal requirements for a smooth relationship with the Han. Such behavior suggests that Southern Yue submission to the Han – in the early years of both empires – was considered to be a diplomatic formality that ensured peaceful relations, trade, and communication with their northern neighbor. The first two "Emperors" of Southern Yue often chose the ways in which they wanted to comply with the terms of the agreement, demonstrating that they did not hold it binding in many ways. Though the *Shi ji* merely hints at it, Zhao Hu was also, effectively, the *Di* of Southern Yue.

Looking at the lavish tomb associated with Hu found at Xianggang Hill in modern-day Guangzhou City, we gain significant insights into the way in which its primary occupant, Zhao Hu, wished to represent himself in the afterworld. Through extensive appropriation of northern symbols of empire, Hu made his imperial aspirations clear. The tomb's layout and many of its grave goods reveal a significant northern influence, which

[42] Yü, "Han Foreign Relations," p. 452. For more on the civil, rather than military duties of the prince, see A. F. P. Hulsewé, *Remnants of Han Law* (Leiden: E. J. Brill, 1955), p. 154, note 87.

[43] See Guangzhou shi wenwu guanli weiyuanhui, *Xi-Han Nanyue wang mu*, p. 324.

Figure 8.1: Jade suit for king's corpse.

makes sense in light of the Zhao family's northern roots, but also supports the notion that early Zhao rulers employed tools and regalia to echo northern imperial power and better bolster their control.[44] The tomb, dug into the top of a hill, contains chambers and uses large stones to line the chamber walls, which Francis Allard states is reminiscent of "slightly earlier developments in funerary architecture in the North of China."[45] Furthermore, of the over 1,000 objects found in the tomb, a jade funerary suit and the inclusion of cooking and serving containers reveal the influence of mortuary practices and other cultural links to the north (Figure 8.1).[46]

Other objects, such as the "Yue-style" ding tripods, bronze buckets, *goudiao* 句鑃 bells, and the use of human sacrifice in burial ritual, suggest the maintenance and preservation of more native traditions (Figure 8.2). Fifteen human sacrifices were included in the tomb. As of yet, there is no analog in Han tombs for the use of human sacrifices, suggesting that this was either a legacy of Yue culture or perhaps an anachronistic use of

[44] Allard, "Frontiers and Boundaries," pp. 240–244. See also Francis Allard, "Interaction and Social Complexity in Lingnan during the First Millennium B.C.," *Asian Perspectives* 33.2 (1994): 309–326.

[45] Allard, "Frontiers and Boundaries," p. 241. [46] *Ibid.*

Figure 8.2: Southern Yue *goudiao* bells.

Central Plains rituals from much earlier times.[47] The set of eight bronze *goudiao* bells is the first of its kind found among Han Dynasty tombs and demonstrates how musical traditions unique to the Yue might have been enjoyed at the Southern Yue court. In sum, the evidence from Hu's tomb suggests that King Zhao Hu in death was identified primarily with mortuary practices that tied him into the greater ritual traditions of China's central and northern regions, although native traditions, prestige goods, and markers of distinction – as well as pervasive influences from the Chu culture – complicated such an identity considerably.[48]

There are two pieces of evidence, which, taken together, clearly support the view that Zhao Hu also identified himself as Emperor, or *Di*, of Southern Yue, and only minimally as a dependent of the Han. One object is a gold seal belonging to "Emperor Wen (*Wendi*; the Civil Emperor)" of the Southern Yue. Its inscription reads, "administrative seal of the Civil Emperor (*Wendi*

[47] Allard, "Frontiers and Boundaries," p. 241. Lothar von Falkenhausen has commented on the implications of ritual bronze tripods in this southern region in "The Use and Significance of Ritual Bronzes in the Lingnan Region during the Eastern Zhou Period," *Journal of East Asian Archaeology* 3.1–2 (2001): 193–236.

[48] Guangzhou shi wenwu guanli weiyuanhui, *Xi-Han Nanyue wang mu*, p. 1.

xing xi 文帝行璽)" implying that it was to be used by Hu in his capacity as emperor, not king (Figure 8.3).[49] Another piece of evidence that Zhao Hu used the title "Emperor" during his lifetime occurs in the form of a set of eight bronze *goudiao* bells mentioned above (see Figure 8.2), each bearing the inscription: "Produced by Music Bureau Artisans in Year Nine of the Civil Emperor's Reign 文帝九年樂府工造."[50] Here, "Emperor" refers not to the Han Civil Emperor but to the Yue Civil Emperor, Zhao Hu, as such a set of bells – being unique to the Yue – would not have been cast by smiths in Chang'an, much less cast in Chang'an and bestowed as gifts upon the king of Yue.

A key textual source also confirms that such a seal was produced for use during Zhao Hu's life, and that the latter referred to himself as the "Civil Emperor," just as his predecessor and grandfather, Zhao Tuo, had referred to himself as "Martial Emperor." According to the *Han shu*, Hu's son, Zhao Yingqi "hid the seals of his forebears, Emperor Wu and Emperor Wen 臧其先武帝文帝璽" upon taking office as the third king of Southern Yue.[51] Thus, around 122 BCE, when Yingqi ascended the throne, the fact that his two forebears had wrongfully usurped the title "Emperor" had either just come to the attention of the Han, or at the very least had become a matter that threatened to mar Han–Yue relations. Since Yingqi had personally served in the court of Han at Chang'an, it is possible that he was more keenly aware of the possible repercussions of such a transgression, or that he wished to publicly demonstrate his loyalty to Han in order to ameliorate relations with them. Perhaps most importantly, the beginning of Yingqi's reign corresponded to a period in which Han Emperor Wu was engaging in a massive build-up of Han military power (to be employed especially along the northern frontier, against the Xiongnu) and was completing his takeover of the kingdom of Huainan, north of Southern Yue.[52] In any case, both the gold seal and set of *goudiao* bells, as well as this textual reference in the *Han*

[49] Guangdongsheng bowuguan 廣東省博物館, "Guangdong kaogu shi nian gai shu" 廣東考古十年概述, in Wen wu bian ji wei yuan hui, ed., *Wenwu kaogu gongzuo shi nian* 文物考古工作十年, 1979–1989 (Beijing: Wenwu, 1991), pp. 222–223. See also Xiaoneng Yang, ed., *The Golden Age of Chinese Archaeology: Celebrated Discoveries from the People's Republic of China* (New Haven: Yale University Press, 1999), p. 413.

[50] The ninth year of Zhao Hu's reign would correspond to c. 129 BCE. Guangzhoushi wenwu guanli weiyuanhui, *Xi-Han Nanyue wang mu*, pp. 3–4.

[51] *Han shu*, 95.3854.

[52] For more on this, see Griet Vankeerberghen, *The Huainanzi and Liu An's Claim to Moral Authority* (Albany: State University of New York Press, 2001). For an account of Han Emperor Wu's shift of policy toward Southern Yue during this period, see Huang Qingchang 黃慶昌, "Lun Xi Han wangchao yu Nanyue guo de guanxi 論西漢王朝與南越國的関系," *Nanfang wenwu* 南方文物 (2003): 75. See also Nicola di Cosmo, "Han Frontiers: Toward an Integrated View," *Journal of the American Oriental Society* 129.2 (2009): 199–214.

Figure 8.3: Golden seal of Emperor Wen (poster view).

Shu, suggest the double identity of the first two kings of Southern Yue. They corroborate the suspicions of Hu's disloyalty – hinted at above in the *Shi ji* references – and implicate Zhao Tuo's successors in the same identity ruse as Tuo himself.

Drawing upon evidence from textual records and Southern Yue tombs throughout the region, Zhang Rongfang 張榮芳 argues that the early administration of Southern Yue was specifically modeled on that of the Han, using a system comprising small kingdoms and provinces and commanderies regulated in a centralized, bureaucratized style.[53] The *Shi ji* account corroborates this claim by showing how Zhao Tuo, for example, sometimes behaved according to a (Han) imperial model, rather than assume a role more befitting of a king. Not only did he threaten border regions with military force, Tuo also used gifts and bribes to convince regional overlords such as the Min-yue, Western Ou, and Luo-yue to submit to his ultimate authority.[54] This suggests not only that Southern Yue rulers drew upon administrative and political trends of the day, but that they also envisioned Southern Yue as an empire developing in parallel to the Han. By anointing subjects as vassal "kings," Southern Yue rulers such as Tuo and Hu laid claim to the position of *Di* within the Empire of Southern Yue.

Stories concerning Zhao Yingqi, his son, Xing, and Yingqi's "Central States" wife from the Jiu 摎 clan of Handan 邯鄲 continue to pique our curiosity about the dubious and ever-changing relationship between the Zhao family and the Han imperial court.[55] We know from the *Han shu* reference above that Yingqi took measures to hide the seals of his forebears to destroy evidence that they had referred to themselves as *Di*. He also did not fail to send special, exotic gifts to the Han court, such as a trained elephant and a talking bird, which he sent to Han Emperor Wu in 121 BCE. No doubt, Yingqi's personal ties to the Han court were somewhat tight, as he had served the Han Emperor as a palace attendant during his youth and married a woman from the Central States region.[56]

All this notwithstanding, there is reason to believe that the legacy of Southern Yue autonomy from the Han prevailed even during Yingqi's reign. The *Shi ji* informs us that Yingqi, much like his father, Hu, disregarded the admonitions of Han envoys to go to the capital to visit the Emperor. It states:

> Yingqi still took pleasure in unilaterally deciding upon death sentences and acting morally unrestrained, and he feared that if he paid visit [to the Han court] he would be tried [for his offenses] under Han law and be [expected to act] as the other inner lords [of the empire]. So he kept claiming he was ill and thus did not pay a visit.
>
> 嬰齊尚樂擅殺生自恣, 懼入見要用漢法, 比內諸侯, 固稱病, 遂不入見。[57]

[53] Zhang Rongfang, "Han chao zhi li Nanyueguo." [54] *Shi ji*, 113.2969.

[55] Handan was located in the former state of Zhao 趙, in northern China, modern-day Hebei Province.

[56] *Han shu*, 6.176. [57] *Shi ji*, 113.2971.

Insofar as Yingqi did not make personal visits to the Han court, he behaved like Tuo and Hu, enjoying a special status within Southern Yue as de facto sovereign, who stood above Han law itself. Thus, despite the fact that he had never officially claimed to rule as a *Di*, Yingqi seems to have been the last Southern Yue Emperor to have enjoyed de facto sovereignty over his state and a significant amount of distance from the Han court.

The three early rulers of Southern Yue seemed clearly to understand that the distance and climatic differences between them and the Han court were enough to give them some measure of autonomy and protection from its influence – or, at the very least, its military wrath. As long as Yue was not openly rebellious, its kings could abide by this law of avoidance and rule over their own kingdom with absolute power – virtually untouched by Han laws and customs. From within their kingdom, they represented themselves as all-powerful *Di* leaders who were on relatively equal footing with the Han *Di* to their north. Indeed, their identity as *Di* centered power around themselves and the Southern Yue court; while the concept and its expression in politics had been adopted from the North, its use as a tool for consolidating and maintaining imperial power was certainly not limited to Han leaders ruling over the erstwhile Central States regions.

The loss of Southern Yue power and political identity

Southern Yue notions of autonomy and independence changed markedly in 113 BCE, when Emperor Wu adopted a more aggressive, military strategy toward the kingdoms on the margins of the Han. He sent an envoy named Anguo Shaoji 安國少季 to pressure the king of Southern Yue, now Yingqi's son, Xing 興, and his mother, the Queen Dowager, to pay a visit to the Han capital. This must have been a very calculated move on Emperor Wu's part, since years before the Queen Dowager had had an affair with this envoy before marrying King Zhao Yingqi of Southern Yue. Resuming a relationship with Anguo Shaoji, the Queen Dowager acted against the interests of the Yue people, many of whom knew about the illicit affair. A woman from what Sima Qian refers to as the "Central States" and not at all affiliated with Yue, the Queen Dowager had already very little to ingratiate her to the Yue ministers and elites (*guo ren* 國人).[58] They began paying allegiance to the prime minister, Lü Jia, rather than to Zhao Xing and his mother. What ensues is a story of treachery and intrigue, the likes of which are fit for a Shakespearean play, in which Lü

[58] *Shi ji*, 113.2972.

Jia emerges as the true warrior of the Yue, forging an identity associated with Yue independence from Han control. Thus, the family of Zhao, while winning itself the positions of king and emperor over the Southern Yue, eventually succumbed to Han pressures. Zhao Xing and his mother allied themselves with the Han against their own prime minister and his supporters. They represented the "Han" or "Central States" outsiders in a way that Zhao Tuo, Hu, and even Yingqi (who had served for years at the Han court as an imperial attendant) never had.

The language used in the *Shi ji* account of the fall of Southern Yue in 111 BCE reveals Yue concerns about "inner membership" (*nei shu* 內屬) with the Han court. We will recall that Southern Yue had officially been admitted as a dependent kingdom during Gaozu's reign. We also note that Emperor Wen of the Han had succeeded in having Zhao Tuo formally rescind the title "Emperor" and resume official relations with Han envoys and inspectors as before. All this suggests that Southern Yue was technically an "inner member" of the Han since its early days as a kingdom. Why should Zhao Xing and the Han court be worried about achieving such a status?

It is possible that before Han Emperor Wu, Southern Yue was not inspected or checked upon by the Han in the same vigorous manner as the commanderies, where official inspectors would have been dispatched at irregular intervals to oversee local governments.[59] New references to "inner membership" around 112 BCE show that Han attitudes toward its kingdoms were changing and that it wished to tighten its grip over even the most far-flung kingdoms. One might look to the imperial government's reforms of 145 BCE – which abolished many administrative offices in the kingdoms and stripped each king's ability to appoint most of his administrators – as one of the harbingers of such change.[60] Imperial control over certain, more nearby, kingdoms increased dramatically, and such control, in turn, might have had the unintended result of pushing the most distant kingdoms from the center – like those of the various Yue kingdoms – even farther away from imperial reach. In such a way, the status of Southern Yue might have regressed from being considered an "inner member" to being thought of as a peripheral, non-participating kingdom.

Nonetheless, "inner membership" with the Han was something that the Yue could still try to establish, and that they did. Perhaps out of fear that his own power at home was at risk, or, afraid of the increasing military arsenal and ambitions of Han Emperor Wu, Zhao Xing sent envoys to

59 *Han shu*, 95.3850. Bielenstein, *The Bureaucracy of Han Times*, p. 90.
60 *Shi ji*, 113.2972–73. Bielenstein, *The Bureaucracy of Han Times*, pp. 106–107.

memorialize the Han throne, asking that he be given the status of an "inner lord (*nei zhu hou* 內諸候)."[61] This marked Xing's willingness to submit to the Han central state and accede to its political authority. When his request to Emperor Wu was granted, Xing made efforts to remove any stigma of Southern Yue as remote, backward, and different from the Han. Effectively, he took steps to transform Southern Yue identity and customs vis-à-vis the Han so as to make his kingdom truly more amenable to Han laws and systems of control.

First, he asked that the Emperor remove the border controls between Southern Yue and Han. Second, King Zhao Xing abolished the ancient laws of tattooing and cutting the noses off of criminals, using Han laws instead.[62] And third, he vowed to act in accordance with the rites appropriate to other "inner lords," which included making a journey to court in person once every three years to bring tribute, ensure loyalty, and pay one's respects.[63] This increased frequency and amount of contact between the two courts through better road networks and regular royal tributes would have made it far more difficult for the king to get away with calling himself an emperor in his own lands. The new measures were clearly intended to weaken Xing's royal power, increasing his accountability to the Han Emperor, and giving the latter better access and control over Southern Yue than ever before.

The allegiance of Zhao Xing to the Han, unlike the nominal allegiance of his forefathers, seems not to have been duplicitous, demonstrating an abandonment of the Zhao family's so-called "secret" identity as *Di* of Southern Yue. In consequence, it appears that Xing's affiliation with the Yue people (*Yue ren* 越人) declined, since, as the *Shi ji* account relates, around this time his subjects shifted their loyalty away from the king and increasingly gave it to his prime minister, Lü Jia, whom we will discuss in the next chapter.[64] It is possible that the reference here to "Yue people" does not really imply the Yue population at large, but the regional Yue

[61] *Shi ji*, 113.2972.

[62] Despite this change, there must have been many statutes of the Yue that remained in place for quite some time. For example, we know that around 40 CE, The General Who Calms the Waves, Ma Yuan 馬援, was still explaining to the natives the differences between Han and Yue statutes. Michael Loewe, *The Government of the Qin and Han Empires: 221 B.C.E.–220 CE* (Indianapolis: Hackett Publishing Company, 2006), p. 58. The "ancient" practices referred to in this passage were not exclusive to the Yue but were widespread among the states of the Zhou sphere before the rise of the Han. For an explanation of the Han abolition of tattooing as a punishment in 167 BC. – as opposed to a stigma – see Hulsewé, *Remnants of Han Law*, pp. 124–125. Also, the court of Southern Yue did not sustain itself through tax collection but most likely through forced labor on royal fields, corvée labor projects, royal monopolies on maritime trade, etc. See Lü, *Nanyue wang mu*, pp. 148–149.

[63] *Shi ji*, 113.2972. [64] *Shi ji*, 113.2972.

leaders (local chieftains and lords) who might have provided the court with support and military backing. Regardless, this loss of Yue support suggests that Xing either no longer presented himself as Yue, or no longer aligned himself with certain Southern Yue elite interests in the same way his forefathers had. Allied with an outsider mother from the "Central States" and various Han envoys, the young king more or less embraced the identity of the loyal Han minister, thereby helping bring the Zhao lineage of Yue Emperors to an end.

Conclusion

Through a detailed discussion of several royal figures of the Southern Yue empire and kingdom, I analyze variable types of responses to the Han imperial state and its associated, more northern cultures. I show how each constituted a different mode of asserting and expressing one's identity, which was contingent upon contemporary, local conditions and the perceived benefits of cultural or political adoption and resistance. In particular, I underscore instances in which individuals appropriated or implicitly accepted the values and habits associated with either the Huaxia or the local Yue culture, paying heed to their likely reasons for choosing – or, indeed, falling into – any given mode of doing so.

We might interpret certain acts of appropriating Yue culture or Han political trappings, titles, and symbols of power as a form of political masquerading intended to increase and strengthen one's local control. The risky act of usurping the title "Emperor" at home while at the same time doing one's utmost to cover up such an act vis-à-vis the Han imperial world is one that demands great political finesse. Maintaining two different and contradictory identities – each of which served a beneficial purpose to the beholder but posed considerable risks – could only be successfully pulled off by a relative outlier such as the Southern Yue. Both its physical distance from the Han court and its relative strength vis-à-vis the early Han (Han was at this time, after all, still a new empire with many other problems to attend) were facilitating factors in Zhao Tuo's and Zhao Hu's successes in this area. Even though the kingdom of Southern Yue would not last past a century, the precedent had been set for the existence of a powerful southern imperial regime. Despite (and also, perhaps in part, because of) borrowing from northern templates of imperial rule and ritual symbols of authority, the Southern Yue court successfully established itself as the first empire south of the Yangzi.

By referring to themselves as emperors rather than kings subordinate to the Han, Zhao Tuo and Zhao Hu forged more of a political than cultural identity for themselves. The use of the nomenclature, *Di* ("Emperor"), by the first two Southern Yue rulers, while borrowed from the North, was an act of appropriation that wholly served Southern Yue imperial designs, lending power to the users and reflecting the strength of their own agency from within their own realms of power. No doubt, however, the mere use of the title *Di* would have influenced the way Yue elites, not to mention the Southern Yue Emperor himself, viewed their own independence and status vis-à-vis the Han Empire. In this way, the political identity of emperor would have influenced and strengthened elite claims to a legitimate, powerful Southern Yue identity. By conceiving of oneself as a member of an empire, the ruling classes and elite of Southern Yue would have imagined themselves as being at the center of an important polity in its own right, with its own characteristic identity, rather than at the periphery in a center–periphery conceptual scheme.

In terms of Han influence on Yue customs and identity, it is important to examine the clues concerning the nature of "inner membership" in the Han imperium. By Emperor Wu's time, the Han court had hoped to secure its control over wayward, far-out kingdoms by holding them accountable to Han systems of laws and ritual protocols, which required that such kingdoms spend considerable resources to participate as a member of the larger imperial community. Such measures were intended to unify customs, laws, and administrative practices throughout the empire, therefore contributing to the eventual demise of local, Southern Yue habits of government control. Both the Queen Dowager and King Zhao Xing chose to submit themselves wholesale to the Han by accepting the rules and status of inner membership, which affected taxation, laws, border controls, and more. Such situations support the notion that the Han Empire was successful at sinicization measures temporarily and on some counts, especially with respect to laws, administration, and certain rituals related to the court.

Our sources also show that in time the military power of the Han grew to become formidable to the rulers of Southern Yue, especially under the rule of Han Emperor Wu. Yet the accounts in the *Shi ji* and *Han shu* give us reason to suspect that Yue culture and identity were hardly pushed aside for Han ways, even in the later years of the Southern Yue. The fact that the early Zhao kings conducted much of their business without reference to themselves as subjects of the Han points to the construction of a rather autonomous sense of the state of Southern Yue – this, despite the fact that they often employed Central Plains administrative or military technologies to bolster the power at home. Their use as well of native cultural symbols (such as the *goudiao* bells) to reinforce local prestige bespeaks the agency of the early Southern Yue rulers, underscoring their abilities to draw expediently from local and non-local technologies of control.

It is unlikely that the first two Zhao rulers "went native" in the manner that our histories would like for us to believe. A more measured evaluation of the evidence suggests that these rulers acted and viewed themselves as sovereigns with nearly complete power over their people. Even though they accepted formal positions as subject kingdoms to the larger Han Empire, this seemed to have been done to receive certain trade and military benefits, not to mention to mollify and maintain a peaceful relationship with their powerful northern neighbor.

Rather than "going native," these rulers "went sovereign," or "went imperial" – employing every bit of a claim to authority available to establish and maintain control over their large empire/kingdom. So whereas the Han viewed Southern Yue affiliation as a sign of the latter's ultimate subservience and allegiance to the Han and its ritual protocols, the constant flouting of such protocols and the various acts of independent sovereignty by the first two Zhao rulers suggest that such an affiliation could mean something quite different back home. Indeed, to them it could serve as an important piece of external, exotic sanction and ritual legitimacy that could be used to boost their own control – as Southern Yue kings and emperors – over their peoples.

9 Yue identity as armed resistance to the Han imperium

Identity is often created, maintained, and solidified through acts of resistance or armed engagement. Having examined the complexities of the formation of political identities in Southern Yue during the early imperial period, we now turn our attention to an analysis of moments of intense standoff and struggle – moments of armed resistance that often go hand-in-hand with the formulation of Yue identity against neighboring powers or the status quo. In the brief period of almost a century during the early Han period (c. 200–110 BCE), and then again in 40 CE, we have textual records and descriptions of at least four different rebellions or defensive, armed encounters launched by certain Yue individuals or states against the Han. All of them count as attempts at extrication from the power of the Han court and lay claim to an independent, Yue kingdom. In what follows, I discuss these armed engagements, highlighting the ways in which the outright rejection of imperialist forces served perhaps as one of the strongest factors in the creation of a more lasting Yue identity in the South.

The four armed encounters are as follows: 1) 138 and 135 BCE, Min-yue attacks on its neighbors and the Han response, 2) 113 BCE, the rebellion of Prime Minister Lü Jia 呂嘉 of the Southern Yue and fight for Southern Yue independence, 3) 111 BCE, the rebellion of King Zou Yushan and fight for Eastern Yue independence, and 4) 40–43 CE, the rebellion of the Trung sisters in Guangxi. While there were other armed encounters among various Yue kingdoms or forces in the early imperial period, we do not have enough information concerning some of these engagements to warrant an extended discussion of identity.[1]

[1] *Shi ji*, 114. One such example is that of Eastern Ou's involvement in the Rebellion of the Seven Kingdoms in 154 BCE. For this latter incident, the *Shi ji* merely alerts us to Eastern Ou's involvement in an unsuccessful attempt to over-throw Han authority, which was spearheaded by King Liu Pi of Wu in alliance with many other powerful neighbors (excepting Min-yue and Southern Yue). Of interest is the fact that it was the men of Eastern Ou – likely in the face of certain defeat – who were successfully bribed by the Han to assassinate the instigator, the king of Wu. After this last stand of rebellion, the kingdom of Eastern Ou (also known as Eastern Sea) did not create very much trouble for its Hua-xia

Min-yue aggression toward its southern neighbors

Two military standoffs in 138 and 135 BCE concerning a cluster of interconnected powers – the Min-yue, Southern Yue, Eastern Ou, and Han – are worth examining in greater detail to gain a better understanding of the many political identities associated with the Yue in the early imperial period. In Sima Qian's *Shi ji*, this period witnessed the development of a kingdom of Min-yue that pursued aggressive, expansionist policies and attacked its Yue neighbors: first the Eastern Ou, and then the Southern Yue. The account does not give us many of the reasons for such aggression, although if one considers the multiple accounts spread throughout the *Shi ji* of the various Yue states, one may find enough clues to piece together some inconspicuous elements of the story.

In 138 BCE, the then-reigning king of Min-yue attacked Eastern Ou by surrounding the capital city with Min-yue troops. This attack was instigated by the refugee son of Liu Pi 劉濞 (King of Wu), who had spearheaded the Rebellion of the Seven Kingdoms (against the Han Empire) in 154 BCE. The son's name was Liu Ziju. Eastern Ou had aided in the assassination of Ziju's father, and so Ziju sought revenge for this through the help of the state of Min-yue, where he had been taking refuge after the rebellion. The *Shi ji* reads: "[Liu Ziju] always tried to persuade Min-yue to attack Eastern Ou 常勸閩越擊東甌."[2] Whether or not this was the primary motivating factor behind the attack in 138 BCE, we cannot know. There is very little in the historiography of the period that suggests any other reason for this attack, although it would have been likely that the very transition from Han Emperor Jing to Han Emperor Wu in 141 BCE would have aroused further anxiety among leaders of frontier kingdoms concerning the imperial aims of the Han. The Min-yue attack on Eastern Ou might have been an attempt by the king of Min-yue to strike a weaker target in the hopes of annexing it and gaining more political leverage against an increasingly threatening Han state. This interpretation is bolstered by the fact that the Han did not merely ignore the advances of Min-yue. They promptly responded by sending military troops to staunch the siege. So rather than view this inter-Yue attack as something concerning exclusively Yue business (with a smattering of revenge by Wu thrown in),

neighbors to the north. Eastern Ou's status as a seat of Yue culture and political power seems to have waned thereafter, especially since many of the elite and key members of the population were moved farther inland, as the political history outlined in Chapter 4 tells us. The case of Eastern Ou is a case of short-lived defiance (but never on its own) and then total submission to Han leadership and protection. Indeed, Eastern Ou resistance was not carried out in extended or extreme ways.

[2] *Shi ji*, 14.2980.

we might surmise that the real power struggle at issue involved Min-yue and the Han, not Min-yue and the Eastern Ou.

In 135 BCE King Zou Ying of Min-yue attacked Southern Yue for reasons that are not clearly stated in the histories. We know from the account of Southern Yue, however, that during Empress Lü's reign roughly forty-five to fifty years earlier, King/Emperor Zhao Tuo of the Southern Yue attacked border areas in the Changsha region, and that after the Empress' death around 180 BCE, he continued to attack in all directions around his borders, including Min-yue. In combination with military force, Tuo used material bribes to force kingdoms like Min-yue to submit (at least in name, or perhaps only yielding their border regions – the record is unclear about this) to his authority. Given this bad history between Southern Yue and Min-yue, it is no doubt of great significance that King Zou Ying of the Min-yue attacked Southern Yue shortly after King Zhao Tuo's death (the date for Zhao Tuo's death is 137 BCE). In this light, the Min-yue attack on Southern Yue might be understood to have been part of a long-standing feud concerning territorial claims and authority over the Min-yue and Southern Yue frontier.

Min-yue military action against the Southern Yue may have served the double goal of increasing Min-yue territory and authority vis-à-vis the Han while simultaneously decreasing that of its southern rival. We should therefore consider Min-yue aggression in the 130s in terms of a series of pre-emptive, southerly strikes intended to stave off Han encroachment and potential takeover. With the dissolution of the kingdom of Eastern Ou, Min-yue lost an important buffer zone between itself and the Han. One way of recouping the loss of its protection against Han incursion was to expand itself in perhaps the only other direction it deemed feasible: southward toward Southern Yue. So while Min-yue aggression appears in the history books as the spontaneous whim of a foolhardy and greedy king, Zou Ying, a more careful look at the geopolitical circumstances facing the state (which potentially also included revenge as a motive) reveals that such aggression may justifiably be interpreted as a state's pre-emptive, defensive move and bid for survival.

What does this say about Min-yue identity? The incident as described in the *Shi ji* unfortunately says nothing from the perspective of the players in Min-yue. Instead, it describes the actions of the key Min-yue leaders (Zou Ying and his brother, Zou Yushan) in the third person and in terms of political expediencies: Zou Ying and Zou Yushan are both implicated in plotting revolts; Zou Yushan later reconsiders and assassinates his brother, presenting his head to the Han in an effort at reconciliation; the Han thanks Yushan but names its own puppet as king of the region (now called "Yue-yao"); and Zou Yushan defies the Han by declaring himself king and forcing Han to acknowledge him formally as "King of Eastern Yue."[3] From this we learn that regional lords such as the king of Yao, who descended from former Yue kings, were ruling over indigenous populations and could be cherry-picked by the Han to disrupt local power in Min-yue. We also learn that the Han had a difficult time enforcing its contrivances from afar, since King Yushan was the leader of choice in the region, and not the Han Emperor's pick. Intriguingly, Zou Yushan and his brother are presented as disloyal subjects who stood in opposition to Han interests. This is especially hinted at when Sima Qian depicts Yushan as a greedy and conniving warlord, saying that the latter "displayed his might in his country so that he garnered many followers, and he secretly declared himself king 威行於國, 國民多屬, 竊自立為王."[4]

Given that Yue or indigenous supporters of Yushan versus Chou divided themselves along political, not ethnic lines, it seems fair to say that the operating identity implied in this story is not Yue in any generic sense of ethnicity or culture, but Yue-yao, or Eastern Yue. Such an identity was political and based on the king or state with which one was aligned or allied. Despite such paltry information about identity beyond the political sphere, it is possible to conclude that the Min-yue state was trying to survive and stake out its own claims to independence or self-sovereignty at this time. This is clear from its aggressive acts toward its neighbors in 138 and 135 BCE, and from Zou Yushan's secret acts of proclaiming himself king despite the Han attempt to unseat him from power.

Lü Jia and the Rebellion of Southern Yue

Though the description of Lü Jia in Southern Yue is extremely brief in comparison with that of the Zhao royal clan (discussed in Chapter 8), it nonetheless provides important information about identity politics relevant to the frontier court from about 112 to 111 BCE, which culminated in the downfall of Southern Yue in 111 BCE. Lü Jia had served in the capacity of prime minister to the last three Zhao rulers: Hu, Yingqi, and Xing. He was not only greatly involved in the politics of Southern Yue, but he was also entwined with the Zhao clan and royal lineage through marriage alliances of various sorts. Many current Chinese scholars claim that Lü was Yue himself, though I have not been able to find confirmation in the early record of this as a fact.[5] The *Shi ji* informs us that over seventy

[3] *Shi ji*, 114.2981–82. [4] *Shi ji*, 114.2981.

[5] See Yang Zhaorong 楊兆榮, "Xi-Han Nanyue xiang Lü Jia yizu ru Dian ji qi lishi yingxiang shitan 西漢南越相呂嘉遺族入滇及其理史影響試探," in *Nanyueguo shiji yan tao hui*, pp. 31–41. Perhaps the fact that our sources take pains to mention Lü's marital

members of his family held high positions at court, and that all of his sons and daughters were married into the royal Zhao family.[6] In addition, Lü had close ties to the military; his younger brother was a general who would serve as a key facilitator in the conflict with Han forces at the end of the Southern Yue Dynasty.[7] We also learn that Lü was related by marriage to another Zhao king, King Qin of Cangwu 蒼梧秦王, a kingdom situated near modern-day northeastern Guangxi and Southern Hunan provinces.[8] Clearly, no matter how local Lü Jia was in terms of his lineage's historical connections with the people of Southern Yue, we know in fact that his family was also deeply inbred with the Zhao family that hailed from north China, as well as other Zhao royalty spread throughout the empire/kingdom.

Though Lü Jia's family history fails to yield definitive evidence of a Yue ancestry, his political identity imparts vital information about conceptions of identity among the people of Southern Yue during the reign of Han Emperor Wu. Indeed, there are several indications in the *Shi ji* account that Lü Jia embodied typical Yue interests. First, Lü had been popular among the Yue even before his revolt against the Han. The *Shi ji* states that he had "obtained the hearts of the masses to a greater degree than the king himself 得眾心愈於王," and that "the people of Yue trusted him 越人信之," so that "many of them acted as his 'ears and eyes 多為耳目者.'"[9] Second, he garnered tremendous support for his revolt against the Han, not just through those members of his family (like his younger brother) who were generals or other key administrators and military commanders, but through ordinary Yue folks living in and around the capital city of Panyu. In one instance, the Southern Yue people contributed to Lü's rebellion by ensnaring an initial band of 2,000 Han soldiers en route to Panyu. The Yue people initially put up a false front by opening up the roads and supplying food to the Han soldiers, allowing the latter to move effortlessly toward the outskirts of Panyu.[10] Then, once lured inside and deep within the Yue borders, Lü and his men pounced on and exterminated all of them.[11]

connections with the expatriot Zhao royal family, we are to assume that most of his other kinsfolk were local.

[6] *Shi ji*, 113.2972. [7] *Shi ji*, 113.2973–74. [8] *Shi ji*, 113.2972.

[9] *Shi ji*, 113.2972. The extent to which "*Yue ren*" refers to the common people is unclear and is complicated by the simultaneous mention of the "masses." It appears that Yue support for Lü extended beyond the elite leadership into the population somewhat.

[10] Sima's account but vaguely refers here to the "Yue," not "Yue people." In this instance, the context seems to imply ordinary "Yue people," as opposed to Lü Jia's military men, in order for the ruse to have been convincing to the Han soldiers.

[11] *Shi ji*, 113.2974.

Third, Lü Jia promoted a vision of Yue independence by appealing throughout the kingdom to a prevailing sense of Yue identity and common purpose against a threatening outsider. Once the Han had invaded the border towns of Southern Yue, Lü Jia attacked the Southern Yue palace, assassinating King Xing, his mother the Queen Dowager, and all the Han envoys present. He then set up a new Yue king, Zhao Jiande 趙建德, who was the eldest son of the previous king and a wife of Yue descent.[12] Given Lü's popularity among the people and renegade status vis-à-vis the Han court, one might think that he would simply have usurped the throne after having ousted the king. Instead, he chose to install a member of the Zhao family with more local ties to the Yue people (than the previous king). While Lü may have done this to keep the remaining members of the Zhao family (many of whom were related to him through marriage) on his side, his particular choice of a king of Yue descent appears to have gone beyond mere respect for individual members of the Zhao family. His actions could be interpreted as a most politically expedient form of identity construction: Lü was gathering forces around a vision of what was at once native (Yue) and linked to the already firmly established imperial identity of the Zhao royal clan.

A sense of Southern Yue identity prevails in the following proclamation from Lü, which Sima Qian claims was sent throughout the kingdom just before Lü committed the above-mentioned regicide:

> The King is very young. The Queen Dowager is from the Central States; in addition, she has had illicit relations with a [Han] envoy. Focused on having [Southern Yue] become an "inner member" [of Han], she intends to take all the former kings' priceless treasures and present them to the Son of Heaven in an effort to curry favor with him. She will be accompanied by many attendants, and when they arrive in Chang'an, they will be seized and placed in bondage. In seizing a momentary advantage for herself, she has neglected the sacred altars of the Zhao family, and has no intent on caring and planning for future generations!
>
> 王年少。太后，中國人也，又與使者亂，專欲內屬，盡持先王寶器入獻天子以自媚，多從人，行至長安，虜賣以為僮僕。取自脫一時之利，無顧趙氏社稷，為萬世慮計之意。[13]

Lü's proclamation reads much like a manifesto of Southern Yue independence, dressed in the language of ritual respect for the Zhao ruling clan. From it, we see that his stance actually runs counter to that held by previous Zhao kings, who had each ceded nominally to the Han. But Lü faced a very different situation than the previous Zhao rulers, who had likely realized that they could successfully keep the Han at bay through

[12] *Ibid.* [13] *Shi ji*, 113.2974.

acts of diplomatic and ritual appeasement. Lü, not a king, served a boy king who had been highly influenced by his "Central States" mother, the Queen Dowager, and an unequivocal advocate of Han control. King Xing's act of writing the Emperor to request the status of inner lord marked a watershed moment in Yue history in which the kingdom was placed under obligation to follow Han laws in addition to ritual protocols as never before.[14] From that moment on, it would have been unlikely that Southern Yue, under the control of Lü Jia, could have recovered or retreated to past types of relationships with the Han. So, unlike for the earliest Yue kings, submission to the Han was now an all-or-nothing game. In analyzing Lü's declaration, we must therefore keep in mind these new choices facing Southern Yue as a kingdom, as well as the highly politicized context of the statement.

Lü's divisive statements distinguish Southern Yue from Han identity in no uncertain terms, thus clarifying his intent to sever the connection to the Han. Southern Yue identity is marked by its own treasures, history, and, especially, a sacred, royal lineage. The Queen Dowager, he claims, is not trustworthy because her loyalties are aligned with the Central States, as opposed to the Southern Yue polity, its people, and its royal line. Moreover, in referring to the Central States and not the Han, Lü conjures up the general, cultural and political superpowers of the past, pitting Southern Yue against an outsider that transcends political boundaries.[15] He also plays upon local pride by invoking the imagery of bondage and subservience to alien overlords, especially since many of the attendants who were to be sent up to Chang'an would have been local Yue people. He notes how the Queen Dowager plans to use Southern Yue treasures and people as tokens to gain favor with the Han overlords. Lastly, he criticizes the Queen Dowager for betraying the efforts and labors of past Zhao rulers in planning for the future of Southern Yue. In other words, Lü rhetorically points out that the Zhao clan would not have wished for the destruction of their own ruling house, the loss of Southern Yue treasures, and the complete subservience of Southern Yue to Han. In short, earlier Zhao rulers would not have sold Southern Yue as a slave to Han interests, as the Queen Dowager was doing.

One will recall how the people of Southern Yue ensnared the first 2,000 advancing troops sent by the Han to punish Lü's misdeeds. With the help

[14] The *Shi ji* informs us that from that moment on, the Yue abandoned their old laws of branding and cutting off the noses of those convicted of certain crimes.

[15] Such an identification of the Queen Dowager as a person from the "Central States" (*zhong guo ren* 中 國 人), and not the Han state or people, is intriguing. It suggests that a person's identity could be associated with historical, geographic regions, and not necessarily the current empire or their specific hometown.

of local people, Lü's soldiers were able to slaughter and defeat them before they made it to the capital of Panyu. This suggests that Lü's actions, and quite possibly his manifesto, struck a chord with the Southern Yue people at the time, that they identified with the call for outrage intimated by it, that they supported Southern Yue independence, and that they joined in the fight against Han forces to try to achieve it. It therefore seems fair to claim that such a manifesto resonated with what many elites and people thought it meant to be Southern Yue as opposed to Han or "Central States," and that Lü's metaphor of Southern Yue bondage vis-à-vis the Han may have been something that the Yue people of the time understood and responded to by choosing to act and fight on Lü's side.

One should note that, like the last Southern Yue king, Zhao Xing, there were also a few Yue leaders and people who chose not to identify themselves with local interests and rally behind the cause of Southern Yue autonomy. The *Shi ji* account also tells us that at least three military generals from Yue fought for the Han against Lü's rebels in Southern Yue: two served as naval generals, and one was charged with leading newly released convicts from the southwest regions of Ba and Shu.[16] Though we are in want of information regarding the histories of these so-called Yue men, we may justifiably conclude that one's home region did not necessarily define one's personal identity or political loyalties. Also, as Han generals lay siege and set fire to the capital city of Panyu, they offered defectors the seals of marquises and other titles in exchange for their loyalty and surrender.[17] Many inhabitants of the capital chose such enticing reward over death and the stigma of being on the losing side. Those who defected were sent back to canvass for more Yue people to do the same.[18] Such stories indicate to us that preserving outward loyalty to the Yue was not something many individuals were willing to die for. Indeed, the *Shi ji* account gives the impression that the goal of Southern Yue independence was rather easily relinquished in the face of Han military might, but this is likely a bias of our sources.

[16] *Shi ji*, 113.2975. These would have been beneficiaries of Emperor Wudi's general amnesty. The *Han shu* states that all the Han generals led convicts. *Han shu*, 6.186–87.

[17] Archaeological remains of the "Southern Yue Palace" in former Panyu, now in downtown Guangzhou City, corroborate historical accounts of the burning of the city. See Allard, "Frontiers and Boundaries," p. 239. The flames had been so ferocious that they even burnt the stone sides of a canal. (Personal visit to the site, 5/2008.) See also Wu Hongqi 吳宏岐, "Nanyue guo du Panyu cheng hui yu zhan huo kao shi 南越國都番禺城毀於戰火考實," *Jinan xuebao* 暨南學報, (2008): 5.

[18] *Shi ji*, 113.2976.

The die-hard followers of Lü Jia, which included hundreds of people, did not switch sides. Together with Lü Jia, they first escaped the burning city of Panyu by ship, only to be captured at sea by Han forces in the brief aftermath of the siege.[19] Clearly, by embodying a certain local Southern Yue identity and fighting to the death to preserve Southern Yue independence, Lü Jia proved himself to be even more "Yue" than local city inhabitants who defected when Panyu was sacked. After all, it was Lü's war to wage, and his actions of regicide and rebellion toward the Han placed him in a unique position with little recourse except to fight or flee. Since Lü had effectively used Southern Yue identity as a weapon in his rebellion against the Han, his defeat was tantamount to a quashing – at least for the time being – of the legitimacy of such an identity at the political level.[20]

King Zou Yushan and the last fight for Eastern Yue

Roughly twenty-three years after the Min-yue attack on Southern Yue in 135 BCE, King Zou Yushan was still in power as the king of Eastern Yue. Emperor Wudi of the Han was also still in power and had just declared war on Southern Yue in 112 BCE. As there was no apparent loyalty between Eastern Yue and Southern Yue, King Zou Yushan initially took sides with the Han and asked to send 8,000 of his own troops to help Han General Yang Pu of the Towered Ships attack Lü Jia and his forces (請以卒八千人從樓船將軍擊呂嘉等).[21] Instead, according to the *Shi ji*, Yushan ended up blatantly betraying the Han by stationing his troops at Jieyang and not budging, refusing to take sides and secretly communicating with Southern Yue just as he was communicating with the Han (不行, 持兩端, 陰使南越).[22]

While one can argue that the Eastern Yue may have been doomed anyway, such a flagrant act of betrayal against the Han was the beginning of a most certain end for the Eastern Yue, especially in light of the Han

[19] *Shi ji*, 113.2976. The *Han shu* mentions a message from Han Wudi to the Xiongnu *Shanyu* 單于 shortly after his victory over Southern Yue, claiming that the "head of the King of Southern Yue already hangs from the northern Gate of the Han [Palace] 南越王頭已縣於漢北闕矣." *Han shu*, 6.189.

[20] This says nothing of the persistence of Yue cultural values and practices at the local level. We know for sure that certain Yue ways continued to thrive throughout and beyond the Han, as there is evidence of later Han officials encountering and trying to change various Yue practices. See Fan Ye 范曄, *Hou Han shu* 後漢書 (Beijing: Zhonghua shu ju, 1995), p. 76, which describes the Chinese prefect, Xi Guang 錫光, and his policies of introducing Han-style marriage rites, the wearing of sandals and hats, and other rituals. *Hou Han shu*, 76.2457 and 76.2462. Cited in Keith Taylor, *The Birth of Vietnam* (Berkeley: University of California Press, 1983), p. 33.

[21] *Shi ji*, 114.2982. [22] *Ibid.*

defeat of Southern Yue. Zou Yushan's wavering and defiance of his own stated commitment to the Han reveals what seems in retrospect to be a fantastic miscalculation on his part. It also reveals the fact that the conquest of Southern Yue was not at all an easy affair for the Han. Although the Han would emerge victorious in this campaign, we can see that from where Yushan was standing in Jieyang – at the southern periphery of the mainland – Lü Jia's Southern Yue forces must have seemed formidable and likely to win. How else might one explain Zou Yushan's behavior?

Let us consider the situation in more detail. Pinned between two very powerful foes, it was a matter of life and death for Eastern Yue to side with the eventual victor. If it appeared that Southern Yue was going to win, then it makes sense that Yushan would turn back on his promises to aid a failing Han campaign against the Southern Yue. If, on the other hand, Yushan had thought there was a strong chance that the Han would win, then one might expect him to have sided more fully with the Han, and at the very least come through on his promises. But by failing to act and sitting out on a battle when he had promised to support the Han, Yushan's actions inadvertently reveal, I think, that he was probably not hedging his bets. Stationed at Jieyang, he was somehow persuaded that Southern Yue would win.

As mentioned above, the possibility of a Southern Yue defeat of the Han is not at all hinted at in the historical records. The *Shi ji* describes the devastation wreaked on the capital city of Panyu, much of which has been confirmed by archaeological excavations of the palace and its environs. Thus, one of the only clues we have that the Southern Yue was so powerful that even its neighbor thought it wise to sit out on the fight and avoid aiding the Han is the description of Zou Yushan's bizarre act of defiance against Han. Such a clue gives us pause; it asks us to step away from the standard presentation of Han strength in the historiography and take on the perspective of political agents who at the time had their own survival and interests in mind.

In the ending to the saga of Zou Yushan, we are presented with a complicated picture of what Min-yue/Eastern Yue identity may have been, if it meant anything at all beyond loyalties to specific political leaders. After the defeat of Southern Yue, Han forces were too depleted to attack Eastern Yue, but Zou Yushan's insecurities concerning an impending Han attack compelled him to take the offensive and declare open revolt against the Han. Yushan made all the necessary preparations to bolster his authority within Eastern Yue and fight the Han. Part of this offensive involved assuming the status of an imperial overlord, "Emperor Wu [this time, of Eastern Yue]," and, according to the Han perspective, "deluding his people and promulgating false stories 詐其民, 為妄言."[23] In addition, Yushan named some of his generals "Han-swallowing Generals 吞漢將軍," and "attacked the areas of Baisha, Wulin, and Meilin, killing the three [Han] Commanders stationed there 入白沙、武林、梅嶺, 殺漢三校尉."[24]

That Zou Yushan began a concerted campaign to revolt against the Han is nothing new. But the manner in which he tried to garner the authority of an Emperor and translate that into military power is stunning and worthy of analysis. As discussed in the previous section, while revolting against the Han, Lü Jia of Southern Yue, who himself was not a king, made no attempt to usurp the title of Southern Yue king, let alone Emperor, for himself. Even during the Revolt of the Seven Kingdoms in 154 BCE, King Liu Pi of Wu did not usurp imperial titles and fight the Han in the name of a new empire. In terms of precedent, then, the closest act we have to that of Zou Yushan takes us back to the period of Han Empress Lü, around 183 BCE, when King Zhao Tuo of Southern Yue declared himself Emperor and attacked the region of Changsha to the north of his frontier. But even in such a case, Zhao Tuo was not directly attacking the Han – only a southern sub-division of Han that could conceivably have been contested territory. Seen in such a context, it follows that Zou Yushan's response to an impending Han attack on Eastern Yue was to "go for broke" and try to establish his own empire in competition with the Han to the north. One might even claim that Yushan's appeal to the identity of an "Emperor Wu" of Eastern Yue was an integral part of the process of amassing supporters back in the homeland, since, as emperor, Yushan would have been able to promise to bestow on local lords even more grandiose titles and rewards.

The *Shi ji* also mentions that Zou Yushan's army of rebels included local Yue leaders who were to fight on behalf of Yushan and, thus presumably, a greater Eastern Yue Empire. As the text describes the early stages of a significant military standoff between Han and Eastern Yue (one in which Eastern Yue was actually making headway and defeating several Han commanders at a key pass at Wulin), it turns to a dialog to impart information about the actions of three Yue conspirators – each a local leader in or around the region of Eastern Yue. We must be wary of dialogs in these early histories. Most likely, Sima Qian was crafting a justificatory rationale for these men's betrayal and attempting, without proof of course, to get into the minds of these Yue conspirators. Here are their alleged words:

[23] *Ibid.* [24] *Shi ji*, 114.2983.

Zou Yushan is a tyrant who imposed his authority over our territories. Now the Han armies arrive in great strength and number. If we plot together to assassinate Yushan and surrender to the various Han generals, perhaps we will be lucky and get exonerated.

餘善首惡, 劫守吾屬。今漢兵至, 眾彊, 計殺餘善, 自歸諸將, 儻幸得脫.[25]

Just as Zou Yushan had betrayed his brother and committed fratricide to avoid a military confrontation with Han some twenty-five years earlier, local Yue leaders did the same to him, bringing about the effective conquest of the Eastern Yue and the massive resettlement of much of its population to inland, Han-controlled regions around the Yangzi and Huai Rivers.[26] As would be expected, all three Yue assassins were rewarded generously by the Han with marquisates in the newly conquered territories of erstwhile Min-yue/Eastern Yue.

Here we have a story of intense military confrontation, especially along the coast and passes of Eastern Yue, combined with an imagined dialog that explains the political machinations and betrayals of local Yue leaders against Zou Yushan. Rather than suffer through an intense war that could devastate their cities, as in the case of Southern Yue and its great capital of Panyu (and the case of Southern Yue would have been fresh on their minds), local Yue leaders sided at the last minute with the victor and did what it took to ensure their own future survival and success. Ostensibly, loyalty to any abstract Yue identity did not exist in the minds of the local lords who turned against Yushan. They expressed concern for their own territories and survival, for their own authority as Yue leaders, and not for the survival of a political entity such as the Eastern Yue Empire or a would-be Min-yue kingdom.

So while the imperial aspirations of the Eastern Yue Emperor Zou Yushan did not bring about a lasting empire, this brief moment of Min-yue/Eastern Yue resistance is noteworthy and reminds us of how historically contingent various identities are on political and military successes. Certainly, the area around Fujian would remain culturally distinct from more northern areas for many more centuries to come. The story of how the region identified as Yue (or Min-yue, or Ou) continues well into the first and second millennia CE, even though leaders after the fall of Eastern Ou, Min-yue, and Eastern Yue never really managed to set up their own independent Yue states after this time. Had Zou Yushan and his predecessors, including the brother he killed, Zou Ying, been successful, their successes no doubt would have

[25] *Ibid.* [26] *Shi ji*, 114.2983–84.

affected and improved the long-term outcomes and preservation of a more self-conscious Yue identity in the region.

The rebellion of the Zheng/Trung sisters

The history of the frontier in the Southwest during the Han is less well documented than either that of the Min-yue/Eastern Yue or Southern Yue. Since this region includes areas around contemporary Vietnam, this history has been much sought after, and there are many speculations concerning the early period. Unfortunately, the earliest histories of Vietnam are unlikely to contain reliable information concerning the history of the early imperial period, since these texts date to the thirteenth through fifteenth centuries CE. While scholars believe the main works of early Vietnamese historiography draw from Chinese texts dating to the Sui-Tang period (sixth–ninth centuries CE), such as Li Daoyuan's *Commentary on the Classic of Waterways* (*Shuijing zhu* 水經注), the earliest one can trace its source material to is the third or fourth centuries CE.[27] Texts that are more contemporary to the early imperial period, such as the *Shi ji* and *Han shu*, write sparingly about such regions.

One of the great rebellions of the Han period, which dates to 40–43 CE (early Eastern Han), concerns two sisters who garnered support from the entire commandery of ancient Jiaozhi (Vietnamese: Giao Chỉ), as well as areas around Jiuzhen (Vietnamese: Cửu Chân), Rinan (Vietnamese: Nhật Nam), and Hepu commanderies. Jiaozhi lay along on the Red River Delta, and its capital, Longbian (Vietnamese: Long Biên), was located near modern Hanoi, while Jiuzhen and Rinan lay to the south of that, and Hepu north along the coast in modern-day Guangxi Province.[28] Stephen O'Harrow provides a very good outline of scholarship (up to 1979) on the sisters, which includes discussion of the possible reasons for their rebellion, their background, etc.[29] But the truth is that we know virtually nothing about these two sisters from the early record itself. The earliest references to the rebellion can be found in a fifth-century history, the

[27] Important passages concerning the Hung kings (in the Red River Delta region) of pre-Qin times in the *Shuijing zhu* cite even earlier texts such as the *Record of the Outer Territory of Jiaozhou* (*Jiaozhou waiyu ji*), which dates to the third and fourth century CE but is no longer extant. See Liam Kelley, "Tai Words and the Place of the Tai in the Vietnamese Past," *Journal of the Siam Society* 101 (2013): 55–84.

[28] De Crespigny, *Generals of the South: The Foundation and Early History of the Three Kingdoms State of Wu* (Canberra: Australian National University, Faculty of Asian Studies, 1990), Chapter 1. The capital of Jiuzhen was Xupu, near Thanh Hoa in northern Vietnam. The commandery of Rinan was centered around Xiquan, near present-day Quang Tri.

[29] Stephen O'Harrow, "From Co-loa to the Trung Sisters' Revolt: Vietnam as the Chinese Found it," *Asian Perspectives* 22.2 (1979): 140–164.

Hou Han shu (History of the Later Han), compiled about 400 years after the alleged event (40 CE), by Fan Ye 范曄. Even though such a source drew upon earlier Han period documents and histories that are no longer extant, it barely mentions anything aside from the sisters' names, their father's status, the elder's marital status, and hometown. Other references from early Vietnamese histories date to the second millennium CE and, while they may draw on some sources dating to the Tang period (c. sixth–eighth centuries CE), the information contained therein can hardly be considered to be reliable source material.[30]

A *Hou Han shu* passage provides one of the best summaries of the rebellion – in particular, Han involvement in quelling it through the military campaigns of Generals Ma Yuan 馬援 and Duan Zhi 段志. I cite it in full to provide a glimpse of just how little is said about the Zheng sisters themselves, and how we have virtually no access to their own voices or perspectives on the events of that period:

In the 2nd year of Jianwu (26 CE), Chief Zhang You of the Man barbarians beyond the Jiuzhen border ordered the various peoples to respect and become inner members [of the Han]. For this he was enfeoffed as "Chief-ruler who is loyal to Han." The next year, the borderland regions outside of the Southern Yue sent white pheasants and white creepers as tribute to the Han. During the 16th year (41 CE), Madame Zheng (Trung 徵) from Jiaozhi and her younger sister Zheng Er [the "Second"] (Trung Nhi 徵貳) rebelled and attacked the entire commandery. Zheng Ce (徵側, Trung Trac) (the older) was from Meiling County and a daughter of a Luo General. She married a man from Zhugou named Shi Suo (詩索, Thi Sach). She was very heroic and courageous. The Grand Commandant of Jiaozhi, Su Ding 蘇定, used laws to ensnare her (literally, "to rope"). Enraged, Madame Zheng rebelled. The Man 蠻 local leaders of Jiuzhen, Rinan, and Hepu commanderies all joined her. With control over about 65 towns total, she established herself as king. The Inspector of Jiaozhi and all the various Grand Commandants could only rule their own people. The Guangwu Emperor thus ordered that [workers in] the regions of Changsha, Hepu, and Jiaozhi assemble all the vehicles and boats, repair all roads and bridges, make it so that all blockages and ravines can be traversed, and create reserves of food and grain. In the 18th year (43 CE), he sent the General Who Calms the Waves, Ma Yuan, along with the General of the Towered Ships, Duan Zhi, down to lead over 10,000 troops from Changsha, Guiyang, Lingling, and Cangwu [areas just north and south of the Wuling Mountains] in an attack on the rebels. The next summer, in the 4th month [44 CE], Ma Yuan succeeded in conquering Jiaozhi and beheading the two sisters and their lot, allowing the rest to surrender or scatter into the countryside. He then advanced further to attack the traitor from Jiuzhen, Du Yang都陽, and company. He defeated them and obtained their surrender. The Han then exiled over 300 local chieftains up to Lingling [farther north near the

30 See Liam Kelley, "Tai Words."

Wuling mountain range, away from their bases of power]. Thereupon the Lingbiao (i.e., Lingnan) region was pacified.

建武十二年, 九真徼外蠻里張游, 率種人慕化內屬, 封為歸漢里君。明年, 南越徼外蠻夷獻白雉、白菟。至十六年, 交阯女子徵側及其妹徵貳反, 攻郡。徵側者, 麊泠縣雒將之女也。嫁為朱䳒人詩索妻, 甚雄勇。交阯太守蘇定以法繩之, 側忿, 故反。於是九真、日南、合浦蠻里皆應之, 凡略六十五城, 自立為王。交阯刺史及諸太守僅得自守。光武乃詔長沙、合浦、交阯具車船, 修道橋, 通障谿, 儲糧穀。十八年, 遣伏波將軍馬援、樓船將軍段志, 發長沙、桂陽、零陵、蒼梧兵萬餘人討 之。明年夏四月, 援破交阯, 斬徵側、徵貳等, 餘皆降散。進擊九真賊都陽等, 破降之。徙其渠帥三百餘口於零陵。於是領表悉平。[31]

From such a passage we learn about the rise and fall of the Zheng/Trung sisters. Our source clearly comments on the Luo (ethnic/tribal) heritage of the sisters, as well as the fact that the starting point for the rebellion was located in the Jiaozhi region. Meiling County, the native place of the sisters, was one of ten counties in the Han commandery of Jiaozhi (including Zhugou, where Zheng Ce's husband came from), and the passage implies that the original center of Zheng/Trung power lay in Jiaozhi commandery.[32] The sisters drew further upon non-Han support from an area stretching from the coastal regions of modern-day Guangxi Province (the ancient region of Hepu) to central Vietnam (the ancient region of Rinan). This native Luo versus Han distinction is brought out by the text's allusion to the fact that Han officials still retained limited power in the region, or "self-governance 自守," a likely reference to power that was circumscribed to Han immigrants and official emigrés living in the region. It is also brought out by the text's mention of the sisters' Luo heritage; they were daughters of a "Luo general 雒將." This "Luo" seems to be the same "luo 駱" – an alternative form of the graph – that is used in Sima Qian's discussion of the Ou-luo 甌駱(Vietnamese: Au Lac) peoples and Luo-luo 駱裸peoples.[33] It appears to be some sort of tribal name for a particular southern group of Yue peoples that inhabited areas around the coast of Guangxi and northern Vietnam (see Chapter 1).

As daughters of a general, the Zheng/Trung sisters were members of the local nobility with direct ties to the military. While we are not privy to information about the kind of legal entanglement that spawned the Zheng sisters' rebellion, the passage suggests that the older sister, Zheng Ce,

[31] *Hou Han shu*, pp. 2836–2837.

[32] The ten counties included Leilou 羸婁, Anding 安定, Goulou 苟屚, Miling 麊泠, Quyang 曲易, Beidai 北帶, Jixu 稽徐, Xiyu 西于, Longbian 龍編, Zhugou 朱䳒. See the "Treatise on Geography" in the *Han shu*, p. 1629.

[33] *Shi ji*, 113.2969–70, 2977. The term is used four times in the chapter on Southern Yue, sometimes in the two-word compound, 甌駱, sometimes on its own, and once in the compound, Luo-luo 駱裸.

somehow came to loggerheads with the highest Han official in Jiaozhi, the Grand Commandant, Su Ding 蘇定. Evidence concerning their followers – local leaders of the Man ("southern barbarians") from Hepu to Rinan – suggests that native self-sovereignty and independence were a prominent issue at stake.

The scale and scope of this rebellion cannot be understated, as it would have been no mere frustration for the Han to lose control of sixty-five cities along one of its most populous borders and important centers for maritime trade. Moreover, the region of Jiaozhi had in the early centuries of the first millennium become one of the major entrepots for maritime trade, overshadowing even Hepu, which had been so important in the pearl trade of the early imperial period.[34] One need only compare the population registries of 2 CE for Nanhai (erstwhile center for the kingdom of Southern Yue, with allegedly 19,613 households and 94,253 individuals) with Jiaozhi (with 92, 440 households and 746,237 individuals) in the *Han shu* "Treatise on Geography" to see that Jiaozhi was a budding metropolis of the middle Han era.[35]

The strategic importance of Jiaozhi is underscored by the fact that the Han sent one of their most trusted teams of generals, Ma Yuan and Duan Zhi, to quell the rebellion. Both generals had seen success in a military campaign against upstart religious leaders who were causing trouble in Lujiang commandery 廬江 (in modern-day Anhui Province), beheading the shaman Li Guang 妖巫李廣 and others, only a year before (42 CE) they were sent down to attack the Zheng/Trung sisters.[36] General Ma Yuan would later go down in Chinese history as a great official who brought Han civilization to the barbarians.[37]

From this passage we also learn of a figure who does not feature prominently in the history of Vietnam, a certain Du Yang 都陽, associated

[34] As de Crespigny states:

> The earliest description of the sea trade, preserved in the Treatise of Geography of Han shu, emphasises the importance of Hepu commandery, and sailing distances were apparently counted from that territory. By the first centuries AD, however, the natural advantages of Longbian, with its fertile and open ground for settlement, and its access to a network of transport routes, had given it pride of place: the descriptions of the city under the rule of Shi Xie at the end of Han, and the records of Jiaozhi's population and prosperity, indicate a dominant position as market and entrepot for goods brought by land and sea, with a flourishing trade, along the coast of China and beyond to the lands of southeast Asia and the Indian Ocean. (*Generals of the South*, Chapter 1)

See also Li Tana, "The Tongking Gulf Through History: A Geopolitical Overview," in Nola Cooke, Li Tana, and James Anderson, eds., *The Tonking Gulf Through History* (Philadephia: University of Pennsylvania Press, 2011), pp. 39–52.

[35] *Han shu*, pp. 1628–1629.

[36] *Hou Han shu*, "Record of Emperor Guangwu, Lower 光武帝紀下," p. 68.

[37] See de Crespigny, *Generals of the South*, Chapter 1 and Taylor, *The Birth of Vietnam*.

with the now northern Vietnamese area of Jiuzhen (Cuu-chan), a bit farther to the south. Intriguingly, the Trung sisters are given all the credit for this rebellion, even though it seems clear from our source that there were more rebel leaders who had either collaborated with the Trung sisters or took advantage of a vacuum of local leadership in their own regions to rise up and maintain sort of independence from the Han. Certainly the notion that two rebellious women leaders were entirely responsible for a campaign for independence against the Han serves as a much more compelling story than that of random military upstarts (Du Yang among them – important enough to be named while the others were not), about whom we know even less than we know about the Trung sisters. One can imagine the large number of rebel leaders who were actually involved, which reminds us that the situation that the Han faced with certain kinds of Yue peoples in its frontier zones was much more complicated than the Chinese histories reveal.

What is interesting in this account is that references to Yue are sparse. Still, there is proof that authors of this later date still considered these groups to be part of a larger Yue mega-culture. For one thing, the author of this passage specifies the location of unrest to be near Southern Yue. In other passages from the *Hou Han shu* (specifically in the account on General Ma Yuan) both the terms "Yue" and a relatively new term, "Luo-yue 駱越," are used to discuss the cultural changes that Ma Yuan imposed on the region.[38] The following statement provides some insights into how these Yue were seen as culturally distinct from the Han in terms of laws and statutes, levels of technological achievement (especially in the area of agricultural techniques and technologies), and other social systems:

> General Ma Yuan commandeered over 2,000 large and small towered ships and conquered over 20,000 enemy troops. He attacked the traitor Zheng Ce [the older Trung sister] and the factions associated with Du Yang [this time, different graphs are used for his name: 都羊]. From Wucheng to Jufeng, he killed or captured over 5,000 people, pacifying the entire region South of the Passes. Ma Yuan memorialized the throne requesting that the county of Xiyu – having over 32,000 inhabitants and lying over 1,000 li from the provincial capital – be divided into the counties of Fengxi and Wanghai, which the Emperor granted. The remaining territories were made into provinces and commanderies. He made cities and towns orderly and built canals and irrigation systems to benefit the people. On ten occasions he also memorialized the throne to refine Yue statutes by adapting them to Han statutes. He had the old protocols clarified and spread out to the Yue people so as to bind and restrain them. From that time on, the Luo-yue served and carried out General Ma's traditional ways of running affairs of the state.

[38] This term appears in texts dating from the Later Han, possibly slightly earlier.

援將樓船大小二千餘艘, 戰士二萬餘人, 進擊九真賊徵側餘黨都羊等, 自無功至居風, 斬獲五千餘人, 嶠南悉平。援奏言西于縣戶有三萬二千, 遠界去庭千餘里, 請分為封溪、望海二縣, 許之。援所過輒為郡縣治城郭, 穿渠灌溉, 以利其民。條奏越律與漢律駮者十餘事, 與越人申明舊制以約束之, 自後駱越奉行馬將軍故事.[39]

This section also mentions the extensive reach of the rebellion, along with the fact that the Trung sisters were not the only leaders and groups involved. Unlike in the previous passage, where the general term "Man" was used (to refer to ethnic others from the South), the author here refers to the same groups of people as the "Yue." Since the topic at hand concerns culture, laws, and technologies, it seems likely that Han authors considered the appellation "Yue" more appropriate, and that the term "Yue" had some sort of value as a marker for a certain cultural system that was specific to particular groups of southerners.

From both passages in the *Hou Han shu*, we gain a sense that authors distinguished the Han from these southwestern Yue peoples not only in terms of the differences in political systems, but in terms of a cross-cultural and, quite possibly, cross-ethnic divide as well. The Luo-yue of the region were clearly Man whose traditions, values, administrative methods, laws, and technological achievements were drastically non-Hua-xia. In the discussion of Ma Yuan's reforms above, words such as "benefit," "make orderly," and "pacify" all suggest that such colonial measures were completely justified and ultimately beneficial to the native peoples. This reveals the primary assumptions concerning sinicization embedded deeply in the ancient historiographical traditions. Similarly, it reveals a fundamental assumption about Hua-xia identity and culture as superior to that of the Southern Yue natives. It is only by paying close attention to the scope and intensity of the rebellion, along with oblique references to the many local leaders who participated in it and the strong Han response that ensued, that we might more fully realize how Yue agency and instances of rebellion like these constituted watershed moments in the history of the creation of a more permanent Yue identity. Even though the earliest accounts of the Trung sisters ostensibly glorify Chinese victory and the cultural and administrative successes of the Hua-xia colonizers, and even though they tell us virtually nothing of local efforts at identity construction, we need only ponder for a moment the gravity of the situation as well as the potential motives of the rebels to fathom how, in the midst of such massive military encounters, self-sovereignty and the consolidation of Yue identity was at stake.

[39] *Hou Han shu*, 24.839.

Conclusion

The historical accounts of southern armed resistance are usually brief, especially when compared to the northern frontier. It seems clear that the military power of the Han was ultimately superior to that of the rulers of the various Yue kingdoms, but one should be careful not to overstate their supremacy in this area. The sheer fact that the Han campaign to quell the revolt of the Trung sisters in Jiaozhi and surrounding regions lasted for over a year tells us that certain Yue groups were very serious about their own sovereignty, and that they had the will and military wherewithal to defend it. Many local Yue leaders rebelled only under threat of total destruction, as in the case of Lü Jia and Zou Yushan, who up until the time of rebellion were happy to serve as kings or high officials with only a nominal connection to imperial Han overlords. Others initiated their own revolts out of dissatisfaction with some aspect of Han control or colonization, as in the Trung sisters' case. In either case, armed resistance meant taking a clear and definite stand on one's political identity and pledging allegiance to a certain way of ruling and being ruled. Because one is willing to sacrifice bloodshed and fight to the death for independent rule, armed resistance is an ultimate expression of the act of carving out one's own identity and space for self-sovereignty.

Our sources give us very little information about specific formulations of Yue identity during times of armed resistance, although Sima Qian provides one example of a proclamation by Lü Jia that hints strongly at the creation of a Southern Yue political self. In it, Lü referred to a powerful and lasting political lineage and identity that held legitimacy as the ruling dynasty of the region. His performance of Southern Yue identity in this manifesto no doubt served as in important tool by which he could justify certain violations of Han protocol and consolidate his power against the Han. Lü Jia in particular invoked the loss of Yue resources and the status of Yue peoples to the Han. His use of local identity over and against the people from the Central States demonstrates how identity could be appropriated to gain support for rebellion and self-sovereignty.

From this analysis we also gained a sense of the non-sacred, permeable nature of Yue identity. Support for its non-sacred nature lies in the fact that people could, and often would, switch loyalties according to political or economic exigencies. Some of the key military generals who helped invade and destroy the kingdoms of Southern Yue were originally "Yue people," according to our sources. Also, the fact that many Southern Yue inhabitants of Panyu could be lured into betraying the Yue before the city was captured suggests that most people were not willing to die or suffer indignities merely based on their associations with the kingdom of Southern Yue. In Eastern Yue, leaders deemed by our sources to be local Yue leaders betrayed would-be imperialists like Zou Yushan and his brother in their campaigns for Yue suzerainty by assassinating the incumbent power-holders, submitting to Han rule, and getting rewarded for it with marquisates and official Han recognition of their own local power.

Precisely because external Han authority and all its accoutrements were a primary means for local southern chieftains or kings to bolster their own identity and authority, it was particularly lethal for the creation of independent states. Indeed, there was always somebody in the region who could be bribed by the Han with promises for future rewards – rewards such as enfeoffments and titles – that would support their own regional authority. The Han needed but to exploit local factionalism and a lack of a sense of greater Yue unity to their benefit, which they did in the Southeast and South (Eastern and Southern Yue regions) with great success.

That Yue identity was permeable and difficult to unify is suggested by the fact that various forms of this identity were easily co-opted by Central States outsiders, just as Yue identities were easily abandoned by some Yue insiders. Relatively easy to adopt and abandon, Yue identity could also be mixed, diluted, and otherwise transformed. Many members of the ruling class of Southern Yue were of mixed, Yue–Central States blood. We recall that Lü Jia set up as king an eldest son of the Zhao lineage with a Yue wife, and that his own family – which may have been of Yue origin – was related by marriage to the ruling Zhao clan. This shows that even members of the ruling elite were intermarrying with local peoples, and so it is likely that intermarriage at lower levels was a commonplace phenomenon as well. Most scholars tend to cite the purported 50,000 male soldiers and workers sent by the Qin state south of the Wuling mountain range (compared with the 10,000 Central States females ordered to migrate there as their possible partners) as evidence of the dearth of Central States females and the necessary intermixing of such lower-class men with local Yue women.[40]

The above notwithstanding, armed rebellions and moments of intense Yue resistance to conquest, encroachments, and colonization remind us of a constant attempt on the southern frontier to reclaim Yue identities through the formation of local kingdoms and, even, imperial authorities. The fact that so many people supported Lü Jia's, Zou Yushan's, and the Zheng/Trung sisters' bids for independence from the Han helps support

[40] Liu Min 劉 敏, "'Kai guan' ding lun – cong 'Wendi xing xi' kan Han-Yue guanxi 開棺定論 – 從 文帝行璽看漢越關系," in *Nanyueguo shiji yan tao hui*, 26.

the notion that more lasting Yue states had been real possibilities on numerous occasions in the past. To take an example from later history, local Yue/Viet lords of the tenth-century CE Red River region were able to stave off Song conquest and establish their own regional dynasties, leading to a more lasting era of Vietnamese identity and self-sovereignty. While the Yue lords and chieftains of the Han period were ultimately not successful in fighting off the Han, such later victories attest to the occasional and sometimes hugely decisive efforts of local, southern peoples. They also confirm the continuation of some form of Yue/Viet identity in later history.

Even from the ostensibly Han, Central States, or Hua-xia perspective of the textual sources we use, we can gain a sense of Yue agency. The various acts of appeasement, subterfuge, diplomacy, and rebellion that many Yue leaders demonstrated toward the Han reveal some of the political contingencies surrounding the construction of Yue political and ruling-class identities in the South. Furthermore, the invocation of local and Han laws and customs, intermarriage with local women, and valuing of local and Han goods – all while appropriating tools, symbols, and ranks/emoluments from northern imperial rule – suggest attempts at creating one's own, local form of Yue identity, although the details of such local processes in this early period are often lost to history.

Conclusion

The early twentieth-century anthropologist Fei Xiaotong 费孝通 provided a summary of the origins of Chinese culture in terms of ethnic diversity, which was later adopted more officially as an explanatory concept for Chinese ethnic unity amid diversity. He spoke of a "single body with multitudinous origins (多元一体)," in which the "body" refers not merely to a political but also ethnic unity: the "Chinese ethnicity" *Zhonghua minzu* (中華民族).[1] This panoptic perspective on what it means to be Chinese, one that became relevant for certain contexts in the twentieth century, stresses unity and wholeness at the expense of uniqueness and a diversity of parts.[2] Countless other conceptual models of the relationship between Hua-xia/Chinese unity and the diversity of the "other" have been proposed throughout the ages. Regardless of how authors from different eras may have formulated such models, the fundamental act of mapping out a particular relationship between unity and diversity has complemented colonial goals, helped in the task of governing a large and extremely diverse empire, and aided in cultural management and control since the time of the birth of empire over 2,000 years ago.

In this book we analyzed a dominant, ancient ethnonym for the southern other: Yue. Through both an introductory analysis of current social science research and an in-depth look at the concept and representation of Yue identity in ancient texts, we found that the ancient southern frontier of what is now China was far from unified and undifferentiated, as the ancient ethnonym "Yue" suggests. Yet it was precisely through the formulation of broad labels like Hua-xia and Yue that we learned about the power dynamics and ways of remaking the Chinese self and other in history.

[1] *Fei Xiaotong wenji* 费孝通文集 (Collected works of Fei Xiaotong), 15 vols. (Beijing: Qunyan chubanshe, 1999).

[2] For more on the history of ethnic classification and the state in recent times, see Thomas Mullaney, *Coming to Terms with the Nation: Ethnic Classification in Modern China* (Berkeley: University of California Press, 2010).

Even though ethnic diversity was likely the norm, Hua-xia authors did not always wish to see or admit it. They lumped the peoples of the South together under the rubric of "Yue" or "Bai-yue" (Hundred Yue), so that the entire South and Southeast appeared to be a homogeneous mass of southern others, foreign to the Zhou sphere of culture. As I have shown in this book, creating such a generic, undifferentiated other seems to have been done in the interest of building a broad, ethnic concept of the self, one that would be very useful later in fulfilling colonial interests. In other words, the concept of the "Yue" and "Bai-yue" often served as a foil to the imagined Hua-xia self, and, like the Hua-xia, such terms were defined according to broad, sweeping cultural and genealogical criteria.

The foregoing examination of the Yue is therefore not a history of the ancient Yue as they were in reality but an evaluation of the knowledge that we have about who they might have been, as well as how they were depicted and identified in ancient texts. I have shown that the textual record on Yue is spotty, limited, and fraught with problems, and that, in earlier texts especially (i.e., texts from the Warring States), we may not even encounter much about the Yue that was factually true. However, rather than throw out the data because of their obvious biases, I make use of such distortions to shed light on the concerns and agendas of Central States authors as they try to categorize the Yue. In so doing, I provide a historical context for understanding Yue identity as a function of the creation of a Hua-xia self.

My analysis reveals how the Hua-xia positioned themselves spatially at the center of their world, with special access to all the trappings of enlightenment and civilization: order, morality, normalcy, moderation, balance, etc. At the same time, we gain insights into the changing history of Hua-xia perceptions of the self and other, and we come to appreciate the extent to which our authors were either coming into direct contact with southern others or obtaining reliable information through some sort of lived cultural encounter of the time.

While much more work in the areas of archaeology, linguistics, biology, and anthropology must be done to obtain more data and a greater understanding of who the southern inhabitants of ancient China and parts of Southeast Asia were, we must not neglect listening closely and critically to what the textual record can teach us. Indeed, it reveals a process whereby Hua-xia and Yue identities become entwined in a duet that spotlights the self while making a shadow of the other, and centers the self while decentering the other. It also tells a narrative of the beginnings of a permeable, malleable, and diffuse sense of Yue self-identity at the start of the imperial period. These are important and profound stories concerning the first formulations of Hua-xia and Yue identities, and they reflect early solutions in the Chinese record to the problem of creating and maintaining a sense of ethnic unity in light of the radical diversity of the ancient landscape.

As problematic and vague as the ethnonym, "Yue" is, a couple reasons justify our using it as a lens through which to understand the intellectual history of the southern frontier. For one thing, our analysis of the breadth of the term "Yue" and its implications for drawing connections among various cultures and peoples across the ancient South forced us to take a step back from more manageable and coherent micro-research on individual sites, cities, provincial regions, or states. The sweeping nature of the term challenged us to see the southern frontier as our ancient Chinese elite authors did, and to try to understand how many disparate regions may have fit or been linked together as a larger network in their minds. For another, the ancient characterization of the Yue highlighted in many instances a real distinction in habitat and economy; it distinguished the predominantly inland and agricultural networks of the Central States from the predominantly maritime and coastal networks in the South.[3]

Much of the history of the South involves and cannot be separated from the vital, interactive maritime spheres that pervaded the southern and southeastern coastal-riverine regions. Just as the life of steppe nomads to the north of the Yellow River regions differed significantly from that of settled agriculturalists in the Central Plains, the life of primarily coastal-riverine peoples south of the Yangzi might be contrasted with those of the Central Plains regions as well. In particular, many regions of the South might be characterized in terms of a distinctive, sub-tropical flora and fauna, high humidity, and mountainous terrain cut by small river valleys – all of which contributed to particular styles of agriculture and ways of life in which sea-faring and a close relationship to water were common. In light of this, the term "Yue" provides us with a means of addressing the history of the southern frontier in terms of shared traits and similarities among southern regions and peoples – similarities that resulted from extensive communication, trade, and cross-cultural, cross-ethnic interactions across the riverine and seaboard regions of the South.

[3] Note that this interpretation differs from Magnus Fiskesjö's claim that the peoples on the ancient southern frontier "were culturally, linguistically, and ethnically different, but not necessarily in terms of habitat or mode of subsistence." Magnus Fiskesjö, "On the 'Raw' and 'Cooked': Barbarians of Imperial China," *Inner China* 1–2 (1999): 142. The interpretation that I present here suggests that the highland–lowland, maritime and riverine economies of the South did, on the whole, constitute a rather different type of habitat from the intensively agricultural regions of the Central Plains.

Hua-xia identity as a function of the logic of centrality

Specific articulations of the Hua-xia self and Yue other appear to have been motivated by a logic of centrality that constructed the self as a central, primary, and normative agent in relationship to a peripheral, secondary, and peculiar (or morally deviant) other. The Hua-xia self was formulated early on by Ru such as Confucius and his disciples in terms of an ethnic concept that employed cultural capital as the main prerequisite for group membership. In some Warring States texts, the Yue appeared in an ecliptic relationship to the Hua-xia, helping give definition to the known world but serving as a distant, strange, and sometimes more powerful foil to the central self. In such formulations, the Yue were not always made out to be barbarian others – sometimes they were praised so as to criticize the self – but the assumption of their spatio-temporal distance from the center nonetheless placed them in an inferior position vis-à-vis the leading target, voice, and agent: the Hua-xia self.

Why might the ethnic formulation of "Hua-xia" have had such a strong link to conceptions of centrality? The term "Hua-xia," after all, merely refers to a lineage of variegated peoples who descend from the Xia cultural spheres. Although there may not be a direct etymological connection between "Hua-xia" and notions of centrality, there were certainly many other ways in which such centrality was asserted and reinforced in our texts. Perhaps most obvious are the equivalencies drawn between the Hua-xia people and such geopolitical and geographical markers as the Central States.[4] Indeed, our texts demonstrated in no uncertain terms that the self resided in the Central States and was the central, substantial entity in comparison to its shadowy others on the periphery.

Given this positioning of the Hua-xia self, it makes sense that Hua-xia authors often referred to others through directional ethnonyms or slurs that underscored their lesser importance. Peoples were labeled according to the four directions from which they came: the Yi of the East, the Di of the North, the Rong of the West, and the Man of the South. This "Four Quadrant (Sifang 四方)" mode of dividing up the world has deep roots in Shang period cosmology, and Wang Aihe has shown how such a cosmology was further refined and developed to incorporate the center in the "Five Phases (Wuxing 五行)" cosmology of the later Warring States

[4] Though the term "Central States" referred more to a geopolitical reality than an ethnic one, nonetheless, it was also a widespread way of referring to the "self" that paralleled the "self" understood to be "Hua-xia." The term "Central Plains" is used much less frequently than "Central States" in Warring States and early imperial texts, and I am hesitant to say that it had ethnic connotations in early times. "Central Plains" may in fact have had a much more circumscribed, geographical meaning early on, and only later was it co-opted to represent the Hua-xia or Han ethnicity.

period.[5] Rather than view each directional label as representing an actual ethnic group (and not precluding the possibility that the label may have specified an ethnic group at one point in its history), it is perhaps more fruitful to consider this nomenclature to be part and parcel of what Mark Lewis has called an imperializing, ruler-centered cosmology that emphasized Grand Unity among disparate parts.[6] Such a cosmography – one that was symbolized in the very layout of the imperial palace (which situated the Bright Hall [Ming Tang 明堂] and Dark Palace [Xuan Gong 玄宮] at the very center of the world) – arranged the cosmic and social order according to a physical, geographic taxonomy of place and direction, and not merely lineage.[7]

By the Han period, the Hua-xia were also considered to be the central lineage of many possible lineages – a schema that again highlighted unity among disparate parts, or branches. We see this most prominently in Sima Qian's grand history, which represents all (people) under Heaven through multiple lineages stemming from a similar source. While Hua-xia centrality seems to be assumed, the Yue are included in the "many varied lineages of the Xia" (Zhu-xia) by dint of their descent from Yu the Great: the founding ancestor of the Hua-xia. The addition of alternative lineages and family trees gave aliens in the periphery claims to the same or associated ancestors as the Hua-xia while clearly differentiating them from the main, central Xia branch of ancestors. Sima Qian's approach justifies the incorporation of others into a single diverse whole while at the same time relegating them to a subordinate line and reserving the center for the self. In this sense, Sima Qian's method of mapping the known world through mythological lineage and descent also hinges upon the logic of Hua-xia centrality.

In addition to spotlighting the centrality of the self, notions and representations of the Yue served to enhance the role of the Hua-xia self in the greater cosmos. Hua-xia authors often thought of the Yue other as inhabiting the same universe and abiding by the same universal rules, but as being prone to extremes within such a context. The center of gravity – indeed, the locus of harmony and balance in the cosmos – was attached to the self, while the Yue other was off-balance and lacking such harmony and gravity. To use Chinese cosmological language to frame this conceptual structure, the Yue were the *yin*-shadow that served to enhance Hua-xia *yang*-brightness. Cast as a background but nonetheless necessary

[5] Wang Aihe, *Cosmology and Political Culture in Early China* (Cambridge: Cambridge University Press, 2000), pp. 23–128.

[6] Mark Lewis discusses the mapping and ordering of spatial cosmologies in his chapter, "World and Cosmos," in *The Construction of Space in Early China* (Albany: State University of New York Press, 2006), pp. 245–273.

[7] *Ibid.*

contrapuntal figure on a cosmic stage, the Yue served as an undifferentiated, all-inclusive southern other that made it possible for the Hua-xia to play the starring role.

Cosmographic conceptions of southerners as Man-yi, or "non-Central States peoples hailing from the southerly direction," support the claim of Hua-xia centrality and render the specific term "Yue" even more important and intriguing. To be sure, the Yue were also Man-yi. But even though Yue identity might be conflated with that of the Man-yi of the South, it was different in a significant way. Rather than ubiquitously pointing to any alien southerner, the Yue were a specific type of Man-yi who formed an alternative, southern, ethnic foil to Hua-xia culture and ethnicity. In other words, they were more than the cosmographic other occupying the South (as is referenced by "Man-yi"); the Yue were an ethnic and cultural counterpart to the Hua-xia who confirmed and highlighted not only the latter's cosmic centrality but its cultural achievements and ethnic coherence as well. In such a sense, the term "Yue" should not be separated from its role as a partner in the making of Hua-xia identity, not just Hua-xia centrality.

On the historically constructed nature of Hua-xia and Yue identities

In our search for the origins of a Chinese sense of ethnicity, I took us back to the ancient text attributed to Confucius, the *Analects*. I showed how a myth of descent, geography, and cultural capital were the primary criteria for early Ru formulations of the Zhu-xia, or Hua-xia, identity in such a text. Later, by the early Han period, influential authors such as Sima Qian created alternative lineages for alien peoples surrounding the Hua-xia, thereby granting them a legitimate space in the ethnic imaginary – alongside (and sharing) the main ancestors and primary branch of the Hua-xia. Southern people thus occupied both a physical space on the margins as well as an abstract connection to founding lineages associated with the Hua-xia.

Han authors also began incorporating certain types of spatial thinking into their formulations on ethnicity, drawing up formulas for categorizing peoples according their environments and geography. This environmental determinism – one that fixed human traits according to factors of habitat and space – no doubt served to reinforce the logic of centrality that shaped the conceptualization of Hua-xia ethnicity. The Hua-xia self, after all, was not only from the "Central States," or "Central Plains" regions, it was the home of a civilized Xia, Shang, Zhou cultural heritage that represented physical moderation and balance through ritual comportment, as opposed to marginality and the lack of restraints.

Various Yue political identities moved from region to region and time period to time period in part because they offered a convenient, native, counter-Hua-xia tool for independent state-building and rebellion. The historically potent legacy of the Spring and Autumn/Warring States kingdom of Yue also lent caché and a sense of local, pan-regional (southern) power to any who would adopt such an identity for political purposes. But, as we saw, when Yue efforts at state-building failed, hopes for a political identity associated with the Yue were often dissolved or transformed beyond obvious recognition.[8]

The ultimately superior forces of the Han Empire seem to have further hindered the growth of a sustained, unified, and unfractured sense of Yue identity – one that befitted the Yue as imagined by early Hua-xia authors. In such a period, nascent forms of Yue identity were temporary, porous, and malleable; in other words, they coalesced and dissolved depending on the success of political structures and military forces, and they were easily abandoned or altered when certain enticements or threats (such as death) came to challenge one's formal or official allegiances. Thus, the histories of various early imperial Yue polities reveal an intriguing trend: whenever Yue states tried to claim complete independence from the Han, they may have achieved short-term success, but they were always stopped in the end by the Han. Thus, to the extent that Yue identity was espoused by Yue people themselves, such an identity was usually linked to non-Han state-building. Unfortunately, after Han Emperor Wu's conquests of the entire southern frontier, it was simply not advantageous or in an individual's interests to express publicly or cling too tightly to an identity that had lost to Han forces, though many still tried throughout the ages.

From the beginning of the imperial period, the process of state-building in the South relied very heavily on external forms of legitimation from farther north. The Han knew this and made good use of bribes, enticements, and possibilities for an individual's own personal gain, so that there was great incentive for greedy, self-interested, or self-protective local leaders to rebel against their neighbors or other local leaders and earn titles, emoluments, external legitimation, and land. Given that the temptations and reasons for defection or cooperation with the Han were great, it was no doubt very hard for enterprising local Yue leaders to use

[8] A sense of greater Yue identity associated with the entire area inhabited by the Hundred Yue was, in fact, never even a historical possibility. We may wonder whether this was testament to the fact that the concept of the Hundred Yue was merely a northern fiction that was never really embraced by locals, or whether it might be attributed to other historical contingencies throughout the ages (such as, the absence of a charismatic leader who, under the right circumstances, could have united the Yue under a single front, as the Xiongnu chieftains [*shanyu* 單于], had done along the northern frontier during the Han).

Yue identity as a tool to unite various groups of locals under a single cause. This was especially the case when most such leaders lacked an army that could defeat the Han troops in the long run.

In sum, the divisions among so-called Yue (i.e., native, non-Hua-xia) groups across the South were great. Unity was constantly undermined and mitigated against by many political and military factors. Not only did the Han state end up winning most of its wars against those southern kingdoms and commanderies that were of geographic and strategic value to them; Han foreign policy also exploited the political situation among rival Yue leaders and factions by playing locals off each other and enticing them with bribes or prospects for holding power as a Han subordinate.

While the various Yue political identities of the Han period were destroyed by 110 BCE, native, cultural identities of peoples in the South (note: not necessarily "Yue" identities) undoubtedly possessed a much more tenacious hold and would not have changed overnight. Even when powerful Han colonialists such as General Ma Yuan tried to enforce the adoption of Han statutes and select customs in the first century CE, it was likely that the scope of such changes was limited to certain metropolitan regions where the Han presence could be felt and where real consequences for non-compliance were enforced through military action. In reality, there were very few Han officials and colonists compared to the population of indigenous peoples at the time. So any acculturation that took place was likely to have occurred in a direction that favored the perpetuation of native habits and the assimilation of such native habits by minority Han outsiders in the South, at least at this early date.

The process of incorporating native identities and cultural practices into the Han fold took thousands of years. This process was clearly not always one of sinicization, whereby native identities vanished without a trace and became Hua-xia in their stead. Even early descriptions of attempts to establish local control suggest that the process of cultural change was highly varied, and it did not involve wholesale substitution of one culture for another. Nor did such a process occur immediately, and especially not during the period of Han colonial rule, despite the temporary obliteration of all the major Yue political entities.

While many more of the histories of cross-cultural interactions and blending along the southern frontier still need to be written, it seems fairly clear from our study that the concept of sinicization is of limited use, and that the early southern frontier was far from being Hua-xia or sinicized during the period we have considered.[9] Given the minority of

[9] The history of pre-modern, southern, cross-cultural relations is currently being studied by an ever-widening circle of scholars. For the history of the pre-Song and Song period, see

Hua-xia immigrants (government workers, traders, or new settlers) in southern communities and cities throughout the early imperial period, the peoples associated with the erstwhile Yue lands no doubt remained more a part of their native, local cultures than Central Plains cultures. It was only after the Eastern Han that the southern frontier of China became a crucible for the formation of the specific blends of Sinitic and native cultures and identities that are very much a part of the legacies we might still see in Vietnamese and southern Chinese cultures today.

the work of Hugh Clark, or the articles in the volume edited by Nola Cooke, Li Tana, and James A. Anderson, *The Tongking Gulf Through History* (Philadelphia: University of Pennsylvania Press, 2011). See also the works of James A. Anderson and Sean Marsh. For histories concerning the Ming and Qing southern frontiers, see the work by C. Michele Thompson, Li Tana, Robert Antony, Liam Kelley, John Whitmore, Niu Junkai, Kathlene Baldanza, and many more.

Select bibliography

Abramson, Marc. *Ethnic Identity in Tang China*. Philadelphia: University of Pennsylvania Press, 2008.

Allan, Sarah, ed. *The Formation of Chinese Civilization: An Archaeological Perspective*. New Haven: Yale University Press, 2005.

Allard, Francis. "Early Complex Societies in Southern China." Chapter 8 in *The Cambridge World Prehistory*, vol. II, eds. Colin Renfrew and Paul Bahn, 797–823. Cambridge: Cambridge University Press, 2014.

"Frontiers and Boundaries: The Han Empire from Its Southern Periphery." In *Archaeology of Asia*, ed. M. Stark, 233–255. Malden: Blackwell Publishers, 2005.

"Stirrings at the Periphery: History, Archaeology and the Study of Dian." *International Journal of Historical Archaeology* 2.4 (1998): 321–341.

"The Archaeology of Dian: Trends and Tradition." *Antiquity* 73.279 (1998): 77–85.

"Interaction and the Emergence of Complex Societies in Lingnan During the Late Neolithic and Bronze Age." Ph.D. dissertation, University of Pittsburgh, 1995.

"Interaction and Social Complexity in Lingnan during the First Millennium B.C." *Asian Perspectives* 33.2 (1994): 309–326.

Allen, John, Doreen Massey, and Allan Cochrane. *Rethinking the Region*. London: Routledge, 1998.

Anderson, James A. *The Rebel Den of Nung Tri Cao: Loyalty and Identity Along the Sino-Vietnamese Frontier*. Seattle: University of Washington Press, 2007.

"A Special Relationship: 10th–13th Century Sino-Vietnamese Tribute Relations and the Traditional Chinese Notion of World Order." Ph.D. dissertation, 1999, University of Washington.

Archeological Discovery in Eastern Kwangtung: The Major Writings of Fr. Rafael Maglioni (1891–1953). Hong Kong: Hong Kong Archeological Society, 1975.

Aurousseau, Leonard. "La première conquêt chinoise de pays annamites (III Siècle avant notre èra)." *Bulletin de l'École Française D'Extrême-Orient* 23 (1924): 137–266.

Bagley, Robert, ed. *Ancient Sichuan: Treasures from a Lost Civilization*. Princeton: Princeton University Press, 2001.

Ban Gu. *Han Shu* (History of the Han). 12 vols. Beijing: Zhonghua shu ju, 1995.

Bang, P. F. and C. Bayly. "Introduction: Comparing Pre-modern Empires." *Medieval History Journal* 6 (2003): 169–187.

Barbieri-Low, Anthony. *Artisans in Early Imperial China*. Seattle: University of Washington Press, 2007.

Barfield, Thomas. "The Shadow Empires: Imperial State Formation Along the Chinese–Nomad Frontier." In *Empires: Perspectives from Archaeology and History*, eds. Susan E. Alcock *et al.*, 10–41. New York: Cambridge University Press, 2001.

"The Hsiung-nu Imperial Confederacy: Organization and Foreign Policy." *Journal of Asian Studies* 41 (1981): 45–61.

Barkey, Karen. *Empire of Difference: The Ottomans in Comparative Perspective*. Cambridge: Cambridge University Press, 2008.

Beck, B. J. Mansvelt. *The Treatises of Later Han: Their Author, Sources, Contents and Place in Chinese Historiography*. Leiden: E. J. Brill, 1990.

Behr, Wolfgang. "Etymologisches zur Herkunft des ältesten chinesischen Staatsnamens." *AS/EA* 61.3 (2007): 727–754.

"'To Translate' is 'To Exchange' 譯者言易也 – Linguistic Diversity and the Terms for Translation in Ancient China." In *Mapping Meanings: The Field of New Learning in Late Qing China*, eds. N. Vittinghoff and M. Lackner, 173–209. Leiden: E. J. Brill, 2004.

Bellwood, Peter. "Southeast China and the Prehistory of the Austronesians." In *Lost Maritime Cultures: China and the Pacific*, ed. Jiao Tianlong. Honolulu: Bishop Museum Press, 2007.

"Asian Farming Diasporas? Agriculture, Languages, and Genes in China and Southeast Asia." In *Archaeology of Asia*, ed. M. Stark, 96–118. Blackwell Publishing, 2006.

"The Dispersal of Neolithic Cultures from China into Island Southeast Asia: Stand Stills, Slow Moves, and Fast Spreads." In *Huanan ji dongnan ya diqu shiqian kaogu* (Prehistoric Archaeology of South China and Southeast Asia), eds. Institute of Archaeology, Chinese Academy of Social Sciences, 223–234. Beijing: Wenwe chubanshe, 2006.

"The Origins and Dispersals of Agricultural Communities in Southeast Asia." In *Southeast Asia: From Prehistory to History*, eds. I. Glover and P. Bellwood. London: Routledge Curzon, 2004.

"Formosan Prehistory and Austronesian Dispersal." In *Austronesian Taiwan*, ed. D. Blundell, 337–365. Berkeley: The Regents of the University of California, 2000.

Prehistory of the Indo-Malaysian Archipelago. Honolulu: University of Hawaii Press, 1997.

"Austronesian Prehistory in Southeast Asia: Homeland, Expansion, and Transformation." In *The Austronesians: Historical and Comparative Perspectives*, eds. P. Bellwood, J. Fox, and D. Tryon, 96–111. Canberra: Australian National University, 1995.

Bellwood, Peter, and E. Dizon. "The Batanes Archaeological Project and the Out of Taiwan Hypothesis for Austronesian Dispersal." *Journal of Austronesian Studies* 1 (2005): 1–33.

Benedict, Paul. "Austro-Thai; Austro-Thai Studies." *Behavior Science Notes* 1.4 (1967–1968): 227–261.

"Thai, Kadai, and Indonesian: A New Alignment in Southeastern Asia." *American Anthropologist*, New Series, 44.4, Part 1 (1942): 576–601.

Bhabha, Homi. *The Location of Culture*. London: Routledge, 1994.

Bielenstein, Hans. *The Bureaucracy of Han Times*. Cambridge: Cambridge University Press, 1980.

"The Chinese Colonization of Fukien Until the End of T'ang." In *Studia Serica Bernhard Kargren Dedicata*, eds. Soren Egerod and Else Glahn, 98–122. Copenhagen: Ejnar Munksgaard, 1959.

Bin Wong, R. *China Transformed: Historical Change and the Limits of European Experience*. Ithaca: Cornell University Press, 1997.

"Chinese Historical Demography A.D. 2–1982." *Bulletin of the Museum of Far Eastern Antiquities* 59 (1987): 1–288.

Blench, Roger. "The Prehistory of the Daic (Tai-Kadai) Speaking Peoples and the Hypothesis of an Austronesian Connection." Presented at the 12th EURASEAA meeting Leiden, 1–5 September, 2008, and subsequently revised for publication; printout, July 12, 2009.

"Stratification in the Peopling of China: How Far Does the Linguistic Evidence Match Genetics and Archaeology?" Paper presented at the symposium, "Human Migrations in Continental East Asia and Taiwan: Genetic, Linguistic and Archaeological Evidence," June 10–13, 2004, Université de Genève, Switzerland, pp. 12–13.

Blust, Robert. "Austronesian Culture History: The Window of Language." In *Prehistoric Settlement of the Pacific*, ed. Ward H. Goodenough, 28–35. Philadelphia: American Philosophical Society, 1996.

"Beyond the Austronesian Homeland: The Austric Hypothesis and its Implications for Archaeology." In *Prehistoric Settlement of the Pacific*, ed. Ward H. Goodenough, 117–140. Philadelphia: American Philosophical Society, 1996.

"The Prehistory of the Austronesian-speaking Peoples: A View from Language." *Journal of World Prehistory* 9.4 (1995): 453–510.

"The Austronesian Homeland: A Linguistic Perspective." *Asian Perspectives* 26 (1984/5): 45–67.

Brindley, Erica. "Layers of Meaning: Hairstyle and Yue Identity in Ancient Chinese Texts." In *Imperial China and Its Southern Neighbors*, Nalanda-Srivijaya Series, eds. Victor Mair and Liam Kelley. Singapore: Institute for Southeast Asian Studies, 2014.

"Representations and Uses of Yue 越 Identity Along the Southern Frontier of the Han, ~200–111 BCE." *Early China* 33–34 (2010–11): 1–35.

"Barbarians or Not? Ethnicity and Changing Conceptions of the Ancient Yue (Viet) Peoples (~400–50 B.C.)." *Asia Major* 16.1 (2003): 1–32.

Brown, Miranda. "Neither 'Primitive' nor 'Others,' But Somehow Not Quite Like 'Us': The Fortunes of Psychic Unity and Essentialism in Chinese Studies." *Journal of the Economic and Social History of the Orient* 49.2 (2006): 219–252.

Butler, Judith. *Gender Trouble: Feminism and the Subversion of Identity*. New York: Routledge, 1990.

Cao, Jinyan 曹錦炎. 曹錦炎.春秋初期越為徐地說新證 ("A New Examination of the Claim 'Yue is Xu territory during the early Spring and Autumn Period'").

Chapter in *Wu-yue lishi yu kaogu luncong* 吳越歷史與考古論叢. Beijing: Wenwu, 2007.

Chang, K. C. "China on the Eve of the Historical Period." In *The Cambridge History of Ancient China*, eds. Edward Shaughnessy and Michael Loewe, 37–73. Cambridge: Cambridge University Press, 1999.

The Archaeology of Ancient China. 3rd edn. New Haven: Yale University Press, 1978.

Early Chinese Civilization: Anthropological Perspectives. Cambridge, MA: Harvard University Press, 1976.

"Ancient Trade as Economics or as Ecology." In *Ancient Civilization and Trade*, eds. J. A. Sabloff and C. C. Lamberg-Karlovsky, 211–224. Albuquerque: University of New Mexico Press, 1975.

Fengpitou, Tapenkeng and the Prehistory of Taiwan. New Haven: Yale University Press, 1969.

Chang, K. C. and Ward H. Goodenough. "Archaeology of Southeastern Coastal China and its Bearing on the Austronesian Homeland." In *Prehistoric Settlement of the Pacific*, ed. Ward H. Goodenough, 36–56. Philadelphia: American Philosophical Society, 1996.

Chen Guoqiang 陳國強, *et al. Baiyue minzu shi* 百越民族史. Beijing: Zhongguo shehui kexue, 1988.

Chen Qiyou 陳奇猷. *Lüshi chunqiu jiaoshi* 吕氏春秋校釋. Shanghai: Xuelin Publishing, 1984.

Churchman, Michael. "'The People in Beween': The Li and Lao from the Han to the Sui." In *The Tongking Gulf Through History*, eds. Nola Cooke, Li Tana, and James Anderson, 67–83. Philadelphia: University of Pennsylvania Press, 2011.

Clark, Hugh R. "Frontier Discourse and China's Maritime Frontier: China's Frontiers and the Encounter with the Sea Through Early Imperial History." *Journal of World History* 20:1 (2009): 1–33.

Portrait of a Community: Society, Culture, and the Structures of Kinship in the Mulan River Valley (Fujian) from the Late Tang through the Song. Hong Kong: The Chinese University Press, 2007.

Community, Trade, and Networks: Southern Fujian Province from the Third to the Thirteenth Century. Cambridge: Cambridge University Press, 1991.

Coedes, Georges. *The Making of South East Asia*, trans. H. M. Wright. Berkeley and Los Angeles: University of California Press, 1966.

Cohen, David. "The Yueshi Culture, the Dongyi, and the Archaeology of Ethnicity in Early Bronze Age China." Ph.D. dissertation, Harvard University (2001).

Cohen, Paul. *Speaking to History: The Story of King Goujian in Twentieth-century China*. Berkeley: University of California Press, 2009.

Cook, Constance and John Major, eds. *Defining Chu: Image and Reality in Ancient China*. Honolulu: University of Hawaii Press, 1999.

Cooke, Nola, Li Tana, and James A. Anderson, eds. *The Tongking Gulf Through History*. Philadelphia: University of Pennsylvania Press, 2011.

Crossley, Pamela. *A Translucent Mirror: History and Identity in Qing Imperial Ideology*. Berkeley: University of California Press, 1999.

The Manchus. Cambridge, MA: Blackwell Publishers, 1997.

"Thinking about Ethnicity in Early Modern China." *Late Imperial China* 11.1 (June 1990): 1–35.

Csete, Ann. "A Frontier Minority in the Chinese World: The Li People of Hainan Island from the Han through the High Qing." Ph.D. dissertation, SUNY Buffalo, 1995.

Cushman, Richard. "Rebel Haunts and Lotus Huts: Problems in the Ethnohistory of the Yao." Ph.D. dissertation, Cornell University, 1970.

Davidson, J. C. S. "Recent Archaeological Activity in Vietnam." *Journal of the Hong Kong Archaeological Society* 6 (1975): 80–99.

De Crespigny, Rafe. *Generals of the South: The Foundation and Early History of the Three Kingdoms State of Wu.* Canberra: Australian National University, Faculty of Asian Studies, 1990.

Northern Frontier: The Policies and Strategy of the Later Han Empire. Canberra: Australian National University, Faculty of Asian Studies, 1984.

Deagan, Kathleen. *Spanish St. Augustine: The Archaeology of a Colonial Creole Community.* New York: Academic Press, 1983.

Demiéville, P. "Philosophy and Religion from Han to Sui." In *The Cambridge History of China I*, eds. Denis Twitchett and Michael Loewe, 808–872. Cambridge: Cambridge University Press, 1986.

Di Cosmo, Nicola. "Han Frontiers: Toward an Integrated View." *Journal of the American Oriental Society* 129.2 (2009): 199–214.

Ancient China and its Enemies: The Rise of Nomadic Power in East Asian History. Cambridge, Cambridge University Press, 2002.

Dien, Albert E., ed. *State and Society in Early Medieval China.* Stanford: Stanford University Press, 1990.

Dietler, Michael. *Archaeologies of Colonialism: Consumption, Entanglement, and Violence in Ancient Mediterranean France.* Berkeley: University of California Press, 2010.

"Consumption, Agency, and Cultural Entanglement: Theoretical Implications of a Mediterranean Colonial Encounter." In *Studies in Culture Contact: Interaction, Culture Change, and Archaeology*, ed. J. G. Cusick, 288–315. Carbondale: Center for Archaeological Investigations, SIU, 1998.

Diffloth, Gérard. "The Contribution of Linguistic Palaeontology and Austroasiatic." In *The Peopling of East Asia: Putting Together Archaeology, Linguistics and Genetic*, eds. Laurent Sagart, Roger Blench, and Alicia Sanchez-Mazas, 77–80. London: Routledge Curzon, 2005.

"The Lexical Evidence for Austric, So Far." *Oceanic Linguistics* 33 (1994): 309–322.

Dikötter, Frank. *Discourse of Race in Modern China.* Stanford: Stanford University Press, 1994.

Dong Chuping 董楚平. "An Investigation into the Question of Tomb Occupancy at the Great Yingshan Mausoleum, along with Some Comments on the State Affiliation of Shaoxing Tomb 306 關於紹興印山大墓墓主問題的探討—兼說紹興 306 號墓的國屬問題." *Journal of Hangzhou Teachers College (Social Sciences Edition)* 4 (July, 2002): 57–62.

Dubs, Homer H., trans. *The History of the Former Han Dynasty, vols. I and II.* Baltimore: Waverly Press, Inc, 1938.

Eberhard, Wolfram. *The Local Cultures of South and East China*, trans. Alide Eberhard. Leiden: E. J. Brill, 1968.

"Kultur und Siedlung der Randvolkers China." *T'oung Pao*, Supplement to Vol. 36 (1942).

Eberhard, Wolfram, Krysztof Gawlikowski, and Carl-Albrecht Seyschab, eds. *Ethnic Identity and National Characteristics: Studies*. Bremen: Simon & Megiera, 1982.

Eisman, Harriet Lenz. "Shan hai ching (The Classic of Mountains and Seas)." Master's thesis, Cornell University, 1975.

Elliott, Mark. *The Manchu Way: The Eight Banners and Ethnic Identity in Late Imperial China*. Stanford: Stanford University Press, 2001.

Erickson, Susan, Yi Song-mi, and Michael Nylan. "The Archaeology of the Outlying Lands." In *China's Early Empires: A Reappraisal*, eds. Michael Nylan and Michael Loewe, 135–168. Cambridge: Cambridge University Press, 2010.

Falkenhausen, Lothar von. *Chinese Society in the Age of Confucius*. Los Angeles: Cotsen Institute of Archaeology, University of California, 2006.

"The Use and Significance of Ritual Bronzes in the Lingnan Region during the Eastern Zhou Period." *Journal of East Asian Archaeology* 3.1–2 (2001): 193–236.

"The Waning of the Bronze Age: Material Culture and Social Developments, 770–481 B. C." In *Cambridge History of Ancient China: From the Origins of Civilization to 221 B.C.*, eds. Edward Shaughnessy and Michael Loewe, 450–554. Cambridge: Cambridge University Press, 1999.

"The Regionalist Paradigm in Chinese Archaeology." In *Nationalism, Politics and the Practice of Archaeology*, eds. P. L. Kohl and C. Fawcett, 198–217. Cambridge: Cambridge University Press, 1995.

Fang Tie 方鐵. "Nanyueguo de nei-wai guanxi ji qi zhengce 南越國的內外關系及其政策." *Journal of Wenshan Teachers College* 19.2 (2006): 1–7.

Fei Xiaotong wenji 费孝通文集 (Collected works of Fei Xiaotong), 15 vols. Beijing: Qunyan chubanshe, 1999.

Fiskesjö, Magnus. "On the 'Raw' and 'Cooked': Barbarians of Imperial China." *Inner China* 1–2 (1999): 135–168.

FitzGerald, C. P. *The Southern Expansion of the Chinese People*. New York: Praeger Publishers, 1972.

Flad, Rowan, and Pochan Chen, *Ancient Central China: Centers and Peripheries Along the Yangzi River*. Cambridge: Cambridge University Press, 2013.

Fried, Morton. "Tribe to State or State to Tribe in Ancient China?" In *The Origins of Chinese Civilization*, ed. David Keightley. Berkeley: University of California Press, 1983.

Friedman, Sara L. "Embodying Civility: Civilizing Processes and Symbolic Citizenship in Southeastern China." *Journal of Asia Studies* 63:3 (2004): 687–718.

Fujian Bowuyuan 福建博物院 and Fujian Minyue Wangcheng bowuguan 福建閩越王城博物館, eds. *Wuyishan Chengcun Hancheng yizhi fajue baogao 1980–1996* 武夷山城村漢城遺址發掘報告 *(Excavation Report on the Site Remains of the Han City near Chengcun at Wuyishan, 1980–1996)*. Fuzhou: Fujian renmin chubanshe, 2004.

Gladney, Dru. *Ethnic Identity in China: The Making of a Muslim Minority Nationality*. Forth Worth, TX: Harcourt Brace College Publishers, 1998.

Glover, Ian, and Peter Bellwood. *Southeast Asia: From Prehistory to History*. New York: Routledge Curzon, 2004.

Goodenough, Ward H., ed. *Prehistoric Settlement of the Pacific*. Philadelphia: American Philosophical Society, 1996.

Graff, David. *Medieval Chinese Warfare, 300–900*. New York: Routledge, 2001.

Gray, R. D., A. J. Drummond, and S. J. Greenhill. "Language Phylogenies Reveal Expansion Pulses and Pauses in Pacific Settlemen."*Science* 323 (2009): 479.

Guangdongsheng bowuguan 廣東省博物館. "Guangdong kaogu shi nian gaishu 廣東考古十年概述." In *Wenwu kaogu gongzuo shi nian 1979–1989* 文物考古工作十年, ed. Wenwu bianji weiyuanhui, 222–223. Beijing: Wenwu, 1991.

Guangzhou shi wenwu guanli weiyuanhui *et al. Xi-Han Nanyue wang mu* 西漢南越王墓, 2 vols. Beijing: Wenwu, 1991.

Guo Qingfan 郭慶藩. *Zhuangzi ji shi* 莊子集釋. Taipei: Wan juan lou, 1993.

Hagelberg, Erica. "Origins and Affinities of 'Papuan' and 'Austronesian' Genes in the West Pacific." 17th Congress of Indo-Pacific Prehistory Association, Taiwan, 2002.

Hall, Jonathan. *Ethnic Identity in Greek Antiquity*. Cambridge: Cambridge University Press, 1997.

Han Kangxin and Takahiro Nakahashi. "A Comparative Study of Ritual Tooth Ablation in Ancient China and Japan." *Anthropological Science* 104.1 (1996): 43–64.

Hargett, James M. "會稽: Guaiji? Guiji? Huiji? Kuaiji? Some Remarks on an Ancient Chinese Place-Name." *Sino-Platonic Papers* 234 (March 2013): 1–32.

Harper, Donald. "A Chinese Demonography of the Third Century B.C." *Harvard Journal of Asiatic Studies* 45.2 (1985): 459–498.

Harrell, Stevan. *Ways of Being Ethnic in Southwest China*. Seattle: University of Washington Press, 2002.

Hawkes, David. *The Songs of the South: An Ancient Chinese Anthology of Poems by Qu Yuan and Other Poets*. London: Penguin, 1985.

He, Guangyue 何光岳. *Bai Yue yuanliu shi*. Nanchang: Jiangxi jiaoyu chubanshe, 1989.

He Jianzhang 何建章, *Zhanguoce zhushi* 戰國策注釋. Beijing: Zhonghua shuju, 1990.

Henry, Eric. "The Persistence of Yuè in Southeast China." Paper presented at the AAS Annual Conference, March 31, 2011 in Honolulu, Hawaii.

"The Submerged History of Yuè." *Sino-Platonic Papers* 176 (2007): 1–36.

Higham, Charles. "The Prehistory of Southeast Asia: A Retrospective View of 40 Years' Research." *Antiquity* 85 (2011): 639–653.

"Mainland Southeast Asia From the Neolithic to the Iron Age." In *Southeast Asia: From Prehistory to History*, eds. Ian Glover and Peter Bellwood, 41–67. London: Routledge Curzon, 2004.

Early Cultures of Mainland Southeast Asia. Bangkok: River Books, 2002.

"Archaeology and Linguistics in Southeast Asia: Implications of the Austric Hypothesis." *Bulletin of the Indo-Pacific Prehistory Association* 14 (1996): 110–118.

The Bronze Age of Southeast Asia. Cambridge: Cambridge University Press, 1996.

The Archaeology of Mainland Southeast Asia. Cambridge: Cambridge University Press, 1989.

Ho, Chui-mei. "Pottery in South China: River Xijiang and Upper Red River Basins." *World Archaeology* 15.3 (Feb., 1984): 294–325.

Ho, Ping-ti. "In Defense of Sinicization: A Rebuttal of Evelyn Rawski's 'Reenvisioning the Qing.'" *Journal of Asian Studies* 57 (1998): 123–155.

The Cradle of the East: An Inquiry into the Indigenous Origins of Techniques and Ideas of Neolithic and Early Historic China, 5000–1000 B.C. Hong Kong: Chinese University of Hong Kong, 1976.

Holcombe, Charles. "Early Imperial China's Deep South: The Viet Regions through Tang Times." *T'ang Studies* 15–16 (1997–1998): 125–156.

In the Shadow of the Han: Literati Thought and Society at the Beginning of the Southern Dynasties. Honolulu: University of Hawaii Press, 1994.

Holmgren, Jennifer. *Chinese Colonisation of Northern Vietnam*. Canberra: Australian National University Press, 1980.

Hsu, Cho-yun. "The Spring and Autumn Period." In *Cambridge History of Ancient China: From the Origins of Civilization to 221 B. C.*, eds. Edward Shaughnessy and Michael Loewe, 545–586. Cambridge: Cambridge University Press, 1999.

Huang Qingchang 黃慶昌. "Lun Xi Han wangchao yu Nanyue guo de guanxi 論西漢王朝與南越國的関系." *Nanfang wenwu* 南方文物 (2003).

Hulsewé, A. F. P. *Remnants of Han Law*. Leiden: E. J. Brill, 1955.

Izui, Hisanosuke. "Ryu Eko 'Setsu En' Kan ju ichi no Etsuka ni tsuite 劉向'說苑'巻十一の越歌について." *Gengo Kenkyuu* 22/23 (1953): 41–45.

Jao Tsung-i. "Yüeh wen-hua." *The Bulletin of the Institute of History and Philology, Academica Sinica* 41.4 (1969): 609–636.

Jiao, Tianlong. *The Neolithic of Southeast China: Cultural Transformation and Regional Interaction on the Coast*. Youngstown, N.Y.: Cambria, 2007.

"The Neolithic Cultures in Southeast China and the Search for the Austronesian Homeland." In *Southeast Asian Archaeology*, ed. Victor Paz, 565–588. Quezon City: University of Philippines Press, 2004.

Jiao Tianlong 焦天龍 and Fan Xuechun 范雪春. 福建與南島語族 (*Fujian and the Austronesians*). Beijing: Zhonghua shuju, 2010.

Kelley, Liam. "Tai Words and the Place of the Tai in the Vietnamese Past." *Journal of the Siam Society* 101 (2013): 55–84.

"The Biography of the Hong Bang Clan as a Medieval Vietnamese Invented Tradition." *Journal of Vietnamese Studies* 7.2 (2012): 87–130.

"Inventing Traditions in Fifteenth-century Vietnam." Paper presented at "Imperial China and its Southern Neighbours," June 28–29, 2012, Singapore.

Kern, Martin. "Announcements from the Mountains: The Stele Inscriptions of the Qin First Emperor." In *Conceiving the Empire: China and Rome Compared*, eds. Fritz-Heiner Mutschler and Achim Mittag, 217–240. Oxford: Oxford University Press, 2008.

Kieschnick, John. *The Impact of Buddhism on Chinese Material Culture*. Princeton: Princeton University Press, 2003.

Kim, Hyun-jin. *Ethnicity and Foreigners in Ancient Greece and China*. London: Duckworth, 2009.

Kirch P., "Peopling of the Pacific: A Holistic Anthropological Perspective." *Annual Review of Anthropology* 39 (2010): 131–148.

Kiser, E., and Y. Cai. "War and Bureaucratization in Qin China: Exploring an Anomalous Case."*American Sociological Review* 68 (2003): 511–539.

Kleeman, Terry. *Great Perfection: Religion and Ethnicity in a Chinese Millennial Kingdom*. Honolulu: University of Hawaii Press, 1998.

Ko, Albert, and Chung-yu Chen *et al.* "Early Austronesians: Into and Out of Taiwan." *The American Journal of Human Genetics* 94 (March 6, 2014): 426–436.

Lagerwey, John. "A Translation of *The Annals of Wu and Yue*, Part I, with a Study of its Sources." Ph.D. dissertation, Harvard University, 1975.

Lary, Diana. "The Tomb of the King of Nanyue – The Contemporary Agenda of History." *Modern China* 22.1 (1996): 3–27.

Lattimore, Owen. *Inner Asian Frontiers of China*. Boston: Beacon Press, 1962.

Lau, D.C. (trans.). *Confucius, The Analects (Lun yü)*. New York: Penguin, 1979.

Lefebvre, Henri. *The Production of Space*. Oxford: Wiley-Blackwell, 1991.

Leong, Sow-theng. *Migration and Ethnicity in Chinese History: Hakkas, Pengmin, and Their Neighbors*, ed. Tim Wright. Stanford: Stanford University Press, 1997.

Lewis, Mark Edward. *China Between Empires: The Northern and Southern Dynasties*. Cambridge, MA: The Belknap Press of Harvard University Press, 2009.

The Early Chinese Empires: Qin and Han. Cambridge, MA and London: Harvard University Press, 2007.

The Construction of Space in Early China. Albany: State University of New York Press, 2006.

"Warring States Political History." In *Cambridge History of Ancient China: From the Origins of Civilization to 221 B.C.*, eds. Edward Shaughnessy and Michael Loewe, 587–650. Cambridge: Cambridge University Press, 1999.

Sanctioned Violence in Early China. Albany: State University of New York Press, 1990.

Li, Feng. *Landscape and Power in Early China: The Crisis and Fall of the Western Zhou, 1045–771 BC*. Cambridge: Cambridge University Press, 2006. ("Appendix I: The Periphery: The Western Zhou State at Its Maximum Geographical Extent," pp. 300–342.)

Li Ji 李濟. "Gui zuo, dun ju, yu ji ju 跪坐蹲居與箕踞." *Zhongyang yanjiuyuan lishi yuyan yanjiusuo jikan* 中央研究院歷史語言研究所集刊 24 (1953): 283–301.

Li Jinfang 李锦芳. *Buying yu janjiu* 布央语研究. 北京市: 中央民族大学出版社 (Research on Buying Language). Beijing: Zhongyang People's Publishing, 1999.

Li, Tana. "Jiaozhi (Giao Chi) in the Han Period Tongking Gulf." In *The Tongking Gulf Through History*, eds. Nola Cooke, Li Tana, and James A. Anderson, 39–52. Philadelphia: University of Pennsylvania Press, 2011.

Lightfoot, Kent, and Antoinette Martinez. "Frontiers and Boundaries in Archaeological Perspectives." *Annual Review of Anthropology* 24 (1995): 471–492.

Linduff, Katheryn. "Here Today and Gone Tomorrow: The Emergence and Demise of Bronze Producing Cultures Outside the Central Plains." *Bulletin of the Institute of History and Philology* (1996).

Ling, Shunsheng 凌純聲. "Gudai zhongguo yu Taipingyang qu de quanji" (Dog Sacrifice in Ancient China and the Pacific Area). *Bulletin of the Institute of Ethnology, Academia Sinica* 3 (Spring, 1957): 1–40.

Liu, Lydia. "The Question of Meaning-Value in the Political Economy of the Sign." In *Tokens of Exchange: The Problem of Translation in Global Circulations*, ed. Lydia Liu, 34–36 (on *yi*-"barbarians"). Durham, NC: Duke University Press, 1999.

Liu Min 劉敏. "'Kai guan' ding lun – cong 'Wendi xing xi' kan Han-Yue guanxi 開棺定論 – 從 文帝行璽看漢越關系." In *Nanyueguo shiji yan tao hui*.

Liu Rui 劉瑞. "Nanyueguo fei Han zhi zhuhouguo lun 南越國非漢之諸侯國論." In *Nanyueguo shiji yan tao hui*, 9–22.

Liu Wendian 劉文典. *Huainan honglie jijie* 淮南鴻烈集解. Beijing: Zhonghua Publishing, 1989.

Liu Xiaomin 劉曉民. "Nanyueguo shi qi Han-Yue wenhua de bingcun yu ronghe 南越國時期漢越文化的並存輿融合." *Dongnan Wenhua* 東南文化 1.123 (1999): 22–27.

Loewe, Michael. *The Government of the Qin and Han Empires: 221 B.C.E.–220 CE.* Indianapolis: Hackett Publishing Company, 2006.

"Guangzhou: The Evidence of the Standard Histories from the *Shi ji* to the *Chen shu*, A Preliminary Survey." In *Guangdong: Archaeology and Early Texts/ Archäologie und frühe Texte (Zhou – Tang)*, eds. Shing Müller, Thomas Höllmann, and Putao Gui, 51–80. Wiesbaden: Harrassowitz Verlag, 2004 (South China and Maritime Asia, vol. XIII).

The Men Who Governed Han China: Companion to A Biographical Dictionary of the Qin, Former Han and Xin Periods. Leiden: Brill, 2004.

"China's Sense of Unity as Seen in the Early Empires." *T'oung Pao* 80 (1994): 6–26.

ed. *Early Chinese Texts: A Bibliographical Guide*. Berkeley: Society for the Study of Early China and The Institute of East Asian Studies, University of California Press, 1993.

"The Structure and Practice of Government." In *The Cambridge History of China, I: The Ch'in and Han Empires, 221 B.C.–A.D. 200*. eds. Denis Twitchett and Michael Loewe, 463–490. Cambridge: Cambridge University Press, 1986.

Lu Liancheng, "The Eastern Zhou and the Growth of Regionalism." In *The Formation of Chinese Civilization*, ed. Sarah Allan, 202–247. New Haven: Yale University Press, 2005.

Lu Liancheng and Yan Wenming, "Society during the Three Dynasties." In *The Formation of Chinese Civilization*, ed. Sarah Allan, 141–201. New Haven: Yale University Press, 2005.

Lü Liedan 呂烈丹. *Nanyue wang mu yu Nanyue wang guo* 南越王墓與南越王國. Guangzhou: Guangzhou wenhua, 1990.

Luo, Chia-li. "Coastal Culture and Religion in Early China: A Study through Comparison with the Central Plain Region." Ph.D. dissertation, Indiana University, 1999.

Lyons, C. L. and J. K. Papadopoulos, eds. *The Archaeology of Colonialism*. Los Angeles: Getty Research Institute, 2002.

Mann, Michael. *The Sources of Social Power, I: A History of Power from the Beginning to A.D. 1760*. Cambridge: Cambridge University Press, 1986.

Maspero, Henri. "Etudes d'histoire d'Annam." *Bulletin de l'Ecole Francaise d'Extreme-Orient* 16: 1–55, and 18 (1918): 1–36.

Meacham, William. "Defining the Hundred Yue." *Indo-Pacific Prehistory Association Bulletin* 15 (1996; Chiang Mai Papers, vol. II): 93–100.

"On the Improbability of Austronesian Origins in South China." *Asian Perspectives* 26 (1988): 89–106.

"Origins and Development of the Yüeh Coastal Neolithic: A Microcosm of Culture Change on the Mainland of East Asia." In *The Origins of Chinese Civilization*, ed. David Keightley. Berkeley: University of California Press, 1983.

Meng Wentong. *Yueshi congkao*. Beijing: Renmin chubanshe, 1983.

Milburn, Olivia. *The Glory of Yue: An Annotated Translation of the Yuejue shu*. Leiden: Brill, 2010.

Miller, Innes. *The Spice Trade of the Roman Empire, 29 B.C. to A.D. 641*. Oxford: The Clarendon Press, 1969.

Mittag, Achim. "Forging Legacy: The Pact between Empire and Historiography in Ancient China." In *Conceiving the Empire: China and Rome Compared*, eds. Fritz-Heiner Mutschler and Achim Mittag, 143–168. Oxford: Oxford University Press, 2008.

Mittag, Achim and Ye Min. "Empire on the Brink: Chinese Historiography in the Post-Han-Period." In *Conceiving the Empire: China and Rome Compared*, eds. Fritz-Heiner Mutschler and Achim Mittag, 347–372. Oxford: Oxford University Press, 2008.

Moseley, George. *The Consolidation of the South China Frontier*. Berkeley and Los Angeles: University of California Press, 1973.

Mullaney, Thomas. *Coming to Terms with the Nation: Ethnic Classification in Modern China*. Berkeley: University of California Press, 2010.

Müller, Shing, Thomas Höllmann, and Putao Gui, eds. *Guangdong: Archaeology and Early Texts/Archäologie und frühe Texte (Zhou – Tang)*. Wiesbaden: Harrassowitz Verlag, 2004 (South China and Maritime Asia, vol. XIII).

Munson, Rosaria Vignolo. *Telling Wonders: Ethnographic and Political Discourse in the Work of Herodotus*. Ann Arbor: University of Michigan Press, 2001.

Murowchick, Robert E. "The Interplay of Bronze and Ritual in Ancient Southwest China." *JOM* 42.2 (1990): 44–47.

Mutschler, Fritz-Heiner, and Achim Mittag, eds. *Conceiving the Empire: China and Rome Compared*. Oxford: Oxford University Press, 2008.

Nam, Kim, Lai Van Toi, and Trinh Hoang Hiep. "Co Loa: An Investigation of Vietnam's Ancient Capital." *Antiquity* 84 (2010): 1011–1027.

Nylan, Michael. "The Rhetoric of 'Empire' in the Classical Era in China." In *Conceiving the Empire: China and Rome Compared*, eds. Fritz-Heiner

Mutschler and Achim Mittag, 39–66. Oxford: Oxford University Press, 2008.

Nylan, Michael, and Michael Loewe, eds. *China's Early Empires: A Reappraisal.* Cambridge: Cambridge University Press, 2010.

O'Harrow, Stephen. "Men of Hu, Men of Han, Men of the Hundred Man: The Biography of Si Nhiep and the Conceptualization of Early Vietnamese Society." *Bulletin de l'Ecole Francaise D'Extreme-Orient* LXXV (1986): 249–266.

"From Co-loa to the Trung Sisters' Revolt: Vietnam as the Chinese Found it." *Asian Perspectives* 22.2 (1979): 140–164.

"Nguyen-Trai's Bình-Ngo-Dai-Cao of 1428: The Development of a Vietnamese National Identity." *Journal of Southeast Asian Studies* 10.1 (March, 1979): 159–174.

Oppenheimer, S., and M. Richards. "Fast Trains, Slow Boats, and the Ancestry of the Polynesian Islanders." *Science Progress* 84 (2001): 157–181.

Ostapirat, Weera. "Kra-Dai and Austronesian: Notes on Phonological Correspondences and Vocabulary Distribution." In *The Peopling of East Asia: Putting Together Archaeology, Linguistics and Genetics*, eds. L. Sagart, R. M. Blench, and A. Sanchez-Mazas. London: Routledge Curzon, 2005.

Pearce, S., A. Spiro, and P. Ebrey, eds. *Culture and Power in the Reconstitution of the Chinese Realm, 200–600.* Cambridge, MA: Harvard University Asia Center, Harvard University Press, 2001.

Peng Nian 彭年. "'Shufa chuiji' fei Nanyue zhi su – jianlun shufa zhi su de qiyuan ji qita 束髮椎髻非南越之俗—兼論束髮之俗的起源及其他." *Zhong yang min zu da xue xue bao* 中央民族大學學報 (2001).

Peng Shifan 彭適凡. *Zhongguo nanfang daogu yu baiyue minzu yanjiu* 中國南方考古與百越民族研究. Beijing: Kexue chubanshe, 2008.

Peters, Heather. "Ethnicity Along China's Southwestern Frontier." *Journal of East Asian Archaeology* 3.1–2 (2001): 75–102.

"Tattooed Faces and Stilt Houses: Who Were the Ancient Yue?" *Sino-Platonic Papers* 17 (April 1990): 1–28.

Pham, Minh Huyen. "The Metal Age in the North of Vietnam." In *Southeast Asia: From Prehistory to History*, eds. Ian Glover and Peter Bellwood, 189–201. New York: Routledge Curzon, 2004.

Phan, John D. "Re-imagining Annam: A New Analysis of Sino-Vietnamese Contact." *China Southern Diaspora Studies* 4 (2010).

Pines, Yuri. "Imagining the Empire? Concepts of 'Primeval Unity' in Pre-imperial Historiographic Tradition." In *Conceiving the Empire: China and Rome Compared*, eds. Fritz-Heiner Mutschler and Achim Mittag, 67–90. Oxford: Oxford University Press, 2008.

Pirazzoli-t'Serstevens, Michele. "Urbanism." In *China's Early Empires: A Reappraisal*, eds. Michael Nylan and Michael Loewe, 169–185. Cambridge: Cambridge University Press, 2010.

"Imperial Aura and the Image of the Other in Han Art." In *Conceiving the Empire: China and Rome Compared*, eds. Fritz-Heiner Mutschler and Achim Mittag, 299–323. Oxford: Oxford University Press, 2008.

"The Bronze Drums of Shizhai Shan, Their Social and Ritual Significance." In *Early Southeast Asia: Essays in Archaeology, History, and Historical Geography*, eds. R. B. Smith and W. Watson, 125–136. New York: Oxford University Press, 1979.

Provine, Robert. "State Sacrificial Music and Korean Identity." In *Harmony and Counterpoint: Ritual Music in Chinese Context*, eds. Evelyn Rawski, Bell Yung, and Rubie Watson. Stanford: Stanford University Press, 1996.

Pulleyblank, E. G. "Zou 鄒 and Lu 魯 and the Sinification of Shandong." In *Chinese Language, Thought, and Culture: Nivison and His Critics*. ed. Philip J. Ivanhoe, 39–57. Chicago: Open Court, 1996.

"The Chinese and Their Neighbors in Prehistoric and Early Historic Times." In *The Origins of Chinese Civilization*, ed. David Keightley. Berkeley: University of California Press, 1983.

Rao Zongyi. "Wu-Yue wenhua." *The Bulletin of the Institute of History and Philology Academica Sinica* 41.4 (1969): 609–636.

Rawski, Evelyn. "Presidential Address: Reenvisioning the Qing: The Significance of the Qing Period in Chinese History." *Journal of Asian Studies* 55.4 (1996): 829–850.

Renfrew, Colin. "Where Bacteria and Languages Concur." *Science* 323 (January 23, 2009): 467–468.

Richards, M., S. J. Oppenheimer, and B. Sykes. "mtDNA suggests Polynesian Origins in Eastern Indonesia." *American Journal of Human Genetics* 63 (1998): 1234–1236.

Rockhill, W. W. "Notes on the Relations and Trade of China with the Eastern Archipelago and the Coast of the Indian Ocean during the Fourteenth Century," Part II. *T'oung Pao*, second series, 16.1 (1915): 61–159.

Roymans, Nico. *Ethnic Identity and Imperial Power: The Batavians in the Early Roman Empire*. Chicago: University of Chicago Press, 2005.

Sagart, Laurent. "The Austroasiatics: East to West or West to East?" In *Dynamics of Human Diversity*, ed. N. J. Enfield, 345–359. Canberra: Pacific Linguistics, 2011.

"The Expansion of Setaria Farmers in East Asia: A Linguistic and Archaeological Model." In *Past Human Migrations in East Asia: Matching Archaeology, Linguistics and Genetics*, eds. A. Sanchez-Mazas, R. Blench, M. Ross, I. Peiros, and M. Lin, 133–157. London: Routledge, 2008 (Routledge Studies in the Early History of Asia).

"The Higher Phylogeny of Austronesian and the Position of Tai-Kadai." *Oceanic Linguistics* 43 (2004): 411–444.

Sagart, L., R. Blench, and A. Sanchez-Mazas. "Introduction." In *The Peopling of East Asia: Putting Together Archaeology, Linguistics and Genetics*, eds. L. Sagart, R. Blench, and A. Sanchez-Mazas, 1–14. London: Routledge Curzon, 2005.

Sage, Steven F. *Ancient Sichuan and the Unification of China*. Albany: State University of New York Press, 1992.

Schaberg, David. "Travel, Geography, and the Imperial Imagination in Fifth-Century Athens and Han China." *Comparative Literature* 51.2 (1999): 152–191.

Schafer, Edward. *The Vermilion Bird: T'ang Images of the South*. Berkeley: University of California Press, 1967.

The Empire of Min. Rutland, VT.: Published for the Harvard-Yenching Institute by C.E. Tuttle Co., 1954.

Scheidel, Walter, and Ian Morris, eds. *The Dynamics of Ancient Empires: State Power from Assyria to Byzantium*. New York: Oxford University Press, 2009.

Schortman, Edward, and Patricia Urban. "The Place of Interaction Studies in Archaeological Thought." In *Resources, Power, and Interregional Interaction*, eds. Edward Schortman and Patricia Urban, 3–15. New York: Plenum Press, 1992.

Schüssler, Axel. "Das Yüeh-chüeh shu als Hanzeitlicher Quelle zur Geschichte der Chan-kuo-Zeit." Ph.D. dissertation, University of Munich, 1969.

"The *Yüeh-chüeh shu*, An Early Text about South China." *American Oriental Society, Middle West Branch, Semi-centennial volume*, ed. Denis Sinor, 198–210. Bloomington: Indiana University Press, 1969.

Scott, James C. *The Art of Not Being Governed: An Anarchist History of Upland Southeast Asia*. New Haven: Yale University Press, 2009.

Shaughnessy, Edward, and Michael Loewe, eds. *Cambridge History of Ancient China: From the Origins of Civilization to 221 B.C.* Cambridge: Cambridge University Press, 1999.

Shen Jishan 沈佳姗. "Zhanqian Taiwan heichixisu liubian chutan 戰前臺灣黑齒習俗流變初探." *Taiwan yuanzumin yanjiu luncong* 台灣原住民研究論叢 10 (2011): 67–94.

Sherratt, Andrew. "Foreword." In *Southeast Asia: From Prehistory to History*, eds. Ian Glover and Peter Bellwood, xviii–xxi. New York: Routledge Curzon, 2004.

Siu, Helen. "Cultural Identity and the Politics of Difference in Southern China." *Daedalus* (Spring, 1993): 19–43.

Skinner, G. William. "The Structure of Chinese History." *Journal of Asian Studies* 44 (1985): 271–292.

Stark, Miriam. "Early Mainland Southeast Asian Landscapes in the First Millennium AD." *Annual Review of Anthropology* 35 (2006): 407–432.

ed. *Archaeology of Asia*. Malden, MA: Blackwell Publishing, 2006.

Stein, Gil. *Archaeology of Colonial Encounters*. Santa Fe: SAR Press, 2005.

Sun Yirang 孫詒讓. *Mozi jian gu* 墨子閒詁. Taipei: Huaqu shuju, 1987.

Swann, Nancy Lee. *Food and Money in Ancient China*. Princeton: Princeton University Press, 1950.

Tan Shengmin 覃聖敏. "Xi-ou, Luo-yue Xinkao 西甌駱越新考." In *Baiyue Yanjiu* 百越研究, ed. Zhongguo Baiyue Minzushi Yanjiuhui, 中國百越民族史研究會, 1–19. Nanning: Guangxi Kexue Jishu Chubanshe, 2007.

Taylor, Keith Weller. *History of the Vietnamese*. Cambridge: Cambridge University Press, 2013.

"Perceptions of Encounter in *Shui Ching Chu* 37." in *Asia Journal* (published by Seoul National University), 2 (1994): 29–54.

The Birth of Vietnam. Berkeley: University of California Press. 1983.

"Madagascar and the Ancient Malayo-Polynesian Myths." In *Explorations in Early Southeast Asian History: The Origins of Southeast Asian Statecraft*, eds.

K. R. Hall and J. K. Whitmore, 25–60. Ann Arbor: Center for South and Southeast Asian Studies, University of Michigan, 1976 (Michigan Papers on South and Southeast Asia, no. 11).

Tenazas, Rosa. "The Boat-coffin Burial Complex in the Philippines and Its Relation to Similar Practices in Southeast Asia." *Philippine Quarterly of Culture and Society* 1.1 (1973).

Thomas, Rosalind. *Herodotus in Context: Ethnography, Science, and the Art of Persuasion*. Cambridge: Cambridge University Press, 2000.

Thompson, C. Michele. "Scripts, Signs and Swords: The Viet Peoples and the Origins of Nom." *Sino-Platonic Papers* 101 (2000).

Tsang, Cheng-hwa. "Recent Discoveries at the Tapenkeng Culture Sites in Taiwan: Implications for the Problem of Austronesian Origins." In *The Peopling of East Asia: Putting Together Archaeology, Linguistics and Genetics*, eds. L. Sagart, R. Blench, and A. Sanchez-Mazas, 63–71. London: Routledge Curzon, 2005.

Tsu-lin Mei, and Jerry Norman. "The Austroasiatics in Ancient South China: Some Lexical Evidence." *Monumenta Serica* 32 (1976): 274–301.

Turchen, Peter. "A Theory for Formation of Large Empires." *Journal of Global History* 4 (2009): 191–217.

Historical Dynamics: Why States Rise and Fall. Princeton: Princeton University Press, 2003.

Twitchett, Denis and Michael Loewe, eds. *The Cambridge History of China, I: The Ch'in and Han Empires, 221 B.C.–A.D. 200*. Cambridge: Cambridge University Press, 1986.

Underhill, Anne, and Junko Habu. "Early Communities in East Asia: Economic and Sociopolitical Organization at the Local and Regional Levels." In *Archaeology of Asia*, ed. Miriam T. Stark, 121–148. Malden, MA: Blackwell Publishing, 2006.

Van Ess, Hans. *Politik und Geschichtsschreibung im alten China*. Wiesbaden: Harrassowitz, 2014.

Vankeerberghen, Griet. *The Huainanzi and Liu An's Claim to Moral Authority*. Albany: State University of New York Press, 2001.

Wagner, Donald. *Iron and Steel in Ancient China*. Leiden: E. J. Brill, 1993.

Wang Aihe, *Cosmology and Political Culture in Early China*. Cambridge: Cambridge University Press, 2000.

Wang Gungwu. *The Nanhai Trade: Early Chinese Trade in the South China Sea*. Singapore: Eastern Universities Press, 2003. (Originally published in 1958 by the *Journal of the Malayan Branch of the Royal Asiatic Society*.)

"The Chinese Urge to Civilize: Reflections on Change." *Journal of Asian History* 18.1 (1984).

Wang Jian 王健. "Nanyueguo bainian shi de jingshen wenhua xunzong 南越國百年史的精神文化尋踪." In *Nanyueguo shiji yan tao hui* 南越國史跡研討會, ed. Zhongshan Daxue Lishi xi, 56–58. Beijing: Wenwu, 2005.

Wang Mingke 王明珂. Hua-Xia bianyuan: Lishi jiyi yu zuqun rentong *(Frontiers of the Hua-xia: Historical Memory and Ethnic Identity)*. Taipei: Yunchen wenhua, 1997.

"The Ch'iang of Ancient China Through the Han Dynasty: Ecological Frontiers and Ethnic Boundaries." Ph.D. dissertation, Harvard University, 1993.

Watson, Burton. *Courtier and Commoner in Ancient China: Selections from the History of the Former Han by Pan Ku*. New York: Columbia University Press, 1974.

Records of the Grand Historian of China, vol. II: The Age of Emperor Wu 140 to Circa 100 B.C. New York: Columbia University Press, 1961.

Watson, William. *Cultural Frontiers in Ancient East Asia*. Edinburgh: Edinburgh University Press, 1971.

Wiens, Herold. *Han Chinese Expansion in South China*. Hamden, CT: Shoe String Press, 1967.

China's March Toward the Tropics: A Discussion of the Southward Penetration of China's Culture, Peoples, and Political Control in Relation to the Non-Han-Chinese Peoples of South China and in the Perspective of Historical and Cultural Geography. Hamden, CT: Shoe String Press, 1954.

Wilkinson, Endymion. *Chinese History: A Manual*. Cambridge: Harvard University Asia Center, 1998.

Wu Chunming 吴春明. 从百越土著到南岛海洋文化 (*Maritime Cultural Interactions between the Indigenous Yue in Southern China and Austronesians in Southeast Asia and the Pacific*). Beijing: Wenwu, 2012.

"Dongnan Hanmin renwen de baiyue wenhua jichu 東南漢民人文的百越文化基礎." In *Baiyue Yanjiu* 百越研究, Zhongguo Baiyue Minzushi Yanjiuhui 中國百越民族史研究會, 34–45. Nanning: Guangxi Kexue Jishu Chubanshe, 2007.

Wu Haigui 吳海貴. "Xianggang Nanyue wang mu zhu xin kao 象崗南越王墓主新考." *Kaogu Wenwu* 考古興文物 (2000).

Wu Hongqi 吳宏岐. "Nanyue guo du Panyu cheng hui yu zhan huo kao shi 南越國都番禺城毀於戰火考實." *Jinan xuebao* 暨南學報, (2008).

Xie Chongguang 謝重光. "Tang dai Fujian jingnei de tuzhu zhongzu renkou 唐代福建境內的土著種族人口." *Fujian Minzu* 2 (1996).

Xiong Gongzhe 熊公哲. *Xunzi jinzhu jinyi* 荀子今註今譯. Taipei: Shangwu Publishing, 1990.

Xu Songshi 徐松石. *Dongnanya minzu de Zhongguo xuelu* 東南亞民族的中國血路. Hong Kong: Tianfeng yingshua chngyin, 1959.

泰族僮族粵族考 *(Research on the Tai, Tong, and Yue Peoples)*. Beijing: Zhonghua shuju, 1946.

Yue jiang liu yu renmin shi shi 粵江流域人民史 *(History of the Yue River [Pearl River] Delta Peoples)*. Shanghai: Zhonghua shuju, 1939.

Yang Bojun 楊伯峻. *Mengzi yizhu* 孟子譯注. Hong Kong: Zhonghua shuju, 1988.

Lunyu yizhu. Hong Kong: Zhonghua shuju, 1984.

Yang Cong 楊琮. *Minyueguo Wenhua* 閩越國文化. Fuzhou: Fujian Renmin Chubanshe, 1998.

Yang Shangqun 楊善群. *Woxin changdan: Yuewang Goujian xin zhuan* 臥薪嚐膽: 越王勾踐新傳 *(Sleeping on Twigs and Tasting Gall: A New Biography of the Yue King Goujian)*. Taipei: Yunlong chubanshe, 1991.

Yang, Xiaoneng, ed. *The Golden Age of Chinese Archaeology: Celebrated Discoveries from the People's Republic of China*. New Haven: Yale University Press, 1999.

Yang Zhaorong 楊兆榮. "Xi-Han Nanyue xiang Lü Jia yizu ru Dian ji qi lishi yingxiang shitan 西漢南越相呂嘉遺族入滇及其理史影響試探." In *Nanyueguo shiji yan tao hui*, 31–41.

Yao, Alice. "Recent Developments in the Archaeology of Southwestern China." *Journal of Archaeological Research* 18 (2010): 203–239.

"Culture Contact and Social Change Along China's Ancient Southwestern Frontier, 900 B.C.–100 A.D." Ph.D. dissertation, University of Michigan, 2008.

Yü Tianchi 余天熾 *et al. Gu Nan Yue Guo shi* 古南越國史. Nanning: Guangxi renmin Press, 1988.

Yü, Ying-shih. "Han Foreign Relations." In *The Cambridge History of China, vol. I: The Ch'in and Han Empires, 221 B.C.–A.D. 220*, eds. Denis Twitchett and Michael Loewe, 453–457. Cambridge: Cambridge University Press, 1986.

Trade and Expansion in Han China: A Study in the Structure of Sino-Barbarian Economic Relations. Berkeley: University of California Press, 1967.

Yunnan sheng wenwukao yanjiusuo 云南省文物考古研究所. 个旧市黑蚂井墓地第四次发掘报告 *(The Fourth Excavations Report of Heimajing Cemetery Site, Gejiu City)*. Beijing: Science Publishing, 2013.

Zeitoun, Elizabeth, and Paul Jen-kui Li, eds. *Selected Papers from the Eighth International Conference on Austronesian Linguistics*. Taipei: Symposium Series of the Institute of Linguistics, Academia Sinica, 1999.

Zhang Rongfang 張榮芳. "Han chao zhili Nanyueguo moushi tanyuan 漢朝治理南越國謀式探源," in *Nanyueguo shiji yantaohui*, 1–8.

Zhang Rongfang 張榮芳 and Huang Miaozhang 黃淼章. *Nanyueguo shi* 南越國史 Guangdong: Guangdong renmin, 1995.

Zhejiang Wenwu Archaeological Research Group 浙江省文物考古研究所. 绍兴县文物保护管理所. 浙江绍兴印山大墓发掘简報 "Report on the Great Tomb of Yingshan Excavated in Shaoxing, Zhejiang." *Wenwu* 文物 11 (1999).

Zhengzhang, Shangfang 鄭張尚芳. "Some Kam-Tai Words in Place Names of the Ancient Wu and Yue States 古吳越地名中的侗台語成份." *Minzu Yuwen* 6 (1990).

"Decipherment of Yuè-Rén-Ge." *Cahiers de Linguistique Asie Orientale*, 20 (1991): 159–168.

Zhong Zhe 鍾哲. *Han feizi jijie* 韓非子集解. Beijing: Zhonghua shuju, 1998.

Zhongguo Baiyue Minzushi Yanjiuhui 中國百越民族史研究會. *Baiyue Yanjiu* 百越研究. Nanning: Guangxi Kexue Jishu Chubanshe, 2007.

Zhongshan Daxue lishi xi, ed. 中山大學歷史系. *Nanyueguo shiji yan tao hui lunwen xuan ji* 南越國史跡研討會論文選集. Beijing: Wenwu Publishing, 2005.

Ziegler, Delphine. "The Cult of Wuyi Mountain and Its Cultivation of the Past: A Topo-cultural Perspective." *Cahiers d'Extrême Asie* 10 (1998): 255–286.

Zumbroich, Thomas. "'Teeth as Black as a Bumble Bee's Wings': The Ethnobotany of Teeth Blackening in Southeast Asia." *Ethnobotany Research and Applications* 7 (2009): 381–398.

Index

Printed in Great Britain
by Amazon

54405610R00169